THE CATHOLIC UNIVERSITY OF AMERICA
CANON LAW STUDIES
No. 198

THE RECEPTION OF CONVERTS

COMMENTARY WITH HISTORICAL NOTES

BY THE

REV. JOSEPH G. GOODWINE, A.B., S.T.B., J.C.L.
Priest of the Archdiocese of New York

A DISSERTATION

Submitted to the Faculty of the School of Canon Law of the Catholic University of America in Partial Fulfillment of the Requirements for the Degree of Doctor of Canon Law

THE CATHOLIC UNIVERSITY OF AMERICA PRESS
WASHINGTON, D. C.
1944

Nihil Obstat:

LUDOVICUS MOTRY, S.T.D., J.C.D.,
Censor Deputatus.

Washingtonii, D. C., die 5 maii, 1944.

Imprimatur:

✠ FRANCISCUS J. SPELLMAN, D.D.,
Archiepiscopus Neo-Eboracensis.

Neo-Eboraci, die 31 maii, 1944.

Printed by
THE PAULIST PRESS
New York, N. Y.

51

TO

THE

SACRED HEART

OF

JESUS

TABLE OF CONTENTS

FOREWORD

The Church has always held the work of conversion as of primary importance to her fruitful mission among men. In her prudent zeal to make the prayer of Christ, "That they all may be one," a vibrant reality, she has laid down certain rules which must be adhered to in receiving converts into the true fold. It is the purpose of this work to examine the procedure which is applicable in the United States to the reception of converts.

The word *convert* in the sense in which it is generally accepted is used to designate any person born and reared outside the Church who, being moved by divine grace, seeks admission to membership in her society.[1] According to the Code of Canon Law one becomes a member of the Church by the fact of valid baptism: hence, the definition is not strictly canonical, since even non-Catholics who never professed the Catholic Faith are by the very fact of their valid baptism members of the Church. In the eyes of the law they are considered as belonging to either of three groups of delinquent members —apostates, heretics, or schismatics—who because of their defection from the faith and cessation from active membership are penalized with the loss of certain rights and privileges. Because they are members of the Church, though deprived of certain rights, their status is not the same as the status of those who were never validly baptized or who were never baptized at all. A third class of persons, those whose baptism is doubtful, must also receive consideration. Hence the strict definition of *convert* should read: any person born and reared in beliefs opposed to the Church's teaching who, moved by divine grace, embraces the Catholic Faith and seeks active membership in the society of the Church. *Conversion* is defined as the change from non-Catholic belief or from infidelity to acceptance of

[1] Cf. *A Catholic Dictionary*, Donald Attwater, general editor (The Catholic Action Society of the College of St. Robert Bellarmine, Heythrop, New York: Macmillan Co., 1941), v. *Convert*, p. 129.

the truths of the Catholic religion.[2] In this work three classes of converts are considered in order: (1) the unbaptized, including those who never received the sacrament and those whose baptism is invalid; (2) the doubtfully baptized; (3) the validly baptized. Because of their special character, a separate chapter is devoted to the treatment of Oriental converts.

The discussion, however, is limited to persons of adult age. In the canonical definition of the term, an adult is one who at the moment of baptism enjoys the use of reason (canon 745, § 2, 2°). The age at which one is presumed to have the use of reason is seven years.[3] Hence the word "adults" includes minors[4] and those still under the care of their parents or guardians. The importance of this norm is seen in cases wherein the parents of a child who has attained the age of seven years are unwilling that he should be received into the Church. Such a one can be admitted to baptism,[5] although it is not always advisable to admit him to a public profession of faith because of attendant difficulties, such as the danger of perversion and possible grave harm to either the child or the Church.[6] If there is doubt that the minor has attained the age of seven years, or if there is doubt as to his sufficient use of reason, then outside of a case of danger of death the baptism is to be postponed.[7]

[2] *Kirchenlexikon,* Hergenröther-Kaulen (ed. 2, 13 vols., Freiburg in Breisgau: Herder, 1882-1903), Vol. III, col. 1049, v. *Conversion*; col. 1053, v. *Convertiten.*

[3] Cf. canon 12; Benedictus XIV, ep. *Postremo Mense,* 28 febr. 1747—*Codicis Iuris Canonici Fontes* (cura Emi Petri Card. Gasparri editi, 9 vols., Romae: 1923-1939), n. 377; S. Congr. de Prop. Fide, 3 mart. 1703—*Fontes,* n. 4495; Gillmann, "Die *anni discretionis* im Kanon *Omnis utriusque* sexus," *Archiv für katholisches Kirchenrecht,* CVIII (1928), 556-617.

[4] Cf. canon 98.

[5] S. Cong. de Prop. Fide 3 mart. 1703—*Fontes,* n. 4495. Cf. II Prov. Council of Quebec (1854) decr. VII, n. 7—*Acta et Decreta Sacrorum Conciliorum Recentiorum, Collectio Lacensis* (7 vols., Friburgi Brisgoviae: Herder, 1870-1890), III, 635.

[6] Cf. S. C. S. Off., 21 iul. 1880—*Acta Sanctae Sedis* (41 vols., Romae: 1865-1908), XXVII (1894-1895), Appendix II, 193 (hereafter cited *ASS*); *Fontes,* n. 1066.

[7] Benedictus XIV, *Postremo Mense,* 28 febr. 1747—*Fontes,* n. 377.

For infants baptized outside the Church there is not required any formality other than an inquiry into their baptism, so that in the case of the proved invalidity or doubtful validity of the former baptism, they are admitted to the Church by the second baptism, absolute or conditional; if their former baptism is found to be certainly valid they are aggregated to the Church without formalities.[8]

Since it is imperative for uniform practice to have definite regulations guiding the procedure to be followed in each case, it was necessary to treat the subject of procedure in the first chapter. And because the reception of converts is a matter involving jurisdiction, a treatment of the qualifications of those who have competence in this regard forms the subject of the second chapter, both chapters being preliminary to a detailed discussion of the procedure to be followed.

No attempt has been made to discuss the historical aspect of the reception of converts in a treatment separate from the discussion of the present law itself. When it seemed necessary for a better understanding of contemporary legislation to touch on the historical development of the various institutes connected with the reception of converts, this was done.

The matter of non-Catholic baptisms being of such importance in connection with this work, it seemed necessary to include in a separate appendix all the forms of non-Catholic baptismal rites it was possible for the writer to secure. The inclusion of these non-Catholic baptismal rituals in this work is justified on the grounds that the Holy Office itself has repeatedly insisted that an examination be made of the ritual of the sect to which the convert belonged as a preliminary step in the forming of definite conclusions in regard to the validity or invalidity of the convert's baptism. The information given in the appendices is not absolutely complete: the rituals of all non-Catholic sects are not included, but only those which represent the larger denominations. Ready reference to these rituals can be made by the reader in fulfillment of the express commands of the Holy Office.

Because of the nature of the subject, it was necessary also to

[8] Cf. De Smet, *De Sacramentis in Genere—De Baptismo et Confirmatione* (ed. 2a, Brugis: Car. Beyaert, 1925), n. 304. This work is hereafter cited *De Baptismo*.

depart from the strictly canonical sources of information at various points, and to have recourse to works on moral and dogmatic theology as well as liturgy.

The author wishes to express his sincere gratitude to His Excellency, the Most Reverend Francis J. Spellman, Archbishop of New York, for the opportunity to pursue graduate studies at the Catholic University of America, and to the members of the Faculty of the School of Canon Law for their helpful direction and kind assistance. Sincere thanks are also due the Reverend Adolph Marx, J.C.D., for his suggestion of the title of this dissertation, the Reverend John A. Goodwine, J.C.D., and the Reverend Patrick Skehan for their advice in obtaining the non-Catholic rituals included in Appendix I, and the student priests at the Catholic University and the classmates of the author for their kindly interest and helpful criticism.

CHAPTER I

THE PROCEDURE

ARTICLE 1. IN GENERAL

NOWHERE in the Code of Canon Law does one find rules which govern the exact procedure to be followed in all cases for the reception of converts into the Church. This is because the Code does not envisage the definition of *convert* in the sense in which it is understood in this work. The word *conversus* in the Code refers to one in the religious life.[1] Only incidental references are found to the act of conversion as it is understood in this treatment.[2] The definition of conversion in the Code refers to incorporation into the society of the Church by means of baptism.[3]

The most pertinent legislation is found in canon 2314:

> § 1. Omnes a christiana fide apostatae et omnes et singuli haeretici aut schismatici:
> 1°. Incurrunt ipso facto excommunicationem;
> § 2. . . . si tamen delictum apostasiae, haeresis vel schismatis ad forum externum Ordinarii loci quovis modo deductum fuerit, etiam per voluntariam confessionem, idem Ordinarius, non vero Vicarius Generalis sine mandato speciali, resipiscentem, praevia abiuratione iuridice peracta aliisque servatis de iure servandis sua auctoritate ordinaria in foro exteriore absolvere potest; ita vero absolutus, potest deinde a peccato absolvi a quolibet confessario in foro conscientiae. Abiuratio vero habetur iuridice peracta cum fit coram ipso Ordinario loci vel eius delegato et saltem duobus testibus.

[1] Cf. canons 564, § 2; 565, §§ 2, 3.

[2] Cf. canons 300, § 2; 1062; 1070, § 1; 1099, § 1, 1°; 1121, § 1; 1122, § 2.

[3] Canon 87.—Baptismate homo constituitur in Ecclesia Christi persona cum omnibus christianorum iuribus et officiis, nisi, ad iura quod attinet, obstet obex, ecclesiasticae communionis vinculum impediens, vel lata ab Ecclesia censura.

Reference to this canon which penalizes those who have defected from the faith is justified by the presumption that, when a delict is committed, it is presumed in the external forum to have been done with deliberate malice.[4] Thus converts are looked upon in the eyes of the law as apostates, heretics or schismatics, and are governed by the prescriptions of canon 2314.[5]

In this canon the penalty of a *latae sententiae* excommunication is levied against apostates, heretics and schismatics, and the absolution in the external forum is reserved to the Ordinary. In the interpretation of the phrase *servatis de iure servandis* authors generally refer to an Instruction of the Holy Office, issued July 20, 1859.[6] Thus, Augustine,[7] Cappello,[8] Cerato,[9] Coronata,[10] Salucci[11] and Wernz-Vidal[12] clearly state that this phrase must be interpreted exclusively according to the norms of the Instruction. Other authors such as Vermeersch-Creusen,[13] De Smet,[14] Cocchi,[15] Mothon,[16] Geni-

[4] Canon 2200, § 2.

[5] Haring, *Grundzüge des katholischen Kirchenrechtes* (2 vols., Graz: Ulrich Moser, 1924), II, 381.

[6] *Fontes*, n. 953; *Concilii Plenarii Baltimorensis II, in Ecclesia Metropolitana Baltimorensi, a die VII ad diem XXI Octobris, A. D., MDCCCLXVI Habiti et a Sede Apostolica Recogniti, Acta et Decreta* (ed. 2a, Baltimorae: Ioannes Murphy, 1894), Appendix I, pp. 277-279. Hereafter this Instruction will be referred to as "the Instruction" or "the Instruction of 1859."

[7] *A Commentary on the New Code of Canon Law* (8 vols., Vol. VIII, 2. ed., St. Louis: B. Herder Book Co., 1924), VIII, 283.

[8] *Tractatus Canonico-Moralis De Censuris iuxta Codicem Iuris Canonici* (ed. 2a, Taurinorum Augustae: Marietti, 1925), n. 215, 8°.

[9] *Censurae Vigentes Ipso Facto a Codice Iuris Canonici Excerptae* (ed. 2a, Patavii: Typis Seminarii, 1921), p. 144, n. 68.

[10] *Institutiones Iuris Canonici* (5 vols., Taurini: Marietti, 1928-1936), IV, p. 293, n. 1867.

[11] *Il Diritto Penale Secondo Il Codice Di Diritto Canonico* (2 vols. in 1, Subiaco: Tipografia dei Monasteri, 1926-1930), II, 15, nota 1.

[12] *Ius Canonicum* (7 vols. in 8, Romae, 1923-1938), VII, 416-417.

[13] *Epitome Iuris Canonici* (3 vols., Vol. I, ed. 6a, 1937; Vol. II, ed. 5a, 1934; Vol. III, ed. 5a, 1936, Mechliniae-Romae: H. Dessain), III, p. 312, n. 513.

[14] *De Baptismo*, nn. 304, 305.

[15] *Commentarium in Codicem Iuris Canonici* (5 vols. in 8, Taurinorum Augustae: Marietti, 1922-1930), VIII, p. 226, n. 136.

[16] *Institutions Canoniques* (3 vols., Lille-Bruges: Desclée De Brouwer et Cie., 1922-1924), II, art. 2970.

cot-Salsmans,[17] Merkelbach [18] and Lydon [19] explicitly indicate that the procedure outlined in the Instruction is still to be followed in receiving converts, except for the abjuration and the absolution from the censure, which must take place in accordance with the law of canon 2314, § 2.

The authors who form the latter group seem to indicate that in receiving converts, the direct obligation is to follow the procedure outlined in the Instruction, but the law of canon 2314, § 2, is to be observed insofar as it interprets the Instruction. The former group point to canon 2314, § 2, as binding directly, though it is to be interpreted in the light of the Instruction. Both groups concede a mutual interdependence between the law of the Code and the procedure outlined in the Instruction, and thus advocate universal application of the Instruction in receiving converts into the Church. This general consensus of the authors as to the applicability of the Instruction indicates that it is not merely a particular response to an individual doubt, but that it embodies the general practice of the Church and is an application of the general law of the Code.

The Instruction reads:

> To the doubt proposed by the Most Reverend Bishop of Philadelphia concerning the Profession of Faith and the Absolution of heretics when they are converted; on Wednesday, July 20, 1859, the most eminent cardinals decreed that an instruction be given as follows.
>
> In the conversion of heretics there must first be an inquiry into the validity of the Baptism received in heresy. After a diligent examination has been made, if it is found that no baptism was conferred, or that it was conferred invalidly, they are to be baptized absolutely. But if, when the investigation is completed, there still remains a probable doubt concerning the validity of the Baptism, then Baptism is to be repeated conditionally. Finally, if it is established that the Baptism was valid, they are to be received only to the Abjuration, or Profession of Faith.

[17] *Institutiones Theologiae Moralis* (ed. 14a, 2 vols., Dedebec-Buenos Aires: Desclée De Brouwer, 1939), II, n. 153.

[18] *Summa Theologiae Moralis* (ed. 3a, 3 vols., Parisiis: Desclée De Brouwer et Soc., 1942), III, n. 168.

[19] *Ready Answers in Canon Law* (San Francisco: Benziger Bros., 1934), v. *Converts,* p. 176.

Therefore there is a threefold method of procedure in reconciling heretics:

1. If the Baptism is to be absolutely conferred, there is to be no Abjuration, nor Absolution, because of the fact that the Sacrament of Regeneration takes away all stain.

2. If Baptism is to be repeated conditionally, this order of procedure must be followed:

(a) Abjuration or Profession of Faith,

(b) Conditional Baptism,

(c) Sacramental Confession with conditional Absolution.

3. Finally, when the Baptism was judged to be valid only the Abjuration or Profession of Faith is to be made, which will then be followed by the Absolution from censures.

It is to be noted, however, that the Abjuration or Profession of Faith is different from the one set forth in the Bull of Pius IV. For the formula which is attached was prescribed by the Supreme S. C. of the Holy Office for the conversion of heretics, and the Bishop Petitioner is to use this together with the formula of Absolution which is also attached.

Manner of Receiving the Profession of Catholic Faith From Converts

The Priest wearing surplice and violet stole sits on the Epistle side (if the Blessed Sacrament is reserved in the tabernacle), otherwise in front of the tabernacle, and the convert kneels before him, and touching the book of Gospels with his right hand, pronounces the profession of faith as it is set forth below: if he does not know how to read, the Priest is to read it to him slowly, so that the convert can understand it and pronounce the words distinctly after the Priest. (Here follows the Profession of Faith. The text is quoted in the second article of this chapter for purposes of comparison with the more recent formula approved by the Holy Office.)

After this the convert remains kneeling, while the Priest still sitting down recites the psalm *Miserere* or *De Profundis* adding the Gloria Patri at the end. When this is finished, the Priest stands and says: (Here follow certain prayers and the absolution from the excommunication. These are quoted in the footnote and are to be found in the addenda to the Roman Ritual for the use of the clergy of the United States.)

Finally the Priest is to impose a salutary Penance, e. g., certain prayers, a visit to a church, or some other like penances.[20]

[20] The above is the author's translation. The Latin text with the exception of the Profession of Faith is as follows:

Proposito dubio R.P.D. Episcopi Philadelphien. circa Professionem Fidei, ac Absolutionem haereticorum dum convertuntur, Feria IV. die 20. Julii 1859, Emi D.D. decreverunt dandam esse instructionem, prout sequitur.

In conversione haereticorum inquirendum est primo de validitate Baptismi in haeresi suscepti. Instituto igitur diligenti examine, si compertum fuerit, aut nullum, aut nulliter conlatum fuisse, baptizandi erunt absolute. Si autem investigatione peracta, adhuc probabile dubium de Baptismi validitate supersit, tunc sub conditione iteratur. Demum si constiterit validum fuisse, recipiendi erunt tantummodo ad Abjurationem, seu Professionem Fidei. Triplex igitur in conciliandis haereticis distinguitur procedendi methodus:

1. Si Baptismus absolute conferatur, nulla sequitur Abjuratio, nec Absolutio, eo quod omnia abluit Sacramentum Regenerationis.

2. Si Baptismus sit sub conditione iterandus, hoc ordine procedendum erit:
   (a) Abjuratio seu Fidei Professio,
   (b) Baptismus Conditionatus,
   (c) Confessio Sacramentalis cum Absolutione conditionata.

3. Quando denique validum judicatum fuerit Baptisma, sola recipitur Abjuratio seu Fidei Professio, quam Absolutio a censuris sequitur.

Notandum vero Abjurationem, seu Professionem Fidei aliam esse ab ea quae habetur in Bulla Pii IV. Nam a Suprema S. C. S. Officii praescripta fuit illa, quae adnectitur, pro conversione haereticorum, eaque utetur Episcopus Orator, cum formula Absolutionis, quae pariter adjungitur.

MODUS

EXCIPIENDI PROFESSIONEM FIDEI CATHOLICAE A NEO-CONVERSIS

Sacerdos superpelliceo et stola violacei coloris indutus, sedet in cornu Epistolae (si SS. Sacramentum asservetur in tabernaculo) sin minus in medio Altaris, et coram illo genuflectit Neo-conversus; qui codicem Evangelii dextra manu tangens, emittit professionem fidei, prout inferius habetur: vel si nesciat legere, Sacerdos praelegit eidem tarde professionem, ut Conversus eamdem intelligere, et cum Sacerdote distinctis verbis pronuntiare possit.

* * *

Postea, neo-converso genuflexo manente, Sacerdos sedens dicit psalmum Miserere, *sive psalmum* De profundis, *cum* Gloria Patri *in fine. Quo finito, Sacerdos stans dicit:*

Kyrie eleison. Christe eleison. Kyrie eleison. Pater noster, secreto.

V. Et ne nos inducas in tentationem.

R. Sed libera nos a malo.

From the text of the Instruction it is evident that in itself it is an answer to a particular doubt of the Bishop of Philadelphia, and therefore, is of obligation only in that particular diocese for which it was intended. However, from the fact that the Instruction embodies the general law and practice of the Church, it can be said that a certain universal obligation to follow the procedure set forth, at least substantially, does arise. It is the nature of an instruction to explain doubtful points in the law and to set forth certain norms whereby the law may be observed in practice. When, however, an instruction such as the instruction of the Holy Office under discussion intends to recall the common law, a real obligation to obey its prescriptions does arise.[21] Thus it seems that the necessity of an

V. Salvum fac servum tuum (ancillam tuam).
R. Deus meus, sperantem in te.
V. Domine, exaudi orationem meam.
R. Et clamor meus ad te veniat.
V. Dominus vobiscum.
R. Et cum spiritu tuo.

OREMUS

Deus, cui proprium est misereri semper et parcere, suscipe deprecationem nostram, ut hunc famulum tuum (hanc famulam tuam) quem (quam) excommunicationis catena constringit, miseratio tuae pietatis clementer absolvat. Per Dominum nostrum Jesum Christum Filium tuum: qui tecum vivit et regnat in unitate Spiritus Sancti Deus, per omnia saecula saeculorum. *R*. Amen.

Deinde Sacerdos sedet et ad Profitentem genuflexum versus, eum ab haeresi absolvit, dicens:

Auctoritate apostolica, qua fungor in hac parte, absolvo te a vinculo excommunicationis quam(1) incurristi, et restituo te sacrosanctis Ecclesiae sacramentis, communioni et unitati fidelium, in nomine Patris et Filii et Spiritus Sancti. Amen.

Denique abjuranti aliquam Poenitentiam salutarem injungat, e. g. aliquas preces, visitare Ecclesiam, aut similia.

(1) In dubio gravi aut levi, utrum poenitens excommunicationem incurrerit per haeresim professam, sacerdos hic inserat vocabulum *forsan.*

[21] Maroto, *Institutiones Iuris Canonici ad Normam Novi Codicis* (2 vols., Vol. I, ed. 3a, Romae: Apud Commentarium Pro Religiosis, 1921), I, n. 180, a: "Non raro Superiores ecclesiastici suis instructionibus intendunt in mentem subditorum revocare ea quae praecepta sunt vel prohibita ex iure divino vel ecclesiastico, universali aut particulari; tunc illae instructiones . . . sane obligant; quod si obligatio non dicatur promanare ex praescripto Superioris, oritur certe

investigation into the fact and validity of the convert's baptism, and the procedure outlined for the results of that investigation must be adhered to universally. If the Holy See has approved other formulas for the abjuration or profession of faith or for the absolution from censures, and if such formulas were prescribed for particular dioceses, the more recent formulas certainly supersede those in the Instruction. In the absence of any such special regulations the Instruction should be adhered to in these details.

In its prescriptions regarding the profession of faith the Instruction does not indicate the presence of two witnesses. Canon 2314, § 2, on the other hand, definitely demands that at least two witnesses be present. Since the Instruction is opposed to the common law of the Code in this matter, it must be considered as abrogated, even though it remains in force in all its other prescriptions.

Article 2. In the United States

In the United States by reason of the legislation of the Plenary Councils of Baltimore, the Instruction has the status of particular law. The II Plenary Council of Baltimore (1866) decreed:

> In receiving converts from heresy into the faith we desire that that procedure be exactly followed which is contained in the form given by the Sacred Congregation of the Holy Office, July 20, 1859, and which is already printed in several ritual books. That it may be known to everyone, we shall take care to incorporate it in the Appendix. For there it is explicitly stated when Baptism is to be conferred absolutely, when conditionally, and when not at all.[22]

From the text of the decree it may be argued that no strict obligation to comply with the Instruction arises, even though it was the

ex iuribus praeexistentibus. Sub hac ratione censendae sunt obligatoriae plures Instructiones Sacrarum Congregationum, maxime S. Officii et Cong. de Prop. Fide."

[22] *Acta et Decreta*, n. 242: "In conversis ab haeresi ad fidem excipiendis, volumus ut ad amussim servetur modus ille, qui in Forma a Sacr. Congr. S. Officii, die 20 Julii, an. 1859, tradita habetur, et jam in quibusdam libris ritualibus typis impressus invenitur. Hanc, ut neminem lateat, in Appendicem referendam curabimus. Ibi enim explicite declaratur, quando Baptismus absolute, quando sub conditione, quando denique nullo modo sit iterandus."

mind of the Fathers of the Council to institute a uniform practice in this country. From the text of the decree of the III Plenary Council, which repeated the recommendation of the former council, no such latitude of interpretation is allowed.[23]

> That due veneration for Baptism be preserved, and that all appearances of its illegitimate repetition be removed, the Church has prescribed that when one is converted to the faith from error, there must always be a diligent inquiry as to whether he has been baptized before, and whether the Baptism received in heresy was valid. A mere general investigation of the custom or practice of certain sects, from which can be had a presumption as to whether or not the Baptism was conferred, or as to its validity or nullity, is not sufficient; but, as far as it shall be possible, there must be an inquiry into the Baptism of the individual converts, so that the certitude or probability that they were or were not validly baptized may be obtained. When the investigation has been completed, the convert must be received according to the manner described in the Instruction of the Holy Office of the year 1859, which is to be seen in the Appendix of the II Plenary Council of Baltimore and in most ritual books.[24]

[23] Cf. Beste, *Introductio in Codicem* (St. John's Abbey Press, Collegeville, Minn., 1938), pp. 935-936; Ayrinhac-Lydon, *Penal Legislation in the New Code of Canon Law* (revised edition, New York: Benziger, 1936), p. 158; MacKenzie, *The Delict of Heresy in Its Commission, Penalization, Absolution* (The Catholic University of America Canon Law Studies, n. 77, Washington, D. C.: The Catholic University of America, 1932), p. 116. Barrett, however, in his work, *A Comparative Study of the Councils of Baltimore and the Code of Canon Law* (The Catholic University of America Canon Law Studies, n. 83, Washington, D. C.: The Catholic University of America, 1932), omits all mention of the decrees of the II and III Plenary Councils of Baltimore referring to the Instruction.

[24] *Acta et Decreta Concilii Plenarii Baltimorensis Tertii, A. D. MDCCCLXXXIV* (Baltimorae: Typis Joannis Murphy Et Sociorum, 1886), n. 122: "Ut sua igitur Baptismo debita servetur veneratio, atque quam longissime absit vel sola apparentia repetitionis ejus illegitimae, praecipit Ecclesia ut quando quis ab errore ad fidem convertitur, semper diligens fiat investigatio num antea forsan baptizatus fuerit, numque validus fuerit Baptismus in haeresi susceptus. Neque sufficit investigatio mere generalis de consuetudine vel praxi aliquarum sectarum, per quam haberi posset praesumptio de collato vel non collato Baptismo aut de ejus validitate vel nullitate; sed, quantum possibile fuerit, inquirendum est in singulorum neophytorum Baptismum, ut obtineatur, qualis in casu haberi queat, vel certitudo vel probabilitas, eos fuisse vel non

In the Addenda of the Roman Ritual for the use of the clergy of the United States the formula of absolution from the censure of excommunication coincides exactly with that set forth in the Instruction.[25] In the smaller ritual the entire Instruction is included.[26] Thus, additional weight is given to the obligation to observe the procedure outlined in the Instruction.

A practical difficulty arises, however, from a comparison of canon 2314, § 2, with the Instruction. The Instruction requires that the abjuration and profession of faith be made in the presence of the priest, without reference to witnesses, whereas canon 2314, § 2, expressly demands the presence of at least two witnesses in order that the abjuration have juridic value in the external forum. If, as MacKenzie maintains, the Holy Office "in granting the priests of the United States the use of this simple method of reconciling converts, was in reality granting a privilege," [27] then such a practice may still be employed in virtue of canon 4, which safeguards the continuance of privileges granted by the Holy See before the promulgation of the Code, if they were still in use and were not revoked with the advent of the Code. The wording of the response of the Holy Office, however, does not substantiate this interpretation. In the first place the Holy Office did not address the Instruction to the priests of the United States, but to the Bishop of Philadelphia. Secondly, there is no question of the granting of a privilege.

The Holy Office was rather rendering an interpretation of the general law of the Church in a particular case of doubt as to the application or fulfillment of the general law. This is evident from the words, *Proposito dubio R.P.D. Episcopi Philadelphien. circa Professionem Fidei, ac Absolutionem haereticorum dum convertuntur*. The Bishop of Philadelphia was not seeking a privilege, but rather requested a clarification of the law which required converts

fuisse valide baptizatos. Facta investigatione, recipiendus erit neo-conversus juxta modum descriptum in Instructione S. Officii anni 1859 quam videre est in calce Conc. Balt. Plen. II., et in libris Ritualibus communiter."

[25] *Forma Receptionis Neo-Conversi.*

[26] *The Priest's New Ritual* compiled by Rev. Paul Griffith (revised edition, Baltimore, Md.: John Murphy Company, 1940), pp. 48-60.

[27] *The Delict of Heresy,* p. 116.

to make a profession of faith and to be absolved from the censure of excommunication. His doubt as to the application of the law was settled by an official interpretation: *Emi D.D. decreverunt dandam esse instructionem.* The Holy Office in the Instruction applied the prescriptions of the general law and formulated them into a workable procedure.

The Councils of Baltimore extended the prescriptions of the Instruction to every diocese in the United States. With the promulgation of the Code, however, all laws, whether universal or particular, which were opposed to the prescriptions of the Code were immediately and automatically abrogated, unless special provision for their continuance was made by the Code.[28] Since the Instruction had assumed the status of particular law and since this particular law in prescribing merely the presence of the priest for the juridic efficacy of the abjuration was opposed to the provisions of the Code, the practice of receiving the convert's abjuration and profession of faith in the presence of only the priest is abrogated, and the prescriptions of canon 2314, § 2, must be observed. Therefore, while the other prescriptions of the Instruction remain in force as particular law for the United States, the abjuration of heresy and profession of faith must take place in the presence of the bishop or his delegate and two witnesses.[29]

Another difficulty arises by reason of the new formula of profession of faith which was approved by the Holy Office and sent to the Ordinaries of the United States by His Excellency, the Most Reverend Amleto G. Cicognani, Apostolic Delegate, under date of March 26, 1942. Does the more recent formula abrogate the use of the profession of faith which is contained in the Instruction? It seems that the approval given the new formula by the Holy Office acting in the name of the Holy See [30] is sufficient to warrant the abrogation of the formula of the Instruction, just as the Holy Office in the Instruction abrogated the use of the formula of Pius IV. This conclusion seems warranted, whether the formula of the Instruction be considered either as particular law (by reason of the decrees of the

[28] Canon 6, 1°.
[29] Cf. *AER,* LXXXVII (1932), 530.
[30] Canon 7.

Councils of Baltimore which commanded the observance of the Instruction), or as a mere addition to the particular law of the United States (by interpreting the decrees of the Councils of Baltimore as referring only to the manner of procedure and not to the formula for the profession of faith or the prayers and formula for absolution). If in issuing the new formula, the Holy See intended that it be considered as particular law for the United States, this new law certainly abrogated the formula contained in the Instruction; if the law of the Councils of Baltimore is, on the other hand, considered as not embracing the formula in the Instruction, the mere approval of the new formula by the Holy See and its promulgation by the Apostolic Delegate to all the Ordinaries of the United States with the command that it be used is sufficient to supplant the use of the formula in the Instruction.

While the two formulas are essentially the same, the more recent formula is more detailed concerning certain truths and does not follow the same order.

Abjuration and Creed

Instruction Formula

1. I, N.N., having before my eyes the holy Gospels, which I touch with my hand, and knowing that no one can be saved without that faith which the Holy Catholic Apostolic Roman Church holds, believes, and teaches, against which I grieve that I have greatly erred, inasmuch as I have held and believed doctrines opposed to her teaching.

2. I now with grief and contrition for my past errors, profess that I believe the Holy Catholic Apostolic Roman

1942 Formula

1. I .... years of age, born outside the Catholic Church, have held and believed errors contrary to her teaching. Now, enlightened by divine grace, I kneel before you, Reverend Father ...., having before my eyes and touching with my hands the Holy Gospels; and with a firm faith I believe and profess each and all the articles that are contained in the Apostles' Creed; that is: I believe in God, the Father Almighty, Creator of Heaven and Earth; and in Jesus Christ, His only Son, our Lord,

Church to be the only and true Church established on earth by Jesus Christ, to which I submit myself with my whole heart. I believe all the articles that she proposes to my belief, and I reject and condemn all that she rejects and condemns, and I am ready to observe all that she commands me. And especially, I profess that I believe:

3. One only God in three divine Persons, distinct from, and equal to, each other—that is to say, the Father, the Son, and the Holy Ghost;

4. The Catholic doctrine of the Incarnation, Passion, Death, and Resurrection of our Lord Jesus Christ; and the personal union of the two Natures, the divine and the human; the divine Maternity of the most holy Mary, together with her most spotless Virginity;

Who was conceived by the Holy Ghost, born of the Virgin Mary, suffered under Pontius Pilate, was crucified, died and was buried; He descended into hell, the third day He rose again from the dead; He ascended into heaven and sitteth at the right hand of God, the Father Almighty; from thence He will come to judge the living and the dead. I believe in the Holy Ghost; the Holy Catholic Church; the communion of saints; the forgiveness of sins; the resurrection of the body, and life everlasting. Amen.

Tradition, Scripture

10. The authority of the Apostolic and Ecclesiastical Traditions, and of the Holy Scriptures, which we must interpret, and understand only in the sense which our holy mother the Catholic Church has held, and does hold;

2. I admit and embrace most firmly the apostolic and ecclesiastical traditions and all the other constitutions and prescriptions of the Church.

3. I admit the Sacred Scriptures according to the sense which has been held and which is still held by Holy Mother Church, whose duty it is to judge the true sense and interpretation of the Sacred Scriptures, and I shall never accept or interpret them except according to the unanimous consent of the Fathers.

Sacraments

6. The seven Sacraments instituted by Jesus Christ for the salvation of mankind; that is to say, Baptism, Confirmation, Eucharist, Penance, Extreme Unction, Order, Matrimony;

4. I profess that the Sacraments of the New Law are, truly and precisely seven in number, instituted for the salvation of mankind, though all are not necessary[31] for each individual: Baptism, Confirmation, Eucharist, Penance, Extreme Unction, Holy Orders, and Matrimony. I profess that all confer grace and that of these Baptism, Confirmation and Holy Orders cannot be repeated without sacrilege.

5. I also accept and admit the ritual of the Catholic Church in the solemn administration of all the above mentioned Sacraments.

Eucharist

5. The true, real, and substantial presence of the Body, together with the Soul and Divinity of our Lord Jesus Christ, in the most holy Sacrament of the Eucharist;

6. I accept and hold, in each and every part, all that has been defined and declared by the Sacred Council of Trent concerning Original Sin and Justification. I profess that in the Mass is offered to God a true, real and propitiatory sacrifice for the living and the dead; that in the Holy Sacrament of the Eucharist is really, truly and substantially the Body and Blood together with the soul and Divinity of our Lord Jesus Christ, and that there takes place what the Church calls transubstantiation, that is the change of all the substance of bread into the Body and of all substance of wine into the Blood. I confess also that in receiving under either of these species one receives Jesus Christ, whole and entire.

[31] "Though not all are necessary" is suggested as more in keeping with the doctrine of the Church.

Purgatory, Saints

7. Purgatory, the Resurrection of the dead, Everlasting life;

9. The veneration of the Saints, and of their images;

7. I firmly hold that Purgatory exists and that the souls detained there can be helped by the prayers of the faithful. Likewise I hold that the saints, who reign with Jesus Christ, should be venerated and invoked, that they offer prayers to God for us and that their relics are to be venerated.

Primacy

8. The Primacy, not only of honor, but also of jurisdiction of the Roman Pontiff, successor of St. Peter, Prince of the Apostles, Vicar of Jesus Christ;

8. I profess firmly that the images of Jesus Christ and of the Mother of God, ever Virgin, as well as of all the saints should be given due honor and veneration. I also affirm that Jesus Christ left to the Church the faculty to grant Indulgences and that their use is most salutary to the Christian people. I recognize the Holy Roman, Catholic and Apostolic Church as the mother and teacher of all the Churches and I promise and swear true obedience to the Roman Pontiff, successor of St. Peter, Prince of the Apostles, and Vicar of Jesus Christ.

General Councils, Abjuration

11. And everything else, that has been defined, and declared by the sacred Canons, and by the General Councils, especially by the Holy Council of Trent.

12. With a sincere heart, therefore, and with unfeigned faith, I detest and abjure every error, heresy, and sect opposed

9. Besides I accept, without hesitation, and profess all that has been handed down, defined and declared by the Sacred Canons and by the general Councils, especially by the Sacred Council of Trent and by the Vatican General Council, and in a special manner concerning the primacy

to the said Holy Catholic and Apostolic Roman Church. So help me God, and these His holy Gospels, which I touch with my hand!

and infallibility of the Roman Pontiff. At the same time I condemn and reprove all that the Church has condemned and reproved. This same Catholic Faith, outside of which nobody can be saved, which I now freely profess and to which I truly adhere, the same I promise and swear to maintain and profess, with the help of God, entire, inviolate and with firm constancy until the last breath of life; and I shall strive, as far as possible, that this same faith shall be held, taught and publicly professed by all those who depend on me and by those of whom I shall have charge.

So help me God and these Holy Gospels.[32]

[32] The Instruction Formula is to be found in the *Acta et Decreta*, Appendix I, pp. 278-279 of the II Plenary Council of Baltimore. The 1942 Formula may be found in Bouscaren, *Canon Law Digest* (2 vols., Milwaukee: Bruce Publishing Company, 1934-1943), II, pp. 182-184; *The Jurist*, II (1942), 305-307; *AER*, CVI (1942), 355-357; *Conference Bulletin of the Archdiocese of New York*, XIX (1942), 60-61.

CHAPTER II

WHO ARE COMPETENT TO RECEIVE THE CONVERT

CANON 1350, § 1,[1] reminds local Ordinaries and pastors of their special obligation toward non-Catholics residing in their respective dioceses and parishes. The obligation is a general one to procure the conversion of these non-Catholics,[2] and as such is only the canonical repetition of the mandate given by Christ to His Apostles.[3] From this obligation it follows that both local Ordinaries and pastors as well as all priests have the right to instruct the convert and help him on his way to embracing the Faith. The actual reception, however, must follow the definite law of the Code. The question of who may receive the convert in the formal ceremony of Baptism or of Reconciliation depends on the legislation of the Code which singles out those to whom the right to baptize, to receive the abjuration, and to absolve from the censure of excommunication which may be present, belongs. The mere fact that a priest has instructed a convert does not in itself confer on him the right to receive the convert into the Church.

ARTICLE 1. THROUGH BAPTISM

When the investigation relative to the convert's possible earlier baptism discloses the fact that no baptism has been received or that the former baptism was administered invalidly, the convert is to be admitted into the Church through solemn baptism. Canon 744 designates the bishop of local Ordinary as the one to confer the sacrament:

> **Adultorum baptismus, ubi commode fieri possit, ad loci Ordinarium deferatur, ut, si voluerit, ab eo vel ab eius delegato sollemnius conferatur.**

[1] Ordinarii locorum et parochi acatholicos, in suis dioecesibus et paroeciis degentes, commendatos sibi in Domino habeant.

[2] "Qua commendatione, sicut missio quaedam Apostolica Ordinarii set parochis concreditur respectu horum acatholicorum, ita generalis quaedam imponitur obligatio procurandi eorum conversionem."—Wernz-Vidal, *Ius Canonicum,* Tom. IV, Vol. II, 62.

[3] Matt. XXVIII, 19.

When an adult convert, therefore, is ready for baptism, the local Ordinary should be notified, so that he himself or his delegate may perform the ceremony with greater solemnity than would ordinarily attach to the usual ceremony of solemn baptism. From this canon authors agree on the strict right of the Ordinary to baptize adults. He is, therefore, the one to receive the convert into the Church. This right of the local Ordinary is conditioned on his own willingness to perform the ceremony or to have his delegate administer the sacrament, as is evident from the phrase *si voluerit*. If he so wishes, therefore, the local Ordinary can reserve to himself the right to receive all adult converts by means of a diocesan statute, as is done in some parts of Europe.[4]

The obligation, on the other hand, to notify the local Ordinary when the convert is prepared to receive Baptism is not an absolute but only a conditional one, as is evident from the use of the subjunctive form, *deferatur,* coupled with the qualification expressed in the phrase, *ubi commode fieri possit*. Authors interpret this canon as being a relic of the ancient discipline wherein all baptisms were reserved to the bishop of the diocese.[5] It is not on that account to be taken to mean that those who have prepared converts for solemn Baptism may or may not notify the bishop, as Ayrinhac seems to infer.[6]

It is only when it is inconvenient, that the obligation to notify the local Ordinary does not bind. A real obligation, however, does exist. Any reasonable inconvenience either on the part of the priest who has instructed the convert in notifying the bishop, or on the part of the convert himself in waiting till the bishop can baptize

[4] Vermeersch-Creusen, *Epitome,* II, p. 16, n. 28.

[5] "Etiam in memoriam antiquae disciplinae, adultorum baptismus, ubi commode fieri possit, ad loci Ordinarium deferatur. . . ."—Wernz-Vidal, *Ius Canonicum,* Tom. IV, Vol. I, 37; "This canon [744] recalls the discipline of the Church in the early centuries when all baptisms were reserved to the bishop of the diocese."—Woywod, *Commentary,* I, n. 637; cf. O'Kane, *Rubrics of the Roman Ritual,* p. 203, n. 426.

[6] "The Church wishes to surround the baptism of adults with greater solemnity; for this reason the Code, confirming an ancient provision of the Ritual, recommends, without perhaps strictly commanding it, that all such cases be referred to the Ordinary. . . ."—*Legislation on the Sacraments,* p. 21.

him, or on the part of the bishop in conferring the baptism, would excuse from this obligation to notify the bishop. Local circumstances and conditions will in most cases be the determining factors.[7]

When conditions would make impossible the fulfillment of the obligation of canon 744, or render its observance gravely inconvenient, the bishop could notify the pastors of the diocese that he will not insist on his right. This right can be relinquished through legislation in the provincial council[8] or through diocesan statute, so that the right to receive the convert through baptism devolves on the pastor of the parish where the convert lives.[9] The bishop can also delegate all priests to perform the ceremony by means of a diocesan statute,[10] or he may authorize the priests who instruct the converts to act as his delegate in all cases.[11]

In the event that the bishop has not positively relinquished his right or delegated it generally to others, existing custom may empower those who instructed the convert also to receive him into the Church. Such a custom, however, would be contrary to the general law of canon 744, and therefore must meet the requirements of canon 5 which prescribes that only centenary and immemorial cus-

[7] Cf. Vermeersch-Creusen, *op. cit., loc. cit.*

[8] Cf. II Prov. Council of Toronto (1938), decr. 138: "Baptismus adultorum in hac Provincia non reservatur Ordinario"—*Acta et Decreta Concilii Provincialis Torontini Secundi, Toronti in Ecclesia Metropolitana Celebrati Diebus XIII, XIV, XV Decembris MCMXXXVIII*; IV Prov. Council of Oregon (1932), decr. 218: "Baptismus adultorum in hac Provincia non reservatur Ordinario"—*Acta et Decreta Concilii Provincialis Portlandensis in Oregon Quarti, Portlandiae in Ecclesia Metropolitana Celebrati Diebus VIII, IX, X Septembris MCMXXXII*, p. 93.

[9] Canon 738.

[10] Cf. I Diocesan Synod of Fargo (1941), n. 986, 14—*Synodus Dioecesana Fargensis Prima diebus XXIX et XXX Septembris A. D. MCMXLI habita* (Milwaukee: Bruce, 1941), p. 245.

[11] V Diocesan Synod of Seattle (1938), stat. 34: "Adulti baptizari possunt in illa paroecia in qua fidem catholicam docti fuerint."—*Statuta Dioecesis Seattlensis Lata ac Promulgata ab Excellentissimo ac Reverendissimo Geraldo Shaughnessy, S. M. Episcopo Seattlensi in Synodo Dioecesana Seattlensi Quinta, Die prima mensi Junii, A. D. 1938* (Seattle, Washington: Typis Metropolitan Press Printing Co., 1938); II Prov. Council of Toronto (1938), decr. 149: "Adulti baptizari possunt in illa paroecia in qua fidem catholicam docti fuerint."

toms can be tolerated if the Ordinary judges that they cannot be prudently removed because of the peculiar circumstances of the place and of the people.[12]

When the local Ordinary has by statute or through an extant diocesan custom released those who have charge of converts from reporting adult baptisms, and when those who instructed the converts are not empowered by statute or through custom to baptize them, the question of who can receive the convert must be decided in the light of the rule of canon 738, § 1, which reserves this right to the proper pastor of the baptizand. This canon reads:

> **Minister ordinarius baptismi sollemnis est sacerdos; sed eius collatio reservatur parocho vel alii sacerdoti de eiusdem parochi vel Ordinari loci licentia, quae in casu necessitatis legitime praesumitur.**

The pastor is defined as the priest or moral person to whom the parish has been conferred in title with the care of souls to be exercised under the authority of the local Ordinary.[13] Since, however, no moral person can exercise the care of souls, a vicar who acts in the name of the moral person must be provided.[14] To this vicar pertains exclusively all the rights and obligations of pastors.[15] The Code extends the meaning of the term, pastor, to embrace: quasi-pastors, or those who are in charge of quasi-parishes,[16] and parochial vicars, if they have the full powers of a pastor.[17] These latter include besides the actual vicar of an incorporated parish, the substitute vicar,[18] the parish administrator, when the parish is vacant,[19]

[12] " . . . aliae, quae quidem centenariae sint et immemorabiles, tolerari poterunt, si Ordinarii pro locorum ac personarum adiunctis existiment eas prudenter submoveri non posse. . . ." Cf. Schaaf, "The Right to Baptize Converts," *AER*, XCIV (1936), 531.

[13] Canon 451, § 1.

[14] Canons 452, § 2; 471, § 1.

[15] Canon 471, § 4.

[16] Canons 451, § 2, 1°; 216, § 3.

[17] Canon 451, § 2, 2°.

[18] Canons 465, §§ 4, 5; 474.

[19] Canons 472, 1°; 473.

and before the administrator's appointment, the assistant pastor, or in parishes entrusted to religious the local superior resident at the attached parish house,[20] the adjutant vicar, if he is called on to assume full parochial charges,[21] and the assistant pastor when he is given full parochial powers.[22]

The proper pastor is determined by the domicile or quasi-domicile of the convert.[23] If the convert has not yet completed his twenty-first year, he is considered a minor,[24] and consequently retains the domicile of the person to whom he is subject.[25] Hence, the proper minister to receive the convert into the faith by solemn baptism is the convert's proper pastor by reason of the parish in which the convert lives. Outside of his own parish the pastor has need of the proper permission to baptize the convert, even though the convert has established his residence in the pastor's parish.[26]

In general, the pastor has the exclusive legal right to baptize solemnly all converts who have residence in his own parish. There are two notable exceptions to this rule, however: first, when another parish likewise has the right to baptize the converts of the parish; secondly, when a national parish exists within the boundaries of the parish. The first of these exceptions can be present when a filial church has been erected within the boundaries of its mother church.

[20] Canon 472, 2°. This canon makes provision also for meeting additionally possible emergencies in view of further possible situations. It designates in the absence of any assistants in the parish, the nearest neighboring pastor; in the event of several assistants, the one first in rank; in the event of equal rank among them, the one who has served the parish longer than any of the others. It remains for the bishop to determine in a timely fashion, either in or out of synod, which particular parish in relation to any given parish is to be considered as the nearest neighboring parish.

[21] Canon 475, §§ 1, 2.

[22] Canons 451, § 2, 2°; 477, § 2; 1427, §§§ 1, 4, 5. It is evident, however, that in almost all cases, according to the ruling of canon 476 and in the light of canon 1412, 1°, parish assistants do not qualify for classification among those *"qui parochorum nomine in iure veniunt"* (can. 451, § 2) or *"qui parochorum nomine in iure censentur"* (can. 899, § 3).

[23] Canon 94.

[24] Canon 88, § 1.

[25] Canon 93, § 1. Cf. Waldron, *The Minister of Baptism*, pp. 74-75.

[26] Canon 739: In alieno territorio nemini licet, sine debita licentia, baptismum sollemnem conferre ne sui quidem loci incolis.

In such a case the mother church can be permitted to exercise a cumulative right with its affiliated church in the matter of baptizing the converts of the filial parish, and consequently the convert can be received into the faith by the pastor of either one of the two parishes.[27]

Where a national parish exists within the boundaries of an English-speaking parish, both pastors can receive the converts of the nationality of the national parish. The pastor of the national parish cannot, however, baptize converts that are not of the nationality for which the national church exists. The reason for this is that he is limited with regard to jurisdiction to the members of that nationality for which the parish was erected. It is the distinguishing characteristic of a national parish to administer only to those of the nationality for which the parish has been established. The pastor of the national parish cannot insist, as if it were his right, that all converts of his nationality be baptized by him. The convert may make his own choice of the church to which he wishes to belong, and may choose to be baptized by the pastor of the English-speaking parish rather than by the pastor of the church serving his own nationality.

It cannot be argued that there is any obligation on the part of these foreign-speaking people to attend their national church, nor that the pastor of the national church has a right to compel them to attend, if these people can speak and understand English. Pro-

[27] Canon 774, § 1: Quaelibet paroecialis ecclesia, revocato ac reprobato quovis contrario statuto vel privilegio vel consuetudine, baptismalem habeat fontem, salvo legitimo iure cumulativo aliis ecclesiis iam quaesito. The Pontifical Commission for the Authentic Interpretation of the Code on November 12, 1922, explained the meaning of this canon as follows: "The sense of c. 774, § 1, is that a church which has a cumulative right to a font with other parish churches of the whole city, obtains such a right also in regard to the parish churches which have been newly created in the city with baptismal fonts. But the cumulative right to a font cannot in future be acquired by custom, such a custom being regarded as an abuse. But a church which before the promulgation of the Code had the exclusive right to a font over other parish churches, after the promulgation of the Code and the erection of a font in those churches according to the prescription of the aforesaid canon, acquires only a cumulative right, without prejudice to the prescriptions of c. 778."—Bouscaren, *Canon Law Digest,* I, 345; *AAS,* XIV (1922), 662.

vided that they know English sufficiently well, the people of that nationality are free to belong to the national parish or not. If they choose to belong, the pastor then acquires full pastoral jurisdiction over them as his subjects. Until the convert decides not to be baptized by him, then, the pastor of the national parish retains his right to baptize. It cannot be held that the pastor of a national parish can baptize converts of a nationality other than that of the national parish, as Augustine maintains, but rather he is strictly confined to the right and duty of ministering to his own nationals.[28]

Article 2. Through Reconciliation

When the convert is received into the Church through his abjuration of former errors and absolution from the censure of excommunication, the question of who has competence to receive him into the Church depends for its solution on whether the delict belongs to the internal or external forum. In the former instance the delict of heresy, schism and apostasy is reserved *speciali modo* to the Holy See and consequently only the Holy See has the native and inherent power to receive the convert in the internal forum.

There are two possibilities, however, whereby either the bishop or the ordinary confessor may receive the convert. In the first, if the bishop enjoys the faculties granted in the *pagella* of the Sacred Penitentiary, he may absolve from censures incurred by heretics even if the crime is public, provided that the convert has not publicly disseminated heretical doctrines among the faithful.[29] The ordinary confessor may receive the convert in the internal forum by reason

[28] Augustine (*Commentary,* IV, 41) bases his opinion on the allegation that before baptism no convert can be claimed as the subject of any pastor, since before baptism no one is directly bound by the laws of the Church. However, by directly binding her ministers, the Church indirectly, but nonetheless effectively, obligates also the person who is to be baptized. Cf. "National Parishes: Affiliation and Separation," *AER,* LXXXVII (1932), 531-537; Private declaration of the S. C. Conc., Jan. 15, 1938, and the letter of the Apostolic Delegate to all the members of the hierarchy of the United States, Feb. 17, 1938, as reported in Bouscaren, *Canon Law Digest,* II, 78-80.

[29] Cf. Bouscaren, *Canon Law Digest,* II, 38-39.

of the faculties granted him in the common law for urgent cases or when the convert is in danger of death.[30]

In the external forum it is the local Ordinary who can receive the abjuration and absolve from the censure. The term "local Ordinary" includes not only the residential bishop, but the Abbot or Prelate *nullius*, the Administrator, Vicar and Prefect Apostolic and those who succeed the preceding according to the prescriptions of law.[31] The Vicar General, however, cannot receive the convert without a special mandate from the Ordinary.[32] Since this power of the Ordinary pertains to his ordinary power it can be delegated either wholly or in part.[33] By presenting himself for instructions and generally showing his desire to enter the Church, the convert performs what is construed by the law to be a voluntary or spontaneous confession.[34] The recourse is, therefore, to the external non-judicial forum rather than to the judicial forum. Hence, any Ordinary, and not necessarily the proper Ordinary, either by reason of the place where the delict was committed,[35] or by reason of the convert's domicile or quasi-domicile [36] can receive the abjuration and absolve from the censure of excommunication.[37]

30 Canons 2252, 2254.

31 Canon 198. Cf. De Meester, *Compendium*, Vol. III, Pars II, n. 1814, p. 237.

32 Canon 2314, § 2.

33 Canons 2314, § 2; 199, § 1. Cf. *AER*, LXXI (1924), 92; Wernz-Vidal, *Ius Canonicum*, VII, 416.

34 Cf. canon 2314, § 2.

35 Cf. canon 1566, § 1.

36 Cf. canon 1561, § 1.

37 "Delinquens resipiscens, per spontaneam seu voluntariam confessionem potest comparare coram quolibet loci Ordinario ut a censura absolvatur, nec necessarius est recessus ad *proprium* Ordinarium, est autem recursus ad forum externum non praecise ad forum iudiciale. E contra ut post denuntiationem citetur ad forum criminale servandae sunt leges de foro competente."—Wernz-Vidal, *Ius Canonicum*, VII, 416.

CHAPTER III

THE INVESTIGATION

THE Instruction provides for an investigation into the convert's possible previous baptism before all else. In prescribing this formality the Holy Office merely repeated what has been the age-old practice of the Church in receiving converts.[1] This investigation is recommended by the Roman Ritual [2] and was insisted upon by many particular councils.[3] It has also been decreed in responses of the Sacred Congregation of the Council,[4] the Sacred Congregation of the Propagation of the Faith [5] and the Holy Office.[6]

Not only does the Instruction prescribe an examination, but it qualifies it with the word *diligenti.*[7] A conscientious investigation both as to the fact and as to the validity of the convert's baptism was also decreed by the III Plenary Council of Baltimore.[8]

[1] Cf. cc. 28, 38, 44, D. IV, *de cons:*

[2] Tit. 2, cap. 3, *de baptismo adultorum,* n. 10: "Sacerdos diligenter curet, ut certior fiat de statu et conditione eorum, qui baptizari petunt, praesertim exterorum: de quibus facta diligenti inquisitione, num alias, ac rite sint baptizati, caveat, ne quis iam baptizatus, imperitia, vel errore, aut ad quaestum, vel ob aliam causam, fraude, dolove iterum baptizari velit."

[3] Plenary Synod of Irish Bishops at Thurles (1850), decr. XI, c. 10; I Provincial Council of Westminster (1852), decr. XVI, c. 7; The Council of Port of Spain, Island of Trinidad (1854), sec. 1, art. 1, c. 8; Provincial Council of Cassel (1853), tit. III, *de bapt.*; II Prov. Council of Quebec (1854), decr. VII, c. 3—*Coll. Lac.*, III, 779, 929, 1097, 833, 634.

[4] S. C. C., Brixien., 28 nov. 1733; Tarvisina, 28 apr. 1736; Tarvisina, 4 maii 1737; Sutrina, 12 iulii 1794; Brixien., 27 aug. 1796; Brixien., 11 febr. 1797; 16 mart. 1897—*Fontes,* nn. 3412, 3458, 3475, 3890, 3902, 3904, 4302.

[5] S. C. de Prop. Fide, 17 apr. 1777—*Fontes,* n. 4575; instr. (ad Vic. Ap. Mysuren.), 31 dec. 1851—*Collect.*, n. 1069.

[6] S. C. S. Off., 20 nov. 1878; litt. (ad Ep. Harlemen.), 6 apr. 1859; instr. (ad Ep. Nesquallien.), 24 ian. 1877; (ad Vic. Ap. Iaponiae Merid.), 4 febr. 1891 —*Fontes,* nn. 1058, 950, 1050, 1130.

[7] Cf. S. C. S. Off., litt. (ad Ep. Harlemen.), 6 apr. 1859—*Fontes,* n. 950.

[8] N. 122.

> Ut sua igitur Baptismo debita servetur veneratio atque quam longissime absit vel sola apparentia repetitionis ejus illegitimae, praecipit Ecclesia ut quando quis ab errore ad fidem convertitur, semper diligens fiat investigatio num antea forsan baptizatus fuerit, numque validus fuerit Baptismus in haeresi susceptus.

No superficial investigation, then, suffices. Nor is it sufficient to rely on preconceived notions and presumptions of the universal invalidity or doubtful validity of non-Catholic baptism. Rather, each case should receive careful attention with the consideration that, on the one hand, the salvation of a soul is involved, and, on the other, reverence for the sacrament of Baptism demands that it be not administered uselessly. The investigation should concern itself first with the fact of baptism, and secondly, with the validity of the baptism.

Article 1. As to the Fact of Baptism

The practical norm which should guide the investigation of the fact of Baptism is set forth in canon 779:

> **Ad collatum baptismum comprobandum, si nemini fiat praeiudicium, satis est unus testis omni exceptione maior, vel ipsius baptizati iusiurandum, si ipse in adulta aetate baptismum receperit.**

The proof which may be adduced to certify to the fact of the reception of baptism may be divided into three classifications: (a) the certificate of baptism; (b) the testimony of witnesses; (c) the oath of the convert.

To this end, then, the convert should first be questioned as to the sect to which he formerly belonged. If he was born and reared in a sect which does not observe the practice of baptism,[9] and it is certain that he never joined any sect in which baptism was administered, sufficient certitude is had that he was never baptized. If, however, he was a member of a sect which does retain the observance

[9] Cf. Appendix III for a list of sects in the United States which do not observe the practice of baptism.

of baptism, a baptismal certificate should be obtained from the register of the place of baptism. Failing this, inquiry should be made from competent witnesses. The non-Catholic minister who baptized the convert could be such a competent witness, since he is considered qualified to testify to the official acts of his office.[10] Cappello, however, points out that the testimony given by a minister of a non-Catholic sect cannot be considered as conclusive proof in the canonical forum, and, therefore, does not of itself suffice to prove the fact that baptism has been administered or that the sacrament has been administered validly. In certain cases, he admits, such testimony may be sufficient, but its value will always depend on the peculiar circumstances of each case, and it is for the bishop to decide as to the conclusiveness of such proof.[11]

In the absence of a baptismal certificate and the reliable testimony of the one who performed the ceremony, parents, sisters and brothers, close relatives and friends may be presumed capable of giving sufficient proof of the fact of baptism. In evaluating the testimony of witnesses the two qualifying clauses, *si nemini fiat praeiudicium* and *omni exceptione maior* must be taken into consideration before sufficient corroborative proof is had.

[10] Vermeersch-Creusen (*Epitome,* III, n. 189, 1, p. 74) define a *testis qualificatus*: "qui in officio publico et iurato constituitur, si de rebus ex officio gestis deponat." Cf. can. 1791, § 1. The S. R. Rota considered the testimony of a police officer as the testimony of a *testis qualificatus*—S. R. Rota, *Nullitatis Matrimonii,* 4 aug. 1925, *coram R.P.D. Iosepho Florczak,* Decisio XLII, n. 9—*Sacrae Romanae Rotae Decisiones seu Sententiae* (Romae: Typis Polyglottis Vaticanis, 1912-), XVII (1925), p. 332. *A pari* it seems that a non-Catholic minister could also be considered a qualified witness in attesting the fact of a particular baptism.

[11] "Baptismi testimonium traditum a ministro sectae acatholicae nequit in foro canonico plenam fidem facere; ideoque *per se* non sufficit ad comprobandum factum collati Baptismi eiusque valorem. Quinam valor huiusmodi testimonio tribuendus sit, ex peculiaribus circumstantiis pendet. Episcopi erit, omnibus adiunctis accurate perpensis, iudicium ferre de vi atque efficacia probativa praefati testimonii.

"Idem fere dicendum de orali attestatione ministri haeretici aut schismatici." —*Tractatus Canonico-Moralis de Sacramentis* (3 vols. in 6, Vol. I, *De Sacramentis in genere, de Baptismo, Confirmatione et Eucharistiae,* 3. ed., Romae: Marietti, 1938), Vol. I, n. 190, 6, p. 169. (Hereafter cited *De Sacramentis.*)

The phrase *si nemini fiat praeiudicium* is commonly interpreted to mean if no extraneous party will suffer harm thereby.[12] Blat, however, includes even the convert under the word *nemini,* asserting the possibility that such a prejudice could exist for the one baptized, unless the validity of his baptism were proved.[13]

The phrase *omni exceptione maior* is the second qualification in the case of a single witness. To give sufficient proof of the fact of baptism the witness must be above any suspicion regarding his knowledge of the fact, his truthfulness, credibility, or testimony. Special consideration must be given to the circumstances which surround such testimony. Thus, ordinarily, a parent or close relative may be able to attest the fact of baptism.[14] But if the witness were of low moral standards or practiced no religion or were bitterly opposed to the convert's reception into the Church, his testimony could hardly be of sufficient weight to meet the requirements of canon 779.

The final proof mentioned in canon 779 is the sworn testimony of the convert himself, provided that the two necessary conditions are present, namely *si nemini fiat praeiudicium* [15] and *si ipse in adulta aetate baptismum receperit.*

Proof of the reception of baptism is more easily admitted than proof that no baptism was administered. As Wernz-Vidal point out, from their very nature negative facts are proved only with difficulty; and true proof which is tantamount to certitude can only be gleaned from a consideration of the circumstances of the case together with the testimony of close relatives.[16] The Holy Office

[12] "Nullius utilitas laedatur"—Sipos, *Enchiridion Iuris Canonici* (ed. 3a, Pécs: "Haladás R.T.," 1936), p. 448; "quae nullius utilitatem laedit"—Vermeersch-Creusen, *Epitome,* II, n. 56, p. 32; "agitur de damno seu iure tertii"—Cappello, *De Sacramentis,* I, n. 189, p. 167.

[13] "Ad collatum baptismum comprobandum quoad factum, si nemini fiat praeiudicium, uti fieret baptizato, ni validitas ipsius comprobaretur, satis est unus testis de facto et de validitate omni exceptione maior. . . ."—*Commentarium,* Vol. III, Pars I, n. 70, p. 73.

[14] Cf. canon 1974; Doheny, *Canonical Procedure in Matrimonial Cases* (Milwaukee: Bruce, 1938), p. 234.

[15] In discussing this part of the canon Blat excludes the convert: "Quia cum eius salutis valde intersit baptismus, omni exceptione maior est; 'si nemini (alii) fiat praeiudicium.' "—*loc. cit.*

[16] "Specialem difficultatem habet probatio non baptismi . . . de quo facile

on August 1, 1883, listed certain cases wherein the fact of non-baptism might be presumed, namely:

1. When there was question of one whose parents pertained to a sect which did not practice baptism.

2. When the parents belonged to a sect in which baptism was conferred only on adults, provided that there were weighty arguments attesting the fact that baptism was not received after that age (v. g., 30 years).

3. When the parents, while they were alive professed that they did not wish to pertain to any sect.[17] These presumptions, however, were given with regard to forming a judgment on the validity or nullity of a marriage and at a time when all baptized persons, whether they were baptized in the Catholic Church or in a non-Catholic sect, were bound by the impediment of disparity of worship. Of themselves they are not sufficient to prove the fact of non-baptism, and hence an attempt should always be made to obtain certain proof. To this end an investigation of the parish records of the sect to which the convert certainly or probably belonged should be made and the oral testimony of the convert himself together with that of his parents, the sponsors, and close relatives should be taken.[18]

Article 2. As to the Validity of Baptism

When sufficient certitude is had as to the fact of baptism, the examination must center on the validity of the baptism. In this investigation the principles of moral theology and the norms given by the Holy Office at various times serve as a safe guide. Since the validity of the sacrament of Baptism depends on the proper application of the requisite matter and form and the presence of the proper intention in the subject and in the minister, all these points must of necessity come under investigation.

suspicio oritur in locis ubi multae pullulant sectae acatholicae quae baptismum uno vel alio modo admittunt. Difficultas inde oritur, quod ex natura rei facta negativa difficilem habent probationem; vera probatio certitudinem generans solum ex complexu quodam circumstantiarum simul cum attestationibus propinquorum erui potest."—*Ius Canonicum,* Tom. IV, Vol. I, 53.

[17] *Fontes,* n. 1083. Cf. Doheny, *Canonical Procedure in Matrimonial Cases,* pp. 440-441.

[18] Cf. Wernz-Vidal, *loc. cit.*

I. Principles

A. Matter.

All the sacraments of the New Law consist of sensible signs and words which, since the thirteenth century, have been known as the matter and form.[19] The proper matter of Baptism, remote and proximate, is the ablution with true and natural water.[20]

(*a*) *Remote Matter.* The remote matter is natural water in its liquid state. In judging the validity of the remote matter the norm is not to be taken from the deduction of chemists but rather from the common and usual judgment as to what is natural water. It is of no consequence whether it was the result of human ingenuity or of nature, provided that it is commonly considered natural water.[21]

According to the usual opinion the following are recognized as valid matter: the water of rivers, lakes, oceans, wells, fountains, pools, ponds, swamps, marshes, subterranean reservoirs; rain water, distilled water, melted snow, ice, hail; mineral or sulphur water; dew, water from the condensation of mist or fog, water flowing from rocks, leaves, or the wall of a house in damp weather; water chemically produced or obtained by the distillation of some other matter, if it is free from extraneous elements; [22] also water mixed with some extraneous matter in a small quantity, provided that not only chemically but also according to the popular estimation the water is certainly predominant and the mixture can still be called water,[23] even though it is changed as to color, taste and smell,[24] e. g., putrid water, dirty or muddy water. It is of no consequence whether the water is warm or cold,[25] sweet or sour.[26]

[19] William of Auxerre (+1231) is generally considered to have been the first to have used this terminology in his *Summa Aurea* composed between 1215 and 1220, though some authors consider that Stephen Langton was the innovator.

[20] "Baptismus . . . valide non confertur, nisi per ablutionem aquae verae et naturalis cum praescripta verborum forma."—canon 737, § 1.

[21] Cf. Vermeersch, *Theologiae Moralis Principia, Responsa, Consilia* (4 vols., ed. 3a, Romae: Universita Gregoriana, 1933-1937), III, 174, n. 1.

[22] Cf. Merkelbach, *Summa Theologiae Moralis,* III, 101.

[23] S. C. S. Off. (Pondichery), 17 apr. 1839—*Fontes,* n. 879.

[24] Cappello, *De Sacramentis,* I, n. 129, p. 110; Genicot-Salsmans, *Institutiones,* II, 119.

[25] Cf. *Rituale Romanum,* tit. 2, cap. 1, n. 7.

[26] Merkelbach, *loc. cit.*

Matter that is certainly invalid: milk, blood, spittle, saliva, tears, urine, perspiration, phlegm, amniotic liquid [27] and other liquids from the animal or human body; wine, oil, beer, thick soup, gravy, lard, grease; mud, ink, lacquer, shoepolish; strong coffee, tea, broth, lye; the juices of flowers, of herbs, of roots, of seeds, of fruits, or the sap of trees.

Doubtfully valid matter are: very thin soup, broth, coffee, tea, unmelted snow and ice,[28] water produced from salt, from lye, or soapsuds, artificial water extracted by distillation from flowers or herbs, or flowing from vines or trees or other plants.

(*b*) *Proximate Matter.* The proximate matter is the ablution of the baptizand by the one baptizing with water.[29] The ablution or washing may be performed by pouring, immersion or aspersion.[30] A single pouring of the water is sufficient. For validity, the ablution in any of its three forms must meet the following requisites:

(a) The water must immediately and physically touch the body of the person to be baptized, and must flow over a certain portion of the body, so that the subject may be regarded as truly washed.[31]

[27] Merkelbach, *loc. cit.* Waldron, however, admits that the amniotic fluid most probably is not valid matter, though he claims that "it cannot definitely be stated that such a fluid is certainly invalid, for it is not definite that in the common opinion of people it is considered to be not a form of water."—*The Minister of Baptism*, pp. 140-141.

[28] Thus Cappello (*De Sacramentis*, I, p. 111), Noldin-Schmitt (*Summa Theologiae Moralis*, III, 56) and Vermeersch (*Theologia Moralis*, III, 174), as against Merkelbach (*loc. cit.*) who lists unmelted snow and ice as invalid matter, "quia non apta sunt ad ablutionem."

[29] Cf. canon 737, § 1.

[30] Canon 758.

[31] Hence, the baptism would be invalid if the water touched only the clothes. If the water touched only the hair, the baptism would be at least doubtful. Cf. Cappello, *De Sacramentis*, I, p. 114, n. 133; Noldin-Schmitt, *Theologia Moralis*, III, p. 60, n. 61. It is a valid baptism if the water was applied over sores on the head. Because the water must flow, if only one or two drops were applied and remained motionless on the skin, the baptism would be invalid. And one who would baptize by touching the forehead with a moistened finger or hand, or a damp cloth or sponge, would baptize invalidly. The baptism is doubtful if done with the thumb after the manner of anointing, because there is no true washing (S. C. S. Off., 14 dec. 1898—*Fontes*, n. 1211). However, if the forehead of the person is successively touched with the moistened hand of the minister or with

This immediate, physical and successive contact can take place by the movement of the subject in the water or by the movement of the water onto the subject. Hence, in immersion it is required that the subject be moved in or under the water; and in pouring and sprinkling some movement or flowing of the water is necessary.

(b) The water should be applied to the head.[32]

(c) The ablution must be performed by a person other than the one to be baptized, while pronouncing the form. Therefore, if the water is applied by the subject or a third person, while a second person pronounces the formula, or if the ablution is due solely to a natural cause, e. g., rain, or while the subject is bathing, the baptism is invalid. If the minister places the subject under water falling from above, as in a rainstorm, the baptism is invalid; if, however, this is done with the help of a third party who pours the water and who knows and intends that the water flow on the subject, the baptism is doubtful.[33]

B. Form.

The valid formula for Baptism in the Latin rite is: "I baptize thee in the name of the Father, and of the Son, and of the Holy Ghost." The form which is used among the Greeks is also valid: "The servant of Christ is baptized in the name of the Father and of the Son and of the Holy Ghost." [34]

a damp cloth, the common opinion among theologians is that the baptism is valid; likewise, if along with the use of a sponge or a damp cloth some drops of water were squeezed onto the forehead, and these drops actually flowed over a portion of the skin, the baptism is valid.

[32] Cf. canon 746, §§ 2, 3.

[33] The Sacred Congregation of the Sacraments on November 17, 1916, declared invalid a baptism in which the baptizand herself entered the font while the minister pronounced the form but did not pour the water nor submerge the subject. The reason for this pronouncement was the prescription of the Roman Ritual, tit. 2, cap. 1, n. 10, where it is stated: " . . . immergatur in modum crucis uno et eodem tempore, quo verba proferuntur, et idem sit aquam adhibens et verba pronuntians."—*AAS,* IX (1916), 478-480.

[34] Eugenius IV (in Conc. Florentin.) const. *Exultate Deo,* 22 nov. 1439, n. 10: "Non tamen negamus quin et per illa verba, Baptizatur talis servus Christi in nomine Patris, et Filii, et Spiritus Sancti; vel Baptizatur manibus meis talis, in nomine Patris et Filii et Spiritus Sancti, verum perficiatur Baptisma: quoniam cum principalis causa, ex qua baptismus virtutem habet, sit

For validity five elements must receive definite expression: [35]

1. The person baptizing, by either explicit or implicit declaration. The omission of the first personal pronoun would not invalidate the baptism in Latin, Greek or Italian, but in English, French, German or Dutch the baptism would be invalid.[36]

2. The act of baptizing.[37]

3. The person being baptized.[38]

4. The unity of the divine nature.

5. The Trinity of Persons, designated explicitly and distinctly. The general principle ruling the interpretation of the validity of varying forms of baptism is this: an essential or substantial change of the words of the form renders the sacrament invalid; an accidental change, though illicit, does not invalidate the sacrament. The change of the form of baptism is an essential change when the same sense, as conveyed by the valid form, does not remain; the change is accidental when, despite slight changes, the same sense does remain. The sense of the valid form is destroyed when the form which is used does not contain those elements which necessarily must be expressed, or when there is present some false or heretical meaning.[39]

sancta Trinitas, instrumentalis autem sit minister, qui tradit exterius Sacramentum, si exprimetur actus, qui per ipsum exercetur ministrum, cum Sanctae Trinitatis invocatione, perficitur sacramentum."—*Fontes,* n. 52.

[35] Cf. Merkelbach, *Summa,* III, 106.

[36] Cf. Genicot-Salsmans, *Institutiones,* II, 122.

[37] Cf. prop. 27 condemned by Alexander VIII (1689-1691)—Denzinger-Bannwart-Umberg, *Enchiridion Symbolorum* (ed. 21-23, Friburgi Brisgoviae: Herder & Co., 1937, n. 1317). (Hereafter cited D.B.) The use of the synonyms of *Baptizo,* e.g., *abluo, lavo, mergo, tingo, intingo* does not invalidate the form, according to the general opinion. Where, however, the vernacular is used, it is safer to use the word which is derived from the Latin word *baptizo,* unless it has a proper word to signify the sacramental ablution, as *doopen* (Dutch) or *taufen* (German), or *Ia te krstim* (Croatian). If the use of the words *I christen thee* signify the sacramental ablution, the baptism is valid; if they signify the effect of the sacrament, the baptism is invalid. In practice when the doubt cannot be resolved, conditional baptism should be administered. Cf. Waldron, *The Minister of Baptism,* p. 144; Genicot-Salsmans, *Institutiones,* II, 122; *The Clergy Review,* XV (1938), 544.

[38] Cf. S. C. S. Off., 11 mart. 1868, 11 ian. 1882—*Fontes,* nn. 1003, 1072.

[39] That the sacramental form be valid it is necessary that the words be

In practice, nothing can be omitted from the form, without its ceasing to be certainly valid, except the pronoun *I* (unless it must be present in order to determine the person of the minister),[40] the particle *and* before the invocation of the Son, and the adjective *Holy* before the word *Ghost*. If any other word is omitted, the form is substantially changed and the baptism must be repeated.[41] If it is not certain that the form contains all that should necessarily be expressed, or if there is doubt that a false or heretical doctrine is contained therein, the baptism is doubtful and must be repeated conditionally. The form is ambiguous when it can be accepted, as it stands, both in the approved sense and in a false or heretical sense. The validity of the baptism will hinge entirely on the intention of the minister in this case.[42]

suited of themselves to signify what Christ instituted and that the minister intend this; if the minister intends to signify something else, the sacrament is invalid, even though the words are the very same as those which Christ prescribed. Hence, one who uses the legitimate form, but intends to apply it in another sense, e. g., if he did not believe in the eternity of the Father, would baptize invalidly. But the private error of the minister does not impede the validity of the sacrament, provided that the words of themselves and by the at least prevalent intention of the minister signify what Christ intended.—Noldin-Schmitt, *Theologia Moralis,* III, p. 64, n. 63.

[40] Cf. rule 1 above.

[41] Cf. Noldin-Schmitt, *Theologia Moralis,* III, p. 62, n. 62, c.

[42] Authors list the following classifications of forms. The classification is based, however, on the use of these forms by *Catholic* ministers. If a non-Catholic even slightly changed the accepted formula, the baptism would be suspect, and a close investigation would be required to determine whether or not an heretical meaning was intended by the departure from the usual form.

Valid: "cum nomine Patris" (S. C. C., Forosempronien., 24 maii 1823—*Fontes,* n. 3981); "in nomine Patris omnipotentis"; "in nomine Patris qui te creavit"; the transposition of words, provided that the same sense substantially remains; "ego vos baptizo," etc. (if many are baptized at the same time); "in nomen Patris"; "En te baptismo en nome do Padre e do Filio e do Spirito Sancto" (S. C. S. Off. [Siam], 13 maii 1817—*Collect.,* n. 722); "Ego te baptigho in nomine Patri et Firii et Firtui Sancti" (S. C. S. Off. [ad Vic. Ap. Tunkin Occident.], 30 iul.-3 aug. 1880—*Collect.,* n. 1714); "Ego te baptizo in nomine Patris et in nomine Filii et in nomine Spiritus Sancti" (S. C. S. Off., 11 ian. 1882—*Fontes,* n. 1072); "si vis baptizari, ego te baptizo," etc. (S. C. S. Off. [Cochinchin.], 12 iun. 1850—*Collect.,* n. 1043).

The form must be pronounced by the one who administers the baptism, otherwise the words of the form are not verified and the sacrament is consequently invalid. A difference of opinion exists, however, as to the necessity of physical simultaneity in the application of the matter and form. Merkelbach insists that at least part of the form must be pronounced at the same time that the water is applied: otherwise the sacrament is invalid.[43] Genicot-Salsmans, on the other hand, maintain that the baptism is equally valid, if the ablution takes place immediately after the entire form has been pronounced.[44] In view of the instruction of the Holy Office dated May 2, 1858, the former opinion is the one to be followed in practice. This instruction insisted that baptism was to be repeated conditionally if the form was pronounced after the ablution, or if the ablution took place after the pronouncing of the words of the form.[45]

Invalid: The use of the word, *baptizo,* in the past tense (S. C. de Prop. Fide [C. P.], 27 mart. 1631—*Fontes,* n. 4446); if not the manner of the ablution but another mode or only the effects of baptism are expressed, e. g., "ego ungo te," etc.; "ego baptizo in nomine"; "ego baptizo te in nomine Patris maioris et Filii minoris," etc.; "ego volo tibi ministrare sacramentum Baptismi peccatorum in nomine," etc. (S. C. S. Off. [Cochinchin.], 23 iun 1840—*Fontes,* n. 881): "in nomine Dei, Jesu Christi, Dei unius et trini, SS. Trinitatis."

Doubtful: "Ego te baptizo in Patre et Filio"; "cum Patre et Filio"; "in nomine Patris per Filium"; "in nominibus Patris et Filii"; "nomine Patris"; "in virtute, maiestate, auctoritate Patris"; "in nomine Genitoris, et Geniti, et Procedentis ab utroque"; the complete omission of the particle *et*; "ego te christianizo"; "ego te reddo christianum."

[43] "Forma pronuntianda est *simul* cum infusione aquae, non solum moraliter, ita ut una alteri immediate succedat, sed etiam physice. Sic non solum ad liceitatem, sed etiam probabiliter ad validitatem, ita ut saltem partialiter pronuntietur forma durante ablutione. Quod in praxi omnino est tenendum, quia in dubio de *valore* sacramenti faciendum est id quod est tutius."—*Summa,* III, p. 109, n. 129.

[44] "In baptismo . . . *non* requiritur ut actio, quae in (hoc) rationem materiae proximae habet, *omnino eodem instanti physico* ponatur quo verba formae pronuntiantur, sed sufficit ut *partim simultanea* sint, vel ut *actio fiat immediate postquam forma* absoluta est. Nulla enim solida ratione exigitur strictior physica simultaneitas."—*Institutiones,* II, p. 97, n. 109.

[45] S. C. S. Off., instr. (ad Vic. Ap. Abissiniae), 2 maii 1858—*Collect.,* n. 1159.

C. Intention.

(a) In the Subject. For the valid reception of baptism at least an habitual intention is required in adults. This habitual intention may be either explicit or implicit.[46] An explicit habitual intention, which is contained in the wish to embrace the Christian religion, is essential for the validity of the sacrament. Though many theologians maintain that an implicit habitual intention which is expressed in the serious determination to do all that is required for salvation, or in the contrition or attrition of the subject, is sufficient for baptism, it is not a safe opinion to follow in actual practice. One who was baptized with such an intention would be required to receive baptism again conditionally.[47]

(b) In the Minister. In the minister of the sacrament neither probity of life, nor the state of grace, nor, even faith, is required for validity.[48] It is required that he give at least external attention to the rite he is performing,[49] and that he have the proper intention of doing what the Church does.[50]

For the determining of the validity of the minister's intention two fundamental principles must be kept in mind:

1. The required intention is the will, at least virtual and implicit, determined in relation to a certain matter and person for the performance of a sacramental rite.

a. At least virtual and implicit: neither an interpretative inten-

[46] "Dicitur *explicita,* si voluntas intendit id quod clare ac distincte apprehenditur; *implicita,* si id voluntas intendit quod aliquo modo continetur in obiecto explicite cognito et volito, quin tamen illud clare ac distincte apprehendatur."—Cappello, *De Sacramentis,* I, pp. 70-71, n. 84.

[47] Cf. Cappello, *loc. cit.* The question of the subject's intention is treated more fully in article 1, chapter IV.

[48] Cf. Resp. Nicolai I ad consulta Bulgarorum (Nov. 866),—D. B., nn. 334a, 335; Decr. Eugenii IV pro Armenis (22 nov. 1439)—D. B., n. 696; Conc. Trident., sess. VII, *De sacram. in gen.,* can. 12; *De baptismo,* can. 4—D. B., nn. 855, 860.

[49] "Ad validam sacramentorum administrationem requiritur et sufficit *attentio externa*: illa enim attentio requiritur et sufficit, qua administratio est actus vere humanus, ad hoc autem sufficit attentio externa. Ergo etiam minister distractus et de aliis rebus simul cogitans valide confert sacramenta."—Noldin-Schmitt, *Theologia Moralis,* III, 17.

[50] Cf. Conc. Trident., sess. VII, *De sacram. in gen.,* can. 11—D. B., n. 854.

tion, which one would have had, if he had adverted to this, but actually never has, nor an habitual intention, which was once formed and was never retracted but no longer is of sufficient force to influence the sacramental action, suffices. There is not required an actual intention whereby one invariably here and now intends the sacramental rite, since the unexceptable meeting of such a strict requirement would exceed the moral capacity of man. But there is required a virtual intention, whereby the actual intention, formed at some time in the past, is made to influence the sacramental action, though this actual intention is not at the time adverted to. There is also no strict need that the intention to perform the sacrament be explicit. The implicit intention which is contained in some other act suffices, e. g., in the case in which the minister is called for baptism, and proceeds to the church to perform the ceremony, but then does it distractedly. In practice, one who performs the ceremony from force of habit (*de more*) and does not positively exclude the intention, can be said to have an implicit intention.

b. Determined in relation to a certain matter and person: otherwise the action of the minister would be either indifferent, or its application would be misdirected, and either of these two defects would leave the action without sacramental force and effect.

c. For the performance of a sacramental rite: the rite of itself is indifferent and could be performed for a variety of purposes, either sacred or profane. In order that it become a sacrament the rite must be determined by the intention to perform a sacramental rite or of performing it as it is carried out in the true Church.

2. An external intention of simply performing the external act is not sufficient, but it is required that at least implicitly there be present an internal intention to perform the rite as Christ instituted it or as it is performed in the Church.

a. An external intention is not sufficient: the external act, even though it be performed in a sacred place and by a minister clothed in the proper vestments, can have a variety of ends. It can be a serious or a simulated act, a profane or a sacrilegious performance of a sacred action, and can be performed either in one's own name or in the name of Christ. It becomes a sacrament only through the internal intention which is conformable to the external rite.[51]

b. An internal intention to perform the rite as Christ instituted it or as it is performed in the Church is required: this intention is required because it is necessary that the intention to confer the sacrament be present, that the matter and form be determined through the intention of the minister as a sacramental action, and that the minister become through his intention the instrumental cause of the sacrament. This is what is implied in the intention to perform the rite in accord with the practice of the Church. As Pourrat points out, "It is not, however, required that the minister have as complete a knowledge of the Sacraments as the Church has,—else a pagan or a heretic could not validly baptize. It suffices, but it is indispensable, that he really consider the sacrament which he confers to be a sacred rite of the Church. . . . In a word, the minister of the sacrament is the representative, the legate of Christ and the Church; in the sacramental action he must conform his will to that of Christ and the Church."[52] To have the internal intention of acting in accord with the practice of the Church is interpreted to mean the intention so to perform the rite that by performing it the minister positively wills what the Church wills, or at least has the will to perform the rite as an act to which the Church accredits a sacred character with

[51] Cf. Merkelbach, *Summa,* III, 74-76; Prop. 28 damnata in Decr. S. C. S. Off., 7 dec. 1690: "Valet Baptismus collatus a ministro qui omnem ritum externum formamque baptizandi observat, intus vero in corde suo apud se resolvit: non intendo quod facit Ecclesia."—D. B., n. 1318. The condemnation of this proposition by Alexander VIII (1689-1691) furnishes a most weighty argument for the necessity of the proper internal intention. Inasmuch as the positive intention *"non faciendi quod facit Ecclesia"* is at least implicit with the one who has a mere negative internal intention, the opinion which demands a proper and positive internal intention must be followed in practice under pain of invalidity of the sacrament. Cf. Benedictus XIV, *De Synodo Dioecesana,* Lib. VII, cap. 4, n. 8.

[52] *Theology of the Sacraments* (4. ed., St. Louis: B. Herder Book Co., 1930), p. 389. "Ut sacramentum sit validum, non sufficit intentio mere externa, terminata nempe ad solum ritum externum cum apparatu sacro peractum; sed necessaria est intentio interna, quae nempe, implicite saltem et in confuso, pro objecto habeat effectum seu finem sacramenti."—Lahousse, *Tractatus De Sacramentis* (2 vols., Brugis, 1899), Vol. I, Thesis XXIII, pp. 309-317.

inherent spiritual effects.[53] This necessary intention was explained by the Holy Office: [54]

> Ad valorem tamen Sacramenti necessariam non esse eam intentionem quam vocant expressam seu determinatam, sed sufficere intentionem tantum *genericam* nimirum *faciendi quod facit Ecclesia* seu *faciendi quod Christus instituit* vel *quod christiani faciunt*, theologi passim docent.

Therefore an implicit intention of performing the rite in accord with the practice of the Church of Christ, in conformity with the purpose of Christ's institution of it, or in agreement with what Christians practice when they administer the sacrament is sufficient, even though the minister errs in thinking that his sect is the true Church.

From the fact that an implicit intention is required it does not follow that the minister is required to have the *explicit* intention of acting in conformity with the mind of the Church, namely, of conferring a sacrament, or of producing its effect. Nor is faith in Christ, in the Church, or in the sacrament required. Whatever be the minister's opinion of Christ, of the sacrament and of its efficacy, he baptizes validly if he wishes to perform the rite which the Church performs and which is held by her to be sacred, even though he himself thinks it to be of no value. Nor is it necessary to have the explicit intention of doing what the Roman Catholic Church does when baptism is administered, but there must be present simply the *general* intention of doing what is commanded by the true Church of Christ. Hence, a heretical minister, by wishing to act in conformity with the will of his church, which he falsely accounts to be the true Church of Christ, implicitly conforms his will to the will of

[53] "Ad habendam autem intentionem faciendi, quod facit ecclesia, sufficit, ut minister velit non mere ritum externum ponere (intentio *externa*), sed hunc ritum ita, ut eum ponendo velit positive id quod vult ecclesia (intentio *interna*) vel saltem ritum quatenus a catholicis habetur ut sacer."—Noldin-Schmitt, *Theologia Moralis*, III, 20.

[54] S. C. S. Off., instr. (ad Custodem Terrae Sanctae), 30 ian. 1833—*Fontes*, n. 871. Cf. Ayrinhac, *Legislation on the Sacraments*, p. 9: "As to his intention it is enough that he should at least implicitly mean to do what the Church does or what Christ had in view when he instituted the rite of baptism, whatever may be his personal views on the nature and efficacy of the sacrament."

the true Church of Christ, that is, to the will of the Roman Catholic Church. It is likewise not required that the minister think expressly of the Church. His intention of accomplishing what can and must be identified with the will of the Church, e. g., what has been left to mankind as Christ's mandate concerning baptism, what is commanded in the gospels regarding it, what is done by Christians who seek salvation through baptism, or what is desired by the petitioner when he asks for baptism in the name of Christ, is substantially sufficient.[55]

It must be remembered that the errors which non-Catholics hold on the necessity, nature and efficacy of baptism do not necessarily militate against the validity of the sacrament, nor do they exclude the proper intention of the minister, whether these errors reflect but the private opinions of individual ministers or even the official teaching of the sect. Nor do these errors in and of themselves furnish any basis for a general presumption that all non-Catholic baptisms are invalid.[56] Even the express mention of the minister to the candi-

[55] Cf. Merkelbach, *Summa*, III, 76-77. Woywod wrongly interprets the phrase *faciendi quod facit Ecclesia*: "The 'due intention' in baptizing, which the Code demands means that the baptizer intends the *end* for which Christ instituted the sacrament . . ."—"The Legislation of The Code on Baptism," *Homiletic*, XX (1920), 1042.

[56] S. C. S. Off., instr. (ad Ep. Nesquallien.), 24 ian. 1877: "Itaque circa Baptismum a ministris sectae methodistarum administratum refers, tot et tales esse horum haereticorum errores circa necessitatem virtutem et efficaciam eiusmodi sacramenti, ut pro certo retineri debeat eos illum habere tamquam ritum mere indifferentem, quem ideo in praeteritis temporibus penitus omittere consueverunt, et in posterioribus reassumpserunt sola prava voluntate homines infideles, vel etiam fideles fallendi, iisdem scilicet ostendendi falsam eorum religionem a nostra unice vera non differre. . . . Etenim novit A. Tua dogma fidei esse Baptismum a quocumque sive schismatico, sive haeretico, sive etiam infideli administratum validum esse habendum, dummodo in eiusdem administratione singula concurrerint, quibus sacramentum perficitur, scilicet debita materia, praescripta forma, et persona ministri cum intentione faciendi quod facit Ecclesia. Hinc consequitur errores peculiares, quos ministrantes sive privatim, sive etiam publice profitentur nihil officere posse validitati baptismi, vel cuiuscumque sacramenti, quia ut loquitur S. Augustinus, sacramenta ubique integra sunt, etiamsi prave intelligantur, et discordiose tractentur (S. August., *de Bapt.*, lib. 3, cap. 15, n. 20). Imo, quod praesertim in casu de quo agitur notandum est, peculiares errores ministrantium, per se et propria ratione, neque

date before baptism that the rite will have no effect on his soul, since it is to be regarded merely as an external sign of aggregation to the sect, does not exclude the proper intention to perform the rite in accordance with the practice of the true Church.[57] Nor do the presumptions of the old law regarding the validity or invalidity of a doubtful baptism with regard to its consequent effect on the status of marriage have place in the present procedure.[58]

Lehmkuhl[59] maintains, however, that the carelessness prevailing

excludunt illam intentionem, quam minister sacramentorum debet habere, faciendi nempe quod facit Ecclesia. . . . Vidit igitur A. Tua quomodo in Ecclesia semper traditum inveniatur, errores quos haeretici sive privatim, sive etiam publice profitentur, non esse incompossibiles cum illa intentione, quam sacramentorum ministri de necessitate eorumdem tenentur habere, faciendi nempe quod facit Ecclesia, vel faciendi quod Christus voluit ut fieri; et eosdem errores per se non posse inducere generalem praesumptionem contra validitatem sacramentorum in genere, et Baptismi in specie ita ut ea ipsa sola statui possit practicum principium omnibus casibus applicandum, vi cuius quasi a priori, ut aiunt, baptismus sit iterum conferendus."—*Fontes*, n. 1050. Cf. S. C. S. Off., instr. (ad Custodem Terrae Sanctae), 30 ian. 1833—*Fontes*, n. 1024; S. C. de Prop. Fide, instr. (ad Vic. Ap. Siam), 23 iun. 1830—*Fontes*, n. 4748; S. C. de Prop. Fide, instr. (ad Vic. Ap. Pondicher.), 26 iul. 1845—*Fontes*, n. 4815.

[57] S. C. S. Off., instr. (ad Vic. Ap. Oceaniae Central.), 18 dec. 1872: "Denique A. Tua quartum adiecit classem dubiorum circa baptismum, quae haec fuere: '*In quibusdam locis nonnulli* (haeretici) *baptizant cum materia et forma debitis, simultanee applicatis, sed expresse monent baptizandos, ne credant baptismum habere ullum effectum in animum: dicunt enim ipsum esse signum mere externum aggregationis illorum sectae. Itaque illi saepe catholicos in derisum vertunt circa eorum fidem de effectibus baptismi, quam vocant quidem superstitiosam. Quaeritur:*

"1. *Utrum baptismus ab illis haereticis administratus sit dubius propter defectum intentionis faciendi quod voluit Christus, si expresse declaratum fuerit a ministro, antequam baptizet, baptismum nullum habere effectum in animam.*

"2. *Utrum dubius sit baptismus sic collatus, si praedicta declaratio non expresse facta fuerit immediate, antequam baptismus conferretur, sed illa saepe pronuntiata fuerit a ministro, et illa doctrina aperte praedicetur in illa secta.*
R. Ad 1. Negative: quia, non obstante errore quoad effectus baptismi, non excluditur intentio faciendi quod facit Ecclesia.

Ad. 2. Provisum in primo."—*Fontes*, n. 1024; *Collect.*, n. 1392.

[58] Cf. Schenk, *Mixed Religion and Disparity of Cult*, p. 131.

[59] *Theologia Moralis*, II, n. 19, 1.

among Protestants in the administration of baptism creates an *a priori* derived presumption against the validity of the sacrament, and therefore, unless a trustworthy witness is at hand to testify that everythin was done validly, in practice baptism must be again administered. This opinion, says Cappello, is to be accepted only *cum debita discretione.*[60] Such general presumptions are of little or no value. The practice of the Holy See has been to examine whether the particular rite of baptism has been administered properly. When proof of its integrity is furnished, the proper internal intention is to be presumed, unless there is evidence so compelling as to foster a prudent doubt to the contrary. Since the intention of the minister is of its nature internal and intangible, the rule here proposed is the only possible solution for avoiding constant anxieties and scruples.[61]

II. Procedure

The investigation concerning the validity of the convert's baptism must cover two points:

A. An examination of the ritual of the sect in which the convert was baptized.[62]

B. A further examination to ascertain whether the recognized ritual of the sect was actually observed in this particular case.

[60] *De Sacramentis,* I, p. 151, n. 173.

[61] S. C. S. Off., instr. (Ad Custodem Terrae Sanctae), 30 ian. 1833: "Hae autem cautelae ac diligentiae omnes in ferendo iudicio de baptismo iam collato, de cuius validitate dubitatur, ut adhibeantur, tum Sacramenti eiusdem dignitas et sanctitas, tum fidelium utilitas, et animarum quies, atque tranquillitas cui in primis consulendum est, omnino suadent. Quandoquidem si nimia, seu imprudenti quadam facilitate, dubia quae circa huius Sacramenti validitatem in dies nascuntur excipiantur, homines timidi et scupulosi de suscepti baptismi valore semper dubitabunt, seque iterum baptizari requirent. Horum exemplum alii atque alii imitabuntur, ideoque multa eaque gravia in religionem orirentur incommoda et scandala, quae omnino evitari debent."—*Fontes,* n. 871.

[62] "In forming our judgment in any proposed case we must be guided very much by the ritual, or authorized mode of baptizing in the sect from which the convert comes."—O'Kane-Fallon, *Notes on the Rubrics of the Roman Ritual* (new edition revised in accordance with the latest [1925] *Editio Typica* of the *Rituale Romanum* and the Decrees of the Sacred Congregations, Dublin: James Duffy & Co., 1938), p. 210.

A. Examination of the Ritual.

This method is approved by the practice of the Holy Office. When asked about the validity of Anglican baptisms, the Holy Office commanded an examination of the individual rituals to determine their manner of baptism, but added that each case had to be examined individually.[63] In the discussion on Methodist baptism, in the same instruction, it was declared that the solution hinged on two points:

> (1) Whether the rite of administering baptism contained anything which could induce the nullity of the sacrament;
> (2) Whether the ministers of that sect actually conformed to the prescriptions contained in their ritual books.

As to the first point, an inspection of the ritual books will decide. As to the second question, an accurate and prudent investigation in individual instances is necessary, by means of which knowledge both of the fact and the validity of baptism will be obtained. The same Congregation was asked whether those persons who lived in places where Protestant baptisms were doubtful were to be considered as infidels, so that in their prospective marriages with Catholics there was present the impediment of disparity of cult. The answer was given in relation to the then existing marriage law, but it confirms the procedure to be followed in investigating the baptism of converts:

> Resp. Ad 1. Quoad haereticos quorum sectae ritualia praescribunt collationem Baptismi absque necessario usu materiae et formae essentialis, debet examinari casus particularis.
> Ad 2. Quoad alios qui iuxta eorum rituale baptizant valide, validum censendum est Baptisma.[64]

The presumption established in the answer to the second question was concerned with the validity of baptism only in its relation to marriage, and did not suffice as an equivalent for certainty when there was question of the eternal salvation of the convert.

In various responses of the Congregations an examination of the matter and form of non-Catholic baptisms is required; the implica-

[63] 24 ian. 1877—*Fontes*, n. 1050.

[64] S. C. S. Off., 17 nov. 1830—*Fontes*, n. 869.

tion is that this is to be done through an examination of the ritual of the sect and by means of a further investigation to ascertain whether the ritual was actually followed in its prescriptions.[65]

Cappello also approves this mode of procedure:

> Non sufficit attendere ad rituale sectae et examinare num aliquid validitati Baptismi contrarium contineat, sed praeterea inquirendum est singulis in casibus sive de facto, i. e., de collato Baptismo, sive de modo quo a ministro servatae fuerint praescriptiones ritualis sectae proprii.[66]

Waldron states: [67] "Those sects which prescribe baptism must first be examined with regard to their ritual before any presumption can be formed. If valid matter and form are prescribed by the ritual, the initial presumption will be for the validity of the baptism conferred as a ceremony within that sect. If the ceremony prescribed in the ritual is of doubtful validity or definite invalidity, the initial presumption will likewise be for doubtful or invalid baptism. . . . The initial presumption is of use only in determining the nature and extent of the future investigation to be made." Schenk also demands this form of procedure: [68]

> Only those Baptisms, therefore, which are conferred in those sects that repudiate Baptism are under an initial presumption of doubt. On the other hand, those sects which prescribe Baptism must first be examined with regard to their ritual before forming any presumption. If the ritual prescribes a valid matter and form, the initial presumption will be for the validity of the Baptism. If the rite prescribed is of doubtful validity or of manifest invalidity, the initial presumption will bear the corresponding character of doubt or of invalidity.
>
> The term "initial presumption" is used advisedly, for the Church does not permit the investigation to stop with a presumption regarding a sect. Each individual case must be examined to determine the value of the initial presumption.

[65] Cf. S. C. S. Off. (Bulgariae), 5 iul. 1853—*Fontes,* n. 925; S. C. de Prop. Fide instr. (ad Vic. Ap. Siam), 23 iun. 1830—*Fontes,* n. 4748.

[66] *De Sacramentis,* I, p. 150, n. 173, 2.

[67] *The Minister of Baptism,* p. 154.

[68] *Mixed Religion and Disparity of Cult,* p. 129, nn. 197, 198.

This method is also, at least implicitly, decreed by the III Plenary Council of Baltimore: [69]

> Neque sufficit investigatio mere generalis de consuetudine vel praxi aliquarum sectarum, per quam haberi posset praesumptio de collato vel non collato Baptismo aut de eius validitate vel nullitate; sed, quantum possibile fuerit, inquirendum est in singulorum neophytorum Baptismum, ut obtineatur, qualis in casu haberi queat, vel certitudo vel probabilitas, eos fuisse vel non fuisse valide baptizatos.

It is true that the decree does not explicitly use the word *ritual*, but it is obvious that it is principally through a study of the rituals of the various sects that one can arrive at a knowledge of the general practice and the accustomed manner of baptizing in those sects.[70]

When it is impossible to obtain the ritual of a certain sect, or when no ritual exists, the investigation will of necessity be more detailed and will cover all the points concerning validity mentioned in the first part of this chapter.[71] The examination of the ritual will give rise to definite presumptions of validity or invalidity. But since these presumptions do not lead to anything more than an ultimate conjecture, they are of themselves of insufficient weight to warrant either a rebaptism, whether conditional or absolute, or the omission of rebaptism. Further investigation as to the manner in which the baptism was actually conferred in this particular instance is demanded.

B. Individual Investigation.

The Holy Office has repeatedly demanded an individual investigation of each case and has strongly condemned the practice of relying solely on presumptions.[72] On February 21, 1883, the Holy

[69] N. 122.

[70] Because of the importance of knowing the baptismal rites of the various sects, extracts from the rituals ot certain non-Catholics bodies have been arranged in Appendix I.

[71] The sample questionnaire as contained in Appendix IV may be consulted.

[72] Cf. Instr. (ad Ep. Nesquallien.), 24 ian., 1877: "In singulis casibus faciendas esse accuratas investigationes. . . . Spectandos tamen esse casus par-

Office published a response containing the decree of the same Congregation under date of November 20, 1878, which reads: [73]

> Proposito dubio utrum conferri debeat baptismus sub conditione haereticis qui ad catholicam fidem convertuntur e quocumque loco proveniant et ad quamcumque sectam pertineant—Emi Patres responderunt—Negative: Sed in conversione haereticorum a quocumque loco vel a quacumque secta venerint inquirendum est de validitate baptismi in haeresi suscepti. Instituto igitur in singulis casibus examine, si compertum fuerit aut nullum, aut nulliter collatum fuisse, bapizandi erunt absolute: Si autem pro temporum et locorum ratione, investigatione peracta, nihil sive pro validitate, sive pro invaliditate detegatur, aut adhuc probabile dubium de baptismi validitate supersit, tunc sub conditione secreto baptizentur. Demum si constiterit validum fuisse, recipiendi erunt tantummodo ad abiurationem seu professionem fidei.

The insufficiency of an examination of the ritual and the necessity of further accurate investigation is commonly insisted upon by theologians,[74] and was urged by the II Plenary Council of Baltimore (1866): [75]

> Haeretici autem plerique, cum de Baptismo parum recte sentiant, eamque merae caeremoniae loco habeant, quae nihil ad animae salutem consequendam juvet, ritus quosdam, qui maximi momenti sunt, et sine quibus haud consistit sacramenti ratio, negligere saepissime solent. Ideoque eos, quos singularis Dei gratia ex illorum castris evocat atque educit, quum Ecclesiae nomen dant, iterum baptizari fere semper oportet. Neque tamen omnes ab haereticis olim baptizati, statim temere a sacerdote ad quem accedant, iterum baptizari debent. . . . Neque de omnibus, nullo discrimine, per principia quaedam, ut ajunt, generalia

ticulares de quibus agitur."—*Fontes*, n. 1050; litt. (ad Ep. Harlemen.), 6 apr. 1859—*Fontes*, n. 950; instr. (ad Vic. Ap. Iaponiae Merid.), 4 febr. 1891—*Fontes*, n. 1130; S. C. de Prop. Fide, instr. (ad Vic. Ap. Pondicher.), 26 iul. 1845: "Ergo nonnisi post institutum singulorum casuum examen."—*Fontes*, n. 4815.

[73] *Fontes*, n. 1058.

[74] Cf., e. g., Genicot-Salsmans: "Non sufficit attendere ad Rituale sectae et examinare num aliquid validitati baptismi contrarium contineat, sed insuper indagandum in singulis casibus tam de facto, seu de collato baptismo, quam de modo quo a ministro praescriptiones huius Ritualis observatae fuerint."—*Institutiones*, II, p. 135, n. 153.

[75] N. 240.

> judicandum est: sed in singulos, qui oblati fuerint, casus, non levi quidem aut perfunctorio, sed diligenti examine, inquirendum est explorandumque, num in singulis servata fuerit debita materia et forma.

The result of the investigation will determine which of the three methods mentioned in the Instruction must be used. If it is found that no baptism was ever conferred or that it was administered invalidly, reception will be through absolute baptism; in the event of a prior valid baptism, only the formalities of abjuration, of absolution (absolute or conditional) from the censures and of sacramental absolution from the sins need be observed. When the investigation results in a probable doubt as to the validity of the prior baptism, conditional baptism, in addition to the other formalities must be employed.[76]

Scholion I. The Intention of the Minister.

In the investigation some consideration must be given to the intention of the minister when he applies the rite of his sect. Therefore it is imperative to have a practical norm applicable to all cases. Such a rule was set forth by Pope Leo XIII (1878-1903) and applied by him in forming his decision on the invalidity of Anglican Orders. This rule is expressed under n. 10 of his apostolic letter, *Apostolicae Curae,* issued September 13, 1896:

> De mente vel intentione, utpote quae per se quiddam est interius, Ecclesia non iudicat: at quatenus extra proditur, iudicare de ea debet. Iamvero quum quis ad sacramentum conficiendum et conferendum materiam formamque debitam serio ac rite adhibuit, eo ipso censetur id nimirum facere intendisse quod facit Ecclesia. Quo sane principio innitur doctrina quae tenet esse vere sacramentum vel illud, quod ministerio hominis haeretici aut non baptizati, dummodo ritu catholico, conferatur. Contra, si ritus immutetur, eo manifesto consilio ut alius inducatur ab Ecclesia non receptus, utque id repellatur quod facit Ecclesia et quod ex institutione Christi ad naturam attinet sacramenti, tunc palam est, non solum necessariam sacramento intentionem deesse, sed intentionem immo haberi sacramento adversam et repugnantem.[77]

[76] Cf. Instruction of July 20, 1859, and canon 2314, § 2.

[77] *Fontes,* n. 631.

Since therefore, a judgment as to the presence of the proper intention must be made, the practical rule is this: when the valid matter and form of the sacrament are present, by that very fact the minister of the sacrament is presumed to have the proper intention; if however, the rite is so changed, with the manifest intention of substituting another rite not approved by the Church, that what Christ instituted and the Church practices is deliberately changed or omitted, not only is the proper intention lacking, but there is present a positive contrary intention.

This principle of Pope Leo XIII is the same as that which was invoked by the Sacred Congregation of the Propagation of the Faith in 1830 in an instruction on non-Catholic baptisms: [78]

> In illa vero disquisitione facienda de validitate vel invaliditate prioris baptismatis, antequam sub conditionata forma iteretur, debent animarum pastores inquirere praesertim super formam et materiam adhibitam in priori baptismate. Nam relate ad intentionem . . . *nisi prudens de ea fuerit dubitatio, praesumenda illa est.*

The same instruction, in application of the principle, cited Pius V (1566-1572) as maintaining that a general intention of fulfilling Christ's mandate in regard to baptism, even though the particular interpretation and intention in regard to Baptism should be erroneous, was sufficient for the validity of the sacrament.

In a response of the same year the Holy Office rendered a decision in which it presumed the baptism valid when all the essentials for validity were found in the ritual.[79] Three years later the Holy Office issued an instruction on the same subject, in which it upheld the principle that the private error of the minister over which prevails the general intention of performing the baptismal rite in obedience to Christ's command or in accordance with the practice of the true Church of Christ does not affect the validity of the intention, and consequently, not the validity of the sacrament.[80] As Schenk

[78] S. C. de Prop. Fide, instr. (ad Vic. Ap. Siam), 23 iun. 1830—*Fontes*, n. 4748.

[79] S. C. S. Off., 17 nov. 1830—*Fontes*, n. 869.

[80] S. C. S. Off., instr. (ad Custodem Terrae Sanctae), 30 ian. 1833—*Fontes*, n. 871.

remarks, "The primary concern of the Church is centered upon the rite of Baptism, and when proof of its integrity is furnished, the intention is to be presumed. Since the intention is of its nature internal and hidden, the rule established by the Church is the only possible solution of avoiding constant anxieties and scruples." [81]

In judging the validity of the convert's baptism, then, if from an examination of the ritual of his sect, the proper matter (remote and proximate) and form are found to be present, one will presume a valid intention on the part of the minister. This presumption is of such force that only a positive indication of the presence of an improper intention is sufficient to destroy it, and thus render the baptism at least doubtful. Such a positive indication may show itself in the examination of the minister who performed the ceremony. For if the rite prescribed by the sect contains nothing contrary to the valid rite, there is no indication, much less a positive indication, that an improper intention is present. Only when the rite is changed substantially can it be argued that there is present a positive contrary intention which is sufficient to destroy the validity of the sacrament.

It has been alleged that the majority of non-Catholic sects in the United States do not administer baptism validly because by their heretical notions on the nature and efficacy of baptism they interpolate into the form a meaning which is essentially at variance with the Church's sense. It is implied thereby that there is present in the minister a positive intention not to perform the rite of baptism in accordance with the practice of the Church.[82] It is sufficiently clear, from what has been said in the first part of this chapter on the intention of the minister, that no matter how erroneous may be the views of non-Catholic sects concerning the nature and effects of baptism, if there is present the serious intention faithfully to administer the rite as Christ's instituted mandate (the application of the valid matter and form being duly presupposed), the baptism

[81] *Mixed Religion and Disparity of Cult,* pp. 125-126.

[82] Cf. Donovan-Schaaf controversy in *AER,* LXXIV (1926), 158-180; LXXV (1926), 136-151; 358-370; LXXVI (1927), 155-165; 496-504; LXXXIV (1931), 124-139; 282-285; 371-387; Bouscaren, "De Validitate Baptismi apud Baptistas"—*Gregorianum,* VIII (1927), 41-54.

must be considered valid. That this intention is generally present is indicated from the examination of the several ritual formulas found in Appendix I. In general it may be said that it does not appear from these ritual formulas that there is present a positive intention not to perform the rite in obedience to Christ's mandate or in conformity to the practice of the true Church of Christ. Such a positive contrary intention, were it present, could certainly be expected to appear in the very rite itself, which rite would of necessity reflect an essential change and departure from the Catholic rite. But such an essential change or departure from the Catholic rite does not as a rule appear.

SCHOLION II. The Historical Aspect of Non-Catholic Baptism.

The question of the validity of heretical baptism was first raised in the third century. On the occasion of the Montanist heresy, Agrippinus, the Bishop of Carthage, decreed that all converts from heresy were to be rebaptized, thinking that all baptisms conferred outside the true faith were invalid. Tertullian, Clement of Alexandria and Hippolytus approved this doctrine and further confirmation came from the Provincial Council of Carthage (218 or 222). Councils held in Asia Minor a few years later also adopted this practice.[83] St. Cyprian, who succeeded Agrippinus in the See of Carthage, confirmed the practice of his predecessor in three particular councils, as did Firmilianus, the Bishop of Caesarea in Cappadochia. St. Cyprian based this decision on three arguments: (a) outside the Church there is no salvation, and therefore no grace. Since heretics are outside the Church, they cannot be the instruments of grace. (b) Since no one can confer what he does not possess himself, and since heretics have neither faith nor the Holy Ghost, they cannot baptize effectually. (c) Because true faith is a necessary condition for the reception of the sacraments, those baptized in heresy are not validly baptized.

St. Stephen I (254-257) condemned this error, without, however,

[83] Cf. Corblet, *Histoire Dogmatique, Liturgique et Archéologique du Sacrament de Baptême* (2 vols., Genève, 1881-1882), I, 325-351; Hefele-Leclerq, *Histore des Conciles* (10 vols. in 19, Paris: Letouzey et Ané, 1907-1938), I, 172-191.

excommunicating those who adhered to it, because of the intervention of St. Dionysius.[84] The error was adopted by the Donatists in the following century and refuted by St. Augustine, who pointed out that the validity of baptism did not depend on the dispositions of the minister but on the application of the proper matter and form.[85] The Council of Arles (314) in canon 8 expressly condemned the practice of the Donatists.[86] The first Council of Nicaea (325) decreed that converts from Novatianism were to receive only the ceremony of the imposition of hands.[87]

After the pronouncement of Pope Siricius (384-398) the controversy on rebaptism was practically ended.[88] Thus, the I Council of Carthage (348) [89] had prohibited rebaptism, while the Council of Laodicaea (ca. 340) had distinguished between converts from sects in which the proper matter and form were used and converts in whose administration of baptism there was some defect. This same distinction had been made in the I Council of Nicaea and was later explained by Innocent I (402-417) [90] as attributable to the fact that one sect, the Paulianists, rejected the Trinitarian formula, while the other, the Novatianists, held it in great reverence: only

[84] A fragment of the Pope's letter to St. Cyprian reads: "Si qui ergo a quacumque haeresi venient ad vos, nihil innovetur nisi quod traditum est, ut manus illis imponatur in poenitentiam, cum ipsi haeretici proprie alterutrum ad se venientes non baptizent, sed communicent tantum." Cf. Jaffé, n. 125; *MPL,* III, 1128, 1161, 1169.

[85] *De Baptismo contra Donatistas,* lib. IV, cap. xv, n. 22: ". . . iam satis ostendimus ad Baptismum qui verbis evangelicis consecratur, non pertinere cuiusquam vel dantis vel accipientis errorem, sive de Patre, sive de Filio, sive de Spiritu sancto aliter sentiat, quam coelestis doctrina insinuat."—*MPL,* XLIII, 168.

[86] "De Afris, quod propria lege sua utuntur, ut rebaptizent, placuit, ut si ad Ecclesiam aliquis de haeresi venerit, interrogent eum symbolum, et si perviderint eum in Patre et Filio et Spiritu Sancto esse baptizatum, manus ei tantum imponatur, ut accipiat Spiritum Sanctum. Quodsi interrogatus non responderit hanc Trinitatem, baptizetur."—Hefele-Leclerq, *Histoire des Conciles,* I, 209.

[87] Hefele-Leclerq, *Op. cit.,* I, 407.

[88] Cf. D. B., n. 88, nota 3.

[89] Canon 1—Mansi, III, 145 B.

[90] Letter to Rufus and other bishops of Macedonia, December 13, 414—Jaffé, n. 303.

the former, therefore, were to be rebaptized. The traditional doctrine was reiterated by Pope Leo I (440-461) when he wrote that Arian converts were not to be rebaptized, but only the omitted ceremonies were to be supplied. Thus, Arians in the East who had not been anointed, on their reception into the Church were to be anointed; Arians in the West, who had been anointed, were to be received only with the imposition of hands.[91]

The error of the Donatists was revived by the Albigensians in the twelfth century, and by the Waldensians in the thirteenth, and again by Wycliff in the fifteenth century. The former error was condemned by Lucius III (1181-1185) in the Council of Verona (1184),[92] while the IV General Council of the Lateran (1215), John XXII (1316-1334) and the Council of Constance (1414-1418) upheld the traditional doctrine of the Church against the Waldensians and Wycliff.[93] The IV General Council of the Lateran (1215) distinctly forbade rebaptism,[94] as did the II Council of Lyons (1274) [95] and subsequent authoritative pronouncements. It was definitely established that the traditional teaching of the Church was not to rebaptize converts from heresy, simply because they were baptized in heresy, but only if the proper matter and form were not applied.[96]

In the ninth century Pope Nicholas I (858-867) wrote that baptism was valid even when it was conferred by infidels, as long as they used the proper matter and the Trinitarian formula, and that rebaptism in such a case who wholly unwarranted.[97] After the definitions of the Lateran Council (1215), of the Council of Florence (1438-

[91] *Ep. CLXVII* (ad Rusticum, a. 458-459)—c. 38, D. IV, *de cons.;* Jaffé, n. 544.

[92] C. 9, X, *de haereticis,* V, 7; Jaffé, n. 15109.

[93] Cf. D. B., nn. 420; 428; 488; 581 sqq.

[94] Cap. 4, *De superbia Graecorum contra Latinos*—Mansi, XXII, 990.

[95] D. B., n. 464.

[96] This is the testimony of St. Vincent of Lerins: "Agrippinus, Carthaginiensis episcopus, primus omnium mortalium, contra divinum canonem, contra universalis Ecclesiae regulam, contra sensum omnium consacerdotum, contra morem ac instituta majorum, rebaptizandum esse censebat. . . ."—quoted in Tanqueray, *Synopsis Theologiae Dogmaticae,* III, p. 287, n. 409.

[97] C. 24, D. IV, *de cons.;* Jaffé, n. 2821.

[98] D. B., n. 430; *Fontes,* n. 52; D. B., n. 860.

1445) and of the Council of Trent (1545-1563) [98] the discussions on baptisms outside the Church centered on the question of the intention of the minister. In the twelfth century theologians were divided in their opinions as to whether an intention was necessary or not. According to some, no intention was required on the part of the minister for the valid conferring of the sacrament, if the proper matter and form were applied. Hugh of St. Victor and Peter Lombard championed the thesis that not only must there be present the proper matter and form, but the minister must have the intention to confer the sacrament. The scholastics of the next century, following the lead of Peter Lombard, arrived at the doctrine which is now the common teaching of the Church. William of Auxerre (1223) explained the necessary intention as being that which attached to the baptismal rite the same meaning and purpose that the Church attached to it. St. Thomas held to the same opinion, explaining that the minister was not an inanimate instrument *(qui) non solum movetur, sed etiam quodammodo movet seipsum, inquantum sua voluntate movet membra ad operandum; et ideo requiritur eius intentio, qua se subiiciat principali agenti, ut scilicet intendat facere quod facit Christus et Ecclesia.*[99]

Against the opinion of St. Thomas it was argued that, if an intention was required in the minister, the recipient of the sacrament could never have any certitude that he really received the sacrament, and consequently could not know that he would be saved. To this objection St. Thomas replied that he favored the opinion of those who claimed that the minister of the sacrament acted in the person of the whole Church whose minister he was; in the words which he pronounced, there was expressed the intention of the Church which sufficed for the perfection of the sacrament, unless the contrary was externally expressed either by the minister or by the subject.[100]

The Council of Constance (1414-1418) clearly insisted on the intention *faciendi quod facit Ecclesia* as an essential part of the sac-

[99] *Summa,* III, q. 64, a. 8, ad 1. Cf. Pourrat, *Theology of the Sacraments,* pp. 366-388.

[100] *Summa,* III, q. 64, a. 8, ad 2.

[101] D. B., n. 672.

rament together with the matter and form.[101] In the Decree for the Armenians (November 22, 1439) the Council of Florence (1438-1445) [102] declared:

> In causa autem necessitatis non solum sacerdos vel diaconus, sed etiam laicus vel mulier, immo etiam paganus et haereticus baptizare potest, dummodo formam servet Ecclesiae et *facere intendat quod facit Ecclesia.*

The Dominican scholar Catharinus (1484-1553) in the following century introduced a distinction between an internal intention and an external intention. In his opinion the external intention as manifested in the material performance of the external rite, provided that it was freely and seriously done, even though inwardly, the minister had the intention of not conferring the sacrament, was in and of itself sufficient for the validity of the sacrament. Those who followed St. Thomas more strictly opposed this opinion. When Luther went so far as to declare that the correct administration of the ceremonies alone was the essence of the sacrament to the exclusion of any intention on the part of the minister, the Council of Trent solemnly decreed, as had the Councils of Constance and of Florence, that at least there was necessary the intention of performing the baptismal rite as it is performed in the Church.[103]

The Council of Trent, however, did not settle the controversy, since it considered only the necessity of the intention.[104] Continuing the controversy Francis Farvacques (1622-1689) of the University of Louvain adopted the thesis:

> Valet baptismus collatus a ministro, qui omnem ritum externum formamque baptizandi observat, intus vero in corde suo apud se resolvit: Non intendo, quod facit Ecclesia.

[102] D. B., n. 696.

[103] Sessio VII, *de sacramentis in genere,* canon 11: "Si quis dixerit, in ministris, dum sacramenta conficiunt et conferunt, non requiri intentionem, saltem faciendi quod facit ecclesia: anathema sit."—D. B., n. 854.

[104] Cf. Pallavicino, *Istoria del Concilio di Trento* (ed. Francesco Antonio Zaccaria, 4 vols. Romae: nel collegio urbano di Propaganda Fide, 1883), Vol. II, lib. IX, cap. vi, n. 2.

At this point Pope Alexander VIII (1689-1691) entered the controversy and on December 7, 1690, condemned Farvacques' proposition.[105] The opinion of Catharinus, though not directly affected by this condemnation, because he did not postulate a positive contrary intention as did Farvacques, did, however, receive a setback, as Benedict XIV attests,[106] and was never again in great favor, though, on the other hand, it was never officially condemned.

Theologians who since that time have treated the question have not been able to give a satisfactory answer to the question which was proposed to St. Thomas, whereby the presence of the proper internal intention of the minister could be determined with certitude. As a practical rule the Sacred Congregation of the Propagation of the Faith proposed the principle that, when the proper matter and form of the sacrament have been observed, the proper intention is to be presumed, unless there is a prudent doubt to the contrary.[107] In determining the question of the validity or invalidity of baptism in various non-Catholic sects, this has always been the norm used by the Sacred Congregations in issuing their decisions.

[105] S. C. S. Off., decr. 7 dec. 1690, n. 28—*Fontes,* n. 760.

[106] *De Synodo Dioecesana,* Lib. VII, cap. 4, n. 8.

[107] S. C. de Prop. Fide, instr. (ad Vic. Ap. Siam), 23 ian. 1830: "In illa vero disquisitione facienda de validitate vel invaliditate prioris baptismatis, antequam sub conditionata forma iteretur, debent animarum pastores inquirere praesertim super formam et materiam adhibitam in priore baptismate. Nam relate ad intentionem, quae ex superius expositis necessaria est ad valorem baptismi, *nisi prudens de ea fuerit dubitatio, praesumenda illa est,* ut recte observat Card. Petra inquiens de baptismo haereticorum: 'Si materiam et formam adhibeant, praesumendum est habere intentionem baptizandi, alias non baptizarent; quod etiam satis est, ut baptisma collatum a calvinistis sit validum, quamvis ipsi nullam efficaciam Baptismo tribuant!' "—*Fontes,* n. 4748.

CHAPTER IV

THE UNBAPTIZED

WHEN the investigation establishes the fact that the prospective convert has not received baptism at all or that his reception of it was certainly invalid, then he is to be admitted into the Church through the reception of the sacrament of baptism.[1] Neither the abjuration of former errors, nor the absolution from censures (which bind only the subjects of the Church) [2] or from sins is required.[3]

ARTICLE 1. REQUISITE DISPOSITIONS

For the valid and fruitful reception of baptism three conditions must necessarily be present in the adult convert: the intention to receive the sacrament, faith in the principal revealed truths, and repentance for past sins. The convert, therefore, is not to be baptized unless he knowingly and willingly consents to it, has received the proper instruction, and has been advised to renounce his past sins. But while the three dispositions of intention, faith and sorrow for sin are generally insisted upon, it is only the proper intention that is a requisite for validity.[4]

The necessity for these dispositions and their evaluation were set forth in an instruction of the Holy Office:

[1] "Instituto igitur diligenti examine, si compertum fuerit, aut nullum, aut nulliter conlatum fuisse, baptizandi erunt absolute."—Instructio, 20 iul. 1859. Cf. chapter I, footnote 20.

[2] Canons 87; 2226, § 1.

[3] Instructio, 20 iul. 1859: "1. Si Baptismus absolute conferatur, nulla sequitur Abjuratio, nec Absolutio, eo quod omnia abluit sacramentum regenerationis."—Cf. chapter I, footnote 20. In England, however, the profession of faith is insisted upon in this case. Cf. Fortescue, *Ceremonies of the Roman Rite*, p. 424.

[4] *Summa*, III, q. 68, aa. 4, 6, 7, 8; Innocentius III, ep. *Maiores Ecclesiae Causas*, a. 1201—D. B., n. 411; Conc. Trident., sess. VI, cap. 6, *de iustificatione* —D. B., n. 798.

> Explorata res est tres in adulto requiri dispositiones ad Baptismum rite suscipiendum: fidem nempe, poenitentiam et intentionem illum percipiendi. Fides profecto necessaria est qua adultus debet esse sufficienter instructus, iuxta propriae intelligentiae mensuram de mysteriis christianae religionis, et ea firmiter credere; et necessaria item est poenitentia qua debet peccata sua dolere, et actum elicere vel contritionis, vel attritionis; ac tertio necessario requiritur intentio seu voluntas suscipiendi hoc sacramentum, eaque deficiente, non imprimitur in adulto baptismatis character. At enim vero fides et poenitentia in adulto requiruntur, ut licite sacramentum suscipiat, et fructum sacramenti consequatur: intentio vero necessaria est ad illud valide consequendum, adeo ut qui baptizatur adultus sine fide ac poenitentia, illicite quidem at valide baptizatur; et contra qui baptizatur absque voluntate sacramentum suscipiendi, nec licite nec valide baptizatur.[5]

Hence if the intention is lacking, neither the grace of the sacrament is conferred nor the character impressed on the soul; if only faith and sorrow for sin are lacking, the character is impressed but grace is not conferred.

Concerning the presence of these necessary dispositions in the subject, it should be noted that it is not required that the minister have moral certitude of their existence; it is sufficient that he is able to form a prudent judgment that they are really present. In practice, such a judgment, if not formed during the course of instructions, can be had from the responses the convert must pronounce during the actual ceremony of Baptism.[6] Whatever be the minister's

[5] S. C. S. Off., instr. (ad Vic. Ap. Tche-Kiang), 1 aug. 1860—*Fontes,* n. 963.

[6] Intention: "N. quid petis?
R. Baptismum.
Vis baptizari?
R. Volo."—*Rituale Romanum,* Tit. 2, cap. 4, *Ordo baptismi adultorum,* n. 38; Tit. 2, cap. 2, *Ordo baptismi parvulorum,* n. 18.

Faith: "Credis in Deum Patrem omnipotentem, creatorem coeli et terrae?
R. Credo.
Credis in Iesum Christum, Filium eius unicum Dominum nostrum, natum, et passum?
R. Credo.

judgment, however, in itself it cannot influence the validity of the sacrament, since the intention which alone is required for validity, if not actually present, will invalidate the sacrament.[7]

I. Intention

In the discussion regarding the necessary intention for the valid reception of baptism it is important to distinguish between the intention *ex parte subjecti* and that *ex parte objecti,* that is, between the subjective intention and the objective intention.

A. Subjective Intention.

For the valid reception of baptism it is necessary that the convert have at least an habitual intention, which may be only implicit, to receive the sacrament.[8] It is clear from the words of canon 752, § 1, that the positive consent of the will is required.[9] This positive consent is necessary for the removal of any impediment of a contrary will or desire not to receive the sacrament, and because no adult can be saved without his consent.[10]

This intention or positive consent need not necessarily be an

Credis et in Spiritum Sanctum, sanctam Ecclesiam catholicam, Sanctorum communionem, remissionem peccatorum, carnis resurrectionem, et vitam aeternam?
R. Credo."—*Ibid.,* n. 38, also n. 5; *ibid.,* n. 17, also n. 1.

Penance: "N. Abrenuntias satanae?
Abrenuntio.
Et omnibus pompis eius?
Abrenuntio.
Et omnibus operibus eius?
Abrenuntio."—*Ibid.,* n. 35; *ibid.,* n. 14.

[7] Cf. Waldron, *The Minister of Baptism,* p. 84.

[8] Aertnys-Damen, *Theologia Moralis* (ed. 13a, 2 vols., Taurini, Romae: Marietti, 1939), II, pp. 26-27, n. 32; Noldin-Schmitt, *Theologia Moralis,* III, p. 38, n. 41; Vermeersch, *Theologia Moralis,* III, p. 161, n. 182; Cappello, *De Sacramentis,* I, p. 71, n. 85, et auctores communiter.

[9] "Adultus, nisi sciens et volens . . . ne baptizetur."

[10] Cf. Conc. Trident., sess. VI, c. 7; I Council of Orange (441), can. 12; *Rituale Romanum,* tit. 2, cap. 4, n. 1; S. C. de Prop. Fide, instr. (ad Vic. Ap. Siam), 23 iun. 1830—*Fontes,* n. 4748; S. C. S. Off., 28 nov. 1900—*Fontes,* n. 1248.

actual intention or even a virtual intention, which acts as a cause or active principle in relation to the object. The reason for this is the fact that in the subject receiving the sacrament the intention is a *condition* of the voluntary reception of the sacrament, the absence of which renders the sacrament invalid. In baptism, the subject is not the active principle of the sacrament but only the passive recipient, and hence an intention (such as an actual or virtual intention) which is the active principle or cause of the sacramental action is not required. The intention to receive baptism formed at some time in the past and never retracted, though not actual or even virtual at the time of the reception of the sacrament, is nevertheless a true intention, and therefore sufficient. On the other hand, a mere negative or passive attitude does not suffice, and if the sacrament is fictitiously or unwillingly received through force or fear it is invalid.

The habitual intention is not to be confused with an interpretative intention, i. e., one that does not really exist, but would exist if the mind had adverted to the matter at hand. The interpretative intention is generally exemplified with the formula: *si scirem, vellem.* Such an intention is plainly insufficient. It must, however, be carefully distinguished from a presumed intention. The former is one that does not actually exist at the present time, but may exist at some time in the future; the latter is one whose actual presence is indicated by certain circumstances from which it may legitimately be presumed.

B. Objective Intention.

The habitual intention is explicit if at some time in the past the desire to receive baptism was formed; it is implicit, if not the baptism itself was intended, but rather something of a more general character which contained in it the desire for baptism, such as the desire to embrace the Christian religion. With regard to the object intended, there must be present in the subject the same kind of intention that is required in the minister, namely, at least the implicit will to receive the sacrament of baptism or the baptismal rite as something sacred. This implicit intention is contained in the explicit and more general desire of receiving through baptism what Christ connected with it in its very institution by Him, or of gaining through it the effects which the Church recognizes in it, or of profiting by it in the manner in which Catholics or Christians do, or even in the express will to live and die as a Christian.

Whether the general intention of using the means necessary for salvation, which intention is included in the act of contrition or attrition for sins committed, constitutes a sufficient intention is a matter of controversy among authors. Authors of great authority argue that in this intention is included the will to observe all the precepts and therefore also the implicit will to receive baptism. Such an intention, they maintain, is sufficient.[11] Others hold that such a general intention is not sufficiently determined as to the specific means of salvation, nor is it an absolute but a mere conditional intention about a future event, and therefore cannot constitute a proper intention for the valid reception of the sacrament.[12] It is difficult to reconcile the former opinion with the principles enunciated above on the nature of the necessary intention. It is certainly never licit to confer baptism absolutely, whether in ordinary circumstances or in danger of death, on a subject who has merely a profound sorrow for all his wrongdoings. If the sacrament is nevertheless conferred, there is a strong probability which approaches moral certitude that the baptism is invalid. The former opinion may only be acted upon in a case of necessity, when it is impossible to elicit a more definite intention. In such an instance baptism may only be conferred conditionally.[13]

[11] Vermeersch, "Practica disquisitio de sacramentis conferendis vel negandis acatholico," *Periodica,* XVIII (1929), 123*-148*; Genicot-Salsmans, *Institutiones,* II, p. 113, n. 126.

[12] Merkelbach, *Summa,* III, pp. 86-87, n. 93; Noldin-Schmitt, *Theologia Moralis,* III, p. 39, n. 41; Aertnys-Damen, *Theologia Moralis,* II, 27-28; Prümmer, *Manuale Theologia Moralis* (ed. 4a et 5a, 3 vols., Friburgi Brisoviae: Herder & Co., 1929), III, n. 875; Cappello, *De Sacramentis,* I, p. 71, n. 85; Umberg, "Quo iure haereticis et schismaticis sacramenta sint neganda," *Periodica,* XVIII (1929), 97*-122*, and others. A good summary of the exact nature of the proper intention is found in the article entitled "Was there sufficient intention for baptism?" by the Rev. Clement V. Bastnagel, J.U.D., in *AER,* CI (1939), 360-361.

[13] "Hanc opinionem, ob exstrinsecam auctoritatem, improbabilem, dicere non audemus; proinde in casu necessitatis, *si aliter fieri nequeat,* potes et debes eiusmodi opinione uti ad vitam aeternam moribundi sensibus destituti, quantum

It is important also to distinguish between the motives which urge a convert to embrace the faith and his intention to receive Baptism. It is known that non-Catholics are attracted to the Church on varied occasions and for a variety of reasons. They may have been favorably impressed with the good Catholic example of their spouse in a mixed marriage, or with the edifying lives of their Catholic friends, associates and acquaintances. They may have won esteeem for the Church through their attendance at Catholic services or through contact with a priest of noble character. They may have been drawn close to the Church through an act of kindness or Christian charity bestowed on them by a Catholic neighbor. They may have learned to respect the Church in view of demands which were made of them by a young man or woman during the time of courtship. Perhaps as married people they sensed a certain unwillingness ultimately to lie buried apart from their Catholic spouse or children. Perhaps even a troubled and prodding conscience has made them turn to the Church with the hope of finding remedy and relief.[14]

Motives such as these may initially lack the full commendation which would warrant a completely unselfish and fully sincere intention in the matter of conversion to the Church. But with careful direction, encouragement and stimulation such motives can frequently under God's grace be given their opportunity to develop into supernatural motives. The convert should certainly possess supernatural motives for entering the Church, and any superstitious, temporal or purely natural motives should be dispelled by proper instruction. But whatever the motive be, whether natural or supernatural, the baptism is certainly valid, provided only that the right and requisite intention is present.

Waldron seems to confuse *motive* with *intention* when he states the insufficiency of "an intention which is purely superstitious or temporal," and then concludes: "It will not be a valid baptism, if the intention which is purely superstitious is the principal one, and

in te est, procurandum. Palam est Baptismum esse conferendum sub conditione."—Cappello, *De Sacramentis,* I, p. 134, n. 155.

[14] "Pastoral Instruction of Converts," *AER,* LXXVI (1927), 579-587; Weaver, *Hints for the Instruction of Converts* (London: Burns, Oates & Washbourne, Lt., 1933), p. 2.

there is a positive exclusion of the right intention."[15] If he designates the intention as "purely superstitious" or "temporal" by reason of the object or thing intended, i. e., the convert does not intend to receive baptism as a sacrament or as a sacred rite, or to receive it in the meaning and import of Christ's institution of it, or in the manner in which Christians receive it, but simply as something purely magical or temporal in character, then certainly such an intention is insufficient. If, however, he refers to the motive or reason which impels the candidate in his intention to receive the sacrament as something sacred, or as the means of salvation which Christ meant it to be, or in the manner in which Christians receive it, then the designation is misleading. The motive is the reason for the action of the will by which the convert intends to receive the sacrament. If the motive is purely natural in character, the subsequent act of faith will not be supernatural, and consequently the fruit of the sacrament will not be conferred. The sacrament, however, will be valid, because of the presence of the proper intention, which alone is required for validity.

II. Faith

Adults who are obliged by divine law to receive baptism cannot licitly receive the sacrament unless they have, besides the intention necessary for the valid reception of baptism, the necessary dispositions and preparation which are required by the very nature of the sacrament and the law of the Church. Hence, before all else the convert must receive due instruction.[16]

The amount of instruction and the period of time to be consumed in imparting the instruction are not determined by the Code. Of necessity these elements depend on the capacities of the individual and on other circumstances. In an instruction to the Vicar Apostolic of China, the Sacred Congregation of the Propagation of the Faith declared that the time and the curriculum of the catechumenate was to be determined by the prudent judgment of the Vicar Apostolic, but the period of instruction should not be extensively

[15] *Minister of Baptism*, p. 84.

[16] Cf. Wernz-Vidal, *Ius Canonicum*, Tom. IV, Vol. I, 40-41.

prolonged in the case of old people, of the infirm, of those who showed extraordinary signs of conversion, or of those who gave an outstanding example of fortitude in time of persecution.[17] The Holy Office also decided that the time of the catechumenate depended on the ability of the convert to assimilate the necessary truths.[18]

Individual bishops may, however, decide the length of time for ordinary cases by diocesan statute.[19] In the absence of any diocesan regulation, the pastor or priest in charge may decide on the necessary period of time, according to the Instruction of the Sacred Congregation of the Propagation of the Faith.[20]

The instructions should be given with as much dispatch and thoroughness as possible, but unless there are present some specific urgent reasons, baptism should not be administered before the course of instruction is completed.[21] Though no definite amount of instruction has been specifically established for all cases by the Church, one can arrive at some practical conclusions from the common belief and practice of the Church. In general, a complete course in Catholic doctrine should be explained. To this end detailed instructions on the articles contained in the Profession of Faith could be given. If this is not possible, the convert should be taught the basic truths of faith and be made to promise to continue further instruction after baptism.

For the unbaptized convert, an act of faith is indispensable as a necessary means, before he can be justified by baptism. The Council of Trent in defending and explaining the Catholic concept of justification, asserted: "Faith is the beginning of man's salvation, the foundation and root of all justification." [22] As a general rule, then, one may argue that the catechumen should know and believe

[17] S. C. de Prop. Fide, instr. (ad Vic. Ap. Sin.), 18 oct. 1883—*Fontes,* n. 4903.

[18] S. C. S. Off. (Sutchuen.), 28 sept. 1724—*Fontes,* n. 783; S. C. S. Off. (Quebec), 10 maii 1703, ad 2—*Fontes,* n. 765.

[19] Synodus Fargensis I (1941), n. 214: "Neo-conversi per tres plus minusve menses, secundum personarum necessitates duabus horis per hebdomadam de doctrina catholica bene edoceantur."

[20] Cf. *supra,* footnote 17.

[21] Cf. *AER,* LXXVI (1927), 581-582.

[22] Sess. VI, *de iustificatione,* c. 8—D. B., n. 801.

fide divina et catholica all the essential truths which are contained in the Scriptures and in Tradition, as proposed by the Church, either in solemn judgment or by the ordinary and universal magisterium, to be believed as divinely revealed.[23] To deny or even doubt any of these truths would be to lapse into heresy.[24]

It is not necessary, though certainly it is desirable, that the convert know and believe all these revealed truths *explicitly*. Substantially it suffices that all of them are believed implicitly. In the determination of the degree of explicit faith which is required, it is necessary to distinguish between those truths which must be believed *de necessitate medii* and those concerning which belief is necessary *de necessitate praecepti*. The unanimous consent of theologians, confirmed by ecclesiastical decisions, affirms that every convert, however, illiterate he may be, must as a necessary means believe explicitly, and with an understanding of the terms in which they are expressed, at least two truths: the existence of God and His remunerative justice.[25]

Whether explicit belief in the Holy Trinity and in the mystery of the Incarnation is also absolutely necessary as a means of justification is still a matter of controversy among theologians. The majority opinion denies the necessity for explicit belief. The opposing view seems more probable, however, and since there is question of a means to eternal life, the *pars tutior* must be followed in practice. This conclusion is supported by two responses of the Holy Office. This Supreme Congregation was asked whether the minister is obliged to explain all the mysteries of faith before he confers baptism on an adult, especially if he is near death, when such an explanation would disturb his peace of mind, or whether it suffices if the adult promises that, when he has recovered from his illness, he shall take in-

23 Canon 1323, § 1.

24 Canon 1325, § 2.

25 Heb., xi: 6; prop. 22 damnata ab Innocentio XI in decr. S. Off., 4 martii 1679—D. B., n. 1172; prop. 64—D. B., n. 1214. What degree of explicit faith is necessary has been a subject of controversy among theologians for many centuries. Some of the earliest scholastics, as William of Paris and William of Auxerre, held that mere implicit faith in all that the Church teaches was sufficient for uneducated persons. This opinion is now untenable. Cf. Mazzella, *De Virtutibus Infusis* (Romae, 1879), n. 864.

structions and practice faithfully what is demanded of him. To this the Holy Office replied that a mere promise did not suffice, but that the missionary was obliged to explain to the adult convert—even if he was near death—as long as he was not wholly incapable of comprehension, the mysteries of faith regarding which knowledge was indispensable as a means of salvation, as are especially the mysteries of the Trinity and the Incarnation.[26] A few months later the Holy Office insisted that one who does not explicitly believe in Jesus Christ cannot be permitted to receive baptism.[27] It is important to note that the obligation on the one imparting the instructions is not merely to propose these four necessary truths, but to explain them, so that the convert can be said to understand the essence of these mysteries. To determine the exact degree of explicit faith required in the convert, a consideration of the truths necessary as an absolute means of justification and those which are necessary because God and His Church have commanded belief in them is most pertinent: hence, the following consideration of those truths which are called essential doctrines, and those which are termed preceptive doctrines.[28]

[26] S. C. S. Off. (Quebec), 25 ian. 1703, n. 2: "Utrum, antequam adulto conferatur baptisma, minister ei teneatur explicare omnia fidei nostrae mysteria, praesertim si est moribundus, quia hoc perturbaret mentem illius. An non sufficeret, si moribundus promitteret fore, ut ubi e morbo convalesceret, instruendum se curet, ut in praxim redigat, quod ei praeceptum fuerit.

"*Resp.*: Non sufficere promissionem, sed missionarium teneri adulto, etiam moribundo, qui incapax omnino non sit, explicare mysteria fidei, quae sunt necessaria necessitate medii, ut sunt praecipue mysteria Trinitatis et Incarnationis."—*Fontes,* n. 764.

[27] S. C. S. Off. (Quebec), 10 maii 1703, n. 2: "An possit baptizari adultus rudis et stupidus, ut contigit in barbaro, si ei datur sola Dei cognitio et aliquorum eius attributorum, praesertim iustitiae remunerativae et vindicativae, iuxta hunc Apostoli locum: *Accedentem ad Deum oportet credere, quia est et remunerator est* (Heb. 11, 6), ex quo infertur, adultum barbarum in certo casu urgentis necessitatis posse baptizari, quamvis non credat explicite in Iesum Christum.

"*Resp.*: Missionarium non posse baptizare non credentem explicite in Dominum Iesum Christum, sed teneri illum instruere de omnibus iis, quae sunt necessaria necessitate medii iuxta captum baptizandi."—*Fontes,* n. 765.

[28] The "essential doctrines" are necessary *de necessitate medii;* the "preceptive doctrines" are necessary *de necessitate praecepti.*

A. Essential Doctrines.

The Existence of God. To elicit an act of faith in the existence of God the convert must be taught to recognize God as the Supreme Being, Who created all things outside Himself and possesses full rights over all creation, Who can never deceive nor be deceived. He must be shown as the Creator and Sustainer of the universe, distinct from all created things. Explicit recognition of the other divine attributes, e. g., His infinity, does not seem to be necessary, and there are those who hold that an inculpable error regarding some divine attribute, as His freedom to create, would not nullify a true act of faith, provided that the convert had a true concept of God as the uncreated First Cause and Supreme Ruler.[29]

The Remunerative Justice of God. For explicit belief and understanding of this truth it is sufficient that the convert conceive of God as the rewarder, after death, of those whose lives have been good, and as the punisher of those who have been wicked. The specific nature of the reward and punishment, namely, that the reward consists in the vision of God, and the punishment in the pain of fire and in separation from God, need not be known, nor is it necessary that the doctrine of the existence and nature of Purgatory be explained.[30]

The common teaching of theologians is that it is not sufficient to believe these two doctrines as natural truths, inasmuch as they can be known by the light of human reason, but as pertaining to the supernatural order. To make the act of faith a supernatural assent, it is necessary that these truths be believed as supernatural truths, and not as the clear deductions of human reasoning. In practice, however, this point offers no difficulty, since the very motive of faith—the authority of God revealing—raises the assent from the purely natural to the supernatural order.[31]

The Holy Trinity. Here it must be explained that there is only one God with one divine nature, Who is in some way really and

[29] Mazzella, *De Virtutibus Infusis,* n. 865.

[30] Connell, "Priestly Ministry of the Essentials of Faith," *AER,* LXXVI (1927), 570-579.

[31] Cf. Van Noort, *De Fontibus Revelationis* (ed. 2a, Amstelodami: C. L. Van Langenhuysen, 1911), n. 330; Merkelbach, *Summa,* I, 549.

distinctly three Persons, each of Whom is God, though there are not three gods but only one. The names of the three divine Persons should also be known.[32] The meaning of nature and person need not be understood, nor the way in which one Person is distinguished from the other.

The Incarnation. To understand this mystery it is necessary to know that God became man for the sake of men, though at the same time he remained God. Connell thinks this sufficient.[33] However, there are theologians of high authority who require a knowledge of other facts related to this mystery: that the God-Man died to redeem us from sin, rose from the dead, ascended into heaven to reign, and will finally judge all men according to their works.[34] Since the authority of those who sponsor this opinion is such as to make this view probable, it must be followed in practice as the *pars tutior*.

In these four truths—the existence of God, His remunerative justice, the Holy Trinity, and the Incarnation—is contained the absolute minimum of Catholic doctrine which must be explicitly believed before baptism can be administered. In unusual cases the instruction may be limited to these truths. In these instances, however, while explicit faith is demanded, the convert should be instructed to accept implicitly all the other doctrines of faith by giving his general assent to all that God has revealed.

B. Preceptive Doctrines.

All the faithful are bound by a grave obligation arising from the command of Christ [35] to know and believe explicitly the principal mysteries of faith. The common teaching and practice of the Church interprets these essential doctrines as including the Apostles' Creed, which contains the summary of Christian belief, the Ten Commandments, which must be observed by all, the Lord's Prayer,

[32] Cf. S. C. S. Off. (Quebec), 10 maii 1703, quoted in footnote 27 of this chapter; Lehmkuhl, *Theologia Moralis*, I, n. 279. Connell (*loc. cit.*), however, is of the opinion that it is not necessary that the names of the Trinity be known.

[33] *Loc. cit.*

[34] Salmanticenses, *Cursus Theologicus* (ed. nova, 20 vols., Genève, 1870-1883), XVII, Tract. XXII, disp. vii; Lehmkuhl, *Theologia Moralis*, I, n. 279.

[35] Mark, xvi: 15, 16; Matt. xxviii: 19, 20.

and a knowledge of the sacraments which are necessary for all Christians.

The Apostles' Creed. The obligation to know at least substantially the articles contained in the Creed is certainly a grave one. That is, the convert should have at least a common knowledge of these truths. If questioned concerning them, he should be able to relate the substance of the doctrines set forth, though not necessarily in the exact words of the Creed or in the order there followed.[36] The obligation to believe explicitly certain truths, however, is grave or light according to the mental capacities of the convert and the degree of instruction. These truths specifically are: the *perpetual* virginity of the Blessed Mother; the burial of Christ and His descent into hell; His sitting at the right hand of the Father; the communion of saints; [37] Christ's condemnation by *Pontius Pilate;* His resurrection on the *third day;* His judgment of the *living and the dead.*[38] The following articles must be explicitly believed:

1. art. I believe in God: one God Who is three Persons, each of Whom is God, without being three gods; these three Persons are called the Father, the Son and the Holy Ghost.

The Father Almighty, Creator of heaven and earth: the creation of all things outside of God Himself, and therefore the omnipotence of God.

2. art. And in Jesus Christ, His only Son, our Lord: Jesus Christ is man and God, the Son is equal to the Father; He is *one* Lord.

3. art. Who was conceived by the Holy Ghost: the miraculous conception of Christ.

Born of the Virgin Mary: the virginity of the Mother of God.

4. art. Suffered under Pontius Pilate, was crucified, died, and was buried: the death of our Saviour and the manner of His death by crucifixion.

5. art. He descended into hell. The third day he rose again from the dead: Christ's resurrection from the dead.

6. art. He ascended into heaven, sitteth at the right hand of

[36] Lehmkuhl, *Theologia Moralis,* I, n. 279.

[37] Noldin-Schmitt, *Theologia Moralis,* II, 14.

[38] Merkelbach, *Summa,* I, 551.

God, the Father Almighty: Christ's glorious reign in heaven, in a glory which is greater than any other since He is the God-Man.

7. art. From thence He shall come to judge the living and the dead: universal judgment will be exercised by Christ.

8. art. I believe in the Holy Ghost: cf. 1. art. above.

9. art. The Holy Catholic Church, the Communion of Saints: the necessity of remaining in union with the Church.

10. art. The Forgiveness of sins: the ability to obtain remission of sins through the sacraments of baptism and penance.

11. art. The resurrection of the body: all who live and die on earth will one day rise again from the grave.

12. art. And life everlasting: the reward of the good and the punishment of the wicked will be without end for all eternity.[39]

The Ten Commandments. The precepts of the decalogue must not only be known but must be believed and observed by all, since they have come to mankind by divine revelation and are, therefore, part of the depository of divine faith. It suffices to know the substance of what they prescribe, so that upon questioning one would be able to answer whether a certain thing is commanded or prohibited. This necessary knowledge must be sufficiently comprehensive to extend to those things which are formally enunciated in the list of the commandments and also those things which can easily and proximately be deduced from them, but not the more remote conclusions which theologians can derive. The precepts of the Church, while they are not the object of faith, since they do not form a part of revelation, should also form part of the instruction because they contain the norms of proper conduct.[40]

The Our Father. The very special importance of this prayer arises from the fact that it was revealed by Christ Himself. Theologians generally acknowledge that not only should the *Our Father*

[39] Lehmkuhl, *Theologia Moralis,* I, n. 281.

[40] S. C. S. Off. (Quebec), 10 maii 1703, n. 3: "Utrum missionarius teneatur barbaris adultis baptizatis aut baptizandis omnia praecepta legis positivae divinae intimare, praesertim ea omnia quibus sese submittere difficultatem haberent, ut eiusmodi barbari securitate conscientiae fruantur, licet ea praecepta non observent quae ignorant, eo nitentes iuris axiomate: *Lex non obligat nisi fuerit promulgata.*

"R. Teneri omnia praecepta legis positivae divinae intimare."—*Fontes,* n. 765.

be known and believed, but they also recognize a certain obligation of committing it to memory. The source of the obligation is traced to the practice of the Church which ordinarily demanded from catechumens a knowledge both of the Creed and the Lord's Prayer before admitting them to baptism. The obligation, however, is held commonly not to be a grave one. A serious obligation does exist, however, of knowing that one must pray to God with trust and firm hope that He may grant the things which man needs both natural and supernatural, and that He may bestow the necessary graces for avoiding evil.[41]

Sacraments Necessary for All. Knowledge of the doctrine concerning the sacraments of baptism, penance and the Eucharist is generally considered to be of obligation for all converts and Christians alike. Knowledge and belief in the other sacraments is necessary only insofar as it is required as a condition for their lawful reception. Belief in the three mentioned sacraments must be explicit. Concerning baptism, its necessity for salvation and its effects on the soul—the infusion of sanctifying grace, the impression of an indelible character, the remission of all sin and penalties due to sin—must be known at least substantially. The necessity of the sacrament of penance in regard to its principal effect of restoring the soul to the state of grace is likewise the material object of a required explicit belief. With regard to the sacrament of the Eucharist, the convert must know that Christ is really present, whole and entire under the form of bread and wine, and must recognize the fact that the consecrated host is no longer bread but the true and living body of Christ. The convert must also explictly assent to the fact that in the confection of this sacrament, there is contained the essence of the divine sacrifice, which fact enables him to satisfy the divine and ecclesiastical precept by assistance at Mass. The Holy Office, however, exempted certain pious catechumens from the obligation to learn the doctrine of the Holy Eucharist because of the necessity for baptism and the mental tardiness of the converts.[42]

[41] "Cum omnes aliquando ad orandum obligentur, oportet ut Orationem Dominicam *sciant* quod ad substantiam, quatenus hoc necessarium est ad intelligendum quid possint et debeant orando petere."—Genicot-Salsmans, *Institutiones*, p. 143, n. 192. Cf. Lehmkuhl, *Theologia Moralis*, I, n. 280.

[42] S. C. S. Off. (Yunnan), 20 sept. 1854: "1. Novi Dei cultores, qui pie

It must be remembered that the assent to these necessary truths must be reasonable. Since reason precedes faith and leads men to it,[43] certain facts easy to recognize should be proposed as motives of credibility.[44] The explicit act of faith need not be made in all the essential truths at one and the same time, but they can be proposed and assented to by the convert individually as in the profession of faith at the baptismal ceremony. The inability of the convert to give a satisfactory explanation of the four essential truths later on does not render the act of faith invalid, for, as Connell asserts, "if he had sufficient understanding of these doctrines when he made his act of faith, this knowledge *virtually* perseveres, and satisfies, at least for a time, his obligation of explicit faith, even though his present ideas are obscure and confused." [45]

In addition to the truths which both as a means of salvation and also as the fulfillment of a precept must be known, the Sacred Congregation of the Propagation of the Faith instructed Chinese missionaries to teach the acts and the motives of the theological virtues.[46]

vivunt, et iam doctrinam ad Baptismum absolute necessariam callent, debentne statim baptizari, etiamsi nondum Sacra Eucharistia refici possint? . . . Post Baptismum suum doctrinam de aliis sacramentis addiscere poterunt. Aliunde multi sunt ita tardi ingenii, ut statim non possint integram sacramentorum callere doctrinam.

"*Resp.* Ad 1. Novos Dei cultores qui pie vivunt, et iam sunt bene instituti, et necessitas postulabit, posse baptizari, etiamsi S. Eucharistia nondum refici possint."—*Fontes,* n. 927.

[43] S. C. S. Off. 11 (15) iun. 1855: "Rationis usus fidem praecedit et ad eam hominem ope revelationis et gratiae conducit."—D.B., n. 1651. Cf. 5th thesis subscribed to by Louis Bautain at the command of his bishop on November 18, 1835, and again in Rome, September 8, 1840—D.B., n. 1626.

[44] E. g., the order of the universe or man's desire for happiness as proof of God's existence; the miracles of Christ especially His Resurrection, as proof of His divinity and truthfulness. Weaver (*Hints for the Instruction of Converts,* p. 24) suggests the following scheme: "(a) God, source of wisdom and knowledge; (b) God *could* reveal His mysteries; (c) God *did* reveal some knowledge through Christ: the truthfulness of Whom is attested by miracles; (d) to reach all people Christ *could* found a Church; (e) this He *did*; (f) hence the duty to find the Church and submit to her. This must be the conviction of the convert before proceeding with instruction."

[45] *AER,* LXXVI (1927), 575.

[46] S. C. de Prop. Fide, instr. (ad Vic. Ap. Sin.), 18 oct. 1883—*Fontes,* n. 4903.

The converts should be both warned and fortified against the particular dangers to which their new found faith might be exposed. They should also be instructed in the obligation of their state in life. If married converts present themselves for instruction, or if the converts are contemplating marriage, they should be diligently taught the doctrine of the Church concerning the sacrament of matrimony, with special stress on the unity and indissolubility of the sacred contract.[47]

III. Penance

Since the convert will be called upon in the baptismal ceremony to renounce Satan and all his works, it is necessary that we have contrition or at least attrition for all his past sins. This sorrow for sin must be true, sincere, supernatural, sovereign, and at least habitual.[48]

The Holy Office explained that the penance which is necessary for the fruitful reception of the sacrament is a complete recession from the state of sin.[49] If the catechumen persists in his state of sin, the sacrament must be denied him.[50] The Holy Office insisted that the missionary is obliged to induce the convert to elicit an act of contrition or attrition, even though it be much easier to teach and obtain an act of love of God or a firm resolution not to repeat sins already committed.[51] One who did not dismiss his illegitimate wife,[52] or who did not abandon his superstitious practices,[53] even though certain inconveniences would necessarily result,[54] or who continued to practice usury or an unlawful trade,[55] could not be admitted to bap-

[47] Cf. Payen, *De Matrimonio* (ed. 2a, 3 vols., Zi-ka-wei: T òu-sè-wè, 1935), I, pp. 270-271, nn. 349, 350.

[48] Merkelbach, *Summa,* III, p. 120, n. 144 c.

[49] S. C. S. Off., instr. (ad Vic. Ap. Gallas), 28 mart. 1860: " . . . quatenus a statu peccati omnino recedere debeat suscepturus Baptismum, ut gratiam consequatur."—*Fontes,* n. 957.

[50] S. C. S. Off., *loc. cit.*

[51] S. C. S. Off. (Quebec), 10 maii 1703, ad 5—*Fontes,* n. 765.

[52] S. C. S. Off., *ibidem,* ad 6.

[53] S. C. S. Off. (Perth.), 18 sept. 1850, ad 1—*Fontes,* n. 912.

[54] S. C. de Prop. Fide (Sinarum), 12 sept. 1645, nn. 6-17—*Fontes,* n. 4459.

[55] *Ibidem,* nn. 3-5—*Fontes,* n. 4459.

tism. It is interesting to note that the Holy Office did not bar from the reception of baptism any opium smokers who could not immediately desist from the habit without danger of death or of grave sickness, provided that they tried to amend their ways and were otherwise properly disposed.[56] If there was foreseen a proximate danger of perversion for the faith of the convert, baptism had to be deferred.[57]

No works of satisfaction are to be imposed on the convert, however, since baptism washes away all sin; nor is a special oral confession of sins to be made to the priest, for the general renunciation of Satan, his works and pomps as made during the ceremony suffices.[58] Since true sorrow for sin cannot exist without the virtue of hope for eternal life, this disposition must also be fostered in the soul of the convert. To ascertain the presence of the necessary dispositions, canonists recommend a period of probation for the convert.[59] He should be educated in Christian customs and practices, especially in attendance at Mass, benediction and other services, in the recitation of the rosary, and of morning and evening prayers, and should likewise be introduced to Catholic literature.[60]

Article 2. The Baptismal Formula

When there is no danger of death for the prospective recipient, baptism must always be conferred solemnly, i. e., with all the rites and ceremonies prescribed by the ritual for the reception of unbaptized adult converts.[61] The ceremonies to be observed are contained in the Roman Ritual under the title *Ordo Baptismi adultorum*.[62]

[56] S. C. S. Off. (Yunnan), 20 sept. 1854, ad 2—*Fontes,* n. 927.

[57] S. C. S. Off. instr. (pro Vic. Ap. ad Gallas), 20 iun. 1866, III, ad 10—*Fontes,* n. 994.

[58] Merkelbach, *Summa,* III, p. 120, n. 144.

[59] "Etiam praevium in moribus christianis exercitium per aliquod tempus praemitti debet, ut adulti baptizati se ad novam vitam ducendam idoneos ostendant."—Cappello, *De Sacramentis,* I, p. 133, n. 154; cf. Wernz-Vidal, *Ius Canonicum,* Tom. IV, Vol. II, 41.

[60] Cf. Weaver, *Hints for the Instruction of Converts,* p. 4.

[61] Canons 755, § 1; 737, § 2.

[62] Tit. 2, cap. 4.

The obligation to observe these rites and ceremonies is a grave one,[63] and holds also for baptism administered in private homes,[64] so that the entire or notable omission or change of these prescriptions would be a mortal offense. The essential ceremonies besides the actual baptism, are the anointings, the breathing on the subject, the touching of his ears and nostrils with the thumb moistened with saliva and the placing of a pinch of salt upon his tongue, the use of consecrated water, the profession of faith, and, at least probably, the conferring of the white garment and of the candle.[65] A just and grave cause such as the lack of time, or a grave inconvenience would justify the omission of some non-essential ceremony.[66]

The Holy Office directed missionaries to conform to the ritual as much as possible in cases wherein the full observance of the baptismal ceremony was impossible, but not to postpone the administration of the sacrament on this account with notable inconvenience to the convert or other interested persons.[67] On April 30, 1929, Pope Pius XI included among the faculties given to all Ordinaries of Latin America the permission to allow pastors and missionaries to omit certain ceremonies because of lack of time or great fatigue or for other grave causes.[68]

Ordinarily the form for adult baptism is to be used in the case of an adult convert. The word *adult* is to be interpreted according to the norms of canons 745, § 2, and 752, § 1, as anyone who has the use of reason and who with full understanding asks for the reception of the sacrament. This definition includes not only those who have reached their majority, but also minors. All persons,

[63] The source of the obligation is traceable to the importance and antiquity of the rite and the reverence due to the sacrament. Cf. Benedictus XIV, const. *Inter omnigenas,* 2 febr. 1744, const. *Omnium sollicitudinum,* 12 sept. 1744—*Fontes,* nn. 339, 348.

[64] S.R.C., Bellunen, 17 ian. 1914—*AAS,* VI (1914), 32. This particular response is not found in the *Decreta Authentica* (1898-1927) of the Sacred Congregation of Rites.

[65] Cappello, *De Sacramentis,* I, p. 153, n. 175.

[66] S. C. de Prop. Fide (C.P. pro Sin.), 21 ian. 1789, ad 1—*Fontes,* n. 4625.

[67] S. C. S. Off. (Vic. Ap. Sandwic.), 11 dec. 1850, ad 9-11—*Fontes,* n. 913.

[68] *AAS,* XXI (1929), 555. These faculties were extended by the Sacred Congregation of the Consistory for 10 years on April 28, 1939—*AAS,* XXXI (1939), 224.

therefore, except infants who have not attained their seventh year, or who are not yet considered to have the use of reason, are according to the general rule to be received into the Church according to the formula for adults. However, Cappello and others hold that youths who are properly not converted from a heretical or a schismatical sect which they never professed, inasmuch as they were never *confirmed* in it, may be baptized as infants.[69] Such a distinction is not found in the common law and therefore is without juridical basis. If the convert is an adult in the canonical sense of the term, he is to receive baptism according to the formula for adults.

The local Ordinary can for a grave and reasonable cause grant the faculty to substitute the baptismal formula for infants.[70] Before the promulgation of the Code the granting of this faculty was reserved to the Holy See. Thus, the Fathers of the II Plenary Council of Baltimore (1866) petitioned the Holy See to extend the privilege of using the formula for infants—which privilege had been granted to certain dioceses of America up to the year 1870—to all the dioceses for a period of ten or twenty years.[71] Permission to use the infant formula is now frequently conceded by the local Ordinaries in the formulary of diocesan faculties,[72] or by diocesan statute.[73] The priest who receives the convert as the delegate of the Ordinary or with his permission [74] cannot use the formula for infants according to his own discretion, since the words of the canon clearly assign the Ordinary as the one to grant this privilege.

[69] Cappello, *De Sacramentis,* I, p. 154, n. 175, III, f; Schaaf, in *AER,* XCVII (1937), 175-176.

[70] Canon 755, § 2.

[71] N. 243. To this request the Sacred Congregation for the Propagation of the Faith replied, "Porro S. Cong. censuit Episcopos recurrere debere, expleto tempore postremae concessionis."—*Acta et Decreta,* p. lxix, III.

[72] E. g., Facultates ab Ordinario Concessae Clero Philadelphiensi, n. 3: "Adhibendi in baptismo adultorum, justa de causa, caeremonias pro baptismo infantium praescriptas."

[73] E. g., Synodus Fargensis I, Statutum 213, 3: "Conversi ad fidem iuxta normas in sacra doctrina traditas recipiantur: ob consuetudinem autem jamdudum in Dioecesi vigentem indulgemus ut caeremoniae praescriptae pro baptismo infantium adhibeantur in baptismo adultorum."

[74] Canon 744.

The concession of this faculty must be attended by a grave and reasonable cause. Not any light excuse, but the presence of a weighty reason is demanded. Lack of time, great fatigue, the illness of either the minister (even though another priest could easily have been asked to administer the sacrament), or of the subject would be a sufficient warrant for the granting of the faculty to use the formula for infants.[75] The determination of the sufficiency of the cause for omitting the formula for adults will depend in every case on the prudent judgment of the local Ordinary, who must weigh the special circumstances in their relation to the sacred rites. The demand for a weighty reason before any substitution may be made which makes possible the use of the infant formula is perhaps traceable to the beauty, antiquity and sacred character of the formula for adults, which preserves in a shortened form the whole scheme and framework of the ancient initiation ceremony.[76]

Article 3. Time and Place of Baptism

The Code allows the solemn conferring of baptism on any day, but recommends as more fitting and more intimately in keeping with the ancient rite of the Church that it be conferred on the vigils of Easter and Pentecost, if it is at all convenient to do so.[77] Hence, in keeping with the recommendation of the Church, converts who have completed their instructions and have the necessary dispositions for

[75] *Decreta Authentica Congregationis Sacrorum Rituum* (5 vols., Romae: Ex Typographia Polyglotta, 1898-1901, Appendix I, 1912, Appendix II, 1927), II, n. 3051, ad 3.

[76] The rites which remain are: the preliminary instruction and admission to the catechumenate, the series of exorcisms and prayers belonging to each of the scrutinies, a small relic of the special rites of the great scrutiny, the *redditio symboli* and the *Pater,* almost all the rites of the final scrutiny and the initiation proper. For infants this summary is even shorter. Of the instruction preliminary to the catechumenate there remains only what refers to the great precept of Christ: love of God and of one's neighbor; of the admissory rites, the exorcisms, the imposition of the sign of the cross on forehead and breast, the resting of the hand upon the head and the giving of the blessed salt have been retained. Only the *redditio symboli* and the recitation of the Pater Noster by the sponsor have been retained from the scrutinies. Cf. *AER,* CI (1939), 274.

[77] Canon 772. Cf. *Rit. Rom.,* tit. 2, cap. 3, *de bapt. adult.,* n. 3.

baptism before the Paschal season would be received into the Church on these days. If they have completed their preparation only a short time before these vigils and there is no particular reason for admitting them to baptism immediately, they should be made to wait the few days before the sacrament is administered to them. But if before or after the time of Pentecost there are converts for whom it would be a great hardship to put off their baptism for a long period of time, they need not be made to wait for the recurrence of these vigils.[78] The Code, however, imposes no obligation that its recommendations be strictly observed, and hence any reasonable cause would justify the conferring of solemn baptism on any day other than the vigils of Easter and Pentecost.

The Code calls it seemly and fitting that at the actual ceremony both the minister and the subjects who are in good health be fasting.[79] This recommendation is evidently in keeping with the ancient practice in accord with which baptism was administered on the vigils of Easter and Pentecost. Since canon 753, § 1, merely uses the words *decet esse ieiunos,* there is no strict obligation for either the minister or the recipient of the sacrament to be fasting. From the wording of canon 753, § 2, however, there arises a strict obligation on the part of the adult convert to assist immediately after his baptism at the Holy Sacrifice of the Mass and to receive Holy Communion. Only a grave *and* urgent cause really excuses him from fulfilling these two precepts.[80] Vermeersch benignly interprets the word *statim* to mean practically an interval of one, two or three days, and therefore argues that the fast, necessary for the reception of Holy Communion, is not properly commanded for the ceremony of baptism. Based on this interpretation the practice has arisen of

[78] *Rit. Rom.,* tit. 2, cap. 3, nn. 4, 5: "Quare si circa haec tempora Catechumeni sint baptizandi, in ipsos dies, si nihil impediat, Baptismum differi convenit.

"Verum si circa, seu post tempus Pentecostes aliqui conversi fuerint, qui aegre ferant suum Baptismum in longum tempus differi, et ad illud festinent, instructique, ac rite parati esse noscantur, citius baptizari possunt."

[79] Canon 753, § 1: Tam sacerdotem qui adultos baptizaturus est, quam ipsos adultos qui sani sunt, decet esse ieiunos. Cf. *Rit. Rom.,* tit. 2, cap. 3, n. 7.

[80] Canon 753, § 2: Nisi graves urgentesque causae obsint, adultus baptizatus statim Missae sacrificio assistat et sacram communionem percipiat.

baptizing adults in the evening, followed by their attendance at Mass and reception of Holy Communion the next day, or even several days later.[81] Ayrinhac claims that since this opinion bears extrinsic probability it may be followed in practice.[82]

This opinion, however, seems to lack intrinsic probability. The Code states on the one hand that it is fitting that the convert be fasting when he receives the sacrament of baptism; on the other hand, it commands that the convert assist at Mass and receive Holy Communion immediately after the ceremony. The word *statim* is to be interpreted in its proper sense according to the norm of canon 18. Hence, an interval of even an hour or two would seem to offend against the law.

By reason of the fact that the convert must assist at Mass and receive Holy Communion immediately after his baptism, and because Mass must be offered in the morning (canon 821, § 1), the baptism of the convert must also take place in the morning. This conclusion is supported by the clear prescription of the Roman Ritual. After repeating verbatim the words of canon 753, it concludes that the converts should be baptized before noon—*quare non post epulas, aut prandia, sed ante meridiem*—unless a reasonable cause excuses.[83]

In the absence of grave and urgent reasons preventing his reception of Holy Communion immediately after Baptism, is the convert, because of his obligation to receive Holy Communion, also under an obligation to observe the Eucharistic fast before his baptism? The Code makes no direct mention of the Eucharistic fast in this canon. The first paragraph of canon 753 refers to the baptismal fast, and it merely recommends that both the minister and the convert be fasting when the sacrament is administered whether it be in the morning, as in ordinary cases, or at any other time of the day, as in the exceptional case wherein the presence of grave and urgent reasons would prevent attendance at Mass and the reception of Holy Communion immediately after the conferral of baptism. The sec-

[81] Vermeersch-Creusen, *Epitome,* II, p. 24, n. 39.

[82] *Legislation on the Sacraments,* I, 34.

[83] *Rit. Rom.,* tit. 2, cap. 3, nn. 7, 8.

ond paragraph does impose a strict obligation to receive Holy Communion immediately after the baptismal ceremony.

It seems, therefore, that the convert is not bound by the Eucharistic fast. The law of the Eucharistic fast is purely ecclesiastical in its origin. Before his baptism, this law as all other purely ecclesiastical laws has no binding force (canon 12). Immediately after his baptism he does become subject to purely ecclesiastical laws, both the law of the Eucharistic fast and the law which commands his immediate attendance at Mass and the reception of Holy Communion. He cannot, in the supposition that he has already broken his fast, fulfill both laws. It seems, therefore, that since the Code imposes the strict obligation to attend Mass and to receive Holy Communion immediately after the baptismal ceremony, it thereby implicitly dispenses the convert from the fast necessary for the reception of Holy Communion. This interpretation is supported by the fact that the salt consumed by the convert during the actual ceremony of baptism does actually break the fast, and yet no one will hold that as a consequence the fulfillment of the obligation to receive Holy Communion immediately after the ceremony becomes automatically impossible. If, therefore, the convert should break his fast before his solemn baptism, he nevertheless can receive Holy Communion the same morning immediately after his reception into the Church.[84]

According to the Code there must be grave and urgent reason present to exempt the convert from attendance at Mass and the reception of Holy Communion immediately after the ceremony of baptism. Such grave and urgent reasons may easily exist today. Because of varied conditions, it might easily prove a grave inconvenience or an impossibility for the convert to be baptized, to attend Mass and to receive Holy Communion in the same morning. When such conditions exist the baptism may take place at whatever time of day its reception proves most convenient for the convert. The

[84] Cf. Cappello, *De Sacramentis,* I, p. 142, n. 161: "Ex verbis eiusdem can. 753, § 2, 'nisi graves urgentesque causae obsint,' manifesto patet haberi veram obligationem assistendi Missae et sumendi sacram communionem. Baptizatus ex ritu collationis sacramenti recipit sal; ideoque implicite dispensatur, ut, licet ieiunium naturale forte laeserit, nihilominus tuta conscientia SS. Eucharistiam sumere possit."

obligation to attend Mass and receive Holy Communion may then be fulfilled the succeeding day.[85]

The proper place for the solemn administration of baptism is the baptistry in any church or public oratory,[86] but especially in the metropolitan or cathedral churches, when it is convenient.[87] Hence, ordinarily, baptism is forbidden to be solemnly administered in semi-private oratories and in private residences. The Code abstracts from the latter requirement of this general rule when sons or grandsons of actual rulers or of their lawful successors are to be baptized, as often as the request is rightly made; or when in some extraordinary case, the local Ordinary for a just and reasonable cause, such as the infirmity of the convert or the avoidance of unfavorable publicity, prudently and conscientiously sees fit to grant the exception. In these unusual cases, however, the Church insists that the baptism be conferred in the house chapel, or at least in a proper place.[88]

Every parish church must have its own baptismal font. Formerly certain churches by reason of a special statute, privilege or custom had the right of administering baptism to the exclusion of the parish churches. All statutes, privileges and customs of this kind have been abrogated by the Code to the extent that these churches no longer possess an exclusive right, but only a cumulative right with the parish churches.[89]

For the convenience of the faithful the local Ordinary can permit or even command that baptismal fonts be erected even in a church or public oratory other than the parish church, provided that it be within the limits of the parish. Such a church or public oratory, then, would enjoy equal rights with the parish church in the administration of solemn baptism.[90] If for reasons of great distance, grave inconvenience or danger, or other circumstances, it would be impossible for the candidate to go or to be brought to the parish church

[85] Cf. Leroux, "Les Baptêmes d'Adultes,"—*Revue Ecclésiastique de Liége*, XVII (1925-1926), 341-352.

[86] Canon 773.

[87] Canon 772.

[88] Canon 776.

[89] Canon 774, § 1.

[90] Canon 774, § 2.

or to another which has a baptismal font, the pastor can and should confer solemn baptism in the nearest church or public oratory within the parish limits, even though this church or oratory have no baptismal font.[91] In this disposition of the law the Church shows her great solicitude that all means be taken to have the administration of solemn baptism take place in church rather than in some profane place.

Article 4. In Danger of Death

The law of the Church stated in the Code[92] and in the ritual concerning the baptism of those in danger of death is brief and concise:

> In mortis autem periculo, si nequeat in praecipuis fidei mysteriis diligentius instrui, satis est, ad baptismum conferendum, ut aliquo modo ostendat se eisdem assentire serioque promittat se christianae religionis mandata servaturum.
>
> Quod si baptismum ne petere quidem queat, sed vel antea vel in praesenti statu manifestaverit aliquo probabili modo intentionem illum suscipiendi, baptizandus est sub conditione; si deinde convaluerit et dubium de valore baptismi collati permaneat, sub conditione baptismus rursus conferatur.

A true danger of death is present not only when it is positively probable that death will ensue, but also when it remains only probable that it will not ensue.[93] This danger can arise from any cause, whether intrinsic, such as a disease, a wound, a difficult birth, or advanced age, or extrinsic, such as war, an operation, or a dangerous voyage. It is to be morally estimated so that in the event of a positive doubt as to whether a person is really in danger of death, the person must be given the benefit of the doubt.[94]

[91] Canon 775.

[92] Canon 752, §§ 2, 3.

[93] "Periculum mortis est illud rerum discrimen, in quo cum quis constitutus est, ipsum et superesse et occumbere posse, utrumque est vere graviterque probabile."—Cappello, *De Censuris*, n.114.

[94] Thus the Sacred Penitentiary declared on May 29, 1915, that every sol-

The first concern of the Church is to see to it that the one who is in danger of death has the proper dispositions for baptism: the right intention, the requisite faith and the necessary sorrow for sin. Careful instruction of the convert should be given so that, as a minimum for eternal salvation, he will have the proper intention to receive the sacrament, and that he believe those truths which are necessary of belief as a means of salvation.

Canon 752, § 2, demands diligent instruction in the principal mysteries of faith, presupposing that the convert has the proper intention. In this case it is sufficient, if a fuller explanation of these mysteries is impossible, that the convert show in some way—by a nod, by simply answering in the affirmative, or by some other sign [95]—his assent to these fundamental truths, and that he give his serious promise to observe all the precepts of God and the Church. Since explicit faith in the mysteries of God's existence and His remunerative justice are absolutely necessary for salvation, and since there is a strong probability that the mysteries of the Trinity and the Incarnation are with a like necessity to be professed with an explicit faith, assent must by all means be given to these truths.

The Holy Office was asked by the Bishop of Quebec in 1703, whether or not a promise on the part of the convert to take instructions and to practice what was demanded of him after his recovery was sufficient to warrant the conferring of the baptism. In reply the Sacred Congregation declared that such a promise was not sufficient of itself, but that the convert had to be taught the mysteries of faith which as a means of salvation are necessary of belief, as are especially the mysteries of the Trinity and the Incarnation.[96] Likewise, a missionary was forbidden to baptize either conditionally or absolutely an adult Mohammedan *in articulo mortis,* but fully conscious, by only arousing in him solely some sentiments of sorrow and trust apart from all mention of the mysteries of faith.[97]

dier when mobilized for war, can be considered by that very fact to be in a status equivalent with those who are in danger of death.—*AAS,* VII (1915), 282.

[95] Cf. S. C. S. Off. (Tchely Meridio-Oriental.), 10 apr. 1861, ad 1—*Fontes,* n. 965.

[96] S. C. S. Off. (Quebec), 25 ian. 1703—D.B., n. 1349a.

[97] S. C. S. Off., 30 mart. 1898: "Utrum missionarius conferre possit Bap-

Since, however, faith is necessary only for the fruitful reception of the sacrament, converts who have the desire for baptism and sorrow for their sins can be baptized, even though, because of lack of time, they cannot be fully instructed in the mysteries of faith, provided that they show their assent to these mysteries by a simple affirmation or nod of the head.[98] In an instruction of the year 1860 the Holy Office, drawing its conclusions from the fact that only the proper intention is necessary for the valid reception of baptism, declared that when there was doubt as to the presence of sufficient faith or of sincere sorrow for sin, the baptism was to be conferred absolutely. It was only when there was doubt as to whether the convert intended to receive the sacrament that baptism was to be administered conditionally.[99] In practice these three rules will prove helpful.

tismum in articulo mortis mahumedano adulto, qui in suis erroribus supponitur in bona fide: 1. Si habeat adhuc plenam advertentiam, tantum illum adhortando ad dolorem et ad confidentiam, minime loquendo de nostris mysteris; 2. Quacumque habeat advertentiam, nihil ei dicendo, cum ex una parte supponitur illi non deesse contritionem, ex alia vero prudens non esse loqui cum eo de nostris mysteriis.

"*Resp.* Ad 1 et 2: Negative, i. e., non licere huiusmodi madhumedanis, de quibus in primo et secundo quaesito agitur, sive absolute sive conditionate administrare Baptismum."—*ASS,* XXX (1897/98), 700; *Fontes,* n. 1197.

[98] S. C. S. Off. (Tchely Meridio-Oriental.), 10 apr. 1861; (Mission. Loang et Kacong), 8 mart. 1770—*Fontes,* nn. 965, 827.

[99] S. C. S. Off., instr. (ad Vic. Ap. Tche-Kiang), 1 aug. 1860: "In dubio enim utrum adultus morti proximus sufficienter instructus sit de fidei mysteriis, et ea sufficienter crediderit, atque in dubio utrum ipsum ante-actae vitae sincere poeniteat, quum mortis necessitas urgeat, sacramentum absolute administrare ei debet absque ulla conditione. In dubio vero utrum ipse vere intendat Baptismum suscipere, si praevio diligenti examine de hac intentione adhuc dubitetur, Baptismus conferri debet sub conditione dummodo sit capax baptismi."—*Fontes,* n. 963. This decision apparently contradicts that of May 10, 1703, to the bishop of Quebec (*Fontes,* n. 765) wherein a missionary was instructed to baptize conditionally, instead of absolutely, an infidel concerning whose dispositions of faith and sorrow there was some doubt. Lehmkuhl (*Theologia Moralis,* I, n. 391) tried to harmonize the two decrees by maintaining that the latter refers to ignorance so extreme as to render the intention doubtful. But De Smet (*De Baptismo,* n. 278) claims that the Holy Office reversed its former decision.

1. It is never lawful to administer the sacrament to an adult who has certainly never made an act of explicit faith in the first two, at least, of the four essential truths.[100]

2. When there is doubt as to the sufficiency of an adult's explicit belief, the priest is bound to furnish the necessary instruction and assistance for the act of faith; if, however, it is impossible to give instruction and the need is urgent, the sacrament may be conferred.

3. If there is even a slight probability that the minimum of dispositions for the fruitful reception is present, the needed sacraments should be conferred.[101]

The Code insists that the convert even in danger of death have the intention to receive baptism. Since the minister cannot baptize even conditionally, unless he has good reason to conjecture the presence of the right intention, the convert must manifest his desire for baptism in some way. Hence, when he cannot even petition for baptism, but has manifested an intention either before or in his present state in some probable manner—*aliquo probabili modo*—he is to receive the sacrament conditionally.[102] If he then recovers, and the doubt as to the validity of the baptism persists, baptism is to be again administered conditionally.

Theologians give the widest possible interpretation to the words *aliquo probabili modo* which is compatible with the divine purpose of saving all men and of having instituted the sacraments for this end. As a general rule it may be stated that when the presumption is in favor of the convert's desire for baptism, and there are no indications to the contrary, conditional baptism may be administered; if, however, no intention was manifested, baptism cannot be administered even conditionally. The fact that one in danger of death

[100] This holds good even in the case of persons who are dying in the state of unconsciousness. For it is inherently unlawful to confer a sacrament on one who is certainly indisposed—as is the case in the present supposition—even though the sacrament could be validly received. Cf. De Smet, *De Baptismo,* n. 278.

[101] Connell, "Priestly Ministry of the Essentials of Faith"—*AER,* LXXVI (1927), 575, 576.

[102] The condition "si dispositus es" is never to be used and is expressly condemned by the Holy Office. Cf. S. C. S. Off., instr. (ad Vic. Ap. Tche-Kiang), 1 aug. 1860—*Fontes,* n. 963.

goes to a Catholic hospital can be a possible, though certainly it is not of necessity a positive, indication of his desire to receive baptism. But it is not correct to assume a right intention as long as no contrary intention was expressed.[103] The Code does not insist on some ***positive*** nor on a ***possible*** manifestation, but demands a ***probable*** indication of the proper intention. From the use of the word *aliquo,* it is clear that even a slight probability is meant to be included in the consideration of the law. Hence the moral principle that inasmuch as the sacraments have been given for man's salvation, they can be conditionally administered to one who is in danger of death with even a slight probability that they will be conferred validly. Therefore, so long as there is a true probability, even though it be very weak, of the proper intention, conditional baptism not only may but should be administered.

The interpretation regarding the probable presence of a desire to receive the sacrament presents a divergence of theory and practice in the case of persons who are in danger of death and are destitute of their senses, and who, therefore, in their present condition can no longer give any sign of their intention to receive baptism. The judgment that such a probable desire is present can be formed only from the circumstances of the place, the person, his condition in life, his attitude towards the Church, etc. It is not permitted to baptize all such persons indiscriminately, but only those who are prudently considered to have at least the implicit desire for baptism. Hence, if the person is unknown to the priest, the latter must interrogate others as to whether they know anything of his dispositions, whether he had ever asked for baptism or had any Christian instruction, or at least had shown some inclination toward the Church. An affirmative answer to any of these questions would indicate at least a probable intention to receive baptism.

It is not lawful to presume a right intention without any assurance of even a probable sign of a desire for baptism.[104] In condemnation of this practice the Holy Office on September 18, 1850, declared that only when, after a consideration of all the circumstances, the missionary prudently judged that a desire for baptism

[103] This is opposed to the view expressed in *AER,* LXIV (1921), 624.
[104] Cf. Noldin-Schmitt, *Theologia Moralis,* III, 74-75.

was present could baptism be conferred conditionally.[105] This response was repeated and upheld by the same Congregation on March 30, 1898.[106] Therefore, the fact of having led a good life without ever showing any inclination to the Christian religion does not of itself seem to be sufficient evidence of a right intention.[107]

Notwithstanding the clear response of the Holy Office, some authors maintain that in certain cases conditional baptism may be administered. If an unconscious pagan had heard of the Christian religion, a presumption of his desire for baptism is easily had, Vermeersch maintains.[108] Hence in a Christian country he would uphold the practice of baptizing conditionally all unconscious persons in danger of death if it is probable that they have not yet been baptized.[109] In pagan lands the presumption would not be so secure. In this instance, Vermeersch demands that there be present supernatural attrition in addition to some knowledge of God and His remunerative justice to indicate the probability that a sufficient implicit intention for baptism is present. If such were the case the administration of conditional baptism would, he maintains, be justified.[110] This opinion is justified by its proponents with the explanation that the responses of the Holy Office do not condemn this

[105] S. C. S. Off. (Perth.), 18 sept. 1850: "Ad 2. Si antea dederit signa velle baptizari, vel in praesenti statu nutu aut alio modo eamdem dispositionem ostenderit, baptizari posse sub conditione, quatenus tamen missionarius, cunctis rerum adiunctis inspectis ita prudenter iudicaverit."—*Fontes,* n. 912.

[106] *ASS,* XXX (1897/98), 700; *Fontes,* n. 1197.

[107] Prümmer, *Theologia Moralis,* III, 104. In the article entitled "Bedingte Sakramentenspendung an sterbende Akatholiken" in *LQS,* LXXXII (1929), 327-334, Prümmer seems to reverse this opinion when he claims that Protestants, who lived ordinary lives and were not fanatic haters of Catholicism, can be baptized conditionally in danger of death; but that the sacrament is to be denied irreligious Protestants, Jews, and pagans unless they explicitly or implicitly signified their desire for baptism.

[108] *Theologia Moralis,* III, 223; *Epitome,* II, p. 21, n. 35; *Periodica,* XVIII (1929), 141*.

[109] *Loc. cit.* Also Ayrinhac, *Legislation on the Sacraments,* I, 32.

[110] *Loc. cit.* This opinion is shared by Lehmkuhl (*Theologia Moralis,* II, 78), Genicot-Salsmans (*Institutiones,* II, p. 132, n. 150), Cappello (*De Sacramentis,* I, p. 142, n. 159) and Ayrinhac (*loc. cit.*).

practice but only commend a more secure mode of action, and that even the Code does not clearly exclude or forbid this theory.[111]

The Code in canon 752, §§ 2, 3, however, does not speak of instances in which there is no positive indication contrary to a desire for baptism, but of instances in which there is a positive indication, slight though it may be, in conformity with at least a probable manifestation of a desire for baptism. Hence, the argument which maintains that as long as there are no indications that the unconscious person ever manifested a contrary attitude, there is the probability that he did have a positive desire for baptism is untenable.[112]

From the words of the Code and the declarations of the Holy Office an obligation to administer baptism conditionally arises provided that some probable sign of the proper intention was given by the subject who is incapable of manifesting a clear desire for the sacrament. If the subject should afterwards recover, he is to be again baptized conditionally, in the event that a doubt concerning the validity of the previous baptism persists. In this case, however, a certainly valid intention must be elicited before administering the sacrament.

Children in danger of death, even those as old as eight or nine years, may be baptized conditionally even if they manifested no dispositions or intention, when it is impossible to instruct them even in the very fundamentals of the faith. "For unless they have given certain proof of the full use of reason (in the theological sense), there is some probability that they may still be infants in the eyes of God, and hence capable of receiving Baptism validly and fruitfully without any subjective requirements." [113]

In regard to the weak-minded, if they are judged capable of

[111] Genicot-Salsmans, *loc. cit.*; Cappello, *loc. cit.*, *AER,* LXIV (1921), 624: "The administration of conditional baptism is, therefore, not contrary to the Code in cases where the presumption, or general principles of true charity, is in favor of the patient's desire, that is to say, when there are no indications to the contrary."

[112] Umberg, "Quo Iure Haereticis et Schismaticis Sacramenta Sint Neganda" —*Periodica,* XVIII (1929), 97*-122*.

[113] Connell, *AER,* LXXVI (1927), 576.

a prudent judgment of sin, they are to be baptized as any adult.[114] When their mental growth has been subnormal and this condition is judged to be perpetual, they are to be baptized as infants in danger of death.[115] If there is hope that they will recover, and there is no proximate danger of death, baptism must be deferred, so that they can be baptized as adults. If the signs are only doubtful, the rule is that in cases of urgent necessity the doubt must be resolved in favor of the faith and the salvation of the individual.[116]

SCHOLION. Historical Synopsis of Baptism.

In the early Church the right to confer solemn baptism pertained to the bishops. Priests and deacons by the fact of their ordination had this power, but its exercise was dependent on the permission of the bishop. This conclusion is drawn from the testimony of St. Ignatius Martyr,[117] St. Jerome,[118] St. Augustine[119] and many other Fathers, including Tertullian.[120] That the bishop retained exclusive power to baptize is evident as late as the fifth century, for an instruction was inserted in the acts of the Council of Chalcedon (451), drawn up by the clergy of Edessa, petitioning the Bishops Photius and Eustathius for the return of their own bishop because of the proximity of Easter and the necessity of administering baptism to the catechumens.[121]

With the passing of the centuries and the expansion of the

[114] Cf. St. Thomas Aquinas, *Summa,* III, q. 68, a. 12.

[115] Canon 754, § 1.

[116] S. C. de Prop. Fide, instr. 17 apr. 1777: "Si necessitas non urgeat expectari potest et debet commodior et maior cognitio; si autem necessitas urgeat; tunc in casu dubio inclinandum in favorem religionis et fidei christianae, et spiritualis salutis baptizandi."—*Fontes,* n. 4575.

[117] *Ep. ad Smyrnaeas,* 8, 1: "Non esse licitum sine episcopo neque baptizare, neque agapes facere."—*MPG,* V, 714.

[118] *Dialogus adversus Luciferianos,* cap. 9: "Unde venit ut sine episcopi iussione neque presbyter neque diaconus ius habeant baptismi."—*MPL,* XXIII, 165.

[119] *De Civitate Dei,* Lib. 22, cap. 8—*MPL,* CLI, 767.

[120] Cf. Martene, *De Antiquis Ecclesiae Ritibus* (4 vols., Rotomagi, 1700), I, 14-16.

[121] Actio X: " . . . propter catechismos, et propter eos qui digni sunt sancto baptismate, opus est eius praesentia."—Mansi, VII, 251.

Church, the bishops were content to entrust the office of solemn baptism to the priests and deacons, so that in the thirteenth century the bishops, who had been looked upon as the only ones in the early Church having the right to baptize (so much so that many people died without baptism, in their absence,[122]) now almost never baptized. In Milan, however, the custom of having the bishop officiate at solemn baptism on two days of the year, viz., the vigils of Easter and Pentecost, was retained.[123] The reason that priests were granted the right to baptize, first by individual bishops and later by the common law,[124] was the simple fact that the great numbers of people to be baptized exceeded the physical strength of the bishops, especially in the larger cities. Thus one finds that in Rome there were many churches which had several baptismal fonts, so that the bishop and the priests could administer the sacrament to the multitudes simultaneously.[125] Another cogent contributing factor was the rise and importance of individual parishes.

Solemn baptism was conferred on only two days in the early Church: on the vigil of Easter and the vigil of Pentecost. On all other days it was forbidden to use the solemn ceremonies, though the conferring of the sacrament itself was not forbidden if the occasion demanded it. Pope Siricius (384-399) wrote to the Bishop of Tarragona to condemn those who baptized on other feast days.[126] Pope Leo I (440-461) in a letter to the Bishops of Sicily, written on October 21, 447, repeated the regulations of his predecessor, Siricius, expressly prescribing the vigils of Easter and Pentecost.[127] At the end of the fifth century Pope Gelasius I (492-496) in 496

[122] Cf. Letter of the clergy of Italy to the legates of the Franks, demanding the return of Dacius, Bishop of Milan, who had been exiled for many years: "quia cum pene omnes episcopi, quos ordinare solet . . . mortui sint, immensa populi multitudo sine baptismo moritur."—Mansi, IX, 155.

[123] Cf. Martene, *De Antiq. Eccles. Rit.*, I, 16.

[124] Cf. c. 19, D. IV, *de cons.*, from Isidorus, *De Officiis Ecclesiasticis*, lib. 2, c. 24.

[125] Martene, *De Antiq. Eccles. Rit.*, I, 19; Corblet, *Histoire de Baptême*, I, 301.

[126] *Ep. ad Himerium*, Ep. Tarraconen., 10 febr. 385—c. 11, D. IV, *de cons.*; Jaffé, n. 255.

[127] C. 12, D. IV, *de cons.*—Jaffé, n. 414.

warned bishops not to presume to baptize between Easter and Pentecost, unless there was a cogent necessity for the sacrament.[128]

Despite the papal designation of these days, there grew up early in the East the custom of conferring solemn baptism also on the feast of the Epiphany, and this custom was soon transferred to Africa and France, where Christmas and the feast of John the Baptist were added. The outbreak of the persecutions caused the law to be relaxed, so that whenever persecution threatened, the bishops gathered the unbaptized together in order that they might not die without the sacrament.[129] In addition, Pope Leo the Great (440-461) declared that any grave necessity, such as danger of death, sickness, war, or shipwreck, was sufficient reason to depart from the observance of the established days of baptism.[130] The custom of administering the sacrament on certain specified days, especially on the vigils of Easter and Pentecost, persevered until the end of the eleventh century, at which time it began to lapse.[131]

Converts to the faith who were not yet baptized were called catechumens. They were so designated because they were admitted into the church to hear the Word of God, although they were not yet baptized.[132] In the earliest period of the Church there were only two classes, those who were simply catechumens and others who were called *competentes*.[133] A third class was introduced, called *genu-*

[128] "Nisi necessitate cogente inter Pascha et Pentecosten nullus episcopus baptizare presumat."—c. 17, D. IV, *de cons.*; Jaffé, n. 710.

[129] Martene, *De Antiq. Eccles. Rit.*, I, 2-6.

[130] Martene, *loc. cit.*

[131] Corblet, *Histoire de Baptême,* I, 480.

[132] The word *catechumen* was used by St. Paul (I Cor., xiv: 19) in the sense of one being taught the first elements of religion.

[133] "Notandum est quod triplex est differentia ad fidem venientium, scil., competentium, catechumenorum, et baptizatorum. Competentes dicuntur, cum ad ecclesiam primum veniunt fidem petentes; unde appellantur competentes, i. e., simul eandem fidem petentes, quomodo videlicet singuli interrogati: Quod petitis ad ecclesiam, respondent, 'Fidem.' Catechumeni postea vocantur, quando a quarta feria quarte septimane et deinceps simbolantur, id est catechizantur. Baptizati tandum dicuntur, cum in Sabbato magno aqua regenerationis loti fuerint."—Rufinus, *Die Summa Decretorum des Magister Rufinus* (hrsg. von Dr. Heinrich Singer, Paderborn, 1902), p. 565. Cf. Rabanus Maurus, *De Institutione Clericorum* (ed. Aloysius Knoepfler, Veröffentlichungen aus dem kirchen-

flectentes, or those who because of some offense were forced to hear the word of God kneeling down: these, however, did not constitute a special order, but were simple catechumens. Martene (1654-1739) distinguished three different orders in the catechumenate: *audientes,* who were admitted into the church to hear the faith explained; *electi,* who after finishing the time of the catechumenate, were inscribed on the list of those who were to receive the sacrament of baptism; *competentes,* who were diligently instructed in the faith and thoroughly acquainted with Christian doctrine, especially the Creed and the Our Father.[134] They were also called *Christiani, fideles, justi, alumni, auditores, baptizandi, candidati, discipuli, illuminandi, incipientes, infantes, novitii, novitioli, orantes, parvi, parvuli, tyrones.*[135]

The most ancient rite of initiation into the catechumenate consisted of the impression of the sign of the cross on the forehead of the candidate and the imposition of hands. To these were added the exorcisms, breathing on the face, touching the nostrils and ears with spittle, and the anointing of the breast and shoulders, although there was not complete uniformity in all dioceses.[136] In the Western Church all these rites were performed on the same day and outside the Church; in the East, three days were apportioned.[137]

historischen Seminar München, hrsg. von Alois Knoepfler, no. 5, München, 1900), lib. I, c. 26.

[134] *De Antiq. Eccles. Rit.,* I, 29.

[135] Corblet, *Histoire de Baptême,* I, 446.

[136] "At postquam per confessionem verae fidei in alterius commendaverit dominium, et per abrenuntiationem a prioris possessoris se alienaverit servitio, exsufflatur ab eo saeva potestas, ut per pium sacerdotis ministerium spiritu sancto cedat fugiens spiritus malignus; signaturque ipse homo signaculo sanctae crucis tam in fronte quam in corde. . . . Exin jam dicuntur super eum orationes, ut fiat catechumenus. Tunc datur ei sal benedictum in os. . . . Dehinc iterum exorcizatur diabolus. . . . Postea tanguntur et nares et aures cum saliva et dicitur ei illud verbum evangelicum, quod Jesus quando surdum et mutum sanavit, tangens cum sputo linquam eius dixit: 'Epheta, quod est, adaperire.' . . . Deinde benedictione sacerdotali munitur, ut ad sacrum baptismum cum fide accepta custodiatur. Ungitur illius tunc pectus de oleo sanctificato cum invocatione sanctae trinitatis. . . . Ungitur et inter scapulas."—Rabanus Maurus, *De Institutione Clericorum,* lib. I, cap. 27.

[137] I Council of Constantinople (381), cap. 7: "Primo quidem die ipsos Christianos facimus, secundo Catechumenos, deinde tertio exorcisamus sive ad-

The catechumenate was generally of long duration. It was left to the prudent judgment of the bishops and priest to determine the length of time requisite as due preparation for the receiving of the sacrament. Gradually, however, particular legislation set definite limits. The Council of Adge, held in the year 506, decreed that Jewish converts had to spend eight months in the catechumenate.[138] This time was even prolonged to one, two or three years, depending on the faith and sincerity of the convert, and on the hope of his serious observance of the precepts of the Christian religion. But there was never a definite rule. And thus it is not surprising to find that Pope St. Gregory I (590-604) in a letter addressed to Faustinus in May, 598, declared that forty days were sufficient if the eight-month period seemed too long for Jewish converts.[139] Others were required to spend only a twenty-day period in the catechumenate, according to a decree of the II Council of Braga, held in the year 572.[140]

During their probationary period the converts were required to practice penance and abstinence, to abjure the errors of their infidelity, and to receive instruction in the faith. St. Augustine (354-420) stressed the necessity for penance, excusing only infants.[141]

juramus ipsos, ter simul in faciem eorum et aures insufflando; et sic eos catechizamus sive initiamus, et curamus ut longo tempore versentur in ecclesiis, et audiant Scripturas, et tunc eos baptizamus."—quoted in Martene, *De Antiq. Eccles. Rit.*, I, 36.

[138] Canon 34: "Judaeis quorum perfidia frequenter ad vomitum redit, si ad legem catholicam venire voluerint octo menses inter catechumenos ecclesiae limen introeant: et si pura fide noscuntur venire, tunc demum baptismatis gratiam mereantur. Quod si casu aliquo periculum infirmitatis intra praescriptum tempus incurrerint, et desperati fuerint, baptizentur."—c. 93, D. IV, *de cons.*

[139] "Ne, quod absit, longa dilatio Judaeorum retro possit animos revocare, cum fratre nostro episcopo loci ipsius loquere, ut, paenitentia ac abstinentia quadraginta dierum indicta, aut die Dominica, aut si celeberrima festivitas fortassis occurrerit, eos omnipotentis Dei, misericordia protegente baptizes."—c. 98, D. IV, *de cons.*; Jaffé, n. 1511.

[140] Canon 1: "Ante viginti dies baptismi ad purgationem exorcismi currant, in quibus viginti diebus omnino symbolum, quod est: Credo in Deum Patrem omnipotentem, spiritualiter doceantur."—C. 55, D. IV, *de cons.*

[141] *De paenitentiae medicina*, cap. 2, quoted in c. 96, D. IV, *de cons.*: "Omnis qui iam suae voluntatis factus est arbiter, cum accedit ad sacramenta fidelium,

St. Cyril of Jerusalem (ca. 315-387) had insisted on forty days as a sufficient period in which the catechumen was to perform acts of penance. Whether the penance was public or private, however, is a matter of dispute. Corblet held that it was not a public penance, stating that the penance imposed on the catechumens was performed at home.[142] Martene had supported the opinion which held that public penance was performed.[143] The former opinion seems to be the more probable one, especially in view of a text attributed by Gratian to St. Ambrose (ca. 340-397) which insisted that penance was not necessary for the reception of Baptism.[144] The *Glossa Ordinaria* notes that the penance here mentioned refers only to exterior satisfaction.[145] It was only by way of exception that a convert was subjected to the rigors of a public penance.[146] Raymond of Pennafort (1175-1275) made reference to the necessity of penance, but did not insist on exterior penance, since internal sorrow for sin was sufficient.[147]

nisi eum paeniteat vitae veteris, novam non potest inchoare. Ab hac paenitentia, cum baptizantur, soli parvuli immunes sunt."

142 *Histoire de Baptême,* I, 457.

143 *De Antiq. Eccles. Rit.,* I, 75-77.

144 "Sine paenitentia sunt dona et vocatio Dei: quia gratia Dei in baptismate non requirit gemitum: non requirit planctum, vel opus aliquod, sed solam fidem: et omnia gratis condonat."—c. 99, D. IV, *de cons.* Gratian inscribed this canon, "Item Ambrosius super epistolam ad Romanos, ad c. 11." The *Correctores Romani* in a note to the words *sed solam fidem* remark: "Sic in glossa Ordinaria, unde potius videtur hoc loco sumpsisse Gratianus, quam ex Ambrosio, apud quem legitur: *nisi solam ex corde professionem,* quemadmodum etiam refertur supra de paenitentia, dist. L., c. *Quis aliquando,* in vers. *Gratia Dei.*"

145 Ad v. *sine paenitentia*: Idest sine satisfactione exteriori et afflictione, quae solet exigi in paenitentia. Nam sine interiori in adultis, vacuum est baptismi mysterium.

146 "La pénitence des Catéchumènes n'était pas publique; elle s'accomplissait à domicile. Ceux qui ont prétendu le contraire ont cité des faits qui ne peuvent être considérés qui comme la libre et voluntaire expansion du repentir. Ce ne fut qu'exceptionnellement que l'Église soumit à la pénitence publique quelques grands pecheurs non baptises; il en fut ainsi de Dorothee, coupable du martyre de plusieurs Chretiens."—Corblet, *Histoire de Baptême,* I, 457.

147 "Nisi enim baptizandus poeniteat vitae veteris, novam vitam inchoare non potest; sed si baptizetur, recipit caracterem, sed non gratiam et peccatorum remissionem, donec recedat fictio de corde suo: non tamen tenetur iste ad

The Catechumens were admitted to Mass to hear the lessons and the homily or exposition of the gospel. This, however, was not sufficient instruction. A more detailed and gradual course in the principal truths of faith was given.[148] This instruction went under the name of *catechesis*. Priests, deacons, and even laymen were empower to conduct the instruction of the simple catechumens. An idea of what was taught is gathered from St. Augustine's *De Catechezandis Rudibus,* which was written by him at the request of a deacon of Carthage. He first shows the absurdity of paganism and then demonstrates the beauty of the moral teachings of the Gospel; stress is laid on the judgment, the creation of the world, the fall of Adam and Eve; the principal figures of the Old and New Testaments, the life and death of the Saviour, His resurrection, the establishment of the Church. The explanation of the Creed and the Lord's Prayer was reserved for the *competentes.* Similar catecheses were also composed by Eusebius of Caesarea (ca. 263-339), St. Cyril of Jerusalem (ca. 315-387), St. Gregory of Nyssa (ca. 335-ca. 394), St. Ambrose (ca. 340-397), St. Nicetas (ca. 335-414) and St. Cyril of Alexandria (ca. 376-444).

When the time of the catechumenate was finished, there took place the inscription of the convert's name on the official ecclesiastical record and the imposition of a Christian name. This took place about thirty or forty days before Easter, and the catechumens were thereupon called *competentes* or *electi.* During this final period before their baptism, the *competentes* were urged to perform acts of penance and mortification, and even to make a confession of their sins.[149]

exteriorem poenitentiam agendam, quia sufficit ei poenitentia interior."—*Summa,* Lib. III, tit. 34, § 2.

[148] "Sed ante baptismum catechezandi debet in hominem praevenire officium ut fidei primum catecumenus accipiat rudimentum. Nam in evangelio secundum Mattheum legitur, quod post resurrectionem dominus apostolis praeceperit, ut in nomine patris et filii et spiritus sancti docerent et baptizarent omnes gentes, id est, prius fidem Dei illis insinuarent et sic credentes in remissionem peccatorum baptizarent."—Rabanus Maurus, *De Institutione Clericorum,* Lib. I, cap. 25.

[149] Martene, *De Antiq. Eccles. Rit.*, I, 74-78.

The principal formality of these preparatory days was the observance of the scrutinies. This name was given to that procedure which included prayers, exorcisms, instruction and examination of the candidates in the Creed and the *Our Father*. Its purpose was simply to discover those who were prepared to receive the sacrament and those who needed longer preparation. In Rome the first scrutiny was held on the Wednesday of the third week in Lent. After the Collects of the Mass, the deacon called the candidates, who came forward together with their sponsors, the men standing on the right side of the church, the women on the left. At the signal from the deacon they knelt down and prayed. An exorcist then made the sign of the cross on the forehead of each candidate, imposed hands, recited a prayer and performed the exorcism; a second and a third cleric repeated the ceremony. Then the priest imposed hands on all and recited a prayer, after which the candidates returned to their places. After hearing the Epistle they were dismissed. The same ceremony took place at the second scrutiny which was held on the following Saturday.

At the third scrutiny, held on Wednesday of the fourth week in Lent, a more solemn ceremony took place. The candidates remained for the Gospel and received their first instructions in the Creed and the *Our Father*. After the reading of the Epistle, four deacons came from the sacristy carrying four gospel books, which they deposited at four corners of the altar. Each deacon read the beginning of each of the four gospels, after which the priest gave a short instruction. When this had been done, the Creed was explained and all the candidates together with the priest recited it; the same procedure followed for the *Our Father*, with the priest explaining each petition of the prayer. The remaining scrutinies were held on corresponding days of the fourth and fifth weeks of Lent.

The final scrutiny was held on the vigil of Easter, either in the morning or in the afternoon, since Mass was not celebrated on this day. The ceremony began with the imposition of hands by the priest and an exorcism; then followed the touching of the ears and nostrils with saliva, the solemn renunciation of Satan, his works and pomps; the anointing of the breast and shoulders, and the recitation by the candidates of the Creed. The Archdeacon then ordered the catechumens to leave the church, after which the deacon told the *electi* to return to their places and to wait for the time when the baptismal ceremony was to begin.

Before the actual ceremony the Holy Father himself read selections from the Old Testament for the instruction of the *electi,* after which a procession formed to the baptistry. The font was first blessed, with the same rites as are observed today.

The Archdeacon presented the candidates to the Pontiff, who examined them with the triple question which is still used, concerning their belief and their desire to be baptized. Each candidate was then immersed by the Pontiff as he pronounced the formula. If the candidates were too numerous, then priests and deacons also performed some of the baptisms.

Confirmation generally was administered after the baptism. Then a procession was formed to the Basilica. The Pontiff, after prostrating himself before the altar, intoned the *Gloria* and began the first Mass of Easter, at which the converts received their first Holy Communion.[150]

[150] Van der Stappen, *Sacra Liturgia* (Tomus IV, *Tractatus de Administratione Sacramentorum et de Sacramentalibus,* Mechliniae: H. Dessain, 1900), 75-79. Cf. Raymundus, *Summa,* Lib. I, tit. 5, § 8; Hostiensis, *Summa Aurea,* Lib. III, tit. *de bapt.,* § *Quae sit eius forma*; Martene, *De Antiq. Eccles. Rit.,* I, 78-86.

CHAPTER V

THE DOUBTFULLY BAPTIZED

When the preliminary investigation reveals a doubt as to the fact or as to the validity of the convert's former baptism, he is to be received into the Church according to the following procedure:

(a) Abjuration or Profession of Faith,

(b) Conditional baptism,

(c) Scramental confession and conditional absolution.[1]

Before this procedure may be used, the uncertainty of the former baptism or the questionable validity of the former baptism must be definitely established. After stating that the sacraments of baptism, confirmation and holy orders cannot be repeated, the Code demands a prudent doubt as to whether they were actually or whether they were validly conferred, before they can be conditionally administered.[2]

The doubt is prudent, if it is positive, serious and based on some probable evidence, at least extrinsic,[3] if not also intrinsic.[4] A mere suspicion or scruple does not suffice. This point has been consistent-

[1] S. C. S. Off., instr., 20 iul. 1859: "2. Si Baptismus sit sub conditione iterandus, hoc ordine procedendum erit:

(A.) Abjuratio seu Fidei Professio,

(B.) Baptismus Conditionatus,

(C.) Confessio Sacramentalis cum Absolutione conditionata.

[2] Canon 732.

[3] "At non quodlibet placitum seu dubium paucorum theologorum sufficit ad imponendam obligationem repetendi sacramentum, immo ne ad licitam quidem reddendam repetitionem. Ut obligatio iterandi exsistat necesse omnino est, auctoritas theologorum saltem extrinseca tanta sit, ut ipsorum sententia tamquam vere probabilis haberi queat."—Cappello, *De Sacramentis,* I, p. 21, n. 27. Cf. Merkelbach, *Summa,* III, p. 134, n. 164.

[4] Ayrinhac, *Legislation on the Sacraments,* p. 9.

ly emphasized by the Holy Office,[5] by commentators[6] and was decreed by the III Plenary Council of Baltimore (1884):[7]

> Tantopere scilicet exhorruit Ecclesia semper errorem rebaptizantium ut ne sub conditione quidem Baptismum iterari permittat, nisi quando probabile dubium adest sacramentum hoc antea vel nullo modo vel invalide fuisse susceptum. Culpabiliter aut temere dignitati sacramenti huius sic derogantes gravis peccati reatu iuxta omnes se irretiunt.

The doubt is prudent and probable when after a diligent investigation it cannot be dispelled, so that moral certitude regarding the fact or the validity of the baptism cannot be attained. The doubt must be founded on solid reasons, and not on merely negative scruples. If the doubt is wholly inane or imprudent it is illicit to again confer the sacrament, and one who would rashly rebaptize, would commit a grave irreverence to the sacrament. However, because of the primary necessity of baptism for salvation, the reason on which the doubt is based need not be as profound or as decided as that which is required for the repetition of sacraments not absolutely necessary for salvation. Therefore, if after a conscientious investigation it remains uncertain whether the doubt is reasonable or not, it should be resolved in favor of conditional baptism.[8]

Whenever baptism *can* be administered conditionally, it *must*

[5] S. C. S. Off., 5 iul. 1853: "Si autem remaneat prudens dubium circa validitatem,"—*Fontes,* n. 925; 24 ian. 1877: "adhuc prudens dubium de validitate," "Quatenus prudens dubium supersit,"—*Fontes,* n. 1050; 20 nov. 1878: "adhuc probabile dubium de baptismi validitate supersit,"—*Fontes,* n. 1058; 22 iun. 1866, ad 40: "dubium adsit probabile invaliditatis baptismi,"—*Fontes,* n. 994.

[6] Cf. Blat, *Commentarium,* Vol. III, Pars I, p. 17; Cappello, *De Sacramentis,* I, 151, 152; Vermeersch-Creusen, *Epitome,* II, n. 38, and many others.

[7] N. 121. Cf. II Plenary Council of Baltimore, decree n. 240.

[8] Genicot-Salsmans, *Institutiones,* II, 134. Noldin-Schmitt claim that whenever there is not present *full and evident* certitude of the validity of the prior baptism, conditional baptism may be administered: "Fieri potest, ut baptismus ab haeretico collatus repeti non *debeat,* quia nec de recta intentione nec de debita materia et forma exsistit ratio dubitandi, repeti autem *possit,* quia de eius valore plena et evidens certitudo non habetur."—*Theologia Moralis,* III, 24-25. Such an opinion if reduced to practice would destroy the efficacy of the investigation: it can hardly harmonize with the directions of the Holy Office.

be administered conditionally. As a practical rule, it should be remembered that there is an obligation to rebaptize converts conditionally, (1) when positive reasons can be advanced against the validity of the previous baptism, though these reasons are not strong enough to prove conclusively the invalidity of the former baptism; (2) when nothing positive in favor of validity can be ascertained, and at the same time the invalidity cannot be decisively proved.[9]

In practice a prudent doubt may arise in the course of the examination of the ritual of the sect in which the convert was baptized. When it is found that the sect leaves the mode of applying the water to the discretion of the minister or of the subject, or that the sect prescribes sprinkling as the proper manner of baptizing, a doubt can easily arise as to whether the water touched the skin of the head and whether the water actually flowed. In these cases further investigation is peremptory, and if the doubt cannot be resolved from an interrogation of the subject, the minister, the sponsors (if they were present), parents, relatives or friends who attended the ceremony, or if all such further investigation is impossible, conditional baptism is warranted. Also when the examination of the ritual shows the use of a form which differs from the valid form prescribed by the Church, the validity of a baptism conferred with the use of such a form can readily come into question. The Holy Office alone is competent to issue a definite and authoritative pronouncement as to the validity or invalidity of such a form. Meanwhile the priest may resolve the doubt by applying the general principles on the requisites of the valid form to the particular case.[10] If the doubt persists, conditional baptism should be conferred. Again, the examination of the ritual may show that there is too great an interval between the application of the water and the pronouncing of the form to remove all doubt as to the certain validity of the baptism. In the event that with further investigation there cannot be established a certainty concerning the validity or invalidity, baptism is to be administered conditionally. If the ritual prescribes all that is essential for the valid conferring of the sacrament, as is usu-

[9] Schaaf, "The Validity of Protestant Baptisms,"—*AER,* LXXVI (1927), 498.

[10] Cf. Chapter III, art. 2, 1, B.

ally the case, further investigation is necessary to ascertain whether the heretical minister actually used the ritual of his sect in this particular instance, and whether he carried out all the prescriptions or perhaps inserted interpollations which vitiated the sacrament. In this point there is need of careful inquiry, because the erroneous notions of the majority of sects concerning the nature, efficacy or necessity of baptism have led to much carelessness and disregard for the essential elements of the sacrament.[11]

In any case, an investigation of the ritual of a sect must be accompanied by further inquiry to ascertain whether the ritual was faithfully adhered to in practice. If after this investigation a reasonable doubt remains, or if a satisfactory investigation is impossible because of the circumstances of time, place, and persons involved, or if the investigation revealed nothing for the validity and nothing for the invalidity, conditional baptism is to be conferred.[12]

Certain rules will serve as helpful guides in the actual investigation:

1. It is not licit to administer conditional baptism because of any suspicion, scruple or doubt that is wholly inane and without

[11] "The class whose baptism is doubtful, embraces almost all sects that go under the general name of Protestants. Most of them, it is true, in their rituals, prescribe all that is essential to Baptism, and if we had sufficient security that it is always administered by them in exact accordance with their rituals, we should have no reason to doubt its validity. As a matter of fact, the validity of baptism by Protestants at first was generally admitted; and when a doubt was raised in France regarding that conferred by the Calvinists, St. Pius V decided in favour of its validity. But their errors regarding the efficacy and necessity of the sacrament, gradually led to habitual carelessness and frequent substantial defects in its administration, so as to leave reasonable ground for doubting in any given case whether it was rightly conferred."—O'Kane, *The Rubrics of the Roman Ritual*, pp. 212-213.

"Cum baptismus sit sacramentum tam necessarium, cumque defectus fidei tam late grassetur inter ministros haereticos, qui proinde non multum curant de recte applicanda forma ad materiam et de formanda intentione faciendi quod facit Ecclesia, saepe erit melius et securius, condicionate baptizare illos, qui ex haeresi redeunt."—Prümmer, *Manuale Theologiae Moralis*, III, p. 105, n. 137.

[12] "Si examen fieri nequeat, baptismus sub condicione iterandus est; nam, quia magis in dies crescit infidelitas vel, etiam apud bonae fidei acatholicos, incuria, baptismus ab acatholico collatus, practice saltem regulariter repetendus est."—Vermeersch-Creusen, *Epitome*, II, p. 23, n. 38.

rational foundation. The reverence which is due the sacrament concerning whose validity there is moral certainty and also the avoidance and forestalling of all scandal demand this.[13]

2. As often as there is a rational and prudent doubt about the fact of baptism or about its validity which cannot be resolved by a diligent investigation, it is licit to baptize conditionally. Even the slightest doubt suffices, provided that it is based on solid reasons.

3. As long as the validity of the former baptism is not morally certain, conditional baptism must be administered.[14] Full and evident certitude, though it is certainly to be desired, is not required. Nothing more is demanded than a moral certitude, which excludes all reasonable doubt about the validity of the heretical baptism. When no reasonable doubt concerning the matter, form or intention of the minister is present, one cannot administer baptism conditionally without the danger of committing grave sin.[15]

Article 1. Abjuration and Profession of Faith [16]

Before he is received into the Church, the convert must pass some time in preparation. He must be carefully instructed in Catholic doctrine, especially in those truths of which he will make profession during the ceremony of reception, and in addition he must be shown the errors and half-truths of his former beliefs. During

[13] Very often, however, the minister who would conditionally baptize without good reason would be excused from grave sin, especially if he is accustomed to being disturbed by scruples, or if there is no time to conduct a full investigation. But he is obliged to take steps to overcome this irrational manner of acting.—Genicot-Salsmans, *Institutiones,* II, p. 105, n. 118.

[14] Cappello, *De Sacramentis,* I, p. 149, n. 172; p. 21, n. 27.

[15] The irregularity which formerly accompanied the sacrilegious repetition of baptism, since it does not appear in the Code, is abrogated in virtue of the rule mentioned in canon 6, § 5.

[16] In England the order of reception of the doubtfully baptized converts is: abjuration and profession of faith; conditional baptism privately administered with holy water (not baptismal water); absolution from excommunication; sacramental confession. If it is more convenient, the private baptism may follow absolution from censures. Cf. I Provincial Council of Westminster (1852), decr. xvi, c. 8—*Collectio Lacensis,* III, 929; *Ordo administrandi sacramenta et alia quaedam officia peragendi,* Tit. III, cap. iv, nn. 1, 3, 5. The same order is observed in Ireland. Cf. *Rituale Parvum* (2. ed.), pp. 75-85.

this period, the right dispositions for receiving the sacraments of baptism and penance must be cultivated, and the convert should be encouraged to perform acts of piety and devotion as proof of his sincerity.

When the convert has been duly prepared, he is to be received into the Church without delay. Neither the Instruction of 1859, nor the Code, nor the Ritual prescribes any special faculty for receiving the convert's profession of faith. By reason of the fact that the profession and the abjuration are combined to form one formality, however, and also in view of the norm set forth in canon 2314, § 2, governing the juridic efficacy of the abjuration, the delegation of the Ordinary should be obtained before the priest proceeds to act as an official witness to the convert's profession of faith.

At the appointed time, the convert and at least two persons who are to act as witnesses present themselves. The priest wearing surplice and violet stole, sits inside the sanctuary on the Epistle side if the Blessed Sacrament is reserved in the tabernacle; if not, he is to sit in front of the tabernacle. The convert kneels, and placing his right hand on the book of the Gospels, recites the profession of faith. If he is illiterate, the priest must read the formula to him slowly and distinctly in order that the convert may understand and repeat each word.

Since the profession of faith prescribed by the II and III Plenary Councils of Baltimore has given place to the more recent formula approved by the Holy Office, this latter formula is to be used. In other countries, unless special regulations exist, the convert may recite the formula prescribed by the Instruction of July 20, 1859.[17]

Converts who are not yet fourteen years old, are not obliged to make the abjuration. They may do so, but an intelligent recitation of the Apostles' Creed is a sufficient profession of faith on their reception into the Church.[18] This is in keeping with the rule of Cardinal Albizzi (+ 1361), which has been invoked by the Holy

[17] Cappello, *De Censuris,* n. 215; Cocchi, *Commentarium,* VIII, n. 136; Ojetti, *Synopsis,* II, n. 2289; Wernz-Vidal, *Ius Canonicum,* VII, 417.

[18] De Smet, *De Baptismo,* n. 304; Vermeersch, *Theologia Moralis,* II, p. 32, n. 37.

Office[19] and the Congregation of the Propagation of the Faith.[20] According to this rule only converts who are fourteen years of age and over are required to make a formal abjuration of the sect to which they belonged.

It is important that the abjuration and profession of faith, to be of juridical value, be made in the external forum in the presence of the priest and two witnesses. The priest in this case acts as the delegate of the local Ordinary.[21]

Article 2. Conditional Baptism

After the profession of faith, conditional baptism is to be administered. It seems that the baptismal formula for adults must be used, the only change being that the condition, *si non es baptizatus (a),* is prefixed to the usual formula of the words spoken at baptism. In support of this conclusion is the presence of the conditional form in the ritual,[22] and the wording of canons 755, § 1, and 759. Canon 755, § 1, prescribes that baptism is to be conferred solemnly except in the cases mentioned in canon 759, when it is permitted to confer baptism privately, i. e., when not all the rites and ceremonies prescribed by the ritual books are to be observed.[23] These exceptional cases are associated with baptism when its recipient is in danger of death and when baptism is to be given conditionally to adult converts from heresy.[24]

From the fact that canon 755, § 1, uses the word *conferatur,* it is seen that there is present a clear obligation to observe all the

[19] S. C. S. Off., litt. 8 mart. 1882—*Fontes,* n. 1073.

[20] S. C. de Prop. Fide (C.G.), 1 iun. 1885—*Fontes,* n. 4909.

[21] Canon 2314, § 2.

[22] *Rituale Romanum,* Tit. 2, cap. 4, n. 40.

[23] Canon 737, § 2.

[24] Canon 759, § 1. In mortis periculo baptismum privatim conferre licet; et, si conferatur a ministro qui nec sacerdos sit nec diaconus, ea tantum ponantur, quae sunt ad baptismi validitatem necessaria; si a sacerdote vel diacono, serventur quoque, si tempus adsit, caeremoniae quae baptismum sequuntur.

§ 2. Extra mortis periculum baptismum privatum loci Ordinarius permittere nequit, nisi agatur de haereticis qui in adulta aetate sub conditione baptizentur.

§ 3. Caeremoniae autem quae in baptismi collatione praetermissae quavis ratione fuerint, quamprimum in ecclesia suppleantur, nisi in casu de quo in § 2.

rubrics of the ritual for adult baptism. No such obligation to confer conditional baptism privately arises from the wording of canon 759, § 2. This canon denies to the local Ordinary the faculty of permitting private baptism outside a case of danger of death, with one exception, viz., when there is question of conditionally baptizing adult converts. Only in this latter case can the local Ordinary *permit* the ceremonies of solemn baptism to be omitted. Inherently then (i. e., in the absence of any permission from the local Ordinary), all the ceremonies of baptism according to the formula for adults are to be observed.

If the local Ordinary does grant permission to confer the conditional baptism privately, the obligation to observe all the ceremonies no longer holds.[25] In granting the permission to dispense with solemn baptism, the Ordinary has the power to prescribe certain ceremonies which must be observed. In the diocese of Seattle, the ceremonies which follow the actual baptism are to be observed.[26] When the faculty to use private baptism is granted without the prescription of any such additional ceremonies, it is sufficient to pronounce merely the conditional baptismal formula.[27] The formula which is contained in the smaller ritual[28] and which had been granted by indult to the Archbishop of Philadelphia in 1914[29] may also be used.

If the local Ordinary does not grant permission to confer private baptism, but does concede the faculty of using the formula for in-

[25] Cf. II Prov. Council of Toronto (1938), decr. 138; IV Prov. Council of Oregon (1932), decr. 218; V Diocesan Synod of Seattle (1938), n. 34. Hence there is no longer any need for special indults formerly granted to the bishops of several countries, e. g., Ireland (Maynooth Synod [1900], Appendix, pp. 12-14), England (I Prov. Council of Westminster, decr. xvi, 8°).

[26] "Quando agitur de haereticis qui in adulta aetate sub conditione sint baptizandi, baptismum privatim conferre permittitur, quo in casu locum habeat solum ablutio aquae verae et naturalis cum praescripta verborum forma et serventur quoque caeremoniae quae baptismum sequuntur."—V. Dioc. Syn. of Seattle (1938), n. 34.

[27] O'Kane, *Rubrics of the Roman Ritual,* p. 215, n. 441.

[28] *The Priest's New Ritual,* pp. 61-63.

[29] This formula was granted also to Cardinal Gibbons and was permitted in the provinces of Philadelphia and Baltimore. Cf. Schenk, *Mixed Religion and Disparity of Cult,* n. 175, note 62.

fants, because of the presence of a grave and reasonable cause, then all the ceremonies prescribed by the ritual are to be observed.

In the event that there is no episcopal legislation on this matter, the longer formula for adults must be used, with the condition expressed. It depends on the prudent judgment of the bishop whether or not a departure from this solemn ceremony is warranted. Diocesan statutes and faculties are therefore of the utmost importance and should be examined carefully in order that the proper method of administering conditional baptism may be ascertained.

Article 3. Confession

The Instruction provides that sacramental confession and conditional absolution must follow the conditional baptism. Formerly there was a controversy among theologians as to the necessity of confession in this case. The negative opinion based its position on the probable invalidity of the prior baptism, and the fact that the obligation of confession binds only the validly baptized; hence, the conclusion that subsequent sins are not *materia capax* of the sacrament of penance. Those who upheld the necessity for confession argued from the possibility that the prior baptism was valid, and that consequently the sins subsequently committed remained. The III Plenary Council of Baltimore (1884) in adopting the prescriptions of the Instruction as law for the United States, has definitely settled the question for this country.[30]

As to the necessity for an integral confession, however, a difference of opinion among theologians still exists concerning the interpretation of various decrees of the Holy Office on this point. The first of these decrees has to do with the case of a certain Karl Ferdinand Wipperman of Rostock, a Lutheran Quietist, who desired to be reconciled to the Church. The Sacred Congregation was asked if he was bound to confess all the sins of his past life, following his conditional baptism. An affirmative reply was given.[31] Gury (1801-

[30] N. 122. Cf. Sabbetti-Barrett, *Compendium*, p. 677, n. 725, q. 3.

[31] S. C. S. Off., 27 iun. 1715: "Quaeritur, an dictus Wipperman sit rebaptizandus, et quatenus affirmative: an absolute vel sub conditione; et quatenus affirmative: an teneatur confiteri omnia peccata praeteritae vitae; et quatenus

1866) interpreted this obligation of sacramental confession to mean an obligation to make an integral confession and held that this was to be observed in practice. Other authors, however, were of the opinion that, since the first baptism was doubtful, the obligation of making an integral confession was likewise doubtful. Basing their practice on this theory, some confessors in England concluded that a doubtful obligation was no obligation at all, and were satisfied if the converts related only some sins in confession in order to gain the benefit of sacramental absolution, if perchance they were in need of it. On the other hand, it was the constant practice of the greater number of confessors in England to exact an integral confession. To establish a uniform practice and to secure a safe norm of procedure, the Archbishop of Westminster applied to the Holy Office for a solution of the difficulty. The Holy Office replied that an integral confession was to be made by converts, and commanded that the decree of June 27, 1715, be sent to the Archbishop.[32]

In the following year, 1869, the Archbishop of Quebec asked whether the decree of 1868 was of obligation not only in England, for which it was passed, but also in Quebec and in other regions. To this the Sacred Congregation of the Propagation of the Faith replied that the decree of the Holy Office contained a universal law and hence was of obligation not only in England, but in other regions as well, and strictly forbade the contrary opinion to be taught under any circumstances.[33] This response, however, was not included in the official *Collectanea* published in 1893, and hence Genicot (1856-1900) [34] and others concluded that it was spurious.

In interpreting these decrees theologians have sponsored three different opinions. Some hold that these decisions are necessarily to be considered as declarations of the divine law, and hence an in-

affirmative: an confessio praeponenda sit, vel postponenda Baptismo conferendo sub conditione.

"R.: Carolum Ferdinandum esse rebaptizandum sub conditione, et collato Baptismo, eius praeteritae vitae peccata confiteantur, et ab iis sub conditione absolvatur."—*Fontes,* n. 780.

[32] S. C. S. Off., 17 dec. 1868—*ASS,* IV (1868-1869), 320-324; *Collect.,* n. 1338.

[33] S. C. de Prop. Fide, 12 iul. 1869—*Analecta Ecclesiastica,* VII (1899), 489.

[34] *Institutiones,* II, p. 225, n. 259.

tegral confession is demanded.[85] The basis for this opinion is the contention that the doubtfully baptized are considered as subjects of the Church, and therefore the sins committed between the two receptions of baptism are subject to the power of the keys. In criticism of this opinion it can be said that the invoked principle proves that the sins committed between each baptism could be matter for confession, but the conclusion that they must be submitted is unwarranted. It follows that the law which binds the validly baptized should apply also to converts, namely, that the obligation of confession touches only those sins of which certain knowledge is had by the penitent, and in no way touches the sins which have merely a doubtful existence from the viewpoint either of their factual commission, or of their sustained guilt, or of their past forgiveness.[86]

A second opinion maintains that the decrees are neither declaratory of the divine law, nor promulgated as general law for the Church, but bind only those places and territories for which they were issued.[87]

Others hold that these decrees contain a general ecclesiastical precept.[88] That the Church possesses the power to impose the obligation to make an integral confession cannot be denied.[89] But whether these decrees *de facto* contain a general law of the Church is not sufficiently clear, especially since the Code does not solve the controversy, but seems rather to have purposely avoided it.

The cited decrees of the years 1715 and 1868 as issued by the Holy Office regarded a particular case and country. The declara-

[85] Lehmkuhl, *Theologia Moralis,* II, nn. 424 sqq.; Noldin-Schmitt, *Theologia Moralis,* III, p. 238, n. 230.

[86] "Peccata inter utrumque Baptismum commissa probabiliter sunt deleta per alterum Baptisma. Et sane sacramentum baptismale nequit conditionate iterari, nisi primum fuerit probabiliter invalidum; et eo ipso quod primum est probabiliter nullum, novum probabiliter valet et eadem cum probabilitate abstersit peccata praevia."—De Smet, *De Baptismo,* n. 307, nota 100.

[87] Genicot-Salsmans, *Institutiones,* II, 224-225, who cites Ballerini-Palmieri, D'Annibale and Bucceroni as also holding this opinion.

[88] Cf. *AER,* XXXVIII (1908), 508-512.

[89] "Saepe lex positiva statuit aliquid ex prudentiali ratione quae per se sola non induceret necessitatem (ex jure naturali vel divino), est autem sufficiens ad statuendam legem quae necessitatem imponat."—Suarez, *De Censuris,* Disp. XL, sect. vi, n. 9.

tion which was made in the year 1869 by the Sacred Congregation of the Propagation of the Faith does not suffice for a universal law, because of the fact that it was delivered not in a general congregation, but was issued by the secretary of the Congregation *in congressu tantum* and without the previous consultation of the Congregation. In the year 1897 the Cardinal Secretary of the Holy Office publicly declared at S. Apollinaris that this response was not a general decree.[40]

Hence, while the opinion which denies the necessity of an integral confession outside those places for which there has been issued a particular precept either by the Holy See or by the bishop is still probable, and therefore safe in practice, yet it seems that the opinion which demands an integral confession is the safer one, and the one to be followed. Although these decrees are in themselves particular responses and declarations to individual cases, they virtually and equivalently declare that the sins of all doubtfully baptized persons constitute necessary matter for confession, for they were given in wholly different circumstances, and yet the same decision was reached in each case. Even Genicot, who denies any obligation, concludes that the convert should be urged to make an integral confession by which the remission of sins committed after the first baptism is made more certain.[41]

This conclusion is in conformity with a set of principles issued by the Holy Office in connection with its decision of December 17, 1868, and which are still applicable to the question of whether the convert is bound to make an integral confession:

[40] Ojetti, *Synopsis*, III, n. 3164. Cf. Noldin-Schmitt, *Theologia Moralis*, III, n. 238, n. 230.

[41] "Practice: *Ubi S. Sedes vel Episcopi praecipiunt confessionem,* haec regulariter imponenda est neo-conversis; attamen, cum haec lex probabiliter sit mere ecclesiastica, quotiens remanet vere probabile prius baptisma fuisse invalidum, urgenda est cum ea moderatione quae legum positivarum propria est.—*In aliis regionibus,* confessio haec valde consulenda est, quo certior sit peccatorum ante commissorum remissio, sed absque stricto praecepto, excepto casu in quo non vere probabile est prius baptisma fuisse invalidum, ac proinde non est solide probabilis remissio peccatorum per baptismum sub condicione collatum." —*Institutiones,* II, p. 225, n. 259. *Contra,* Donovan, *Homiletic,* XLIII (1943), 1118-1119; XLI (1941), 699.

(1) When there is question of an act which is certainly performed, the presumption is in favor of the validity of the act, unless its nullity is certain; this is especially applicable when there is question of a solemn act which by divine law cannot be repeated or repealed.

(2) All obligations which flow from such an act remain intact, as long as there is no certitude that the act is invalid.

(3) Since after Baptism there is no other sacrament in the Church whereby sinners can effect their reconciliation with God, doubtfully baptized converts must not and cannot be released from this obligation (i. e., integral sacramental confession).

(4) It matters not that they have received conditional baptism after their abjuration of heresy: for what is done in a matter so important for the convert as a proper measure of safety and benefit, cannot be alleged as an argument for the cancellation of obligations which are recognized and understood to be connected with the act (of sin) which was certainly committed.

(5) When there is question of the sacraments, the safer course must always be pursued.[42]

In the United States sacramental confession is prescribed by law. And it is the practice in view of the uniformity of the above decrees to insist on an integral confession.[43]

As regards the time when the confession is to take place some difference of opinion and practice exists because of a decree of the Holy Office, dated December 2, 1874, permitting an integral non-sacramental confession before conditional baptism.[44] Thus in the

[42] *ASS,* IV (1868-1869), 323, 324; *Collect.*, n. 1338.

[43] Cf. Sabetti-Barrett, *Compendium,* pp. 677-678, n. 725, q. 3.

[44] S. C. S. Off., 2 dec. 1874: "An catechumeni confiteri possint sacramentaliter antequam baptizentur sive absolute sive conditionaliter.

"R.: Quoad confessionem ante baptismum absolute conferendum, *negative*; quod si nihilominus catechumenus velit sese confiteri, instruatur id nullatenus haberi posse sub ratione sacramenti, cum nequeat absolutio impertiri, nec teneri missionarium ad secretum servandum. Si vero agatur de iis qui debent baptizari sub conditione, tunc poterunt ad maiorem functionis ecclesiasticae facilitatem prius audiri sacramentaliter quoad eorum culparum accusationem; deinde post collationem baptismi sub conditione confessarius, iterum reassumptis per summa capita cum poenitente iis de quibus iam accusationem fecerit, absolvat sacra-

archdiocese of Dublin an extrasacramental integral confession of sins precedes the conditional baptism; then takes place the sacramental confession of sins at least according to their general headings, and thereupon follows the conditional absolution.[45] In England, conditional baptism is administered after the prayer *Deus cui proprium est,* and confession can either follow the baptism or the recital of *Te Deum laudamus.*[46] The English ritual also permits the custom acording to which the convert makes his confession before receiving conditional baptism; then, after his reception of conditional baptism, he makes a general statement to the effect that he wishes to confess all the sins he has already told, after which conditional absolution is given.[47] In the United States the order prescribed by the Instruction should be followed, i. e., sacramental confession should follow conditional baptism. The practice of following the order used in England and Ireland cannot be wholly censured, if there is a serious and reasonable cause for so acting. The custom of deferring confession and absolution for a few days, however, can hardly be justified.[48]

Because the Instruction, which professedly gives the detailed procedure to be followed, fails to mention the absolution from censures in its direction for the reception of the doubtfully baptized, but explicitly demands this formality for the reception of the validly baptized, the natural conclusion is that no absolution from censures is necessary. Many authors, however, suggest that the absolution, at least a conditional one, from censures be given. De Smet,[49] Wernz-

mentaliter pariter sub conditione."—*Fontes,* n. 1035; *ASS,* XXV (1892-1893), 454; *Collect.,* n. 1426.

[45] *Rituale Parvum,* pp. 73-85.

[46] *Ordo administrandi,* Tit. III, cap. iv, n. 5.

[47] *Ordo administrandi, loc. cit.,* n. 3.

[48] *Contra,* Sabetti-Barrett, *Compendium,* p. 678, n. 725, q. 4: "Verum sicut non videtur esse contra *spiritum* praedictae Instructionis praxis eorum sacerdotum, qui confessionem proprie dictam seu accusationem peccatorum audiunt vel *ante* vel *post* receptam abjurationem, deinde conferunt Baptismum conditionatum, et demum impertiuntur absolutionem, ita praxis eorum qui, justa occurrente causa, confessionem et absolutionem *differunt ad paucos dies,* non videtur esse absona a verbis ipsis Instructionis." Cf. Heuser, *The Parish Priest on Duty,* p. 43.

[49] *De Baptismo,* n. 305.

Vidal,[50] Haring, [51] Cocchi [52] and Mothon [53] among others uphold this practice, which is the custom in England,[54] Ireland,[55] and in the diocese of Seckau.[56]

In the consideration of this question it is important to remember that the discussion concerns only the external forum. In the internal forum, a doubt of fact (whether the convert has ever actually received baptism) or of law (whether the convert was validly baptized) is always resolved in favor of the eternal salvation of the convert.[57] Hence, conditional baptism and absolution from sins are necessary. In the external forum the eternal salvation of the convert is not involved, but merely his subjection to ecclesiastical law. The principle, *in dubio iuris standum est pro valore actus* would seem to have application here, and hence ordinarily the convert would be considered as subject to the law of the Church except in those cases in which he is expressly exempted.[58] Since, however, there is question of an ecclesiastical penalty, the principle enunciated in canon 2219, § 1, is more pertinent and must be applied: *In poenis benignior est interpretatio facienda.*

A censure is defined as a penalty which affects only a *baptized* person, who has committed some crime and is contumacious, by depriving him of certain spiritual benefits.[59] The censure in question is that of excommunication which is attached to the crime of heresy, apostasy and schism.[60] The Code in canon 1325, § 2, explicitly postulates the previous reception of baptism in its definition of these three clases of delinquents. The stricter opinion interprets the words

[50] *Ius Canonicum,* VII, 417.

[51] *Grundzüge des katholischen Kirchenrechtes,* II, p .382, nota 2.

[52] *Commentarium,* VIII, n. 136.

[53] *Institutions Canoniques,* II, art. 1733.

[54] Cf. *Ordo administrandi,* Tit. III, cap. iv.

[55] Cf. *Rituale Parvum,* pp. 75 sqq.

[56] Cf. Haring, *Grundzüge,* II, 382.

[57] Cf. Van Hove, *De Legibus Ecclesiasticis,* p. 198; Beste, *Introductio in Codicem,* p. 70; Michiels, *Normae Generales,* I, 285; Vermeersch-Creusen, *Epitome,* I, p. 6, n. 79; McCloskey, *The Subject of Ecclesiastical Law According to Canon 12,* p. 175.

[58] Canon 12.

[59] Canon 2241, § 1.

[60] Canon 2314, § 1, n. 1.

of this canon *post receptum baptismum* to mean any baptism whatsoever, whether valid, or invalid, or doubtful. The more benign interpretation substitutes or understands the word *validum* after *baptismum*. Since, therefore, one who has been baptized becomes subject to the excommunication, and since in the case of a doubtfully baptized convert this essential condition for incurring the penalty is doubtful, the more benign interpretation favors the principle, *in dubio standum est pro libertate.*[61]

Thus while the doubtfully baptized may generally be subject to the disciplinary and administrative norms of ecclesiastical law,[62] they cannot be considered as being liable to the penal legislation of the Church. "Hence, in practice the factual doubt as to the existence of a valid baptism can be reduced to a legal doubt concerning the person's subjection to ecclesiastical jurisdiction, and so the excommunication may safely be regarded as non-existent." [63]

In view of the fact that absolution from the censure is unnecessary and superfluous, there is no point to the objection that the Instruction suggests that in doubt as to whether the convert incurred the excommunication the word *forsan* may be inserted in the formula of absolution. From the text of the Instruction it is evident that this rubric applies only to the formula used in the reception of those whose baptism is established as valid.[64]

Scholion. Historical Synopsis of Conditional Baptism.

According to the tradition of the Church an investigation of the convert's previous baptism must always precede his reception into the Church. The V Council of Carthage (401) was the first to outline a definite procedure when the convert could not recall being baptized. In this instance, witnesses, including the one who had performed the ceremony, were to be called; if these were not available a further investigation was to be made in an effort to find some-

[61] Cf. *AER*, LXXXVII (1932), 527.

[62] But cf. McCloskey, *The Subject of Ecclesiastical Law*, pp. 80-82, who seems to require valid baptism as an essential requisite for subjection to the laws of the Church.

[63] Waldron, *The Minister of Baptism*, pp. 92-93; Bastnagel, "Validation of a Convert's Marriage,"—*The Jurist*, IV (1944), 146.

[64] *AER*, LXVIII (1933), 419.

one who could testify under oath that baptism had been administered.[65] This was insisted upon by Pope Leo I (440-461) in a letter to Leo, Bishop of Ravenna, written in 458. If there were absolutely no signs to indicate the previous baptism of the convert, he was to be admitted to baptism.[66]

In the conferring of conditional baptism, however, the condition was not formally expressed in the first centuries of the Church, but a tacit condition was used.[67] The form with the condition expressed in it was first used in the eighth century, and was thereupon received in many places. It remained for Alexander III (1159-1181) in the twelfth century to command the universal use of the conditional formula:

> De quibus dubium est, an baptizati fuerint, baptizantur his verbis praemissis: si baptizatus es, non te baptizo: sed si nondum baptizatus es, ego te baptizo, etc.[68]

This was confirmed by John XXII (1316-1334), and has remained as the practice of the Church for the cases wherein there is a serious doubt as to the validity of the former baptism.[69]

In the early Church it was usual for baptism to be conferred conditionally for the reason that doubt as to the fact of baptism then obtained. In the thirteenth century Hostiensis (+ 1271) made a distinction between a doubt of fact (whether the baptism was actually conferred) and a doubt of law (whether the baptism actually conferred was valid).[70] Subsequent legislation followed this distinction. Thus the Congregation of the Council on December 12, 1733, issued a resolution which declared that if the doubt concerned the conferring of baptism in that there was no certificate or document testifying to the reception of baptism, the doubt was not a probable one nor one that sufficed to warrant the repeated conferring

[65] Canon 5—c. 111, D. IV, *de cons.*

[66] C. 113, D. IV, *de cons.*; Jaffé, n. 543.

[67] Cf. Benedictus XIV, *De Synodo Dioecesana,* lib. VII, cap. 6, n. 1.

[68] C. 2, X, *de baptismo,* III, 42.

[69] Cf. Compilatio II, *de baptismo,* V, 20; Jaffé, n. 14200.

[70] *Commentaria in Quinque Libros Decretalium* (8 vols. in 5, Venetiis, 1588), Tom. II, f. 168, c. 2, *De Quibus,* per totum.

of baptism conditionally, if the subject lived among Christians. So strong was the presumption of the fact of baptism in this case, according to Innocent III (1198-1216) as quoted in the decree, that it was to be regarded as the equivalent of certitude until it was disproved by the most evident arguments to the contrary. When, however, it was not known in what place or of what parents the person was born, even though he was instructed in the rudiments of faith, a probable doubt existed and therefore a conditional baptism was to be conferred.[71]

If the doubt concerned the validity of the conferred baptism, such a doubt also had to be a probable doubt before the conferring of conditional baptism became justified.[72]

A previous investigation of the convert's status had been the constant practice of the Church, but with the rise of Protestantism and its branching off into countless sects, and with the consequent misuse of or disregard for the essential requisites of the sacrament of baptism, it became necessary to direct the attention of missionaries and others, laboring in countries where non-Catholic sects had taken root, to this important preliminary formality. One finds many instructions and responses of the Sacred Congregations in the eighteenth and nineteenth centuries to this effect, particularly those of the Sacred Congregation of the Council,[73] of the Sacred Congregation of the Holy Office [74] and of the Sacred Congregation of the

[71] *Thesaurus Resolutionum S. C. Concilii* (167 vols., Urbino, 1718-1749, Romae, 1843-1908), VI (1741), *Ripana*, pp. 206-208; S.C.C., *Ripana*, 12 dec. 1733—*Fontes*, n. 3412.

[72] Petra, *Commentarium ad Const. II, Greg. XI*, n. 10—*Commentaria ad Constitutiones Apostolicas* (5 vols., Venetiis, 1729); S. C. de Prop. Fide, 23 iun. 1830, which related a response of the Sacred Congregation of the Council, 19 dec. 1682, to the effect that conditional baptism was not to be conferred *nisi adsit dubium probabile invaliditatis baptismi*—*Fontes*, n. 4748; Benedictus XIV, *De Synodo Dioecesana*, lib. VII, c. 6.

[73] S.C.C., 12 dec. 1733—*Fontes*, n. 3412; 28 apr. 1736—*Fontes*, n. 3458; 4 maii 1737—*Fontes*, n. 3475; 12 iul. 1794—*Fontes*, n. 3890; 17 dec. 1796—*Fontes*, n. 3902; 11 febr. 1797—*Fontes*, n. 3904; 16 mart. 1897—*Fontes*, n. 4302.

[74] S. C. S. Off., 20 nov. 1878—*Fontes*, n. 1058; 6 apr. 1859—*Fontes*, n. 950; 24 ian. 1877—*Fontes*, n. 1050; 4 febr. 1891—*Fontes*, n. 1130; 2 aug. 1901—*ASS*, XXXIV, 640.

Propagation of the Faith,[75] as well as particular legislation of plenary and provincial councils.[76] The Council of Trent (1545-1563) enacted an excommunication for anyone who rashly rebaptized a convert.[77]

The teaching of the Church regarding baptism by heretics or others outside the Church remained the same as it had always been: such baptisms were held to be valid if the proper matter and form were applied, regardless of the question of the probity of life or the faith of the minister.[78]

In actual practice many heretical baptisms were questioned or declared outright invalid, because of the flagrant disregard for the essentials of the sacrament. The Sacred Congregation of the Propagation of the Faith warned that inasmuch as many Protestants think that the faith of the parents rather than the sacrament of Baptism is necessary for salvation, they neglect the necessary elements, using at times scented water, and at other times having one person pour the water and another pronounce the words or read the Gospel from the pulpit.[79]

The Council of Albi (1850) decreed that because heretics at that time in many places used rose-colored water, or used two ministers, or poured the water on the clothes rather than on the skin of the subject because it was too cold, converts from heresy should be re-baptized conditionally, "nisi in aliquo particulari casu com-

[75] S. C. de Prop. Fide, 17 apr. 1777—*Fontes*, n. 4575; 31 dec. 1851—*Collect.*, n. 1069.

[76] Plenary Synod of Irish Bishops at Thurles (1850), decr. XI, c. 10; I Prov. Council of Westminster (1852), decr. XVI, c. 7; I Council of Port of Spain, Island of Trinidad (1854), sec. 1, art. 1, c. 8; II Plen. Council of Baltimore (1866), n. 240; Prov. Council of Cassel (1853), tit. III, *de bapt.*; II Prov. Council of Quebec (1854), decr. VII, c. 3—*Coll. Lacen.*, III, 779, 929, 1097, 461, 833, 634.

[77] Sessio VII, *de Bapt.*, can. 11—D.B., n. 867.

[78] Cf. IV Council of the Lateran (1215), cap. 1—Mansi, XXII, 982; Council of Trent (1547), Sessio VII, *de bapt.*, c. 4—D.B., n. 860; Decree for the Armenians, November 22, 1439—D.B., n. 696; *Fontes*, nn. 746; 394; 924; 1058; 2116; 2867; 4748; Benedictus XIV, *De Synodo Dioecesana*, lib. VII, c. 7, n. 9; Petra, *Comment. ad Const. II Gregorii XI*, n. 9, who refers to the Council of York (1576) as decreeing an *ipso facto* incurred *suspensio a divinis* for one who would act contrary to this teaching.

[79] 23 iun. 1830—*Fontes*, n. 4748.

pertum haberetur Sacramentum fuisse legitime collatum."[80] In several provinces of France, in view of the grave doubts as to the validity of Protestant baptisms, the bishop was to be consulted in each case.[81] In Ireland all converts were to be conditionally baptized, unless it was plainly evident from trustworthy testimony that the heretical baptism was valid.[82] In England the I Provincial Council of Westminster (1852) renewed the rule that all converts born of and baptized by Protestants after the year 1733 were to be baptized conditionally, "nisi ex indubiis probationibus certissime constet in ipsorum baptismo omnia rite fuisse peracta, quoad materiae et formae applicationem."[83]

The II Plenary Council of Baltimore (1866) accurately summed up the teaching of the Church and the practice that was followed in the last century: since Baptism imprints an indelible character on the soul, one who would rashly presume to rebaptize a convert would be guilty of the gravest crime; since, however, heretics were accustomed to neglect the most essential ceremonies in their administration of Baptism, it became a necessity to rebaptize conditionally practically all converts from heresy. Notwithstanding this condition of affairs an intelligent and diligent investigation of each case was required. If a priest acted on mere general presumptions rather than on the results of an accurate individual examination of the baptism in heresy, he incurred an irregularity for presuming to rebaptize without sufficient reason.[84]

[80] Tit. V, decr. II, c. 4—*Coll. Lacen.*, IV, 432.

[81] Cf. Prov. Council of Lyons (1850), decr. XXI, c. 4; Prov. Council of Rouen (1850), decr. XIII, c. 9; Prov. Council of Bordeaux (1850), Tit. III, cap. 1, c. 3; Prov. Council of Rheims (1849), Tit. V, cap. II; Prov. Council of Aix-la-Chapelle (1850), Tit. VII, cap. II, c. 2—*Coll. Lacen.*, IV, 479, 527, 568, 114, 998.

[82] Plenary Synod of Irish Bishops at Thurles (1850), decr. XI, c. 10—*Coll. Lacen.*, III, 779.

[83] Decr. XVI, c. 7—*Coll. Lacen.*, III, 929. Cf. also I Council of the Port of Spain, Island of Trinidad (1854), Sec. I, art. 1, c. 8—*Coll. Lacen.*, III, 1097.

[84] N. 240.

CHAPTER VI

THE VALIDLY BAPTIZED

In the preliminary investigation it will be found that baptisms administered by Greek schismatics and Oriental heretics are usually valid.[1] Protestant baptisms generally will also be valid if it is discovered that the ritual of the sect is exactly adhered to, at least in the essential acts of applying the water and pronouncing the valid form. Even those sects which do not have an official ritual may be found, after a detailed investigation, to observe all the necessary conditions for the valid conferring of the sacrament. Undue anxiety can be assuaged by certain indications which point out the fact that Protestant sects actually intend to confer the rite which Christ instituted and commanded.[2]

The fact that these sects retain baptism as a sacred rite, that they administer it because of Christ's command to do so,[3] that they

[1] Cf. S. C. S. Off., instr. 8 sept. 1633—*Collect.*, n. 74; *Fontes*, n. 722; instr. (Pro. Vic. Ap. ad Gallos), 20 iun. 1866, ad 40—*Collect.*, n. 1293; *Fontes*, n. 994; Leroux, "Les Baptêmes d'Adultes,"—*Revue Ecclesiastique de Liege*, XVII (1925-1926), 341-352.

[2] As an example of this, the writer learned from correspondence with officials of The First Brethren Church, The Southern Baptist Convention, The General Conference of Seventh Day Baptist Churches, The American Baptist Association and The General Council of the Assembles of God, that while these sects have no official ritual or "Discipline," a uniform method of baptism is obligatory for all ministers, whose intention must be to confer the rite which Christ instituted and commanded to be observed. The Northern Baptist Convention, on the contrary, professedly intends to imitate the method by which Christ was baptized, but it does not admit that Christ instituted the rite.

[3] This command is found in Matthew XXVIII: 18-20. The following sects definitely refer to this command of Christ in their rituals: Evangelical and Reformed Church; Evangelical Church (in adult formula); Evangelical Congregational Church (in adult formula); Evangelical Lutheran Congregations; Evangelical Lutheran Augustana Synod of North America; Norwegian Lutheran Church; Lutheran Missouri Synod; The Finnish American Evangelical Lutheran National Church; The Norwegian Synod of the American Evangelical Lutheran Church; The Evangelical Lutheran Joint Synod of Wisconsin and other States;

substantially retain the rite as set forth in the Roman ritual,[4] that they recognize the application of the water and the pronouncing of the form to be the essence of the ceremony, and that they use the valid form are all serious indications that the proper intention is present in the minister who confers the sacrament according to the prescribed ritual.

When the certain validity of the prior baptism has been established, careful inquiry should be made as to the good faith of the convert so as to form a prudent judgment whether he incurred the censure of excommunication for his heretical beliefs.[5]

The procedure in receiving validly baptized converts includes the following formalities:

(a) Abjuration or Profession of Faith.
(b) Absolution from Censures.
(c) Sacramental confession, absolution.
(d) Supplying of ceremonies omitted in baptism.

Because the absolution from censures implies the presence of a delict of which the censure is the penalty, it seemed advisable to treat these various subjects in order: (1) the abjuration; (2) the nature of delict and censure; (3) the classes of persons affected by the penalty for defection from the faith; (4) the penalty; (5) absolution from the censure in the internal forum; (6) absolution from the censure in the external forum.

Article 1. Abjuration and Profession of Faith

What has been written concerning the abjuration of former errors and the profession of faith in the previous chapter applies here also. The present legislation combines the two formalities, but

The Methodist Protestant Church; The Methodist Episcopal Church; The Methodist Episcopal Church, South (adult formula); The Moravian Church; The Pentecostal Holiness Church; The Presbyterian Church in the U. S. A.; The Orthodox Presbyterian Church; The Cumberland Presbyterian Church; The Protestant Episcopal Church; The Reformed Church in America; The Volunteers of America. Cf. Appendix I.

[4] The most noteworthy features, perhaps, are the recitation of the Apostles' Creed and the Lord's Prayer, and the expression of the renunciation of sin.

[5] Cf. De Meester, *Compendium*, Vol. III, Pars II, p. 235, n. 1814.

this is a comparatively recent development in the law of the Church. The original procedure was to have the returning heretics or schismatics appear before the bishops assembled in a synod or council and, only after renouncing their errors and promising obedience, to subscribe to a formal profession of faith. This was decreed by the I Council of Nicaea held in the year 325,[6] which claimed that it was merely conforming to the tradition of former synods, and was again prescribed by the II Council of Nicaea held in 787.[7]

The abjuration was to be in writing in accordance with the traditional practice of the Church.[8] This was further attested to by the III Council of Soissons celebrated in the year 852.[9] The profession of faith prescribed by the I Council of Nicaea was in the form of an oath of loyalty and obedience to the Holy See.[10] The names of the Consuls were written into the text, but in the time of Gratian it was sufficient to write in the names of the Pope and Emperor, because the office of Consul had ceased to exist.[11] The text was designed for bishops returning to the faith from heresy or schism, but a similar text was used for all converts.[12]

The II Ecumenical Council (I Constantinople, 381) drew up a formulary which is known as the Nicaean Creed.[13] During the four centuries which intervened betwen the two Nicaean Councils, however, other formularies were proposed by various councils. The Council of Laodicaea in Phrygia (343-381) prescribed a profession of faith for heretics returning from the Novatian, Photian, or Quar-

[6] C. 8, C. I, q. 7.

[7] C. 4, C. I, q. 7.

[8] *Ibidem.*

[9] C. 9, C. II, q. 1; Mansi, XV, 983. Gratian's prescription would seem to discount the necessity of a written document: "Praecepit enim Dominus mundandis, ut ostenderent ora sacerdotibus, docens corporali praesentia confitenda peccata, non per nuntium, non per scripturam manifestanda." (c. 88, D. I, *de poenit.*), but there is no contradiction, as the glossator observes (*Glossa Ordinaria* to c. 8, C. I, q. 7, v. *scripturam*), because this regulation does not exclude the observance of a written document afterwards.

[10] C. 9, C. I, q. 7.

[11] *Glossa Ordinaria,* c. 9, C. I, q. 7, v. *consulibus.*

[12] Raymundus, *Summa,* Lib. I, tit. *de haereticis,* § 5.

[13] Canon 1—Mansi, II, 1174; D.B., n. 85.

todeciman sects.[14] A synod held in Hippo Regius in 393 decreed the use of the Nicene formulary.[15] The Antipriscillian Creed, also called the "Faith of Damasus," was written and proposed by the Council of Saragossa in Spain in 380.[16] Various formularies were approved by the Synod of Constantinople held in 448 as being in conformity with that proposed by the I Council of Nicaea.[17] Other examples are found in a Synod of Africa (535),[18] in all the Councils of Toledo in Spain from the beginning of the fifth century to the ninth,[19] and in the Trullan Synod of Constantinople (692).[20]

In the Justinian Code (534) a letter of Pope John I (523-526) demanding the necessity of the profession of faith for all converts is recorded.[21] And in the year 649 Pope Marin I (649-655) instructed the Bishop of Philadelphia in Lydia to receive, after they had signed a profession of faith, certain clerics who had defected from the faith.[22]

Perhaps the most famous profession of faith in the eleventh century was that made by Berengarius of Tours (ca. 1000-1080) before a Council in Rome in the year 1059. He had been condemned by the Council of Rome in 1050 for his erroneous teaching on the Eucharist, and also by the Council of Vercelli held the same year. After signing a retraction at Tours in 1055, he appeared in Rome and signed the document which is preserved in the Decree of Gratian.[23] The formula is noteworthy for the fact that the abjura-

[14] Canon 7—Mansi, II, 565 B.

[15] Canon 20—Mansi, III, 922 B.

[16] D.B., n. 15, nota 1.

[17] Mansi, VI, 679.

[18] Mansi, VIII, 808.

[19] Hinschius, *Decretales Pseudo-Isidori et Capitula Angilramni*, pp. 351, 354, 358, 364, 376, 385, 404-407, 413. Since the *Collectio Hispana* incorporated the canons of the Council of Toledo and was the basis of the famous Pseudo-Isidorean collection, this legislation was evidently in wide use throughout Europe. Cf. Cicognani, *Canon Law*, p. 219, n. 39; p. 239, n. 54.

[20] Cf. canon 47—Mansi, XI, 978.

[21] C. (1.1) 8—*Corpus Iuris Civilis* (3 vols., ed. Krueger-Mommsen-Schoell-Kroll, Berolini, 1928-1929).

[22] Mansi, X, 810 C; Jaffé, n. 2064.

[23] C. 42, D. 11, *de cons.*; Mansi, XIX, 900.

tion of the specific error and the profession of the opposite truth are combined in one document. On December 18, 1208, Durandus of Huesca and his Waldensian companions were obliged to subscribe to a special formulary prepared by Innocent III (1198-1216).[24] That the abjuration and profession of faith had to be performed in the presence of a synod or of a council as late as the twelfth century is evident from a letter of Pope Lucius III (1181-1185) to the assembled bishops at the Council of Verona in 1184.[25]

In the thirteenth century the reconciliation was made before the bishop, either publicly or privately, according to the nature of the heresy of the convert.[26] Before the Council of Trent there is only one instance of the promulgation of a special formulary for converts. This was the profession of faith prescribed for Michael Paleologus (1261-1282) in 1267 by Clement IV (1265-1268) and subscribed to by him in the II Council of Lyons (1274) in the presence of Gregory X (1271-1276).[27] This same formula was proposed by Urban VI (1378-1389) on August 1, 1385, to the orthodox Greeks who returned to the faith.[28] On November 13, 1564, Pius IV (1559-1565) in his Constitution *Iniunctum nobis*[29] prescribed what is known as the Tridentine formula. Promulgated in the Council of Trent, it remained in use up until the issuance of a shorter formula by the Holy Office in its Instruction of July 20, 1589.[30] It still may be used, however, in such places for which no special formulary

[24] D.B., n. 420; Potthast, n. 3571. This formula is noteworthy because it is a general profession of the principal doctrines of faith, but its length defies quotation. The same formula was used again in a letter of the same Pontiff, *Cum inaestimabile pretium,* under date of May 12, 1210, and a third time in a slightly changed form in a letter on the conversion of the Waldensians, June 14, 1210. The latter epistle conveyed the news of the conversion of a certain Bernardus Primus and others and prescribed that the same or a similar formula be used when other converts were received into the Church.—D.B., n. 420, nota 2.

[25] C. 9, X, *de haereticis,* V, 7; Jaffé, n. 9635. Cf. *Comp. I,* c. 11, *hoc. tit.,* V, 6.

[26] Hostiensis, *Summa Aurea,* Lib. V, *de haereticis,* § *Quando et qualiter ecclesiae reconcilietur,* f. 400, col. 1; Raymundus, *Summa,* Lib. I, *de haereticis,* § 5.

[27] D.B., nn. 461-466; Mansi, XXIV, 81 B.

[28] Cf. D.B., n. 461, nota 2.

[29] *Fontes,* n. 108.

[30] Sessio XXV, *de reform.,* cap. 2.

exists.[31] The more recent formula approved by the Holy Office in 1942 is now of obligation in the United States. England and Ireland, however, still use the 1859 profession.[32]

During the period between the Council of Trent (1545-1563) and the present Code (1918) the Sacred Congregations developed many aspects of the abjuration of heresy and the profession of faith through instructions and responses. Thus, on April 7, 1629, the Congregation of the Propagation of the Faith declared that apostates in missionary countries were under no obligation of making a public abjuration before infidels, but it was sufficient for them to make it before the faithful, provided that they discontinued wearing any garb indicative of apostasy, and that they took care that the infidels learned of their abjuration in due time either from themselves or from others, even if this entailed danger to their lives.[33] Ordinarily the abjuration was to be made before the bishop; but the Congregation of the Propagation of the Faith permitted a private abjuration with only a few of the faithful present as witnesses under certain conditions.[34]

[31] Essentially the abjuration consists in the oath of the convert to detest and abandon his former errors; the profession of faith in the explicit assent to the principal mysteries of faith.—Coronata, *Institutiones,* IV, 293; S. C. S. Off., 25 iun. 1715, ad 3, 4—*Fontes,* n. 779.

[32] *Ordo administrandi,* pp. 77-80; *Rituale Parvum,* pp. 75 sqq.

[33] Contained in the response of 28 dec. 1770—*Fontes,* n. 4551. Cf. S. C. S. Off., 5 sept. 1736, ad 2—*Fontes,* n. 790. Vecchiotti (*Institutiones Canonicae ex Operibus Cardinalis Soglia Excerptae* [2 vols., Augustae Taurinorum, 1867] Vol. II, p. 12, n. 10) noted that the Holy Office gave the same response many times almost in the same words, and with regard to the wearing of a distinctive garb stated that the Holy Office granted permission for it to be worn insofar as it was not tantamount to a profession of a false religion.

[34] S. C. de Prop. Fide, litt. (ad Ep. Limericen.), 8 apr. 1786: "Non est necesse ut qui a catholica fide defecerunt, ad eamque postmodum reverti cupiunt, publicam abiurationem praemittant, sed satis est ut privatim coram paucis abiurent, dummodo tamen promissa servent, ac revera abstineant communicare cum haereticis in spiritualibus, aut quidquam facere quod haeresis protestativum sit. Idem sentiendum de iis qui haeresim, in qua usque ab initio educati fuere, privatim abiurent."—*Fontes,* n. 4610. This response was confirmed by the Holy Office on March 28, 1900, with the addition that the abjuration could take place before the bishop or anyone delegated by him as notary.—*Fontes,* n. 1237.

If there was question of scandal, the abjuration necessarily had to be public. The Congregation insisted on this, even at the risk of the loss of temporal goods necessary for the sustenance of the convert and his family, when the retention of these goods connoted an implicit profession of heresy. At the same time, the Congregation declared that no one could be received into the Church, if he wished to keep his Catholicity secret by publicly posing as a heretic. Even when there was a necessity for repairing scandal, however, the abjuration could be made before the bishop and four, five or more witnesses, if certain conditions were fulfilled: the renouncing of all temporal goods and advantages which were the recognized manifestations of heresy; the Catholic education of their children; the promise to observe the precepts of the Church, especially in all those circumstances in which their violation would betoken a profession of heresy or offer scandal to the faithful.[35]

In a letter of March 8, 1882, the Holy Office treated of the question of child converts. It prescribed that those under the age of fourteen years had to make only a profession of faith before being admitted to the sacraments. Those over fourteen, in addition to the profession had to make a formal abjuration of the sect to which they belonged. Then, to counteract the instruction they had received from Schismatics or Protestants, they were to receive special instructions in the faith. When such cases occurred in mission countries, they were to be referred to the Apostolic Delegate, and he in turn could delegate a missionary or the superior of a mission or college to receive the child into the Church.[36]

The Code adopted this distinction as to the age of minors when it excused all persons who have not yet reached the age of puberty,[37] from all *latae sententiae* penalties.[38] The norm set forth by the Holy

[35] S. C. de Prop. Fide, instr. (ad Ep. Miden.), 26 iun. 1790—*Fontes,* n. 4628.

[36] *Fontes,* n. 1073. In this letter of the Holy Office, the rule proposed by Cardinal Albizzi (*De Inconstantia in Fide,* Pars I, cap. xiv, n. 58) is quoted and approved.

[37] The Code established 14 years for boys, 12 years for girls as the age of puberty.—Canon 88, § 2.

[38] Canon 2230.

Office, however, still guides the procedure in receiving child converts into the faith.[39]

The Holy Office determined the juridical form of the abjuration, as it is now prescribed in the Code, in two responses, the former dated March 28, 1900,[40] the latter under date of February 19, 1916.[41] These responses demanded the presence of two witnesses at the abjuration in order that the act would have juridical value in the external forum. As such they went counter to the Instruction of 1859, which omitted reference to witnesses, but prescribed that the abjuration was to take place before the priest. At the time of these latter responses the Instruction had become law for the United States, and as such they were not of sufficient authority to abrogate the practice in this country. It remained for the Code, which adopted the regulation of the two decrees of the Holy Office, to endow this norm with the force of common law obligatory all over the world.

Article 2. Nature of Censure and Delict

Since the penalty inflicted on apostates, heretics and schismatics is the censure of excommunication, it is necessary briefly to explain the nature of a censure. Canon 2241, § 1, defines a censure as the penalty which is inflicted on a baptized person who with contumacious will is guilty of a delict. The existence of the penalty connotes for the culprit the deprivation of certain spiritual or related benefits. The penalty perdures until the penitent, upon abandoning his contumacy, has been absolved from it.[42] Only one who has received baptism can become affected by a censure. This is evident from the fact that the penal laws of the Code are purely ecclesiastical laws which bind only the subjects of the Church: this subjection, however, is concomitant with valid baptism.[43] Therefore, when there is a doubt as to the fact or of the validity of the con-

[39] Coronata, *Institutiones,* IV, 292.

[40] *Fontes,* n. 1237.

[41] *Fontes,* n. 1299.

[42] Censura est poena qua homo baptizatus, delinquens et contumax, quibusdam bonis spiritualibus vel spiritualibus adnexis privatur, donec, a contumacia recedens, absolvatur.

[43] Canons 12; 87.

vert's baptism, such a one is not held by the censure, for the law, which is of an onerous and odious character, receives a strict interpretation.[44] The two conditions essentially required by the Code are that the convert commit a crime penalized by the law; and that he be contumacious directly against the law, and hence indirectly against the authority commanding the observance of the law. The former is required because only one bound by the law is subject to the penalties for its infraction,[45] and because the Church punishes only a delict.[46] The latter is necessary because a censure does not have the nature of a vindictive penalty, which is inflicted to expiate the damage done by the crime, but is a medicinal penalty, designed to break the contumacy of the delinquent; hence it ceases when the delinquent, fully repentant, has received absolution.

That a censure be inflicted, however, the crime must be a true delict, external, grave, consummated and accompanied by contumacy.[47] All these elements must be present simultaneously. If one is lacking, there is no delict in the eyes of the law, and therefore no censure. In the absence of the censure, the absolution is superfluous. Hence it is important fully to comprehend these requisites with a view to evaluating their legal force when they are present in a case that touches the spiritual interests of the individual convert.

(a) A true delict: In the penal law of the Church a delict is the external and morally imputable violation of a law to which is attached a canonical sanction.[48]

(b) External: The necessity of this element follows from the very nature of a delict, and from the practice of the Church. The delict may be externalized by words, signs or actions, even though no one witnessed it and it thus remains wholly occult.[49]

(c) Morally imputable: For the incurring of penalties in general

[44] Cf. canons 19, 2219, § 1; Cappello, *De Censuris*, n. 8, *et alii. Contra*, Cerato, *Censurae Vigentes*, p. 2, n. 1, adn. 3.

[45] Canon 2226, § 1.

[46] Canons 2195, 2198.

[47] Canon 2242, § 1.

[48] Canon 2195, § 1.

[49] Cocchi, *Commentarium*, VIII, n. 135; Cerato, *Censurae Vigentes*, p. 4.

the imputability of a delict is measured by the *dolus* or *culpa* of the delinquent.[50] For incurring a censure, which is the gravest of ecclesiastical penalties, that degree of imputability is always required which is necessary for a mortal sin.[51]

(d) Consummated: This element distinguishes the delict from an attempted or frustrated delict.[52] It must be perfected in act according to the proper sense of the words of the law.[53]

(e) Contumacy: This arises from the malicious will together with a sufficient knowledge of the law. Hence good faith, ignorance of the law which is sufficient to excuse from grave sin, and ignorance of the censure which is sufficient to escape the incurring of a penalty, excuse from contumacy.[54]

These elements must all be present. Otherwise there can be no certainty that the convert contracted the excommunication. On investigation it may often be found that there are present causes of sufficient weight to engender a reasonable doubt. If any of the following cases occurs, there is no penalty: (a) if there is no true delict in the canonical acceptance of the term: (b) if the crime of heresy, apostasy or schism is not external; (c) if there are causes which excuse from grave imputability; (d) if there is good faith or ignorance sufficient to prove the absence of contumacy.

Article 3. Classes of Persons Affected by the Penalty

Three classes of possible and prospective converts are mentioned in canon 2314: apostates, heretics, and schismatics.

[50] Cf. canon 2199. The gravity of a delict is measured not only from the law which is violated, but from the conditions of the subject offending the law, from the damage caused, from the circumstances of time, place and persons.—Teodori, "Condiciones ad censuram incurrendam,"—*Apollinaris,* II (1929), 219.

[51] Cf. Benedictus XIV, *De Synodo Dioecesana,* Lib. X, cap. 1, n. 5.

[52] Canon 2212.

[53] Canon 2228.

[54] Cerato, *Censurae Vigentes,* p. 7: "Contumacia pro censuris *latae sententiae* habetur ex mala voluntate agentis cum cognitione legis sufficiente ad censuram incurrendam.—Quamobrem tum ignorantia legis excusans a gravitate culpae, tum ignorantie censurae relative sufficiens ad censuram vitandam, impediunt contumaciam."

I. Apostates

In its widest interpretation apostasy or infidelity can be understood in a threefold sense: (a) *Negative,* which connotes the status of one who never heard of the Christian religion, or, if he has heard of it, dismissed it entirely in good faith as of no importance. Evidently this is no sin, much less a delict.[55] (b) *Privative,* which connotes the status of one who, although he has not sufficient knowledge of the faith, is culpably negligent in inquiring further. This is a sin, the gravity of which depends on the degree of negligence involved, but it is not a delict. (c) *Contrary,* which connotes the status of one who positively rejects the faith after having sufficiently understood and embraced it. This kind of apostasy is a mortal sin *ex toto genere suo,* and constitutes the delict subject to the penalties of the Code. Thus, in the strictly legal sense, apostates are those who after having received baptism totally defect from the Christian faith.[56]

This total defection may take the form of a total denial or a total doubt of all the truths of the Christian faith.[57] The profession of infidelity or adherence to an un-Christian sect or pagan rite is not required,[58] for in the strict sense the crime consists in a total denial or abandonment of the faith.[59] It matters not, therefore, whether they espouse paganism, judaism, Mohammedanism, atheism, or whether they are mere unbelievers or doubters.[60] Freethinkers, who reject all authority in matters of faith, atheists, skeptics, commu-

[55] The contrary error was condemned in proposition 68 of Baius: "Infidelitas pure negativa, in his quibus Christus non est praedicatus, peccatum est."—D.B. n. 1068.

[56] Canon 1325, § 2.

[57] Ciprotti, "De Consummatione Delictorum attento eorum Elemento Obiectivo,"—*Apollinaris,* VIII (1935), 231.

[58] Wernz-Vidal, *Ius Canonicum,* VII, 411; Beste, *Introductio,* p. 934.

[59] Cf. Reiffenstuel, *Jus Canonicum,* Lib. V, tit. 9, n. 3; Schmalzgrueber, *Jus Ecclesiasticum,* Lib. V, tit. 9, n. 6; Ferraris, *Bibliotheca,* v. *Apostasia*; D'Annibale, *Commentarium in Const. Apost. Sedis,* n. 29.

[60] Augustine, *Commentary,* VIII, 277; Genicot-Salsmans, *Institutiones,* I, 204; Cipollini, *De Censuris,* Lib. II, n. 9. Slater (*A Manual of Moral Theology,* New York: Benziger Bros., 1908, p. 176) wrongly seems to require adherence to an atheistic or un-Christian sect.

nists, deists, pantheists, indifferentists, materialists, naturalists, and all who positively doubt, or directly or indirectly deny either the possibility or the existence of the Christian revelation must be considered as apostates.[61]

Since the delict is committed only by one who through the reception of baptism has embraced and professed the faith, catechumens or persons under instruction who lose interest and pass over to paganism cannot be said to incur the penalty.[62] The delict which is subject to the judgment and penalties of the Church in the external forum is not sufficiently constituted by an internal act: it is necessary that it be manifested by external acts. But the external acts need not be public acts. If internal defection from the faith is indicated externally by words, signs or some other act, the penalty is thereby incurred.[63]

It is important to note that one who follows a practical indifferentism, by wholly neglecting the duties of the Christian religion, is not subject to the penalty for apostasy, unless by word or deed he manifest an intention to break all ties with the true faith. Such an act would be constituted by the drawing up of a will stipulating that the burial be conducted with only a civil funeral.[64] In the external forum, however, anyone guilty of external defection, though he still really believed in the truths of faith, or also anyone who totally neglected his religious duties, would be presumed to have defected from the faith internally also, and hence would be considered an apostate.[65]

[61] Wernz-Vidal list five divergent classes: (1) those who defect from the faith to go over to Judaism; (2) those who give up their faith to embrace Mohammedanism; (3) those who reject their faith in exchange for the superstitions of paganism; (4) those who by rejecting all positive revelation pretend to follow a mere natural religion or moral code; (5) those who without embracing any religion, either natural or revealed, drift along with the tenets of atheism.—*Ius Canonicum,* VII, 410.

[62] Wernz-Vidal, *Ius Canonicum,* VII, 410.

[63] Claeys-Bouuaert-Simenon, *Manuale Juris Canonici* (3 vols., Vols. I, III, ed. 3a, 1930, Vol. II, ed. 1a, 1931, Gandae et Leodii: Dessain), III, p. 378, n. 574; Sole, *De Delictis et Poenis,* n. 312; Cappello, *De Censuris,* n. 208.

[64] Vermeersch-Creusen, *Epitome,* III, p. 310, n. 513; De Meester, *Compendium,* Vol. III, Pars II, p. 236, n. 1814.

[65] Canon 2200, § 2.

II. Heretics.

A heretic is defined in law as one who, having received baptism, pertinaciously either denies or doubts some truth which must be believed with divine and catholic faith, though he still retains the name of a Christian.[66] Essentially there is no distinction between heresy and apostasy because "divine revelation calls for absolute and universal faith in all that is revealed. Rejection of any one truth involves the same blasphemous attitude toward God that is involved when all the truths are rejected." [67]

Certain elements are postulated for the delict:

(a) Valid baptism. In the strict interpretation, all doubtfully and invalidly baptized persons are immediately excluded; hence, a catechumen receding from the faith before baptism is not liable to the penalty. But not only those who were baptized in the Church, but all who have been validly baptized are included.[68]

(b) Error in regard to some revealed truth. Canon 1323, § 1, defines revealed truth as embracing all truths which are contained in Scripture or Tradition and which likewise are proposed by the Church either in solemn judgment or in her ordinary and universal magisterium as divinely revealed. Hence, if one should deny a theological conclusion or a truth not proposed by the Church as divinely revealed, he would not be guilty of heresy.[69] Denial of a truth which one erroneously believed to be proposed by the Church as revealed would constitute a grave sin, but not the delict of heresy, just as the refusal to recognize a truth which the Church in her infallible magisterium has proposed, but not as divinely revealed.[70]

[66] Canon 1325, § 2.

[67] MacKenzie, *The Delict of Heresy*, p. 19.

[68] Wernz-Vidal, *Ius Canonicum*, VII, 423; Ciprotti, *Apollinaris*, VIII (1928), 230.

[69] Cappello, *De Censuris*, n. 208; Chelodi, *Ius Poenale*, p. 75.

[70] Authors generally agree that if one fully embraced the doctrine of Liberalism or its principal tenets, e. g., full and absolute independence of the State from the Church, or the subjection of the Church to the State, he could not be excused from heresy. The same can be said of one who pertinaciously professes certain particular doctrines contrary to divine faith, e. g., the 73rd proposition of the Syllabus of Pius IX: "Vi contractus mere civilis potest inter christianos constare veri nominis matrimonium." Also those who try to divine

(c) Voluntary Error. Though heresy is the result of a wrong judgment by the intellect, its malice comes from the will which moves the intellect to give place to doubt or to a denial of revealed truth. The error in faith must be deliberate, that is, it must be accompanied with the consent of the will.

(d) Pertinacious Will. This qualification refers to that disposition by which one knowingly and willingly opposes the authority of the Church insofar as he adheres to his opinion.[71] Thus one who knows the truth of Catholic teaching, and that his opinion is opposed to the teaching of the Church, but steadfastly refuses to submit his judgment to the decision of the Church, is guilty of heresy on this account. One who doubts or denies a revealed truth because of ignorance, even though it be crassly culpable, indeed, even if it were an affected ignorance,[72] but yet is prepared to submit to the judgment of the Church, is not guilty of the formal sin of heresy, and is therefore excused from the delict. As a general rule uneducated persons would be excused on this account for speaking heresy,[73] though they certainly would be guilty of a grave sin against the virtue of faith.[74]

the hidden things of the heart, the future free actions of men through hypnotism, spiritistic media or other magic arts of this kind, are to be considered as heretics, if in such acts they adverted to their heresy. Cf. C. S. C. Off. (Marianapol.), 28 iul. 1847—*Fontes,* n. 904; litt. encycl., 4 aug. 1856—*Fontes,* n. 937.

[71] Perseverance in this state of mind for a longer or shorter period of time is not required for the commission of the delict. Cf. Vermeersch-Creusen, *Epitome,* III, p. 310, n. 513; Boehm, "Konversion eines vierzehnjährigen Mädchens,"—*LQS,* LXXVI (1923), 118; Chelodi, *Ius Poenale,* p. 75.

[72] Cipollini, *De Censuris,* Lib. II, n. 10.

[73] Cappello, *De Censuris,* n. 208.

[74] "Iamvero qui errant etiam ex ignorantia graviter culpabili, qualis profecto est ignorantia vel supina, vel, eo magis, affectata, ipsam vere non reiicit fidei regulam: nam etsi diligentiam adhibere nolit, ut sciat quae sunt revelata, sive ex pigritia, sive ex inordinato suae opinionis affectu, optime adhuc voluntatem habere potest omnia credendi, quae ipsi sufficienter ut revelata proponuntur ab Ecclesia. Hinc, etsi graviter peccet contra fidem, non est tamen formaliter infidelis vel haereticus, sed fidelis et catholicus, credens omnia, quae a Deo revelata sunt et ab Ecclesia sunt definita et sibi sufficienter proponuntur."—Cipollini, *De Censuris,* Lib. II, n. 10. This author cites De Lugo and St. Alphonsus as also holding this opinion. Cf. Pistocchi, *I Canoni Penali,* p. 8.

(e) Denial or Doubt. This alternative embraces not only the positive rejection of dogmatic truth but also the formal or virtual judgment that a dogma proposed by the Church is uncertain. In both instances subjection to the authoritative teaching of the Church is withdrawn. Only a positive doubt, however, can connote heresy.[75] Doubt is a state of mind which, when faced with two contradictory ideas, does not know whether to affirm or deny either one. In a negative doubt there is simply an absence of any and all willingness to affirm or deny. In the former a definite judgment is present, but not in the latter.[76] Under this heading the sin of heresy is most often committed in our day.[77]

These five elements are present in every delict of heresy. Heresy, however, may be formal or material. The former has all the elements necessary for the delict; the latter consists in the wrong or erroneous assent of a baptized person to some doctrine contrary to the faith because of ignorance, inadvertence or error, but without obstinacy of the will.[78]

Formal heresy may be internal or external. Only formal external heresy falls under the penalties levied by the Church. External heresy may be either occult, public or notorious.[79] If the delict itself is not known publicly, or at least if it is known to only one or two persons, it is materially occult; [80] if the imputability of the delictual act remains secret, it is formally occult. Public heresy is that which is commonly known or which happens in such circumstances

[75] Chelodi, *Ius Poenale,* p. 75.

[76] Cf. D'Annibale, *Commentarium in Const. Apost. Sedis,* n. 23.

[77] Genicot-Salsmans, *Institutiones,* I, n. 203.

[78] Ferraris, *Bibliotheca,* v. *Haeresis*; Reiffenstuel, *Jus Canonicum,* Lib. V, tit. 7, nn. 7, 9. This distinction is also found in the Decree of Gratian, where Augustine is quoted (*Ep. clxii*): c. 29, C. XXIV, q. 3. Cf. Panormitanus, *Commentaria in Quinque Libros Decretalium* (8 vols. in 5, Venetiis, 1588), IV, ad c. 1, X, *de haereticis,* V, 7.

[79] Canon 2197. What is said here of heresy also applies to apostasy and schism.

[80] Ferraris, *Bibliotheca, lic. cit.* Schmalzgrueber (*Jus Ecclesiasticum,* Lib. V, tit. 7, n. 187) maintains, however, that it remains occult not only when it cannot be proved by witnesses, but also when it is known by some and can be proved, provided that it is not known by the major part of the neighborhood, parish, college, or community in which there are at least ten persons.

that a prudent judgment points to the ready and easy divulgement of it. Finally, the delict may be notorious. It is such with the notoriety of law when both the material fact and the formal imputability of the delict are judicially certain, either because the delinquent has been convicted according to the due process of law, or because he himself has confessed his crime before the court. The delict is notorious with the notoriety of fact when it is not only publicly known, but when it was committed in such circumstances that it cannot be concealed by any subterfuge or excused by any judicial patronage or legal favor.

III. Schismatics

A schismatic is defined in law as one who, having received baptism, refuses to be subject to the Roman Pontiff or to communicate with the members of the Church who are subject to him.[81] In the strict sense, a schismatic believes all the articles of faith, even the ones regarding the sovereign power and primacy of the Pope, but from mere malice refuses to subject himself to and obey the Supreme Pontiff as such, that is, as the head of the Church and the Vicar of Christ on earth. Four elements are involved: (a) withdrawal from obedience to the Roman Pontiff or from communion with the faithful, even though there is no joining of a separate schismatical sect; (b) pertinacious rebellion; (c) withdrawal in regard to those things by which the unity of the Church is constituted; (d) notwithstanding this withdrawal of subjection, the continued recognition of the Roman Pontiff as the true shepherd of the universal Church.[82]

Pure schism of this type is practically unknown.[83] Historically schism tends to be coupled with heresy.[84] Greek schismatics, Jansenists, National Italian Catholics and Old Catholics are no less heretical than schismatical.[85] So-called Catholic liberals who act publicly as freed from obedience to the Roman Pontiff are true schis-

[81] Canon 1325, § 2.

[82] Wernz-Vidal, *Ius Canonicum,* VII, 439.

[83] Cf. MacKenzie, *The Delict of Heresy,* p. 16.

[84] Augustine, *Commentary,* VIII, 278; Chelodi, *Ius Poenale,* p. 75; Wernz-Vidal, *Ius Canonicum,* VII, 436; Cipollini, *De Censuris,* Lib. II, n. 1.

[85] Augustine, *Commentary,* VIII, 278; S. C. S. Off., 14 oct. 1676; instr. (ad Ep. Iassien.), 22 aug. 1900—*Fontes,* nn. 753; 1245.

matics and are liable to the censure, provided that they really and maliciously have the intention of refusing obedience to him.[86]

It is commonly admitted that there is no schism if subjection to the Roman Pontiff is refused as to a temporal lord, or if it is disobedience in certain precepts for the reason of the precept itself, or because the person of the Pontiff is displeasing.[87]

Two other classes of delinquents are mentioned in canon 2314. They are (a) Catholics who lapse into apostasy, heresy or schism and who despite canonical warning to abjure their errors and to become reconciled with the Church, remain obdurate in their defection; (b) Catholics who in their defection stray so far from the Church as to have their names inscribed on the registers of a non-Catholic sect or who publicly adhere to some such sect. Since these delinquents are Catholics who have been baptized in the Church, and who in bad faith have knowingly embraced errors contrary to her teaching, they do not come under the term *convert* as understood in this work.[88]

[86] Cappello, *De Censuris*, n. 213.

[87] Reiffenstuel, *Jus Canonicum*, Lib. V, tit. 8, n. 5; Schmalzgrueber, *Jus Ecclesiasticum*, Lib. V, tit. 8, nn. 13-14; Vecchiotti, *Institutiones*, II, 356; D'Annibale, *Commentarium in Const. Apost. Sedis*, n. 33; Sole, *De Delictis et Poenis*, p. 224; Pistocchi, *I Canoni Penali*, p. 11; Ciprotti in *Apollinaris*, VIII (1935), 232.

[88] A treatment of the delicts of obdurate heresy and of adherence to a non-Catholic sect is given in MacKenzie, *The Delict of Heresy*, pp. 50-55. His work does not treat professedly of the reconciliation of these two classes. For the sake of completeness, a brief summary of the canonical procedure in reconciling these delinquents is herewith presented:

(a) *Obdurate Heresy (Apostasy, Schism).* This delict consists in the refusal to heed the canonical warning which is given according to the norms of canons 2143 and 2309, and which is therefore a penal remedy. The penalties which apply both to laymen and to clerics include the privation of any benefice, dignity, pension, office, or other function they may have in the Church, and the declaration of infamy; if a second warning goes unheeded, clerics are to be deposed. As is evident these penalties are *ferendae sententiae* vindictive penalties, and since they presuppose a criminal trial, their infliction is ruled by the norms given in canons 1933-1959. Their remission is by means of dispensation which pertains to the one who imposed the penalty, his competent superior or successor, or his delegate (canon 2236, § 1).

(b) *Adherence to a Non-Catholic Sect.* This delict can be committed either through the inscribing of one's name on the registers of a non-Catholic sect, or

A case could be envisaged, however, wherein a convert would be subject to the penalty of infamy for his adherence to a non-Catholic sect. If such a one were fully cognizant of the law of the Church, and wholly in bad faith, would continue to remain affiliated with some sect, he would not escape the penalty. He would therefore become irregular (canon 985, n. 5), incapable of obtaining any benefice, pension, office or ecclesiastical dignity, of performing any of the legitimate ecclesiastical acts (cf. canon 2256, n. 2) and disqualified for the exercise of any ecclesiastical right or office or any ministry in sacred functions (canon 2294, § 1). Since the dispensation from this penalty is reserved to the Holy See, it follows that if there were need of relaxing the penalty upon the convert's reception into the Church, a petition would of necessity be directed to Rome through the local Ordinary. If the delict was occult, either materially or formally, then the Ordinary can grant the dispensation.

through public and repeated attendance at the functions of the sect, or even through public assertions of affiliation with the sect. The term *secta acatholica* is commonly interpreted to mean a religious body which, though protesting to be Christian, denies the Catholic faith by deed or doctrine; excluded are non-Christian religions and societies which profess no religion; but included are atheistics sects (C. I. C., 30 iul. 1934—*ASS,* XXVI [1934], 494). The penalty for laymen consists in *ipso facto* infamy, the remission of which pertains only to the Holy See (canons 2236, § 1; 2295). Clerics suffer in addition to this penalty the loss of their ecclesiastical office *ipso facto* (can. 188, n. 4), and if a canonical warning goes unheeded they are to be degraded.

Since both these delicts are public, they come under the competence of a judicial trial (canon 1933, § 1), and the infliction of the *ferendae sententiae* penalties follows the norms enacted in canons 1934-1959. The remission of the penalties likewise is public and judicial in nature, i. e., it takes place before the Ordinary or his delegate and at least two witnesses.

In both cases heresy is presupposed. Hence before full restoration of status in the Church there is necessary: (1) The Ordinary's judgment that contumacy no longer exists (cf. canon 2242); (2) A juridic abjuration of the specific errors, and a profession of faith. The formula used by converts could not be employed, as is evident from the words "born outside the Church" in the first paragraph of the new formula; (3) Absolution from the censure according to the form given in the Roman Pontifical (*Ordo excommunicandi et absolvendi*) and in the Roman Ritual (Tit. III, cap. 3); (4) Sacramental confession and absolution; (5) Salutary penance, reparation of scandal or damage, denunciation of any cooperators in the crime.

Article 4. The Penalty

In the matter of liability to penalties there is according to the present law no distinction between apostates, heretics and schismatics. They are equally subject *ipso facto* to simple excommunication.[89] In the pre-Code legislation the penalty for defection from the faith was always excommunication, which was understood in its primary meaning of separation from the body of the faithful. The first recorded reference to this penalty was made by Christ Himself.[90] Other allusions to it are found in the epistles of St. Paul.[91]

Additional penalties were added in the III century by the Council of Carthage (251), which penalties were of the nature of a perpetual penance for those who became reconciled to the Church after their defection during the persecutions.[92] These penalties were re-

[89] "Consulto dicitur simpliciter excommunicatio; nam censura est speciali modo Sedi Apostolicae reservata eo tantum in casu, quo absolutio in *foro conscientiae* sit impertienda; secus non adest huiusmodi reservatio."—Cappello, *De Censuris*, n. 214. The canonical effects of *latae sententiae* excommunication include:

a. exclusion from communion with the faithful (canon 2257, § 1)

b. status of a *toleratus* (canon 2258)

c. loss of the right to assist at divine offices, but not at the preaching of the Word of God (canon 2259, § 1)

d. prohibition to receive the sacraments (canon 2260, § 1)

e. prohibition to confect and administer the sacraments and sacramentals, except in special cases determined by law (canon 2261, § 1)

f. exclusion from participation in indulgences, suffrages, and public prayers of the Church (canon 2262, § 1)

g. removal from ecclesiastical acts; loss of the right to be a plaintiff in ecclesiastical causes; loss of ecclesiastical offices and functions and the enjoyment of privileges (canon 2263).

h. prohibition of acts of jurisdiction (canon 2264)

i. prohibition of electing, presenting, nominating to any office, dignity, benefice or any other position in the Church, or of being appointed thereto, or of receiving orders (canon 2265, § 1).

[90] "And if he will not hear the Church, let him be to thee as the heathen and the publican."—Matt., XVIII: 17.

[91] Cf. Gal., XVIII: 20; Tit., I: 18-20; I Tim., V: 19-20.

[92] These penalties included a probationary period before reconciliation, and the exclusion from all ecclesiastical functions for bishops who had defected.—Mansi, I, 863.

peated in the Council of Ancyra (314).[93] The Council of Nicaea (325) added the penalty of irregularity for orders.[94]

In the first centuries of the Church the penalty of excommunication was inflicted by means of a judicial trial, or at least through the sentence of the bishop. The first reference to an *ipso iure* sustained contraction of the penalty is found in a letter of Pope Gelasius I (492-496) to Faustus in the year 493.[95] This reference of Pope Gelasius to the automatic contraction of the penalty supposes a previous sentence, condemning the error which Achatius revived; by his adherence to this error Achatius immediately came under the penalty which had formerly been lodged against it. This is not quite the same thing as our present concept of *ipso facto* incurred excommunication. Lucius III (1181-1185) in the Council of Verona (1184) seems to have been the first to extend the automatic excommunication so as to embrace those who professed a heresy which had not already been condemned as such by the Church.[96]

Raymond of Pennafort (1175-1275) referred to this legislation with the observation that in the thirteenth century every heretic, whether manifest or occult, was excommunicated *ipso iure,* and in discussing this penalty he referred back to the letter of Pope Gelasius to show that one who adheres to a heresy already condemned, is by

[93] Canons 1-2—Mansi, II, 513.

[94] C. 32, D. L.

[95] C. 1, C. XXIV, q. 1: "Achatius non est factus inventor novi erroris; sed veteris imitator: atque ideo non erat necessarium ut adversus eum nova sententia prodiret, sed antiqua tantummodo renovaretur. Factus sum itaque executor veteris constituti, non promulgator novi. Quicumque enim in haeresim semel damnatum labitur; eius damnatione seipsum involvit." Cf. Jaffé, n. 622.

[96] C. 9, X, *de haereticis,* V, 7: "Ad abolendam . . . Universos, qui de sacramento corporis et sanguinis Domini nostri Jesu Christi, vel de Baptismate, seu de peccatorum confessione, matrimonio vel reliquis Ecclesiasticis sacramentis aliter sentire, aut docere non metuunt, quam sacrosancta Romana Ecclesia praedicat et observat: et generaliter quoscumque eadem Romana Ecclesia, vel singuli Episcopi per dioecesas suas cum consilio clericorum, vel clerici ipsi, sede vacante, cum consilio (si oportuerit) vicinorum Episcoporum haereticos iudicaverint, vinculo perpetui anathematis innodamus." Cf. c. 2, *Compilatio I, de haereticis,* V, 6.

that very fact himself excommunicated.[97] Cardinal Hostiensis (+ 1271), a contemporary of Raymond, confirmed this.[98]

This penalty had been solemnly promulgated in the IV General Council of the Lateran (1215) by Pope Innocent III.[99] The official approval of the decretals in the *Corpus Iuris Canonici* made this penalty universal in its application, and it remained in force continuously up to the present Code through the medium of the *Bullae Coenae*[100] and the Constitution *Apostolicae Sedis* of Pius IX issued on October 12, 1869.[101]

An important change, however, was introduced by the Code. The Constitution *Apostolicae Sedis* had levied the same excommunication on those who believed or gave credence to apostates, heretics and schismatics, and those also who received them or favored them in any way or who defended them.[102] The Code limited the penalty simply to apostates, heretics and schismatics,[103] while the others are now numbered among those who are suspected of heresy.[104]

[97] *Summa,* Lib. I, tit. V, § 2; Lib. III, tit. XXXIII, § 7.

[98] *Summa Aurea,* Lib. V, *de haereticis,* § *Quis dicatur haereticus,* 397v, col. 2.

[99] C. 13, X, *de haereticis,* V, 7, restored from c. 2, *Compilatio IV, de haereticis,* V, 5. Cf. c. 15, X, *de haereticis,* V, 7.

[100] In its origin the *Bulla Coenae* seems to have been solicitous primarily about safeguarding the immunity of the Church and the safety of Christians. (Cf. Urban V, *Apostolatus Officium,* 12 oct. 1363—*Bullarium Romanum,* IV, const. III, p. 520.) Later on, because of the exigencies of the times, it treated of heretics and schismatics. Julius II on March 1, 1511, in his Bull *Consueverunt Romani Pontifices* (*Bull. Rom.,* V, const. XXX, p. 491) excommunicated heretics, using the formula by which all heretical sects were comprehended, but naming the more notorious ones. This formula had been used by Alexander III in the III Lateran Council (1179) and by Innocent III in the IV Lateran Council (1215), by Gregory IX in c. 15, X, *de haereticis,* V, 7, and by subsequent Popes in their constitutions against heretics. Schismatics were included by Gregory XIII, and Paul V in his constitution *Pastoralis Romani Pontificis* of April 8, 1610, added apostates. The promulgation of the *Bulla Coenae* ceased in the pontificate of Clement XIV, 1769, but the penalty of excommunication remained in force.

[101] I, n. 1, *ASS,* V (1869), 287-312; *Fontes,* n. 552.

[102] §§ I, III.—*Fontes,* n. 552; *ASS,* V (1869), 288, 289.

[103] Cf. Crnica, *Modificationes in Tractatu de Censuris per Codicem Iuris Canonici Introductae* (S. Mauritii Agaunensis: Typis Op. S. Augustini, 1919), p. 108.

[104] Cf. canons 2315; 2316.

It is the purpose of canon 2314, § 1, to penalize each and every apostate, heretic and schismatic. It has been argued that all heretics, formal and material, are included under the excommunication. The contention is made that the good of the Church cannot be endangered because of the internal affections of the mind, such as are the good or bad faith of her subjects, which can only with the greatest difficulty be discovered and measured; that therefore, canon 2314, § 1, must regard not the *person* (in whom a determined act can be more or less culpable), but rather the *external quality* of the person (i. e., heresy) which directly affects the public good, and that in consequence of this it is of no import whether good or bad faith is present. The parallel is drawn with canon 731, § 2, in an effort to interpret the words *omnes et singuli haeretici.* The further allegation is made that canons 1323, § 1; 1325, § 2, and 2314, § 1, have the nature of disqualifying laws from which no ignorance excuses.[105]

Because of the nature of the penalty and the spirit of the Church's penal legislation, this opinion seems untenable.[106] Canon 19 demands that penal laws receive a strict interpretation. Since canon 2314, § 1, penalizes the infraction of the law expressed in canon 1323, § 1, the words *omnes et singuli haeretici et schismatici* are to be interpreted according to the strict definition given in canon 1325, § 2. On the one hand, the gravest censure is involved; on the other, the presence of bad faith and malice *(pertinacia)* is postulated. A censure presupposes: (1) a delict, which is the external and morally imputable violation of a law to which is added a canonical sanction; (2) contumacy, which is the formal or virtual contempt for the law. The delict must be certain and perfected in act according to the proper sense of the words of the law. But the imputability of the delict depends on the *dolus,* i. e., the deliberate intention to perform

[105] Pappafava dei Carraresi, "Quaestio Quaedam Circa Haeresim,"—*Jus Pontificium,* XI (1931), 52-53.

[106] Cf. Sole, *De Delictis,* p. 222, n. 314; Vermeersch-Creusen, *Epitome,* III, p. 311, n. 513; De Meester, *Compendium,* Vol. III, Pars II, n. 1814; Beste, *Introductio,* p. 934; Cipollini, *De Censuris,* Lib. II, n. 10; Cerato, *Censurae Vigentes,* n. 90; Cappello, *De Censuris,* n. 210; Cocchi, *Commentarium,* VIII, n. 135.

some action in violation of the law, or the *culpa* of the delinquent, which consists in his culpable ignorance of the law or in the omission of the necessary diligence to acquire a knowledge of the law: therefore, all the causes which increase, diminish or take away *dolus* or *culpa,* by that very fact increase, diminish or take away the imputability of the delict.

Not only those causes which excuse from all imputability, but also those which excuse from grave imputability, equally exempt from all penalty.[107] Such causes are, on the part of the intellect, a substantially defective knowledge of the law, and, on the part of the will, any fundamental lack of freedom or deliberativeness. Principal among these reasons, in practice, are inculpable ignorance and error, or the good faith of the delinquent, according to the norms of canons 2202, 2218, § 2, and 2228, which exclude all contumacy and recalcitrance *(pertinacia).* Hence converts from non-Catholic sects who have been born and educated in heresy can frequently be only material heretics and thus can actually escape the excommunication because of this fact. In the conditions in which they lived, they never perhaps became acquainted with the truth as such, or with the demand mentioned in canon 1323, § 1, and therefore cannot be accused of rejecting the truth of faith deliberately and with obstinacy *(pertinaciter).*[108]

Because of the necessity for obstinacy or recalcitrance in formal heresy, authors agree that canon 2229 does not wholly apply in this case.[109] This canon states that an affected, crass or supine culpable ignorance of the law or also of the penalty alone never excuses from *latae sententiae* penalties. Thus Cipollini, while admitting that a formal heretic certainly incurs the penalty if through voluntary ignorance he does not know of the penalty for his crime, excuses him

[107] Canon 2218, § 2.

[108] Cf. D'Annibale, *Commentarium in Const. Apost. Sedis,* n. 30; De Meester, *Compendium,* Vol. III, Pars II, n. 1814, p. 236; Sole, *De Delictis,* p. 222, n. 314; Cerato, *Censurae Vigentes,* n. 90; Beste, *Introductio,* p. 934; Genicot-Salsmans, *Institutiones,* II, n. 586; Cappello, *De Censuris,* n. 211; Roberti, *De Delictis et Poenis,* I, n. 77; Cocchi, *Commentarium,* VIII, n. 135; Vermeersch-Creusen, *Epitome,* III, p. 311, n. 513; Ciprotti in *Apollinaris,* VIII (1935), 233; *AER,* LXXIV (1925), 315.

[109] Cf., e. g., De Meester, *loc. cit.*; Vermeersch-Creusen, *loc. cit.*; Sole, *loc. cit.*

in the case in which he is ignorant of the law, namely, that the rule of faith is of obligation for him.[110] Vermeersch-Creusen,[111] De Meester [112] and Sole [113] also maintain that even a gravely culpable ignorance is sufficient to assure the absence of obstinacy and therefore the non-incurring of the penalty; but they do not recognize the same legal consequences for an affected ignorance.

Because ignorance of the law is not presumed,[114] and because the violation of any law is presumed to have been perpetrated consciously and deliberately, validly baptized converts, if they have reached the age of fourteen years,[115] are before their reception into the Church to be considered as having contracted the censure of excommunication. Thus their exclusion from the sacraments, the necessity of their abjuration of error and of their profession of faith, and the need of absolution from the censure are sufficiently explained from the necessities and presumptions of the external forum, and also in view of the uncertainty that their good faith was not sufficiently preserved to furnish reliable assurance that they lacked all obstinacy and recalcitrance *(pertinacia)*.[116]

110 "Non sufficit ut peccatum contra eandem virtutem committatur, quae alio et alio modo laedi potest; sed requiritur ut sit illud ipsum peccatum, et quidem consummatum, quod poena, seu ibidem excommunicatione, mulctatur. Iamvero haereticus proprie non est, qui non formaliter despicit regulam fidei; immo neque stricte virtualiter, quia et omnia, quae novit revelata, credit et paratus est alia etiam credere, si ei constet esse revelata. Absonum autem videtur ut talis, qui longe a formali haeresi exsistit, etsi peccet et, forte, etiam graviter peccet ex inquisitionis defectu, poena gravissima mulctetur excommunicationis, et specialiter reservata.—Casus e contra ignorantiae *iuris* non excusantis esset, si quis, sciens volenque, reiiciens veritatem sibi certo revelatam, in tantum desiperet, ut putaret, culpabiliter quidem, fidei virtutem adhuc salvari: quasi scilicet regula fidei eadem permaneret quoad alias veritates, et non potius ratio humana ei substitueretur."—*De Censuris*, Lib. II, n. 12, pp. 97-98.

111 *Epitome*, III, p. 311, n. 513.

112 *Compendium*, Vol. III, Pars II, n. 1814, p. 236.

113 *De Delictis*, p. 222, n. 314.

114 Canon 16, § 2.

115 Cf. Boehm, "Konversion eines vierzehnjährigen Mädchens,"—*LQS*, LXXVI (1923), 120.

116 Cf. Pius IX, Allocutio *Singulari quadam*, 9 dec. 1854: "Tenendum quippe ex fide est, extra Apostolicum Romanum Ecclesiam salvum fieri neminem posse, hanc esse unicam salutis arcam, hanc qui non fuerit ingressus, diluvio periturum;

Does the presumption of *dolus* hold in regard to the penalty of infamy as it does with reference to the censure of excommunication, so that all converts would be considered as laboring under both penalties until contrary proof is brought forward? In treating of the reception of converts, most of the authors are silent on this point, though they do mention the presumption with regard to the censure of excommunication. This is perhaps due to the fact that the penalty of infamy attached to the delict of adherence to a non-Catholic sect is generally interpreted as applying only to lapsed Catholics and not to those who were born and reared outside the Church.[117]

There seems to be no reason for admitting the presumption in regard to one penalty and denying its applicability to the other. For as often as the law has been certainly violated, the delinquent is considered to have acted with full knowledge and perfect liberty. In the external forum, what ordinarily happens and what is manifested externally are the direct concern of the legislation of the Church. Thus in ordinary circumstances everyone who has the use of reason is accustomed to act rationally and freely, doing what he does with full knowledge and volition. When therefore there occurs

sed tamen pro certo pariter habendum est, qui verae religionis ignorantia laborent, si ea sit invincibilis, nulla ipsos obstringi huiusce rei culpa ante oculos Domini. Nunc vero quis tantum sibi arroget, ut huiusmodi ignorantiae designare limites queat iuxta populorum, regionum, ingeniorum aliarumque rerum tam multarum rationem et varietatem?"—D.B., n. 1647.

Pius XI, Allocutio, 10 ian. 1927: "E chi potra mai misurare la buona fede?" Allocutio, 10 mart. 1930, on the occasion of the canonization of Blessed Catharine Thomas: "Dinanzi a tanta grandiositá, il reflesso che vi ci fa sostare non manca di una nota di tristezza, quando si pone mente a tante e tante anime alle quali Iddio non e stato avaro di luce e che vediamo cosi disattente di fronte a si grande testimonianza che Iddio da di perenne presenza: e non inattiva, ma operosa presenza. Veramente, a questa considerazione, vien fatto di pensare che quei disgraziati spiriti siano discesi cosi in basso 'ita ut sint inexcusabiles'; ma non sta a noi di investigare cio: Dio solo conosce 'i limiti della scusabilitá e della buona fede umana' e a Lui bisogna lasciare di decidere e giudicare."—*Jus Pontificium,* XI (1931), 55. Cf. Vermeersch-Creusen, *Epitome,* III, p. 311, n. 513; De Meester, *Compendium,* Vol. III, Pars II, n. 1814, p. 236, nota 4; *AER,* LXXIV (1925), 315.

[117] Cf. Vermeersch-Creusen, *Epitome,* III, n. 513, p. 311; Cocchi, *Commentarium,* VIII, n. 138; De Meester, *Compendium,* Vol. III, Pars II, n. 1814; Augustine, *Commentary,* VIII, 279.

a violation of the law, it is presumed to be a free and deliberate act, i. e., *ex dolo posita,* until from the concrete external circumstances it is proved that the violation took place in ignorance or because of force.[118]

MacKenzie definitely states that the presumption stands in regard to the penalty of infamy: "These individuals (those baptized and educated outside the Church) must be presumed responsible both for the acts of simple heresy which they commit, and likewise for their membership in a non-Catholic sect. . . . Protestants, Nestorians, etc., must be presumed responsible for their external acts in violation of the law of the Church, unless and until the contrary is proved. Consequently, when they formally joined their sect, or publicly lived in accordance with its tenets and its practices, they are presumed to have incurred this juridical infamy, along with the general excommunication for heresy." [119]

Because of the fact that ignorance in this regard generally excuses, the penalty of infamy is usually disregarded in the reception of converts. This has been the practice of the Sacred Congregations. Since the seventeenth century the Congregations of the Holy Office and of the Propagation of the Faith have, when occasion demanded, issued decrees, responses, and instructions dealing with the exact formalities to be observed in the reception of converts, but never has there been mention of this penalty or of its dispensation. Therefore, while the presumption remains, proof of inculpable or even of culpable ignorance will excuse. If the thorough investigation of this delict is omitted, the presumption that also all the consequent penalties were incurred may later affect the status of the convert if he wishes to be a sponsor at baptism or a candidate for holy orders.

Article 5. Absolution in the Internal Forum

The absolution from censures prescribed by the Instruction must be in accordance with the common law, as expressed in canon 2314, § 2:

[118] Cf. Michiels, *De Delictis et Poenis,* I, 113; Berutti, *Institutiones Iuris Canonici* (6 vols., Vol. VI, *De Delictis et Poenis,* Taurini, Romae: Marietti, 1938), VI, 15.

[119] *The Delict of Heresy,* pp. 49, 54.

Absolutio ab excommunicatione de qua in § 1, in foro conscientiae impertienda, est speciali modo Sedi Apostolicae reservata.

In the internal forum, the excommunication is reserved to the Holy See. Hence the norms established in canons 2252-2254 are to be applied.[120]

I. In Danger of Death [121]

All priests including Orientals, even those who are not approved for the hearing of confessions, and even though an approved confessor be present, have the power to absolve from the censure of excommunication.[122] If the convert should recover, then no recourse to the Holy See is necessary, precisely because of the fact that the censure is reserved neither *ab homine* nor *specialissimo modo.*

If the absolution is given in the sacramental forum the usual formula for the absolution from sins is sufficient.[123] In the non-sacramental forum the absolution should be given according to the form prescribed by the Instruction. If time does not permit, the shorter form found in the ritual may be used; [124] if even this is gravely inconvenient or impossible, the absolution may be conveyed in any suitable way.[125]

Both canon 882, which regulates strictly the sacramental forum, and canon 2252, which embraces also the non-sacramental forum, omit the phrase *servatis servandis* as found in canon 2314, § 2. This phrase, however, must be understood.[126] This contention is sup-

[120] S. C. S. Off., declar. 19 febr. 1916—*Fontes,* n. 1299; Cocchi, *Commentarium,* VIII, n. 136; Blat, *De Delictis et Poenis,* p. 200; De Meester, *Compendium,* Vol. III, Pars II, n. 1814, p. 237.

[121] Cf. Moriarty, *The Extraordinary Absolution from Censures,* pp. 69-73.

[122] Canons 882; 2252.

[123] Cf. *Rituale Romanum,* Tit. III, cap. 2; canon 2250, § 3.

[124] *Rituale Romanum,* Tit. III, cap. 3.

[125] Canon 2250, § 3.

[126] Mothon, *Institutions Canoniques,* II, n. 2836; Cipollini, *De Censuris,* Lib. I, n. 52; De Meester (*Compendium,* Vol. III, Pars II, n. 1745, p. 180) commenting on canon 2252, indicates that the phrase *iniunctis de iure iniungendis* of

ported by the fact that canon 731, § 2, expressly forbids the administration of the sacraments to heretics and to schismatics, even those who are in good faith, unless they have first rejected their erroneous beliefs and have become reconciled with the Church.[127] Thus before the absolution from censures the convert should be instructed in the faith, be urged to have perfect sorrow for his sins, and be required to make the abjuration of error and the profession of faith.[128] The absolution from sins should follow the imposition of a salutary penance and the serious promise to repair any damage or scandal.[129]

If the person is already unconscious but has indicated his sorrow for sin and his desire to be reconciled with the Church, he is to be absolved from the censure and the sin. Whenever there is a doubt as to whether he contracted the censure, conditional absolution is to be given; if the doubt concerns his dispositions, conditional absolution from sins is to be administered. The necessary conditions, however, can be prudently presumed in schismatics and also in many heretics who do not belong to a sect which rejects the sacrament of penance. If there is a doubt whether a dying non-Catholic, who is unconscious, admits or rejects confession, he can be absolved conditionally, provided that all danger of scandal is removed.[130]

canon 2254, § 3, is to be understood. Thus a parallel between canons 2252 and 2314, § 2, is also justified.

[127] Cf. response of the S. C. S. Off., 17 maii 1916: "1. An schismaticis materialibus in mortis articulo constitutis *bona fide sive absolutionem sive extremam unctionem petentibus,* ea sacramenta conferri possint sine abiuratione errorum.

"R. Ad 1. *Negative,* sed requiri, ut, meliori quo fieri possit modo, errores reiiciant et professionem fidei faciant."—quoted in Cappello, *De Sacramentis,* Vol. II, Pars I (1. ed., 1926), n. 238, pp. 197-198.

[128] If time does not permit the recitation of the usual formula, this short profession of faith may be used:

I, N.N., do sincerely and solemnly declare that having been brought up in the Protestant Religion (or other Religion as the case may be), but now, by the grace of God, having been brought to the knowledge of the Truth, firmly believe and profess all that the Holy, Catholic, Apostolic, Roman Church believes and teaches, and I reject and condemn whatever she rejects and condemns. —*The Priest's New Ritual,* pp. 60-61.

[129] Cocchi, *Commentarium,* VIII, 78.

[130] Moriarty, *The Extraordinary Absolution from Censures,* pp. 80-81.

II. Ordinary Cases

Since the censure is reserved *speciali modo* to the Holy See, the delinquent is normally required to have recourse to the Sacred Penitentiary for absolution. This recourse may be made in person, or through a letter which may be written by the confessor.[181]

The power which is now reserved to the Holy See was formerly granted by the Council of Trent to bishops but not their vicar-generals in the case of occult heresy.[182] This faculty extended only to those bishops in whose dioceses the decrees of the Council of Trent had been promulgated.[183]

Before this faculty could be used several conditions had to be fulfilled: (1) the bishop had to have a diocese and subjects; (2) he could exercise this power only for his subjects, i. e., those who had a domicile or quasi-domicile in his diocese, and those who actually resided in the diocese as *peregrini* or *vagi;* (3) only the bishop and not the vicar-general could use this power.[184] In the exercise of this faculty, it was the practice to give some instruction and to have the penitent make the abjuration before the absolution from the censure and the sin.[185]

With the appearance of the *Bullae Coenae,* published every year

[181] MacKenzie, *The Delict of Heresy,* p. 107.

[182] Sessio XXIV, cap. 6, *de ref.*: "Liceat episcopis in irregularitatibus omnibus et suspensionibus, ex delicto occulto provenientibus. . . . Idem et in haeresis crimine in eodem foro conscientiae eis tantum, non eorum vicariis, sit permissum."

[183] Pennacchi, *Commentarium in Constitutionem Apostolicae Sedis* (2 vols., Romae, 1883), II, 557. Under the name of bishops were included: (1) bishops who were only elected or confirmed; (2) the chapter of the diocese, when the See was vacant; (3) other inferior prelates who had episcopal or quasi-episcopal jurisdiction in their territories. Cf. Schmalzgrueber, *Jus Ecclesiasticum,* Lib. V, tit. 7, n. 190.

[184] Schmalzgrueber, *Jus Ecclesiasticum,* Lib. V, tit. 7, nn. 191, 192. Garcias (*De Beneficiis Ecclesiasticis,* Caesaraugustae, 1609, Par. II, cap. 10, n. 113) held that this power could be delegated in a special case; Schmalzgrueber (*loc. cit.*) and Pirhing (*Jus Canonicum,* Lib. V, tit. 7, n. 40) maintained that in the absence of a declaration from the Roman Pontiff it could not.

[185] Leone, *Praxis ad Litteras Maioris Poenitentiarii et Officii Sacrae Poenitentiariae Apostolicae* (ed. 2a, Mediolani, 1665), Pars III, *Absolutio pro laico haeretico.*

on Holy Thursday, there arose a controversy among canonists as to whether the power of absolving from occult heresy was abrogated. The majority of canonists favored the opinion that the Tridentine faculty was definitely abrogated. They argued (1) from the tenor of the *Bulla Coenae*:

> Caeterum a praedictis sententiis nullus per alium quam Romanum Pontificem, nisi in mortis periculo constitutus . . . absolvi possit, etiam praetextu quarumvis facultatum et indultorum quibuscumque personis . . . etiam episcopali vel alia maiori dignitate praeditis, per Nos ac dictam Sedem, ac cuiusvis Concilii decreta . . . concessorum.[136]

Cardinal de Lugo (1583-1660) attested that the words "etiam praetextu facultatum aut indultorum per cuiusvis Concilii decreta concessorum" were first found in the Bull of Gregory XIII (1572-1585) and that they were not contained in the Bulls published before the Council of Trent.[137] (2) From the pronouncements of the Popes and of the Sacred Congregations. Benedict XIV (1740-1758) declared that Pius V (1566-1572) and Gregory XIII (1572-1585), when asked, unhesitatingly replied that no one could absolve from heresy, *"etiam occultissima,"* since it was reserved to the Pope through the *Bullae Coenae*.[138] This is borne out by several responses of the Sacred Congregation of the Council[139] and of the Holy Office.[140] Hence Fagnanus (1598-1678) concluded that the question was definitely settled.[141]

136 Text of the Bull of Gregory XV, 1622, quoted in Barbosa, *De Officio et Potestate Episcopi,* Pars III, alleg. 50, nn. 56 sqq.

137 Cf. Bouix, *Tactatus De Episcopo,* II, Pars V, cap. 19. The decree "Liceat" of Session XXIV was read on November 11, 1563.

138 *De Synodo Dioecesana,* Lib. IX, cap. 4, n. 9. Cf. Pignatelli, *Consultationes Canonicae* (6 vols., Coloniae Allobrogum, 1700), I, consult. 291; Garcias, *De Beneficiis,* Pars XI, cap. x, n. 122.

139 S.C.S. (Concordien.), ian. 1585; (Cameracen.), 4 dec. 1632—*Fontes,* nn. 2137; 2548.

140 Mentioned in Pignatelli, *Consultationes Canonicae,* I, consult. 291. Cf. S. C. S. Off., 30 iul. 1806—*Fontes,* n. 850.

141 "Unde frustra nonulli ex recentioribus Theologis hunc articulum in controversiam adducunt, quum habeamus claram determinationem sacrae Congregationis."—*Commentaria in Quinque Libros Decretalium* (4 vols., Venetiis, 1709), Cap. *Quoniam,* n. 29, *de Constitutionibus.*

Sanchez (1550-1610) and others, however, demanded a special revocation of the Tridentine faculty, and this was not found in the *Bullae Coenae*. They also argued that the Tridentine faculty concerned occult heresy, while the *Bullae Coenae* concerned only public heresy.[142] The decree of Alexander VII (1655-1667), however, ended the controversy to a great extent. Among the condemned propositions was the following:

> 3. Sententia asserens, Bulam "Coenae" solum prohibere absolutionem haeresis et aliorum criminum, quando publica sunt, et id non derogare facultati TRIDENTINI, in qua de occultis criminibus sermo est, anno 1629, 18 Iulii in Consistorio sacrae Congregationis Eminentissimorum Cardinalium visa et tolerata est.[143]

The publication of the Constitution *Apostolicae Sedis* by Pius IX on October 12, 1869, led to another divergence of opinion among authors as to the power of the bishop to absolve from occult heresy. The text which occasioned the controversy follows: [144]

> Firmam tamen esse volumus absolvendi facultatem a Tridentina Synodo Episcopis concessam *Sess. XXIV, cap. VI, de Reform.*, in quibuscumque censuris Apostolicae Sedi hac Nostra Constitutione reservatis, iis tantum exceptis, quas Eidem Apostolicae Sedi speciali modo reservatas declaravimus.

Only what had been inserted from the *Bullae Coenae* into the *Apostolicae Sedis* remained in force, Pennacchi (1898) concluded.[145] He argued that, since the faculty of absolving from occult heresy was in no way reserved by the Holy See, the bishops again had that power. The reservation, he pointed out, affected only public heresy and apostasy. Hence the bishop could absolve provided: (a) that the delict was occult; (b) that it was not brought into the contentious forum; (c) that only the subjects of the bishop be absolved;

[142] *Disputationes De Sancto Matrimonii Sacramento* (3 vols. in 1, Antverpiae, 1626), I, lib. III, disp. 26, n. 7. Cf. Reiffenstuel, *Jus Canonicum*, Lib. V, tit. 7, nn. 356-363.

[143] Issued on September 24, 1665—D.B., n. 1103.

[144] *ASS*, V (1869), 311.

[145] *Comment. in Const. Apost. Sedis*, II, 557.

(d) that the absolution be given only by the bishop; (e) that it be given gratuitously; (f) that it be accompanied with the assignment of a salutary penance.[146]

Against Pennacchi, however, Avanzini,[147] Smith [148] and the majority of authors held that the Tridentine faculty was not restored in regard to the bishops' authorization to absolve from occult heresy.

But what was not granted by the common law was conceded by special faculties. Thus the bishops of the United States were granted an apostolic indult whereby they could either personally or through their delegates absolve from every kind of heresy both in the internal and in the external forum. The only restrictions were that the indult was not valid in regard to heretics who had come from places where the inquisitorial tribunals were still in existence, nor for those who had relapsed into heresy after having juridically abjured it.[149] The Holy Office granted similar faculties to Vicars Capitular and to Apostolic Administrators.[150] Missionaries were granted the same faculties that had been conceded to the bishops of the United States.[151] So, too, the Jesuits were granted an apostolic privilege by Julius III (1550-1555) on October 22, 1552, and this was confirmed by Gregory XIII on March 28, 1584, whereby the superior general or also the provincial superior (who could communicate this privilege to his subjects) could absolve from heresy, but only outside of Spain and Italy.[152] The Constitution *Apostolicae Sedis* revoked all real privileges, however, that is, such as had been granted to orders and institutes, but not personal faculties.[153]

[146] Pennacchi, *op. cit.,* II, 558-569.

[147] *Commentarium in Constitutionem Apostolicae Sedis* (ed. 2a, Romae, 1874), pp. 3-7; 98-102.

[148] *Elements of Ecclesiastical Law* (3 vols., Vol. I, 9. ed., 1887; Vol. II, 5. ed., 1887; Vol. III, 3. ed., 1888, New York: Benziger Bros.), I, 363.

[149] Smith, *Elements,* I, 364. Cf. S. C. S. Off., 25 iun. 1715, ad 1; 25 ian. 1627—*Fontes,* nn. 779, 720.

[150] 1 febr. 1865—*Fontes,* n. 981.

[151] S. C. S. Off., 16 iun. 1872. Formula I, n. 15.

[152] Schmalzgrueber, *Jus Ecclesiasticum,* Lib. V, tit. 7, n. 204.

[153] "Nisi de iis formalis, explicita, ac individua mentio facta fuerit."—Pennacchi, *Comment. in Const. Apost. Sedis,* II, 551, 553. Cf. S. Poenitentiaria, 5 dec. 1873—*ASS,* IX (1873-1874), 314, *Fontes,* n. 6431; Tephany, *Constitution Apostolicae Sedis Commentaire* (Tours, 1883), pp. 539-540.

The same restriction imposed by the Constitution *Apostolicae Sedis* has been carried over into the Code. Uusally, however, bishops possess the necessary faculties from the Sacred Penitentiary to receive a convert in the internal forum.[154] According to these faculties the bishops can absolve from all censures and other penalties incurred, whether the heresy be ocult or public. The Holy See reserves only the absolution of those who designedly and maliciously disseminated heretical doctrines among the faithful.[155]

The penitent is bound according to the norms of canons 1935-1937 to denounce those who are teaching the heretical doctrine, if he knows who they are, and any ecclesiastical or religious persons whom he may have had as accomplices in the matter. Ordinarily this denunciation is to take place before absolution; if there are just reasons making this impossible, then a serious promise to do so at the earliest possible opportunity and in a manner that is convenient is sufficient. The fulfillment of certain other conditions is also necessary before absolution can be given. There must be an abjuration of heresy; the convert must accept a salutary penance proportionate to the gravity of the crime, and must promise to frequent the sacraments; finally, he must take upon himself the obligation of retracting his errors in the presence of those before whom he manifested his heresy.

In virtue of these faculties the bishop can absolve and dispense, but only in the internal forum, whether in confession or outside of confession, (1) his own subjects in his own diocese; (2) his own subjects when they or he or both are outside of his diocese; (3) those who are from outside his diocese, but only within the limits of his proper territory. Within the confines of his diocese the bishop can delegate this faculty to his rural deans, even habitually, but only

[154] Cf. Bouscaren, *Canon Law Digest,* II (1943), 38-39.

[155] Cf. S. Poenitentiaria, 3 mart. 1880: "An praefata exceptione (exceptis haereticis publicis, seu publicae dogmatizanibus) comprehendantur haeretici publici, quin sint dogmatizantes; 2° Item, an comprehendantur dogmatizantes non quidem publice, sed privatim, scilicet modo uno, modo altero audiente, modo aliis paucis, et sic deinceps; ita tamen ut computatione facta, numerus dogmatizatorum deprehendatur valde excessivus?

"A. Ad 1. Negative. Ad 2. Affirmative, si notorium sit, haereticum praedicta ratione falsa dogmata spargere."—quoted in Ojetti, *Synopsis,* n. 2290.

in connection with sacramental confession. Unlike the bishop, the rural deans cannot use this delegated power in the non-sacramental internal forum. In particular cases he may also delegate other confessors who petition the faculty. This concession is made ***per modum actus*** and must follow upon the request of the individual confessors. Finally, when special reasons exist this faculty may be delegated to a few selected confessors for a definite period of time.[156]

Power to absolve from heresy is granted by the common law to Cardinals and the priest selected by them for their own and the confessions of those of their household.[157] At the present time Military Vicars or head chaplains also possess this faculty along with the power to subdelegate it to all military chaplains.

It is to be remembered that one who has been absolved in the internal forum can conduct himself in the manner of one who has been absolved in the external forum.[158] If the censure was occult, generally no difficulty will arise. But if it was public or notorious, then the scandal of the faithful[159] or the intervention of the Superior[160] can be an obstacle to such freedom of conduct. The proof of absolution given in the internal forum at first sight seems to be a difficulty. For confessors, not even with the consent of the penitent, can attest to those things which they learned from sacramental confession,[161] and they are exempted from the obligation of submitting

156 Bouscaren, *Canon Law Digest,* II (1943), 41.

157 Canon 239, § 1, nn. 1, 2.

158 Canon 2251.

159 The faithful can suffer scandal because they know of the censure but do not know of the absolution. Hence the one absolved is bound to remove the scandal and must, therefore, avoid all public acts which in the eyes of the faithful would make him appear to be rebellious, until he has given sufficient proof of his absolution. Such proof can be had by means of the confessor's written or declared assurance, or through the testimony of witnesses who saw him go to confession. Cf. Roberti, *De Delictis,* I, n. 310; De Meester, *Compendium,* Vol. III, Pars II, n. 1743, p. 179; Cappello, *De Censuris,* n. 98.

160 The Superior can intervene to urge the observance of the censure which he supposes to be still exstant, and then the delinquent is bound to obey lest the order of jurisdiction be disturbed. In this case, however, a legitimate presumption, such as may be formed from seeing the delinquent frequent the sacraments, living a pious life, etc., can induce the Superior to consider the delinquent as absolved. Cf. Roberti, *op. cit., loc. cit.*; Cappello, *op. cit., loc. cit.*

161 Canon 1757, § 3, n. 2.

testimony of those things which they learned outside sacramental confession. In this instance, however, the confessor acts in the capacity of a public official rather than as the minister of God. Hence, there is nothing to prevent his presenting a written declaration to the effect that absolution was granted, so that the absolution may take effect in the external forum.[162]

III. More Urgent Cases[163]

Under extraordinary circumstances it may be imposible for the penitent to observe the censure in the external forum for the length of time necessary to consult one who has faculties to absolve from the censure. These cases are present: (1) when there is danger of grave scandal or infamy; (2) when the delay would work a hardship on the penitent who is in the state of sin. Authors generally cite the omission of Mass on Sunday, or of the administration or reception of the sacraments, or the loss of one's good reputation among upright and serious-minded people as occasions of scandal or infamy. These could very well apply to Catholics who had defected

[162] Roberti, *De Delictis et Poenis,* I, n. 310.

[163] Can. 2254. 1. In casibus urgentioribus, si nempe censurae latae sententiae exterius servari nequeant sine periculo gravis scandali vel infamiae, aut si durum sit poenitenti in statu gravis peccati permanere per tempus necessarium ut Superior competens provideat, tunc quilibet confessarius in foro sacramentali ab eisdem, quoque modo reservatis absolvere potest, iniuncto onere recurrendi, sub poena reincidentiae, intra mensem saltem per epistolam et per confessarium, si id fieri possit sine gravi incommodo, reticito nomine, ad S. Poenitentiariam vel ad Episcopum aliumve praeditum facultate et standi eius mandatis.

2. Nihil impedit quominus poenitens, etiam post acceptam, ut supra, absolutionem, facto quoque recursu ad Superiorem, alium adeat confessarium facultate praeditum, ab eoque, repetita confessione saltem delicti cum censura, consequatur absolutionem; qua obtenta, mandata ab eodem accipiat.

3. Quod si in casu aliquo extraordinario hic recursus sit moraliter impossibilis, tunc ipsemet confessarius, excepto casu quo agatur de absolutione censurae de qua in can. 2367, potest absolutionem concedere sine onere de quo supra, iniunctis tamen de iure iniungendis, et imposita congrua poenitentia et satisfactione pro censura, ita ut poenitens, nisi intra congruum tempus a confessario praefiniendum poenitentiam egerit ac satisfactionem dederit, recidat in censuram.

Note: Since this canon directly concerns the good of souls, it also affects Orientals, and can be used by confessors of any rite. Cf. Moriarty, *Extraordinary Absolution from Censures,* pp. 155, 156.

from the faith, but not to non-Catholics who are seeking admission into the Church for the first time, and who have never received the sacraments and who are indeed prohibited by law from receiving them.[164]

The second case, however, may be verified in regard to them. It is possible that a non-Catholic who is well informed about the doctrines of the Church, and who knows that his own beliefs are erroneous, may have remorse of conscience and an immediate desire for absolution. The deferring of the absolution would work a hardship on the penitent who is conscious of his state of sin and who is most reluctant to await the necessary time for recourse.[165]

When the delict is occult there is more probability that the faculty granted by canon 2254 can be employed. But even if the delict were public either formally or materially, there might be a hardship of remaining in sin until the confessor could obtain the necessary faculties. In the case wherein absolution has been granted, however, the penitent is bound to avoid any acts which would cause scandal; and if his absolution cannot be proved or legitimately presumed he can be treated as one who still labors under the censure.[166]

Even in the case wherein a convert has presented himself for instructions and has thereby brought the delict into the external forum, canon 2254 can be employed to grant absolution in the sacramental forum. This is substantiated by the fact that canon 2314, § 2, states that the Ordinary *can* grant absolution in the external forum, but does not preclude the possibility of his granting the absolution in the internal forum.[167]

It is generally admitted that the need of having to remain in the state of sin for one day marks a sufficient length of time to substantiate this case.[168] Such a case would not exist, however, if the con-

[164] Cf. canon 731, § 2.

[165] In this theoretical case it is presupposed that the Ordinary has withheld delegation of the necessary faculties in both the internal and external forum, reserving to himself the right to receive all converts into the Church.

[166] Canon 2251.

[167] Cf. Coronata, *Institutiones*, IV, 295-296; Moriarty, *Extraordinary Absolution from Censures*, pp. 263-264.

[168] Coronata, *Institutiones*, IV, 179.

fession were made in the same city in which the bishop resided if he could be approached without difficulty.[169]

In the event that it is a serious hardship for the penitent to remain in the state of sin, any confessor is delegated by the common law to absolve. Before absolution can be given, however, the confessor must notify the penitent of his twofold obligation to have recourse to the proper authorities within a month, unless there is a grave inconvenience in doing so, and of obeying the mandates.[170] This obligation of recourse directly affects the penitent and is clearly a grave one, since if it is neglected it entails the recurrence of the same censure. The penitent may write or go personally to the competent superior for the mandates, or he may have recourse through the confessor by means of a letter.

The period of time allowed is to be computed from the day of confession when the penitent first learned of this obligation. The time as computed must however furnish a genuine occasion for the making of the recourse on any and all the days which coalesce to constitute the month's duration,[171] so that the computation will include only such days on which the penitent could avail himself of the needed opportunity for making the recourse.[172] Thus, canon 2254, § 1, permits an extension of time if there is any grave inconvenience attached to making the recourse. The obligation, however, does not cease. It is only suspended until it can be prudently judged that the inconvenience no longer exists, or that it is no longer grave.

The penitent is also permitted, even if upon the reception of absolution he already had made recourse, to approach another confessor who has the necessary faculty, and upon repeating his confession of at least the delict to receive absolution from him. In this case the penitent is bound to observe the mandates of the confessor without being obliged to await or execute the mandates of the Superior to whom he previously had made recourse.

[169] Vermeersch-Creusen, *Epitome*, III, n. 454, 2°.

[170] The words of canon 2254, § 1, *iniuncto onere recurrendi*, do not, however, affect the validity of the absolution. Cf. Coronata, *Institutiones*, IV, 180; Salucci, *Il Diritto Penale*, I, 232.

[171] Cf. canon 35.

[172] Cf. Coronata, *Institutiones*, IV, 180, 181.

The mandates in either case will enjoin a promise for a fuller instruction and practice of the faith, a complete severance with every and all non-Catholic sects, an abjuration of heretical beliefs, a penance and satisfaction for the censure and the sin, the reparation of any scandal, and the denunciation of any Catholic teachers of heresy or accomplices.

If, however, the confessor who has no special faculties to absolve from the censure foresees at the time of confession that recourse to the proper authorities is morally impossible, then by this very fact of moral impossibility the confessor is endowed by law with the necessary faculty to absolve from the censure without enjoining any obligation of recourse.[173] The confessor must insist, however, on a salutary penance and satisfaction in proportion to the censure, and he must establish, in addition to the other mandates, a period of time in which these must be performed, under pain of the recurrence of the excommunication.[174]

The phrase, *iniunctis de iure iniungendis,* of canon 2254, § 3, is to be interpreted according to the norms of the faculties usually granted by the Sacred Penitentiary. Hence, a promise must be exacted from the penitent to denounce any ecclesiastics or other teachers of heresy; he must abjure all heretical beliefs and sever any and all connections with non-Catholic sects; he must make at

[173] The recourse is morally impossible if neither the confessor nor the penitent can make the recourse even by letter to the Sacred Penitentiary, to the Apostolic Delegate, to the Bishop, or to another who has the faculty to absolve, and at the same time it is hard for the penitent to go to another confessor, e. g., if the penitent cannot come to the same confessor, and it is hard for him to go to another (Cf. S. C. S. Off., 5 sept. 1900—*Fontes,* n. 1247), or if the confessor foresees that the penitent will not return to accept the answer to the recourse, as can happen at the time of a mission or a retreat, or if there is danger of the violation of the seal of confession. Cf. Cocchi, *Commentarium,* VIII, p. 125, n. 79.

[174] For the recurrence of the censure, since it is a new and distinct penalty, there must be a new delict (the deliberate failure to comply with the mandates of the confessor), external, grave, consummated and joined with contumacy. Hence if the mandates are not *maliciously* omitted, there is no delict and consequently no recurrence of the censure. Cf. Blat, *Commentarium,* V, 121; Cerato, *Censurae Vigentes,* p. 38; Chelodi, *Ius Poenale,* p. 43; Coronata, *Institutiones,* IV, 140, 141.

least a short profession of faith; he is to be enjoined to frequent the sacraments, to retract his errors in the presence of those before whom he manifested his heresy, and to repair any scandal he may have caused.

* * * * *

It is important to note that even if in some extraordinary case the conditions for absolution in the internal forum are verified and absolution is given, the absolution will be of little value in the external forum.[175] This is evident from the tenor of the Instruction which requires an investigation of the convert's previous baptism, and prescribes a formula for absolution which clearly pertains to the external forum. Thus, while there is no prohibition against granting absolution in the internal forum, and although the absolution will restore the convert to the state of grace, the absolution will generally be powerless to remove the presumptions of the external forum.[176] It is therefore more practicable, especially in view of the delegation of powers generally conceded by bishops to their parish priests, to receive the convert in the external forum with the full observance of the prescriptions of the Instruction.

Article 6. Absolution in the External Forum

The law regulating the absolution from the censure of excommunication in the external forum is included in canon 2314, § 2:

> **Si tamen delictum apostasiae, haeresis vel schismatis ad forum externum Ordinarii loci quovis modo deductum fuerit, etiam per voluntariam confessionem, idem Ordinarius, non vero Vicarius Generalis sine mandato speciali, resipiscentem, praevia abiuratione iuridice peracta aliisque servatis de iure servandis, sua auctoritate ordinaria in foro exteriore absolvere potest;**

[175] Cf. De Meester, *Compendium*, Vol. III, Pars. II, n. 1742, pp. 174-175.

[176] Moriarty, *The Extraordinary Absolution from Censures*, pp. 262, 265; *contra*, Schenk, *Mixed Religion and Disparity of Cult*, n. 176: "It appears that the reception of the sacraments would serve as sufficient evidence in the absence of the formal abjuration of heresy, the profession of faith, and the absolution from censure in the external forum."

ita vero absolutus, potest deinde a peccato absolvi a quolibet confessario in foro conscientiae. Abiuratio vero habetur iuridice peracta cum fit coram ipso Ordinario loci vel eius delegato et saltem duobus testibus.

The formula to be used is that which is given in the Instruction and reproduced in the *Addenda* to the Roman Ritual for the use of the American clergy. The use of this formula binds at least *sub levi* to the exclusion of the usual formula employed for the absolution from excommunication.[177] For validity, however, no determined form is required in the external forum.[178] Any external sign by which the will of the one absolving is clearly manifested will suffice, whether it be in writing, by word of mouth or by signs.[179]

I. The Local Ordinary

Usually the convert will present himself for instructions to the priest who acts in the capacity of delegate for the local Ordinary. This is tantamount to the voluntary confession mentioned in canon 2314, § 2, for it definitely relegates the procedure of reconciliation to the external forum. No judicial confession is required, since it is sufficient that the delict be brought into the external forum under the competence of the local Ordinary in any manner judicial or non-judicial.

The local Ordinary refered to is usually the residential bishop to the exclusion of the Vicar General, who may not act without a special mandate. Of equal authority with the bishop are the Vicar Capitular, the Apostolic Administrator of the diocese, the Abbot or Prelate *nullius,* and the Vicar and Prefect Apostolic.[180] Religious Ordinaries need special faculties from the Holy See, or delegation from the local Ordinary, to receive converts.[181]

Since this power of the diocesan bishop is an ordinary power

[177] *Rituale Romanum,* Tit. III, cap. 3.

[178] Canon 2250, § 3.

[179] Cf. Cappello, *De Censuris,* n. 91; De Meester, *Compendium,* Vol. III, Pars. II, n. 1743, p. 178.

[180] Canon 198, § 1.

[181] Cf. Augustine, *Commentary,* VIII, 282.

of jurisdiction, it can be delegated generally. Such a general delegation is the usual practice in this country,[182] and hence the parish priest in most instances is empowered to receive converts as the delegate of the bishop. In the absence of a delegation the bishop is the only one who can receive the convert. In granting delegation the bishop may reserve certain cases to himself. Thus it happens that certain ordinaries grant general faculties to receive converts from heresy, but withhold delegation when there is question of those who were educated in the Catholic faith.[183] The power of the local Ordinary to absolve in the external forum is without restriction. The exception mentioned in the *pagella* of the Sacred Penitentiary for the internal forum (*exceptis haereticis haeresim inter fideles e proposito disseminantibus*) does not appear in the Code, and hence, does not hold for the external forum.

Under the old law the bishop also had the power to absolve from the excommunication. This conclusion is drawn from evidence found in the *Corpus Iuris Canonici.* Thus, according to the legislation of Boniface VIII (1294-1303), one finds that the absolution was entrusted to the bishop.[184] In his absence or when the see became vacant, the chapter or the one who filled the see until a successor was appointed was empowered to absolve.[185]

With the development and increased interest in canon law, canonists made certain distinctions in their interpretation of the law. Thus, it was conceded that, since only formal heretics fell under the excom-

[182] Cf., e.g., the Faculties granted to the clergy of New York, Philadelphia, Cincinnati, San Francisco.

[183] Cf. *Formula Facultatum Quae Sacerdotibus Dioeceseos Neo-Eboracensis Concedi Solent* (11 februarii, 1942), n. 14.

[184] C. 17, *de haereticis,* V, 2, in VI°: "Per hoc, quod negotium haereticae pravitatis alicui vel aliquibus ab Apostolicae Sede generaliter in aliqua provincia, civitate vel dioecesi delegatur, dioecesanis Episcopis, quin et ipsi auctoritate ordinaria vel delegata (si habent), in eodem procedere valeant, nolumus derogare."

[185] C. un., *de maioritate et obedientia,* I, 17, in VI°. The glossator to this chapter (v. *iuris*) noted that these persons could absolve from all excommunications, provided that they were not reserved to the bishop. Heresy, however, was not mentioned in the list of sins reserved to the bishop. Cf. *Glossa Ordinaria,* c. 2, X, *de haereticis,* V, 10; c. 4, D. L; c. 7, C. XXXIII, q. 2.

munication, any approved confessor could absolve material heretics,[186] though in many dioceses there existed the custom of sending these to the bishop or others who had special faculties in order that they might be absolved in both forums.[187] In the case of internal heresy, any confessor was likewise empowered to absolve, according to the axiom: *De internis non iudicat praetor.*[188]

When there was question of public or notorious heresy which was brought into the judicial forum bishops and papal inquisitors could absolve.[189] This held not only for the external forum, but for the internal forum as well, for the bishops by their ordinary power in both forums could absolve formal heretics when their crime was brought under their competence.[190] Commenting on the law of Boniface VIII, Benedict XIV stated that both the bishop and the papal inquisitor could absolve from the censure after receiving the abjuration, and then could send the penitent to any simple confessor for sacramental absolution.[191]

The phrase *ad forum contentiosum deductum* was a matter for divided interpretation. Schmalzgrueber (1663-1735) defined the phrase as comprehending not only the accusation, but also the citation of the guilty one.[192] Others held that this element was verified

[186] Pirhing, *Jus Canonicum*, Lib. V, tit. 7, n. 16.

[187] Cf. Reiffenstuel, *Jus Canonicum*, Lib. V, tit. 7, n. 239.

[188] Barbosa, *De Offic. et Potest. Episcopi*, Pars II, alleg. 40, n. 13; Del Bene, *De Officio S. Inquisitionis* (2 vols., Lugduni, 1666), I, Pars I, dub. 49, petit. 3; Petra, *Commentarium*, III, *ad Const. 18 Innoc. IV*, n. 13; Benedictus XIV, *De Syn. Dioec.*, Lib. IX, c. 4, n. 4.

[189] It was generally conceded that the Vicar General shared in this power, an important difference between pre-Code legislation and the present law of the Code. Cf. Crnica, *Modifications in Tractatu de Censuris per Codicem Introductae*, p. 109.

[190] Card. Petra, *Comment.*, III, *ad Const. 18 Innoc. IV*, n. 27; Bouix, *De Episcopo*, II, Pars V, cap. 19, prop. II. Cf. responses of S.C.C., 21 aug. 1609, 7 iul. 1617, 5 nov. 1644, in Petra, *op. cit.*, *loc. cit.* Cf. also Smith, *Elements*, I, 363; Farinacius, *Tractatus de Haeresi* (Romae, 1516), Q. 92, n. 4, c. 52; Del Bene, *De Off. S. Inquis.*, I, dub. 57. That the bishops' power remained unchanged up to the Code is indicated by late responses of the Holy Office: 7 maii 1822, 28 mart. 1900, 8 iun. 1900—*Fontes*, nn. 865, 1237, 1239.

[191] *De Synodo Dioecesana*, Lib. IX, c. 4, n. 3.

[192] *Jus Ecclesiasticum*, Lib. V, tit. 7, n. 188. Cf. Sanchez, *De Matrimonio*, Lib. VIII, c. 34, n. 58.

only after the formal denial of the charge by the accused, since the trial did not properly begin before such a denial was made.[193]

If the heresy was notorious but had not yet been brought into the judicial forum, only the Holy See could grant the absolution.[194] By means of the *Bullae Coenae* the Holy See reserved to itself in a general way the absolution from excommunication which all heretics incurred as a result of any externally manifested heresy. But under this general reservation notorious heresy which had been brought into the judicial forum was not comprehended.[195] Only one year before the promulgation of the Code the Holy Office confirmed the competence of bishops in this matter.[196]

In the present legislation the effect of the absolution is the cessation of the reservation.[197] This entitles the convert to conduct himself in both his public and occult acts as one who has been fully absolved,[198] since the absolution which is granted in the external forum is also valid in and has full legal force for the internal forum.[199] Inasmuch as the sin is reserved by reason of the censure, with the relaxation of the censure, the reservation of the sin also ceases,[200] and thus any approved confessor can impart sacramental absolution.[201]

Before the absolution from censures can be given the Ordinary

[193] Barbosa, *De Off. et Potest. Episcopi*, alleg. 39, n. 29; Pirhing, *Jus Canonicum*, Lib. V, tit. 7, n. 40.

[194] Petra, *Comment.*, III, *ad Const. 18, Innoc. IV*, n. 15; Barbosa, *op. cit.*, alleg. 40, n. 12.

[195] Bouix, *De Episcopo*, II, Pars V, cap. 19; Smith, *Elements*, I, 305.

[196] S. C. S. Off., declar. 19 febr. 1916, n. 2: "Si tamen crimen haeresis vel apostasiae ad forum externum episcopi aut praelati episcopalem vel quasi-episcopalem auctoritatem habentis, aut per spontaneam confessionem vel alio quovis modo deductum fuerit, episcopus vel praelatus sua auctoritate ordinaria resipiscentem haereticum vel apostatam, praevia abiuratione iuridice peracta, aliisque servatis de iure servandis, in foro exteriori absolvere poterit. Absolutus autem in foro exteriori potest deinde absolvi a quolibet confessario in foro conscientiae absolutione sacramentali."—*Fontes*, n. 1299.

[197] Canon 2246, § 3.

[198] Cf. Cappello, *De Censuris*, n. 215.

[199] Canon 2251.

[200] Canon 2250, § 2.

[201] Cf. Blat, *Commentarium*, V, 201.

or his delegate must be certain of the absence of contumacy. According to the norms of the common law contumacy is said to cease simultaneously with the repentance of the delinquent and his congruous or proportionate satisfaction, or, at least, with the serious promise of satisfaction for any damage and scandal he may have caused.[202] The judgment as to the sincerity of the repentance and of the promise of satisfaction is committed to the one from whom the absolution is sought, that is, either the priest who acts as the bishop's delegate or the bishop himself. When the contumacy has definitely been amended, the convert has a strict right to absolution, since his claim rests on a basis of justice.[203]

According to canon 2248, § 2, the one absolving can impose a congruous vindictive penalty or penance if the case merits it. This could happen in the case of grave scandal, or for the repairing of the social order which had been gravely disrupted, or to deter the faithful from imitating the delinquent. To do so, however, the one who absolves would have to be endowed with the power to inflict penalties.[204]

II. Servatis de Iure Servandis

The absolution from censures is also qualified by the performance of the juridical abjuration in the presence of two witnesses,[205] and the observance of the other prescriptions of the law, *servatis de iure servandis*. In the interpretation of this latter condition, authors find a connection between the Code and the Instruction of 1859:

[202] Canon 2242, § 3. This is important, especially in the case in which the convert is taking instructions prior to his marriage with a Catholic.

[203] De Meester, *Compendium*, Vol. III, Pars II, n. 1743, p. 176.

[204] De Meester, *op. cit., loc. cit.*

[205] In contrast to the present law is a response of the Holy Office under date of December 21, 1895, in which the *"ubique locorum usus"* was described as the performance of the abjuration of error and the profession of faith before the pastor and one witness, or if necessity demanded, before the pastor alone, but always in such a manner that the abjuration could be proved in the external forum. The abjuration was considered not so much a judicial or juridical act, as an act of the pastoral office: "idcirco abiuratio non tam actus iudicialis aut iuridicus, sed magis actus pastoralis officii censeri debet, sed semper validus etiam pro exteriori foro."—*Analecta Ecclesiastica,* VIII (1900), 191.

thus before everything else there must be an investigation of the fact and validity of the convert's baptism.[206]

A salutary penance must be imposed in accordance with the gravity of the convert's moral guilt.[207] Since the kind of penance is left to the judgment of the one who receives the convert it is well to recall the cautions urged by Benedict XIV.[208]

> Arbitrium, quod relinquitur Poenitentiario in ordine ad poenitentias individuandas, et iniungendas, non importat meram et liberam voluntatem ita ut possit illas libere iniungere, prout sibi placuerit, sed importat arbitrium regulatum, idest arbitrium boni viri, et iuri conforme.
>
> Quamobrem Confessarius, ut suo muneri recte satisfaciat neque severitatis, neque humanitatis fines excedat, rationem quoque habebit conditionis, aetatis, et sexus illius, cui poena irrogatur.

A penance is any good work whether of religion (prayers, attendance at Mass, frequenting the sacraments), of charity (almsgiving), or of mortification (fasting). A salutary penance is one which is proportionate to the quantity and quality of the delict,[209] and to the condition or ability of the delinquent.[210]

According to the contemporary practice of the Church, a *grave* penance is one which corresponds to a work which is imposed under

[206] Cf. Coronata, *Institutiones,* IV, 293; Beste, *Introductio,* p. 935; Cappello, *De Censuris,* n. 215; De Meester, *Compendium,* Vol. III, Pars II, n. 1814, p. 237.

[207] Cf. Beste, *Introductio,* p. 935; Coronata, *Institutiones, loc. cit.*; De Meester, *Compendium, loc. cit.*; S. C. S. Off., 5 sept. 1736, 30 iul. 1806, 7 maii 1822—*Fontes,* nn. 791, 850, 865; Clemens VII, ep. *Cum sicut,* 15 ian. 1532, § 2—*Fontes,* n. 79.

[208] *Institutiones Ecclesiasticae* (3 vols., Romae, 1784), II, inst. 37, 38.

[209] Cf. canon 2196.

[210] Conc. Trident., sess. XIV, cap. 8: "Debent ergo sacerdotes Domini quantum spiritus et prudentia suggesserit, pro qualitate criminum et poenitentium facultate, *salutares et convenientes satisfactiones iniungere,* ne, si forte peccatis conniveant et indulgentius cum poenitentibus agant, levissima quaedam opera pro gravissimis delictis iniungendo, alienorum peccatorum participes efficiantur (cf. I Tim. V: 22). Habeant autem prae oculis, ut satisfactio, quam imponunt, non sit tantum ad novae vitae custodiam et infirmitatis medicamentum, sed etiam ad praeteritorum peccatorum vindictam et castigationem. . . ."

a grave obligation by the Church, or which would oblige *sub gravi* if it were imposed,[211] e. g., attendance at Mass, fasting, the recitation of the five decades of the rosary, the little office of the Blessed Virgin, the litany of the saints with its accompanying prayers, the reception of the sacraments or an act of generous almsgiving. The penance is *grave and long* if it is to be performed once a month (e. g., confession and communion) for four or five months; or every week for three months (e. g., attendance at Mass); or every day for one month (e. g., recitation of the rosary). It is *grave and very long* if it is to be performed every month for three or two years, or even for one year; every week for six months, or every day for three months. A hard and fast rule does not exist, nor is there any authentic declaration of the Sacred Penitentiary on this point: hence, authors disagree in assigning a time limit. In practice the milder opinion is to be followed. In general the penance which is imposed must be a *grave* one.[212] The imposition and execution of the penance does not affect the validity of the absolution, however.

The bad health, either physical or mental, of the convert; the fear that a graver penance will not be performed, and the wholehearted repentance of the convert are sufficient causes for justifying a diminution of the penance.[213] Penances which exceed the ability of the convert, e. g., fasting for children or laborers who are exhausted by continuous work; prolix prayers, pilgrimages; or penances which are repugnant, such as the tracing of the sign of the cross on the ground with the tongue, should not be imposed.

The natural law demands that in addition to a salutary penance any scandal which may have been caused must be repaired in a manner best suited to achieve this purpose and according to the prudent

[211] Noldin-Schmitt, *Theologia Moralis,* III, n. 303.

[212] Cappello (*De Censuris,* n. 101, nota 53) says that the imposition of a grave penance was commanded by the Sacred Penitentiary, Dec. 10, 1880. Noldin-Schmitt (*Theologia Moralis,* III, n. 303), on the contrary, demand that the penance which is imposed be grave and very long (*gravis et diuturna*).

Note: For a list of salutary penances confer Sabetti-Barrett, *Compendium,* pp. 729-731, n. 768, where they are grouped under three headings: (1) opera pietatis; (2) opera mortificationis; (3) poenitentiae medicinales.

[213] Noldin-Schmitt, *Theologia Moralis,* III, n. 304.

judgment of the one absolving.[214] And all spiritual connections with heretics or those outside the faith must be abruptly abandoned.[215] The denunciation of accomplices or of cooperators in heresy is also demanded whenever it proves necessary, but ordinarily there will be no need for this.[216]

When these specific and general requirements of the law have been fulfilled, the convert is to be absolved in the external forum from the censure of excommunication. If during the investigation of the convert's good or bad faith a reasonable doubt arises, even though it be slight, as to whether the censure was actually contracted, the word *forsan* is to be inserted in the form of absolution according to the rubric of the Instruction.[217] Such a doubt could easily arise because of the possibility that the convert is only a material heretic.

Reiffenstuel (1641-1703)[218] and Lacroix (1652-1714)[219] were of the opinion that great numbers among the mass of non-Catholics were not formal heretics. Some of them were of so simple a mind or so prejudiced by the teaching of their ministers that they were persuaded of the truth of their own religion, and at the same time they were so sincere and conscientious, that if they had known it to be false, they would at once have embraced the true faith.

In the present day, the wide organization and development of the Church in all of the civilized countries of the world make it practically impossible for any non-Catholic in such countries to plead total ignorance of the Church's existence or of all its doctrines and teachings. The final judgment as to whether the good faith of the convert perse-

[214] Cf. De Meester, *Compendium,* Vol. III, Pars II, n. 1814, p. 237; Wernz-Vidal, *Ius Canonicum,* VII, 416; Coronata, *Institutiones,* IV, 293; Chelodi, *Ius Poenale,* p. 76.

[215] S. C. S. Off., 28 mart. 1900—*Fontes,* n. 1237.

[216] "Iure novo censemus denuntiationem *necessario* faciendam non esse, nisi agatur de *clericis* vel *religiosis* qui nomen dederint sectae massonicae aliisque similibus associationibus, iuxta praescriptum can. 2336, 2. Denuntiari debent, aliter ac antea, uni S. Congregationi S. Officii."—Cappello, *De Censuris,* n. 215, nota 27.

[217] "In dubio gravi aut levi, utrum poenitens excommunicationem incurrerit per haeresim professam, sacerdos hic inserat vocabulum *forsan.*"

[218] *Jus Canonicum,* Lib. V, tit. 7, n. 13.

[219] *Theologia Moralis* (3 vols., Venetiis, 1753), II, n. 94.

vered, so as to excuse him from the censure entirely, rests with the one who receives the convert into the Church.

Those converts who are certainly baptized, being already bound by the laws of the Church and coming through their conversion to a knowledge of the obligation of confession, are clearly bound to fulfill the duty of making a sacramental confession if they are conscious of grievous sin. Although the Instruction does not specifically prescribe sacramental confession in this case, the time of the reception of converts into the Church offers a most suitable occasion for them not only to fulfill the precept of annual confession [220] but also to profit from spiritual direction, which is so necessary for them at that time and is nowhere given with such salutary effect as in the tribunal of penance.[221]

The Roman Ritual provides for the supplying of ceremonies which were omitted in the heretical baptism.[222] This is dependent, however, on the judgment of the Ordinary. The direct obligation is to supply the missing ceremonies when the Ordinary has made no definite decision in the matter. If he has decreed that they are to be omitted, as is the case in England,[223] the ceremony of reception will end with the sacramental absolution of the convert. As in the case of the doubtfully baptized, these converts should strongly be urged to attend Mass and to receive Holy Communion at the earliest possible convenience.

[220] Canon 906.

[221] O'Kane, *Rubrics of the Roman Ritual,* 216.

[222] "Ubi vero debita forma et materia servata est, omissa tantum suppleantur, nisi rationabili de causa aliter loci Ordinario videatur."—Tit. II, cap. 3, n. 12.

[223] Fortescue, *Ceremonies of the Roman Rite Described* (6. ed. revised, London: Burns, Oates, and Washbourne, 1937), p. 424.

CHAPTER VII

ORIENTAL CONVERTS

ARTICLE 1. PROCEDURE

ALTHOUGH both uniate and dissident Orientals are not bound generally by the laws of the Latin Church,[1] they are subject to those prescriptions of the Code which of their very nature affect the Oriental Church.[2] Since the prescriptions of canons 1325, § 2 and 2314 explicitly treat of apostates, heretics and schismatics, of their very nature they include Oriental converts. Even before the Code it was the practice of the Sacred Congregation for the Propagation of the Faith to include Orientals under legislation which treated of the faith and defection from the faith. In its celebrated Pamphili response of June 4, 1631,[3] the Sacred Congregation gave answer to a doubt as to whether Oriental dissidents were liable to the penalties of the Bulla *Coenae.* The question was proposed by certain Capuchin missionaries laboring among Catholics and dissidents in the Orient. The two groups were not fully separated but often continued to live under the jurisdiction of the same bishops, some of whom openly professed union with Rome, while others favored it and others opposed it. The response, therefore, embraced not only Catholics, but also dissidents.

> In ea . . . fuit latissime discussus articulus: An Summus Pontifex intendat graecos et alios sedibus patriarcharum schismaticarum subditos comprehendere in Bulla *Coena Domini,* aliisque Constitutionibus Apostolicis, in quibus casus sibi et Sedi Apostolicae reservat. Et. . . . Patres praedicti quoad dictum articulum convenerunt in negativam sententiam, quam tamen limitarunt tripliciter:

[1] Cf. Aemilius Herman, "Reguntume Orientales dissidentes legibus matrimonialibus Ecclesiae Latinae?"—*Periodica,* XXVII (1938), 9-13.

[2] Canon 1.

[3] *Fontes,* n. 4449—so-called because the decision was given in the palace of Cardinal Pamphili.

1—In materia dogmatum fidei;

2—Si Papa explicite faciat mentionem in suis constitutionibus et disponat de praedictis subditis patriarchalium sedium, ut in casu schismaticorum Bullae *Coenae*.

3—Si implicite in eisdem constitutionibus de eis disponat, ut in casibus appellationis ad futurum concilium, et deferentiae armarum ad infideles et similibus.

This response is cited by Benedict XIV in his Constitution *Allatae Sunt*,[4] and served as a norm in a later pronouncement of the same Congregation.[5] The Holy Office also decided that Orientals are bound by the censures of the Constitution *Apostolicae Sedis*,[6] with the same reservations. It is in keeping with pre-Code legislation that Orientals are embraced by the legislation of the Code which regards matters of faith and the preservation of the faith.[7] Since canon 2314 directly concerns those who defect from the faith, Oriental converts must be considered as subject to the prescriptions affecting all apostates, heretics and schismatics,[8] whether they be formally or only materially delinquent. They incur the penalties mentioned in canon 2314 and are absolved from the excommunication in accordance with

[4] *Bullarium*, III, Pars II, § 44, p. 270.

[5] S. C. de Prop. Fide litt. encycl., 5 nov. 1882,—*Collect.*, II, n. 1578.

[6] "Eundo stato promosso il dubbio se gli orientali siano soggetti alla Constituzione Apostolicae Sedis pubblicata dalla f.m. di Pio IX, in data dei 12 Ottobre 1869 la Suprema Congregazione del S. Offizio con successiva approvazione della Santitá di N. S. ha dichiarato quanto seque nella feria IV. 15 Luglio corrente anno:

1. Per Constitutionem Apostolicae Sedis nihil esse innovatum circa censuras earumque reservationes pro fidelibus rituum orientalium.

2. Eosdem fideles subiici omnibus censuris ab Apostolica Sede latis in materia dogmatum et in Constitutionibus in quibus implicite de iis disponitur, nempe ubi materia ipsa demonstrat eos comprehendi, quatenus non de lege mere ecclesiastica agitur, sed ius naturale et divinum declaratur."—S. C. S. Off., 6 aug. 1885,—*Collect.*, n. 1640.

[7] "Nam quod plerumque comprehenduntur, ubi sermo est de acatholicis vel de haereticis et schismaticis, id optime explicatur ex can. 1 CIC. Ut enim ex repetitis declarationibus S. Sedis et ex ipsa rei natura patet, omnes leges quae fidem fideique preservationem spectant, afficiunt etiam Orientales."—Herman, *Peroidica*, XXVII (1938), 19.

[8] Cf. Duskie, *The Canonical Status of Orientals in the United States* (Catholic University of America Canon Law Studies, n. 48, Washington, D. C.: Catholic University of America, 1929), pp. 56 ss.

paragraph 2 of the same canon. As stated above [9] authors agree that the procedure outlined in the Instruction of 1859 is substantially comprehended under the term *servatis servandis* of canon 2314, § 2. This procedure must be followed in receiving Oriental converts. In the United States the Instruction is of obligation by reason of particular law.

I. Investigation of Baptism

Since it is generally recognized that the baptisms conferred by Oriental dissidents are valid,[10] the usual procedure in the reception of an Oriental convert will embrace the abjuration of former errors, the profession of faith and the absolution from the censure of excommunication,[11] if the case warrants it. Before the actual reception of the convert a diligent investigation must be made into the validity of the convert's baptism, and into the fact of his incurring or avoidance of the penalties for espousal of heresy and adherence to an heretical sect.

Concerning the baptisms of dissident Russians, perhaps the largest group of our separated brethren, the Pontifical Commission for Russia advised Ordinaries that "They must recall to mind the replies and decrees of the Holy Office regarding the validity of baptism and confirmation of dissidents." [12] On September 8, 1633, the Holy Office explicitly declared valid the following formulas which were used by schismatic Armenians: [13]

> Baptizat nunc manus mea in nomine Patris et Filii et Spiritus Sancti. Baptizet nunc manus mea in nomine Patris, baptizet nunc manus mea in nomine Filii, baptizet nunc manus mea in nomine Spiritus Sancti.

On June 20, 1886, the Holy Office expressed its disapproval of a de-

[9] Cf. Chapter 1, article 1.

[10] Cf. Chapter VI, footnote 1.

[11] Cf. Letter of Pius IX, *In Suprema Petri Apostoli Sede,* written in 1848: "Itaque non aliud Vobis imponimus oneris, quam haec necessaria; nimirum ut ad unitatem reversi consentiatis Nobiscum in professione verae Fidei, quam Ecclesia catholica tenet et docet, et cum Ecclesia ipsa supremaque hac Petri Sede communionem servetis."—*Acta P. Pii IX,* Vol. I, p. 90.

[12] From English text in Bouscaren, *Canon Law Digest,* I, 851.

[13] *Fontes,* n. 722, *Collect.,* n. 74.

cree of the Vicar Apostolic issued on March 11, 1861, commanding the indiscriminate conditional rebaptism of all Abyssinian converts and declared that the presumption, based on an examination of the schismatic Abyssinian ritual and on the testimony of trustworthy missionaries, was that the baptisms conferred by schismatic Abyssinian priests were valid. At the same time it reported the testimony of the missionaries to the effect that it was possible that in certain provinces there might be a reasonable doubt as to the validity of the sacrament and hence commanded that the baptism of each convert be separately investigated.[14] In the United States eleven dissident Oriental sects are listed under the general heading of Eastern Orthodox Churches. Of these eleven bodies, eight—the Albanian, Bulgarian, Greek, Roumanian, Russian, Serbian, Syrian and Ukrainian—perform the liturgy in their native language, while in the remaining three—the American Holy Orthodox Catholic Eastern Church, the Apostolic Episcopal Church (the Holy Eastern Catholic and Apostolic Orthodox Church) and the Holy Orthodox Church in America—the liturgical books are in English.[15] The investigation of the baptism of converts from the three latter bodies, therefore, will be facilitated. In all these bodies, the seven sacraments are retained and the baptism of infants and adults is by threefold immersion.[16]

[14] S. C. S. Off., instr. (Pro Vic. ad Gallos), 20 iun. 1886, ad 40: "Iamvero rationes quibus permotum se esse dicit Vicarius Apostolicus, ad ferendum decretum de conditionata baptismi iteratione, non sunt profecto eiusmodi ut parere queant probabilem dubitationem de validitate omnium universim baptismorum qui in Abissinia a presbyteris schismaticis administrantur, praesertim cum libri rituales abissinorum, quod ad Baptismum attinet, reprehensione careant et nonnulli fide digni missionarii ad hanc S. C. retulerint, se Baptismo a schismaticis abissinis collato non semel interfuisse nullosque in eo deprehendisse substantiales defectus, tametsi haudquaquam negarent, in aliquibus fortasse abissiniae provinciis locum habere posse talem baptizandi praxim, quae merito ac rationabiliter incertam reddat collati Baptismi validitatem. Revocato igitur suo decreto, stet (Vicarius Ap.) instructioni ab hac Suprema Congregatione ad Apostolicum Abissiniae Vicarium datae die 2 Maii an. 1858: qua ex instructione videbit attendendos esse casus particulares."—*Fontes,* n. 994.

[15] *Religious Bodies, 1936,* Statistics, History, Doctrine, Organization and Work, U. S. Department of Commerce, Bureau of the Census (2 vols., United States Government Printing Office: Washington, D. C., 1941), Vol. II, p. 549.

[16] *Religious Bodies, 1936,* II, 550.

II. Profession of Faith

In accordance with the spirit of canon 1, it is the writer's opinion that the new formula of profession of faith (and in countries other than the United States, the formula given in the Instruction of 1859) would be used only in those instances where an Oriental convert would on his conversion embrace the Latin rite. In the cases where the Oriental would be received into a Catholic Oriental rite the special formulas approved by Gregory XIII and Urban VIII would be of obligation. The formula of Gregory XIII with the added reference to the Vatican Council made in 1868 is to be employed in receiving Greek converts; for all other Oriental converts the longer or more abbreviated formulas of Urban VIII with the additions made in 1899 are to be used.[17] The full texts of these formulas are to be found in the 1893 edition of the *Collectanea*.[18]

Because of the importance of the regulations governing the return of dissident Russians to the Church, it seemed appropriate to quote the Instruction of 1929 issued by the Pontifical Commission for Russia.[19]

I. Lay Persons

Who can receive the convert.

The Pontifical Commission declares that in the case of lay persons the Bishop has power, not only in urgent but also in ordinary cases, to admit and receive them into the unity of the Catholic Church, provided he knows the persons who seek admis-

[17] Wernz-Vidal, *Ius Canonicum,* VII, 417.

[18] N. 1496, nota I, II, III.

[19] English text from Bouscaren, *Canon Law Digest,* I, 850-853. The Latin text is recorded in *ASS,* XXI (1929), 608-610. This Instruction was issued August 26, 1929, as a practical norm for Ordinaries who found it difficult or impossible to comply with the decree of the Pontifical Commission issued January 12 of the same year, whereby every case of a Russian convert who is a cleric must be reported to the Pontifical Commission, or in places where there is one, to the Apostolic Legate. In the Introduction to the Instruction the Commission agreed that the "end and purport of the Decree was to recommend due prudence, so as to forestall any occasion of calumniating the Church on the ground that she was taking advantage of the ill fortune of our brethren in order to draw them to herself." The titles in the text were supplied by the writer.

sion well enough to be able to judge prudently of their right disposition of soul and of their sufficient knowledge of the faith and the Catholic Church.

Validity of Baptism, Confirmation.

They must recall to mind the replies and decrees of the Holy Office regarding the validity of baptism and confirmation of dissidents.

Investigation of marriage.

It is important, however, to inquire whether they contracted matrimony in schism and if so how, before whom, whether with a dispensation from any impediment, and by whom that was granted. Also of what religion was the other party; whether the marriage in question was afterward dissolved, for what reasons, and by whom; whether they have contracted a new marriage. Finally, everything must be investigated so as to find out which marriage was valid.

Instruction.

Likewise a prudent and circumspect investigation should be made to ascertain whether the reasons and motives by which they are drawn to the unity of the Church be spiritual and supernatural, or merely human, such as their present need and poverty; for in this case they should be rather helped as much as possible and very much commended to the charity of the brethren. But in the meantime they should not be rejected nor abandoned, but turned over to some prudent priest who would teach them Catholic doctrine, especially about the unity of the Church, the primacy of the Roman Pontiff, the Immaculate Conception of the Blessed Virgin, purgatory, etc.

Choice of rite.

When they are found sufficiently instructed and disposed they are to be informed of their right to choose their rite, but without presuming to influence them to assume the Latin rite against their inclination. It will be better to explain the dignity and beauty of the Oriental rites, and the doctrine and teaching of the Catholic Church in regard to them, and how solicitous she is for their interests. If, however, any Russian, after duly considering everything, prefers to belong to the Latin rite, he may be admitted to it.

No recourse.

Accordingly if the Most Reverend Ordinaries observe these norms, they need not have recourse in each case to this Commission.

Reception.

When the Ordinaries are sufficiently informed regarding the persons in question, and also regarding their domestic state, and have formed a prudent judgment of their good will and purpose, and of the sufficiency of their disposition and instruction as above prescribed, they may and should admit them to the unity of the Catholic Church, both in ordinary cases and *a fortiori* in urgent ones, for example, when a marriage has to be celebrated with the observance of those formalities which the Holy See requires in abjuration and mixed marriages.

Annual report.

The Most Reverend Ordinaries should, however, remember that this Pontifical Commission is always ready to examine and reply to any doubts or queries regarding the admission of Russians into the Catholic Church. While again praising the prudent zeal of the Ordinaries, this Pontifical Commission earnestly exhorts them to attend with special care to the Christian education of children and young people among the Russians, for these people are rather disposed to truth and goodness. The Ordinaries shall every year inform this Commission regarding the return of young people to the Catholic Church, as well as regarding any inclination manifested by any boy or young man toward embracing the ecclesiastical state.

II. Clerics; That Is, Priests and Deacons

Caution.

Greater caution is to be used in the case of priests or deacons; not that they are to be distrusted, for that is out of the question, but because clerics require a longer period of instruction; and the matter is to be attended to with greater care, especially as regards the future. For experience shows that it is impossible to use too much prudence in these matters.

Investigation.

Hence, besides requiring a more careful and a fuller investigation than that which is prescribed in the case of lay persons, Ordinaries shall make sure of their ordination and their studies;

what language they speak, read, and write, and how well; whether they are sufficiently acquainted with Latin to derive some profit from attending lectures in sacred theology, dogmatic and moral.

They should also find out to what hierarchy of fraction of a hierarchy each one belonged, and whether in the course of time he transferred from one to another; whether he ever belonged to or tried to join any Protestant sect; whether since receiving sacred orders he has lived as a layman without exercising any ecclesiastical ministry.

Moreover, an investigation should be made of each one's morals and rectitude of life. After which the Ordinary should refer the case to this Commission or, if the case is urgent, to the Apostolic Legate in the district, who shall act according to special instructions given him for the purpose.

Report.

Ordinaries shall promptly notify this Pontifical Commission of any clerics who have been admitted to the Catholic Church.

Article 2. Choice of Rite

The sacrament of baptism not only accords the juridical status of personality in ecclesiastical law but at the same time it determines the rite to which the person must adhere.[20] This is in harmony with the rule laid down by Benedict XIV: *Per baptismum fiat suscepti ritus graeci vel latini professio.*[21] This rule which is now incorporated into the Code was evidently established as binding directly on those baptized in the Catholic faith. Petrani,[22] however, is of the opinion that Oriental converts are also comprehended under this norm. His conclusion is based on certain passages from the Constitution of Leo XIII, *Orientalium Dignitas*[23] and from the Constitution of Benedict XIV, *Allatae Sunt*[24] in which missionaries are strictly forbidden to induce any Oriental convert to embrace the Latin rite on

[20] Canons 87, 98, § 1.

[21] Const. *Etsi Pastoralis,* 26 maii, 1742, § 2, n. 4.

[22] *De Relatione Juridica inter Diversos Ritus in Ecclesia Catholica* (Taurini, Romae: Marietti, 1930), p. 33.

[23] 30 nov. 1894,—*Collect.* (1907), n. 1883, n. 1.

[24] § 19, § 21,—*Bullarium,* III, Pars II, p. 267.

his entrance into the Church. From these texts he argues further, that when Oriental converts are in a place where there are Catholic bishops of the Catholic Oriental rite, or at least pastors, or other legitimately authorized Catholic priests, there is no doubt that ordinarily the converts must become subject to the jurisdiction of their Oriental superiors. The texts cited by Petrani seem to presuppose the application of the rule of Benedict XIV to those Orientals baptized outside the true Faith, for in forbidding missionaries to exhort them to join the Latin rite, it is understood that they already are ascribed to some Oriental rite, even though they are not yet admitted to full membership in the Church. In view of several pronouncements of the Holy See, however, the further conclusion of Petrani, seems unwarranted.

The first of these responses was issued by the Sacred Congregation for the Propagation of the Faith on November 20, 1838, in which the Oriental convert was given the privilege of joining any Oriental rite he preferred on his conversion:

> Quod vero ad haereticos et schismaticos pertinet, qui ad Ecclesiae sinum redeunt, permittendum censuit S. C. ut orientalem ritum qui magis iis placuerit amplectantur.[25]

In explaining this decree, the same Congregation declared several years later that this privilege devolved only on those born in schism or heresy and did not pertain to those who defected from the true faith and now wish to be reconciled: these latter must be received into the rite from which they defected.[26] Several years later the same Congregation further interpreted the decree of 1838 as restricting the convert's choice to any one of the Oriental rites to the exclu-

[25] *Collect.*, n. 2007.

[26] S. C. de Prop. Fide, litt. 7 apr. 1859 (ad Ep. Alappen. Moranit.): "Il decreto emanato ai 20 Novembre 1838 riguardo al passagio degli orientali da un rito all' altro, ed alla facoltà che si concede agli eretici ed agli scismatici, di scegliere quel rito orientale che piu loro aggradi nel ritorno dei medesimi al seno della cattolica Chiesa non comprende gli apostati, quelli cioè che essendo cattolici, abbandonarono la vera Chiesa passando all' eresia ed allo scisma, e poi di nuovo si convertono."—*Collect.*, n. 2012.

sion of the Latin rite.[27] The exclusion of the Latin rite was reiterated in a pronouncement of June 1, 1885.[28]

In 1894, however, the privilege accorded the Oriental convert was extended by Leo XIII to include the choice even of the Latin rite, if this were laid down as a necessary condition of conversion. If no such condition were made, the convert could still embrace the Latin rite provided that (1) there were no Oriental priests available to receive him into the Church; (2) as soon as there is a sufficiency of priests of his native rite, he return to this rite.[29]

> Si qua ex dissidentibus communitas vel familia vel persona ad catholicam unitatem venerit, conditione velut necessaria interposita amplectendi latini ritus, huic ritui remaneat ea quidem ad tempus adstricta, in eius tamen potestate sit ad nativum ritum catholicum aliquando redire. Si vero eiusmodi conditio non intercesserit, sed ideo ipsa communitas, familia, persona a latinis presbyteris administretur quia desint orientales, regrediendum ipsi erit ad ritum suum, statim ut sacerdotis orientalis fuerit copia.

In interpreting this faculty granted by Leo XIII, the Sacred Congregation of the Faith declared that the privilege granted Oriental converts on November 20, 1838, remained in force.[30]

This privilege still obtains under the Code because of the fact that it is still in use, has never been revoked, and because an express reprobation is lacking.[31] Duskie argues that nothing should stand

[27] S. C. de Prop. Fide, 15 jul. 1876: "Decretum illud sancitum die 20 nov. 1838 agit de transitu ab aliquo ex ritibus orientalibus ad alterum, et nihil omnino statuit de ritu latino, neque de iis qui hunc ritum habent, vel habere desiderant; et quod ibi statuitur de haereticis et schismaticis ad Ecclesiae sinum redeuntibus, de iis intelligendum est qui ad orientales ritus pertinent."—*Collect.*, n. 2014.

[28] "2. Se il missionario Apostolico in oriente, in forza delle sue facolta ordinarie, possa riconciliare alla Chiesa cattolica *i nati scismatici* compresi nell' ambito della Missione affidatagli.

"Ad 2. Affirmative: suscipiendi tamen sunt ad orientalem ritum, non autem ad latinum absque venia S. Sedis."—*Collect.*, n. 1633.

[29] Const. *Orientalium Dignitas,* 30 nov. 1894, n. 11,—*Collect.*, n. 1883.

[30] *Collect.*, n. 1883, nota 2.

[31] Canon 4. Cf. canon 98, § 3. "Ius istud textu canonis non esse sublatum censemus cum Cappello"—Vermeersch-Creusen, *Epitome,* I, n. 221.

in the way of the convert's reception into the Church, and hence, in the interests of the convert's salvation the privilege is not abolished by the Code.

> In a strict sense the Code is only placing the conditions for a lawful change from one Catholic rite to another. This protects each Catholic group and assures its continuity. The law is intended to govern those already in the fold. Surely nothing should interfere with the choice of the separated Orientals upon their return. If they prefer this or that Oriental rite, they possibly have good reasons. The *bonum fidei* outweighs any objections.[32]

This argument seems to be the basis of the faculty granted by the Pontifical Commission for Russia on August 26, 1929:

> When they are found sufficiently instructed and disposed they are to be informed of their right to choose their rite, but without presuming to influence them to assume the Latin rite against their inclination. It will be better to explain the dignity and beauty of the Oriental rites, and the doctrine and teaching of the Catholic Church in regard to them, and how solicitous she is for their interests. If, however, any Russian, after duly considering everything, prefers to belong to the Latin rite, he may be admitted to it.[33]

It seems equitable to extend this privilege, explicitly granted the converts from Russian Orthodoxy, to all Oriental converts, so that, if they choose to do so, they may on their conversion to the true

[32] *The Canonical Status of Orientals in the United States*, p. 79.

[33] English text in Bouscaren, *Canon Law Digest*, I, 851. It is interesting to note that Bouscaren uses the word "right." Cf. Vermeersch-Creusen's use of the word *"ius"* in footnote 31 above. The Latin text of this passage is as follows:

"Cum sufficienter instructi atque dispositi inveniantur, de ritus electione sunt monendi, quin contra eorum propensionem ad latinum ritum assumendum eos inducere praesumatur. Satius erit dignitatem et pulcritudinem Orientalium rituum explicare, quid Ecclesia catholica de ritibus iisdem sentiat et doceat, et quantum iis favere studeat. Si quis tamen e Russis, omnibus recte perpensis, ritui latino adhaerere maluerit, eidem adscribi poterit."—*ASS,* XXI (1929), 609.

faith join the Latin rite. The conclusions from the pronouncements of the Holy See, therefore, can be summarized in this way:

1. The Oriental convert can join the corresponding Catholic Oriental rite.[84]

2. He may join any Oriental rite he chooses.

3. He may join the Latin rite, if he prefers.

4. After joining the Latin rite, he still retains the right to join his native corresponding Catholic rite.

[84] Cf. Schweigl, "De Unitate Ecclesiae Orientalis et Occidentalis restituenda, documentis S. Sedis ultimi saeculi (1848-1938) illustrata," *Periodica,* XXVIII (1939), 209-233.

CONCLUSIONS

CHAPTER I

By reason of the fact that the Instruction of the Holy Office, July 20, 1859, embodies the general law and practice of the Church, a certain universal obligation arises to follow the procedure for the reception of converts set forth therein. By reason of the legislation of the III Plenary Council of Baltimore, the Instruction has the force of particular law in the United States. The Instruction must be interpreted, however, in the light of canon 2314, § 2.

In the United States the 1942 Formula of Profession of Faith must be used.

CHAPTER II

The fact that a priest has instructed a convert does not in itself confer on him the right to receive the convert into the Church. If the convert is to be received into the Church through solemn baptism the local Ordinary has competence to confer the sacrament. When the local Ordinary has relinquished this right, the proper pastor of the convert has competence. If the formalities of reception into the Church include either the abjuration of former error or absolution from the censure of excommunication, the local Ordinary or his delegate alone are competent to receive the convert.

CHAPTER III

The errors of non-Catholic ministers regarding the nature, efficacy and obligation of Baptism do not exclude the proper intention, nor can such errors form the basis of a general presumption that all non-Catholic baptisms are invalid.

The investigation of the convert's baptism must cover two points: the examination of the ritual of the sect in which the convert was baptized; the further inquiry as to whether the ritual was exactly performed.

CHAPTER IV

The convert is not obliged to observe the Eucharistic fast before his reception into the Church through Solemn Baptism.

Whenever there is a true probability of the proper intention in one who is destitute of his senses, conditional baptism not only can but must be administered. It is not lawful, however, to presume a right intention without any assurance of even a probable sign of a desire for baptism.

CHAPTER V

In the absence of any pontifical or episcopal legislation, doubtfully baptized converts cannot be said to be under any clear obligation to make an integral confession upon their reception into the Church. In practice, however, they are always to be advised to do so.

CHAPTER VI

The opinion which includes all heretics, both formal and material, under the excommunication for heresy is contrary to the spirit of the penal legislation of the Church, and is to be disregarded in practice.

The presumption of *dolus* holds in the external forum not only in regard to the excommunication for heresy, apostasy and schism, but also in regard to the penalty of infamy for adherence to a non-Catholic sect.

CHAPTER VII

Oriental converts may join any rite they choose on their reception into the Church.

APPENDIX I

Non-Catholic Rituals[1]

GENERAL CONFERENCE OF SEVENTH-DAY ADVENTISTS

(Members in U. S. A.: 133,254)

Doctrine: *

Membership Rests on a Spiritual Basis.—The serious, solemn obligations of church membership should be impressed on every one who applies for admittance to the church. All should be faithfully taught what it means to become a member of Christ's body. Thorough instruction on all the great fundamental teachings of the church should be given every candidate for church membership before he is baptized and received. It is due every person seeking admittance to the church that he know the principles for which the church stands. Only those giving evidence of having experienced the new birth into a spiritual experience in the Lord Jesus, are prepared for acceptance into church membership. Church membership is a spiritual relationship. It should be entered into only by those who are converted. In this way only can the purity and spiritual standing of the church be maintained. It is the duty of every minister so to instruct those who accept the principles of the church that prospective members will enter the church on that basis. "As ye have therefore received Christ the Lord, so walk ye in Him: rooted and built up in Him, and established in the faith, as ye have been taught, abounding therein with thanksgiving." Col. 2:6, 7.

Baptism a Gospel Requirement.—"Go ye therefore, and teach all nations, baptizing them in the name of the Father, and of the Son, and of the Holy Ghost: teaching them to observe all things whatsoever I have commanded you: and, lo I am with you alway, even unto the end of the world." Matt. 28:19, 20.

"Then Peter said unto them, Repent, and be baptized every one of you in the name of Jesus Christ for the remission of sins, and ye shall receive the gift of the Holy Ghost." Acts 2:38.

1 The following works proved helpful in obtaining information on the doctrine and manner of administering baptism as held and practiced in the various non-Catholic sects in the United States: *Yearbook of American Churches,* H. C. Weber, editor, 1939 edition, issued under the auspices of the Federal Council of Churches of Christ in America, published by Yearbook of American Churches Press, Elmhurst, New York; *Religious Bodies, 1936,* 2 vols., Dr. T. F. Murphy, general editor, United States Department of Commerce, Bureau of the Census, Washington, D. C.: United States Government Printing Office, 1941.

* *Testimonies to Ministers,* pp. 91-128; *Church Manual,* 77-88. Published by Seventh-Day Adventist Church; Takoma Park, Washington, D. C.

Baptism a Prerequisite to Church Membership.—"Christ has made baptism the sign of entrance to His spiritual kingdom. He has made this a positive condition with which all must comply who wish to be acknowledged as under the authority of the Father, the Son, and the Holy Spirit. Before man can find a home in the church, before passing the threshold of God's spiritual kingdom, he is to receive the impress of the divine name, 'The Lord our Righteousness.'" Jr. 23:6.

Baptism is a most solemn renunciation of the world. Those who are baptized in the threefold name of the Father, the Son, and the Holy Spirit, at the very entrance of their Christian life, declare publicly that they have forsaken the service of Satan, and have become members of the royal family, children of the heavenly King. They have obeyed the command, "Come out from among them, and be ye separate, . . . and touch not the unclean thing." And to them is fulfilled the promise, "I will receive you, and will be a Father unto you, and ye shall be My sons and daughters, saith the Lord Almighty." 2 Cor. 6:17, 18.

Preparation for Baptism.—There is need of a more thorough preparation on the part of candidates for baptism. They are in need of more faithful instruction than has usually been given them. The principles of the Christian life should be made plain to those who have newly come to the truth. None can depend upon their profession of faith as proof that they have a saving connection with Christ. We are not only to say, "I believe," but to practice the truth. It is by conformity to the will of God in our words, our deportment, our character, that we prove our connection with Him.

Mode of Baptism.—Seventh-Day Adventists believe in baptism by immersion, and practice this mode only. When a person has reached a sufficient age to realize his lost state as a sinner, sincerely repents of his sins, and experiences conversion, he may, if otherwise instructed, as provided above, be considered a proper candidate for baptism.

Public Examination.—The church has a right to know concerning the faith and attitude of every individual applying for church membership. It is proper for a public examination of all candidates to be held prior to their baptism, in the presence of the church or before the church board.

The test of discipleship is not brought to bear as closely as it should be upon those who present themselves for baptism. It should be understood whether they are simply taking the name of Seventh-Day Adventists, or whether they are taking their stand on the Lord's side, to come out from the world and be separate, and touch not the unclean thing. Before baptism, there should be a thorough inquiry as to the experience of the candidates. Let this inquiry be made, not in a cold and distant way, but kindly, tenderly, pointing the new converts to the Lamb of God that taketh away the sin of the world. Bring the requirements of the gospel to bear upon the candidates for baptism.

When they give evidence that they fully understand their position, they are to be accepted. But when they show that they are following the customs and fashions and sentiments of the world, they are to be faithfully dealt with. If they feel no burden to change their course of action, they should not be retained as members of the church. The Lord wants those who compose His church to be true, faithful stewards of the grace of Christ.

Ministers Should Thoroughly Instruct Candidates Previous to Baptism.—A minister should not present any candidate for baptism and church membership until he can thoroughly satisfy the church by a public examination of the candidate that he has been well instructed and is ready for such a step. His work is not completed until he has so thoroughly instructed all the candidates that they are familiar with all points of the faith, and are prepared to assume the responsibilities of church membership. Our churches should insist on the application of this as a guiding principle in the reception of new members. One of the best means of giving such instruction is to organize baptismal classes.

Baptismal Covenant.—A summary of Fundamental Beliefs, Baptismal Vow, and Certificate of Baptism have been adopted by the denomination. A printed copy, with the Certificate of Baptism properly filled out, is furnished all those who are accepted for baptism and church membership.

Welcoming of Candidates.—After the candidates have satisfactorily answered the foregoing questions, the church body should be asked to vote their acceptance into the church, subject to baptism, which ordinance should not be unduly delayed, and this should be followed by the right hand of fellowship and a few words of welcome.

Baptismal Ceremony.—At this ceremony the deacons should make the necessary preparation and assist the male candidates into and out of the water. The deaconesses should assist all female candidates. Care should be exercised in seeing that proper attire is provided for all candidates. Robes of suitable heavy material are preferable. If such are not available, the candidates should be instructed to dress in such a manner that they will be modestly attired.

Ritual: **

Baptism is administered only by an ordained minister, or in extreme cases by an ordained church elder in his own church only, where a minister cannot be arranged for. In such cases the local elder will proceed with the administration of the rite of baptism only after he has consulted with the president of the conference or the director of the mission field in which his church is located, and has the approval of the president or superintendent.

In examining candidates for baptism, care should be taken to see that each has had a personal Christian experience, and has learned to exercise faith in God for the forgiveness of sin and for power to live in harmony with His will. The distinctive teachings of the church should be fully understood and accepted.

The following statement in common use among Seventh-Day Adventists will be found useful in placing before a candidate the essential principles which he would accept before coming into the church of which baptism constitutes the door. The minister examining would say in effect:

By going forward in baptism you indicate your purpose—

** *Manual for Ministers* (Seventh-Day Adventist Church, Takoma Park, Washington, D. C.), pp. 54-59.

To keep the commandments of God and the faith of Jesus, forsaking the world with its frivolities and amusements, taking Jesus as your divine Lord and Master, the Bible as your guide, the Holy Spirit as your teacher and sanctifier.

To live the life of a Christian through God's enabling grace, to do all in your power to enlighten others with reference to the truths of the message, and to support this cause with your tithes and offerings.

To adhere loyally to the Seventh-day Adventist Church, endeavoring to make its services a blessing, doing all in your power to maintain its integrity, and to discountenance every attempt to tarnish its fair name.

To give heed to and reverence the instruction given to the church through the Spirit of prophecy.

To live to the best of your ability in accordance with the light God has given with references to healthful and simple dress and living, totally abstaining from the use of alcoholic liquors, tobacco, opium, and other narcotic and habit-forming drugs, as well as from the use of swine's flesh in all its forms, recognizing it as a part of the Christian life to do your utmost to preserve health and strength in order to glorify God in your body as well as in your spirit, which are God's.

To adhere to New Testament simplicity, plainness, and economy in providing things necessary to this life, in order that your manner of life may be a witness to the world that you are preparing to meet the soon-coming Saviour.

The candidate, having signified his acceptance of these principles, is ready for the administration of the ordinance. Suitable robes of heavy material, properly weighted at the bottom with lead, should be kept in our larger churches. Where such garments are not procurable, the deaconess should see that women candidates are robed in sufficiently heavy material. In the absence of weights, the minister should proceed into the water slowly, taking care that the edges of the garment do not float upon the surface. When baptism is administered in a running stream, the candidate should be immersed against the current, or with head upstream. As the minister leads the candidate into the water, instruction should be given him to take a deep, full breath just before being immersed, and to hold the air in the lungs while under the water; also not to flex the knees, but to hold them in a rigid position. The candidate's tightly clasped hands should be held by the minister's left hand, while with his right hand he should firmly grasp the clothing at the back of the neck. He should be lowered carefully into the water, and care should be taken to ensure that the entire person, face and head, is completely immersed. Immediately after the candidate is lifted out of the water, his face and eyes should be dried with a handkerchief.

Before the immersion takes place, the minister should raise his right hand and solemnly utter one of the following formulas:

My brother, upon the profession of your faith in Jesus Christ as your personal Saviour, I now baptize you in the name of the Father, and of the Son, and of the Holy Ghost. Amen.

In harmony with the commandment of our Lord and Saviour, Jesus Christ,

I now baptize you in the name of the Father, and of the Son, and of the Holy Ghost. Amen.

Care should be taken to make the baptismal service as solemn as its importance demands. The administration of the ordinance should be preceded by a hymn and a prayer, and a short address may be given on the meaning of the ordinance. As each candidate is immersed, the congregation may join in singing a stanza of some suitable hymn.

CHURCH OF THE NAZARENE

(Members: 165,000)

Doctrine: *

We believe that Christian baptism is a sacrament signifying acceptance of the benefits of the atonement of Jesus Christ, to be administered to believers, as declarative of the faith in Jesus Christ as their Saviour, and full purpose of obedience in holiness and righteousness.

Baptism being the symbol of the New Testament, young children may be baptized, upon request of parents or guardians who shall give assurance for them of necessary Christian training.

Baptism may be administered by sprinkling, pouring, or immersion, according to the choice of the applicant.

Ritual: *

367. I. The Baptism of Believers

Dearly Beloved: Believing that God has given you forgiveness of sins, and spiritual life through Christ Jesus our Lord and Saviour, and that you are thus graciously prepared to receive Christian baptism, as declarative of your saving faith and covenant of obedience, you will now give avowals of your belief and purpose.

Do you believe in God, the Father Almighty, Maker of heaven and earth, and in Jesus Christ, His only-begotten Son, our Lord? that He was conceived by the Holy Ghost, born of the Virgin Mary? that He suffered under Pontius Pilate, was crucified, dead, and buried? that the third day He rose from the dead? that He ascended into heaven, and sitteth at the right hand of God the Father Almighty, and from thence shall come again to judge the quick and the dead? and

Do you believe in the Holy Ghost? the Church of God? the communion of saints? the remission of sins? the resurrection of the body? and the life everlasting?

* *Manual of the Church of the Nazarene*, History, Constitution, Government, Ritual (Kansas City, Mo.: Nazarene Publishing House, 1940), pp. 30-31; 211-212.

Answer: All this I steadfastly believe.

Will you be baptized in this faith?

Answer: I will.

Do you renounce the devil and all his works? the vain pomp and glory of the world, with all covetous desires of the flesh and of the mind?

Answer: I renounce them all.

Will you then obediently keep God's holy will and commandments, and walk in the same all the days of your life?

Answer: I will.

(The minister, asking the name, shall say):

A. B., I baptize thee in the name of the Father, and of the Son, and of the Holy Ghost. Amen.

368. II. The Baptism of Infants

Dearly Beloved: Baptism is the external seal of the new covenant of grace.

In presenting this child for Christian baptism, you must remember that it is your part and duty to see that he be taught, as soon as he shall be able to learn, the nature and the end of this holy sacrament. You shall call upon him to give reverent attendance upon appointed means of grace; see that he is taught the truth of God as contained in the Holy Scriptures, and help him, as you may be able, in the way of life.

(The minister may then ask the friends of the child to name the child, and baptize it, saying):

I baptize thee in the name of the Father, and of the Son, and of the Holy Ghost. Amen.

(The minister may offer prayer, the congregation uniting in the Lord's Prayer.)

CONGREGATIONAL CHRISTIAN CHURCHES OF THE UNITED STATES OF AMERICA

(Members: 1,049,000)

Doctrine: *

Baptism is considered as an ordinance rather than a sacrament. It is generally regarded as a ceremony of initiation into the life of the church involving four participants: (a) The God and Father of Our Lord Jesus Christ Himself, (b) the child, (c) the parents of the child, (d) the church. Moved by the Holy Spirit, the church accepts the child into the family of Christ and the church and the parents enter into a mutual covenant to bring the child up so far as in them lies in the nurture and admonition of the Lord.

* *Manual of the Congregational and Christian Churches,* Charles Emerson Burton (Boston, Mass.: Pilgrim Press).

It is not customary among us to speak of the baptized child as a member of the church. That awaits the time when on his coming to years of discretion he is "confirmed" or admitted to full standing. Nonetheless, the baptized child is definitely recognized as a member of a sort. He is considered one of the church family.

The rite has nothing magical in it; that is, it is not supposed to compel God to enter into a new relationship to the child. It is rather a response to the loving character of God which is already known and presupposed.

Ritual:

ORDER OF BAPTISM OF INFANTS

While the baptism of children may be performed at home, it is suitable that as a rule the children be brought to the church, and publicly dedicated at the altar of God.

If either parent is a professing Christian, the right of the child to baptism is conceded. Churches differ somewhat in their practice when neither parent is a member of the church. It is the custom of many of our churches to receive for baptism all infants whose parents will assent to the covenant contained in the baptismal service. It is well that the substance of the same covenant be incorporated into the baptismal certificate. Each minister should have his own certificate, neatly printed on good paper. A baptismal certificate has great value in law, in questions of legitimacy and inheritance; and it can be made to have large value in the spiritual life of the home.

Opening Sentences. (To be read by the minister or chanted by the choir as the parents come forward with their children.)

And Jesus said, Suffer little children, And forbid them not to come unto me; For of such is the kingdom of heaven. He shall feed His flock like a shepherd; He shall gather the lambs with His arm and carry them in His bosom. I will pour my spirit upon thy seed, And my blessing upon thine offspring; And they shall spring up as among the grass, As willows by the water-courses. The promise is unto you and to your children; And the righteous God keepeth covenant Unto all generations. Amen.

(The minister shall then read to those who present their children for baptism the following):

Covenant of Parents.

These children, whom God has given to you, you now bring unto Him, that you may consecrate them to Him and enter into covenant with Him in their behalf, engaging to be faithful to them in all spiritual things, and to seek by prayer, by instruction in the Scriptures, by admonition, by persuasion, and especially by a godly life and conversation, to lead them to a saving knowledge of Christ; and you recognize in this rite of Baptism the seal of that covenant, and the sign of the spiritual cleansing which it typifies?

Answer: We do.

The Baptism.

(Then shall the minister, receiving, if he will, each child in turn from the parents, hold the child in his arms and say to the parents):

Will you now name this child?

(One of the parents shall speak audibly the name of the child; and the minister, taking water, shall place it upon the head of the child, and calling the child by the name that has been given, shall say:

N . . . I baptize thee in the name of the Father, and of the Son, and of the Holy Ghost. Amen.

(The rite of baptism having been administered, the church, providing the form is in the hand of the audience, shall rise and repeat the following):

Covenant of the Church.

We also, as your fellow members in this church of Christ, do join with you in the covenant which you make this day in behalf of these your children. We recognize our relation to them as in a peculiar sense the children of the church, desiring with you to watch over them and to care for all their spiritual interests, laboring and praying for their salvation, that they may early become the subjects of that inward grace whose outward sign they have now received.

Prayer. (The Minister may offer a brief prayer for the children and their parents. The following or similar words may be employed):

Almighty God, the God of our fathers, we pray Thee to be also the God of our children. We thank Thee that Thou art our Father, and that in Thee the whole family of heaven and earth is named. Give grace to these parents that they may faithfully perform their promises in behalf of these their children: and grant Thy blessing to abide upon these little ones, that they may be true children of the covenant, heirs of God, and joint heirs with Jesus Christ. Amen.

Recessional. (After prayer by the Minister, the following chant may be sung or read, while the parents and children retire.)

Then will I sprinkle clean water upon you, And ye shall be clean; A new heart also will I give you, And a new spirit will I put within you. The mercy of the Lord is from everlasting to everlasting Upon them that fear Him, And His righteousness unto children's children. To such as keep His covenant, and to those that remember His Commandments to do them. Amen.

EVANGELICAL AND REFORMED CHURCH

(Members: Over 658,000)

Doctrine: *

A sacrament is a holy ordinance instituted by Christ Himself, in which by visible signs and means He imparts and maintains the new life.

Christ instituted two sacraments, the Holy Baptism and the Lord's Supper.

* *Evangelical Catechism,* Heidelberg Press: Philadelphia, Pa.

Holy Baptism is the sacrament by which the triune God imparts the new life unto man. Thereby man is admitted into the communion of God and the whole Christian Church.

The visible sign in Baptism is water, in which the candidate for Baptism is immersed or with which he is sprinkled in the name of the triune God; as it is written Matt. 28, 18-20.

Infants should be baptized because the new life is a divine gift of grace, which the infants are as needy and capable of receiving as adults; hence the Lord has explicitly promised His kingdom unto them.

Ritual: **

Our help is in the Name of the Lord, Who made heaven and earth. Amen.

Dearly Beloved: Our Lord and Saviour Jesus Christ has commanded us, saying, Go ye therefore, and make disciples of all nations, baptizing them in the Name of the Father, and of the Son, and of the Holy Spirit: teaching them to observe all things whatsoever I commanded you: and lo, I am with you always, even unto the end of the world.

Moreover, He has taught us that no one can enter into the kingdom of God except he be born of water and of the Spirit; and has also said, Suffer the little children to come unto Me and forbid them not: for of such is the kingdom of God.

Inasmuch as the promise of the Gospel is not only to us but also to our children, let us call upon God the Father, through our Lord Jesus Christ, that of His bounteous mercy He may grant unto *this child* Baptism with water and the Holy Spirit, receive him into Christ's holy Church, and make *him* a living *member* of the same.

Here the Congregation shall stand.

Let us pray.

Almighty and Everlasting God, the Father of our Lord Jesus Christ, we call upon Thee in behalf of *this child,* and beseech Thee to bestow upon *him* the gift of Thy baptism. Receive *him,* O Lord, into the fellowship of Thy church, and grant unto *him* life everlasting through Jesus Christ our Lord. Amen.

The Minister, addressing the Parents and Sponsors, shall say,

Dearly Beloved: You have brought *this child* here to be baptized and we have prayed that our Lord Jesus Christ would vouchsafe to receive *him,* would purify and sanctify *him* through the Holy Spirit and the washing of water, and would grant unto *him* life everlasting. I therefore ask you:

Do you renounce the vain pomp and glory of the world, the lust of the flesh, and all evil works and ways?

Answer: I do.

** *Book of Worship,* Heidelberg Press: Philadelphia, Pa. The rite here quoted, while not exactly obligatory, is used quite generally.

NOTE: The intention of the minister when baptizing is faithfully to administer the sacrament, its validity, however, not being dependent upon the purity of the minister.

Confess now the Faith into which *this child* is to be baptized.

I believe in God the Father Almighty, Maker of heaven and earth; And in Jesus Christ, His only-begotten Son our Lord: Who was conceived by the Holy Ghost, Born of the Virgin Mary: Suffered under Pontius Pilate, Was crucified, dead, and buried: He descended into hell; the third day He rose again from the dead: He ascended into heaven, and sitteth on the right hand of God the Father Almighty: From thence He shall come to judge the quick and the dead.

I believe in the Holy Ghost; the Holy Catholic Church (one Holy Universal Christian Church may be used); the Communion of Saints; the Forgiveness of sins; the Resurrection of the body; And life everlasting. Amen.

Do you sincerely desire that *this child* be baptized into this Faith?

Answer: I do.

Do you promise to instruct *this child* in the Word of God and by precept and example to bring *him* up in the nurture and admonition of the Lord?

Answer: I do.

Then the Minister shall say,

Name this child.

Thereupon the Minister shall pronounce the Christian name, and baptize the child, applying the water three times, and saying,

N........., I baptize thee in the Name of the Father, and of the Son, and of the Holy Ghost. Amen.

Almighty God, the Father of our Lord Jesus Christ, Who hath begotten thee again of water and the Holy Spirit, bless and sanctify thee unto life everlasting.

Let us pray.

We give Thee hearty thanks, most merciful Father, that it has pleased Thee to grant unto *this child* the gift of Holy Baptism and to receive *him* into Thy Church. Make *him* a living and faithful member of the Body of Christ. Bless, we beseech Thee, the home of this child, and grant wisdom and understanding to all who have the care of *him* that *he* may grow up in Thy constant fear and love and ever walk in the paths of righteousness for Thy Name's sake. Grant that *he* may know Thee to be *his* heavenly Father, through Thy Holy Spirit working in *his* heart, that *he* may be bold to confess the faith of Christ crucified; and that *he* may continue Thy faithful servant all the days of *his* life, and finally enter into Thine everlasting kingdom; through Jesus Christ our Lord. Amen.

The minister shall say,

The Lord bless thee, and keep thee: the Lord make His face to shine upon thee, and be gracious unto thee: the Lord lift up His countenance upon thee, and give thee peace. Amen.

EVANGELICAL CHURCH

(Members: 244,000)

Ritual: *

BAPTISM OF INFANTS

Invocation

In the name of God, the Father, the Son, and the Holy Spirit, we begin this sacred service.

Address to the Congregation

Baptism is a sacrament given us by our Lord as a sign and seal of redemption from sin and of union with Christ. It is to be administered both to believers and their children as belonging to the great family of God. It is our duty as a congregation to receive such children into the care of the Church of Christ and to acknowledge our responsibility to nurture them in the spiritual life, so that they may learn to know God the Father through His Son our Saviour, Jesus Christ.

Scripture

The officiating Minister may then read the following Scripture:

"The loving kindness of Jehovah is from everlasting to everlasting upon them that fear him, and his righteousness unto children's children.

"To such that keep his covenant, and to those that remember his precepts to do them" (Ps. 103:17, 18).

"He will feed his flock like a shepherd, he will gather the lambs in his arm, and carry them in his bosom" (Isa. 40:11).

"For to you is the promise, and to your children, and to all that are afar off, even as many as the Lord our God shall call unto Him" (Acts 2:39).

"And these words, which I command thee this day, shall be upon thy heart; and thou shalt teach them diligently unto thy children, and shalt talk of them when thou sittest in thy house, and when thou walkest by the way, and when thou liest down, and when thou risest up" (Deut. 6:6, 7).

Presentation

The child (children) to be baptized will now be brought forward.

While the parents bring the child (children) to be baptized, a baptismal hymn may be sung.

Address to the Parents

You are presenting this child (these children) to be dedicated to the Lord by Holy Baptism. Baptism is a sacrament given us by our Lord as a sign and

* *Book of Ritual, Evangelical Church,* prepared by Commission on Revision of Ritual (The Evangelical Publishing House, Harrisburg, Pa., 1934), pp. 7-19.

seal of redemption from sin and of union with Christ. You will recognize that this child (these children) thus presented and dedicated will fully experience the larger blessings of the Kingdom of Christ only as you instruct him (her, them) in the knowledge of the Word of God. It is therefore your sacred duty to bring up this child (these children) in the admonition and nurture of the Lord so that he (she, they) may confirm this dedication by personal choice and experience and by godly living perform the duties of a child of God as taught in His Word.

Confession of Our Faith

Let us now confess our Christian faith in the presence of God and this congregation:

I believe in God the Father Almighty, Maker of heaven and earth, and in Jesus Christ His only Son, our Lord; Who was conceived by the Holy Spirit; born of the Virgin Mary, suffered under Pontius Pilate; was crucified, dead, and buried; the third day He rose from the dead; He ascended into heaven and sitteth at the right hand of God, the Father Almighty; from thence He shall come to judge the quick and the dead.

I believe in the Holy Spirit; the holy general Church; the communion of saints; the forgiveness of sins; the resurrection of the body; and the life everlasting. Amen.

Parental Vow

Will you have this child (these children) baptized in this faith and assume your duty of instructing him (her, them) in the principles of the Christian religion as contained in the Scriptures? Will you pray for and with him (her, them), bring him (her, them) up in the fear of the Lord, and by personal example and counsel guide him (her, them) into the fellowship of the Church?

Will you do this to the best of your ability, with the help of God? Then answer:

I will.

Scripture

Let us hear the words of Jesus:

And they were bringing unto Him little children, that He should touch them: and the disciples rebuked them. But when Jesus saw it, He was moved with indignation, and said unto them, Suffer the little children to come unto Me; forbid them not: for to such belongeth the Kingdom of God. Verily I say unto you, Whosoever shall not receive the Kingdom of God as a little child, he shall in no wise enter therein. And He took them in His arms, and blessed them, laying His hands upon them (Mark 10:13-16).

Prayer

Here the Lord's Prayer may be prayed by the officiating Minister, or in unison with the congregation, if desired:

Our Father Who art in heaven, hallowed be Thy name. Thy kingdom come. Thy will be done on earth, as it is in heaven. Give us this day our daily bread. And forgive us our debts, as we forgive our debtors. And lead us not into temptation, but deliver us from evil. For Thine is the kingdom, and the power, and the glory, forever. Amen.

Baptism

Then the officiating Minister, pronouncing the full name of each child, shall baptize him, saying:

N———, I baptize thee in the name of God, the Father, the Son, and the Holy Spirit. Amen.

Prayer

Almighty God, most merciful Father, we thank Thee that Thou dost call our children unto Thee and bestow upon them the mark and seal of this sacrament. Bless this child (these children) dedicated this day unto Thee, and accept him (her, them) as a member (members) of Thy spiritual household. Grant that he (she, they) may be led to a renewal of heart and into a life of faith by the power of the Holy Spirit. Lead him (her, them) safely through the perils of life, that by Thy grace he (she, they) may be kept from all evil, and at last be received into Thine eternal Kingdom.

Bless also these parents who have this day dedicated this child (these children) to Thee. Baptize them with Thy Holy Spirit, that they may faithfully keep the vows made before Thee and this congregation. May they and their family be firmly united in the fellowship of Christ and His Church through a living faith in Thee, in Thy Son, our Saviour Jesus Christ, and in the Holy Spirit; and at least be exalted with the innumerable company of Thy people into the glorious liberty of Thy Kingdom, through Jesus Christ our Lord. Amen.

The officiating Minister shall conclude the service in a suitable manner, with the dedication, or as circumstances may permit.

Briefer Form

Presentation: cf. above.
Scripture: Mark 10:13-16, cf. above.
Address to the Parents: cf. above.
Parental Vow: cf. above.
The Lord's Prayer: cf. above.
Baptism: cf. above.
Prayer.

BAPTISM OF ADULTS

Invocation (cf. above)

Address to the Congregation

Baptism has been regarded from the earliest days of the Church as a sign of the acceptance of Jesus Christ as Saviour and Lord and the token of the renewing grace of God in the heart of the believer. It is a symbol of the Christian profession by which Christians are distinguished from others. By the observance of this sacrament we obligate ourselves to observe every Christian duty. It is also a sign of new birth, for there is a new creation whenever a man comes to be in Christ.

Scripture

The officiating Minister will call by name those who are to be baptized, and while they are standing before him he shall say:

Hear the word of the Lord spoken to His disciples, concerning this holy sacrament: Matt. 28:18-20. . . .

Moreover Peter on the day of Pentecost called upon the people saying: Acts 2:38-42. . . .

Baptismal Vows

The officiating Minister shall say to the persons to be baptized:

It is our earnest prayer that you receive this sacrament of baptism as the sign of your renewal of life through Jesus Christ and of your cleansing from the pollution of sin. In order that we may know that you do accept the obligations of this sacrament, we now ask you to answer the following questions:

Question—Have you confessed and repented of your sins, and do you put all your trust in Christ Jesus as your Saviour? If so, answer:

Yes.

Question—Are you determined by the grace of God to live the Christian life? If you are so determined, answer:

I am.

Question—Do you profess the Christian faith, as contained in the Holy Scriptures, and in this faith do you desire to be baptized? If so, answer:

I do.

Confession of Our Faith

Let us now confess our faith as expressed in the Apostles' Creed: cf. above.

Prayer

Merciful Father, grant to these Thy children (this Thy child) mercy and grace that by Thy Holy Spirit their lives (his, her life) may be made holy. Seal we pray Thee, the solemn vows they take (he, she takes) today and enrich their lives (his, her life) as they grow (he, she grows) in grace and in the knowledge of our Lord and Saviour Jesus Christ and may they (he, she) ever be numbered with Thy faithful children, through Jesus Christ our Lord. Amen.

Baptism

Then, with the congregation standing, shall the officiating Minister take each person to be baptized by the right hand, and placing the candidate conveniently near the water, according to his discretion, shall pronounce the name and then sprinkle or pour water upon him or her, or if desired, immerse in water, saying:

N——, I baptize thee in the name of God, the Father, the Son, and the Holy Spirit. Amen.

Let Us Pray

Almighty and everlasting Father, receive, we beseech Thee, and sanctify by the Holy Spirit, these persons (this person), who have (has) now been baptized in Thy Name according to Thy Word. May they (he, she) continue in the fullness of Thy grace and ever remain among the number of Thy faithful followers through Jesus Christ our Lord. Amen.

The Lord's Prayer: cf. above.

Benediction

Now unto Him that is able to guard you from stumbling, and to set you before the presence of His glory without blemish in exceeding joy, to the only God our Saviour, through Jesus Christ our Lord, be glory, majesty, dominion, and power, before all time and now and forevermore. Amen. Jude 24:25.

THE EVANGELICAL CONGREGATIONAL CHURCH

(Members: 25,000)

Doctrine: *

The sacrament of baptism is the formal application of water to an infant or to an adult believer, in the name of the Father, and of the Son, and of the Holy Spirit, as a visible sign and seal that the person so consecrated stands in a holy covenant relation to God and His people.

Ritual: *

BAPTISM OF INFANTS

Dearly Beloved: In presenting this child for baptism, you not only signify your faith in the Christian religion, which teaches the indispensable necessity of the new birth, of which holy baptism is a sacramental representation, but you also express your earnest desire that . . . may in early life be consecrated to God and His service, and that . . . may continue faithful until death and attain the life everlasting.

In order to accomplish this, it will be your duty as parents (or guardians) to teach . . . early the fear of the Lord: to watch over . . . education that . . . be not led astray; to direct . . . youthful mind to the Holy Scriptures, and . . . feet to the house of God; to restrain . . . from evil associates and habits; and as much as in you lies to bring . . . up in the nurture and admonition of the Lord.

Ques. Will you endeavor so to do, by the help of God?

Ans. I will.

* *The Creed, Ritual and Discipline of the Evangelical Congregational Church,* Adopted by the Annual and General Conferences of 1929 (Myerstown, Pa.: United Evangelical Publishing Company, 1932), pp. 19, 36-40.

Prayer

Eternal God, our Creator and Redeemer, we solemnly present this child to Thee through the ordinance of Christian baptism, pleading the atoning suffering of Thine only-begotten Son, Jesus Christ, by Whom the curse of the transgression of our first parents has been removed, and thus all infants are made heirs of the kingdom of God; and by Whom the element of water has been sanctified for this holy purpose in His own baptism; by Whom also the commandment was given to His disciples to go and teach all nations, baptizing them in the name of the Father, and of the Son, and of the Holy Ghost. Regard mercifully, we beseech Thee, O God, our earnest supplication, and bless both these parents, (or guardians), and this child. Give the parents, (or guardians), wisdom and grace to teach him (her) early, the fear of the Lord. May they first seek the guidance of the Holy Spirit for themselves, so to walk before Thee that by example, as well as precept, they may point him (her) to the life spiritual and eternal. And grant unto this child, now to be baptized, Thy grace as we present him (her) to Thee in prayer. Grant that the Holy Spirit may guide him (her) so that he (she) may follow the path of truth and holiness, and may in the future show himself (herself) an obedient child, firm in the faith, joyful in hope and grounded in love; that, dying to self, Christ may live and reign within, giving him (her) complete victory over the world, the flesh, and the devil. O Thou ever blessed God, give this child the fullness of Thy grace, that he (she) may lead a useful and happy life here, and finally live and reign forever with Thee in Thy glorious kingdom, through Jesus Christ our Lord. *Amen.*

Scripture reading, Mark 10:13-16.

"And they brought young children to Him, that He should touch them. And His disciples rebuked those that brought them; but when Jesus saw it, He was much displeased and said unto them, Suffer the little children to come unto Me, and forbid them not; for of such is the kingdom of God. Verily I say unto you, Whosoever shall not receive the kingdom of God as a little child, he shall not enter therein. And He took them up in His arms, put His hands upon them, and blessed them."—Our Father, etc. (*The parents or guardians shall then name the child.*)

When baptizing the child the Minister shall say:

A.B.—I baptize thee in the name of the Father, and of the Son, and of the Holy Ghost. *Amen.*

Benediction.

Baptism of Adults

Dearly Beloved: Our Lord commanded His Apostles, saying: "Go ye therefore, and teach all nations, baptizing them in the name of the Father, and of the Son, and of the Holy Ghost."

On the day of Pentecost Peter said to the multitude anxiously inquiring for salvation: "Repent and be baptized every one of you, in the name of Jesus

Christ, for the remission of sins, and ye shall receive the gift of the Holy Spirit."

Philip, the evangelist, went down to the city of Samaria and preached Christ to the people. And "when they believed Philip preaching the things concerning the kingdom of God, and the name of Jesus Christ, they were baptized, both men and women."

We trust that it has pleased God, in His infinite mercy, to awaken you to a sense of your guilt and danger, and to lead you to repentance and faith in the Lord Jesus Christ. By presenting yourself for this holy sacrament, you declare your purpose to live the new life, and to seek the inheritance of the saints in light.

Prayer

Eternal God, our gracious Heavenly Father, the helper of all who flee to Thee in time of need, the life of all who put their trust in Thee, and the resurrection of the dead, Thou hast encouraged us through the promise of Thy well-beloved Son, Jesus Christ, to expect great help for Thee, for He said: "Ask, and ye shall receive; seek, and ye shall find; knock, and it shall be opened unto you." Answer now, O Lord, our earnest petition offered in behalf of this person (these persons) now to be consecrated to Thy service by the solemn rite of baptism. As we apply the symbolic water, an emblem of the heavenly washing, apply Thou, O Lord, the Holy Spirit, to purify and sanctify him (her) for holy service in Thy Kingdom. Strengthen within him (her) the new life of faith, so that he (she) may be enabled to overcome the world, the flesh, and the devil; that all carnal affections and lusts may be crucified in him (her), and that the new man may be raised up into spiritual power and usefulness. Regard, we beseech Thee, our supplications in mercy, and grant that the person (these persons) now to be baptized, may receive the fullness of Thy grace, and may he (she) ever remain in the number of Thy faithful and elect children, and finally inherit everlasting life. *Amen.*

(*Then shall the Minister put the following questions to each of the persons to be baptized.*)

Ques. Dost thou believe in God the Father Almighty, Maker of heaven and earth, and in Jesus Christ, His only-begotten Son, our Lord; that He was conceived by the Holy Ghost; born of the Virgin Mary; that He suffered under Pontius Pilate, was crucified, dead, and buried; that He descended into Hades; that the third day He rose from the dead; that He ascended into heaven, and sitteth at the right hand of God, the Father Almighty, and from thence shall come again to judge the quick and the dead?

And dost thou believe in the Holy Spirit, the Holy General Church? the communion of saints? the remission of sins? the resurrection of the body, and the life everlasting?

If so, answer: yes, I do believe it.

If thou wilt be baptized in this faith answer: yes, I will.

Ques. Dost thou renounce the devil and all his works, the vain pomp and glory of the world, with all covetous desires, so that thou wilt not follow them, nor be led by the carnal desires of the flesh?

If so, answer: yes, I renounce them all.

Ques. Wilt thou then obediently keep God's holy will and commandments, and walk in the same all the days of thy life?

If so, answer: yes, by the help of God.

(Then shall the Minister ask the name of the applicant and sprinkle or pour water upon him, or, if he should desire it, immerse him in water saying):

A.B.—I baptize thee in the name of the Father, and of the Son, and of the Holy Ghost. *Amen.*

FIRE BAPTIZED HOLINESS CHURCH OF GOD

(Members: circa 6,000)

Ritual: *

The Minister may read a lesson of his own selection from the Scriptures, after which he shall address the congregation, saying:

Dearly Beloved, the last command of our Risen Lord, was to go into all the world and preach the gospel to every creature. His representative, the blessed Holy Spirit, through the Book of Acts enforced this command through the Apostles in relation to all who believe in Christ: therefore it is our abounding duty, as possessor of His grace to conform to this commission, both in the preaching of the Word and the administration of the ordinance of Baptism, as opportunity affords.

(Here let the candidates for baptism be invited to stand before the congregation, the Minister addressing them as follows):

Dearly Beloved, this act of yours coming seeking baptism in the name of the Lord, is a public testimony of your professed subjection to Christ and the grace vouchsafed you in the pardon and cleansing of your soul from sin.

But you may further declare your determination to the commandments of the Lord in the faith of Christ. You shall, in the presence of God and of this congregation, give answer to the following questions:

1. Have you faith in Christ? Ans. I have.

2. Have you the witness of the Spirit to your acceptance with God? Ans. I have.

3. Will you endeavor to walk in the fear of God and in the way of His commandments to the end of your life? Ans. I will endeavor to do so by His grace.

4. Will you endeavor to seek after the fullness of God, till all His will and good pleasure are fulfilled in you? Ans. I will endeavor to do so by His grace helping me.

* *Discipline* (Fire Baptized Holiness Church of God of the Americas, Atlanta, Ga.: Fuller Press), pp. 39-41.

5. Will you attend divine services as opportunity affords, and contribute of your means for the support and spread of the full gospel? Ans. I will.

6. Do you desire to be baptized in this faith? Ans. That is my desire.

Here the Minister shall proceed to administer the ordinance to the candidate, saying: In obedience to the command of the Word of God, I baptize thee in the name of the Father, and of the Son, and of the Holy Ghost, and may the blessings of the triune of God rest upon you.

(After the baptism of the candidate the congregation shall sing a hymn following which prayer shall be offered and the services closed with benediction.)

EVANGELICAL LUTHERAN CONGREGATIONS

Ritual: *

1. The Baptism of Infants

Dearly Beloved: Forasmuch as all men are conceived and born in sin; and our Saviour Jesus Christ has commanded Baptism, saying unto His disciples, Go ye, therefore, and teach all nations, baptizing them in the name of the Father, and of the Son, and of the Holy Ghost; and has also given the promise, He that believeth and is baptized shall be saved; and has furthermore said, Except a man be born again of water and of the Spirit, he cannot enter into the kingdom of God; I beseech you to call upon God the Father, through our Lord Jesus Christ, that of His goodness and mercy He would receive this child by Baptism into the Church of the Redeemer, and make it a living member of the same. And forasmuch as this child promises, by you its sureties, to renounce the devil and all his works, to believe in God and to serve Him; you must remember that it is your sacred duty to see that it be taught, so soon as it shall be able to learn, what a solemn promise you have made in its name. And that it may know these things the better, you should admonish it to give due heed to the instruction in church and school, and to all those things which a Christian ought to know and believe to his soul's salvation; and that so this child may be brought up to lead a godly and a Christian life; remembering always that Baptism represents unto us our profession; which is, to follow the example of our Saviour Christ, and to be made like unto Him. For as many of us as have been baptized, have put on Christ, that like as He died for us and rose again, so should we die daily unto sin and rise unto righteousness.

Let us pray:

Almighty and everlasting God, the Father of our Lord Jesus Christ, we call Thee for this child, and beseech Thee to bestow upon it the gift of Thy Baptism and Thine everlasting grace by the washing of regeneration. Receive it, O Lord, as Thou hast promised by Thy well-beloved Son, saying: Ask, and it shall be given you; seek, and ye shall find; knock, and it shall be opened unto

* *A Liturgy, for the Use of Evangelical Lutheran Congregations,* prepared by a Committee appointed by the Evan. Luth. Joint Synod of Ohio and other States (Columbus, Ohio: Lutheran Book Concern, 1923), Part II, pp. 217-224.

you. So give now unto us who ask; let us who seek, find; open the gate unto us who knock; that this child may enjoy the everlasting benediction of Thy heavenly washing, and may come to the eternal kingdom which Thou hast promised, through Jesus Christ our Lord. Amen.

Hear the words of the Gospel, written by St. Mark, in the tenth chapter.

They brought young children to Jesus, that He should touch them; etc.

Then the Minister, laying his right hand on the head of the child, shall pray:

Our Father, Who art in heaven; etc.

The Minister shall then demand of the Sponsors, as follows:

Do you, speaking for this child, renounce the devil, and all his works, and all his ways? Then answer, Yes.

Do you believe in God, the Father Almighty, Maker of heaven and earth?

And in Jesus Christ His only Son, our Lord; Who was conceived by the Holy Ghost; born of the Virgin Mary; suffered under Pontius Pilate; was crucified, dead and buried; He descended into hell; the third day He rose again from the dead; He ascended into heaven; and sitteth on the right hand of God the Father Almighty; from thence He shall come to judge the quick and the dead?

Do you believe in the Holy Ghost; the holy Christian Church, the Communion of Saints; the forgiveness of sins; the Resurrection of the body; and the Life everlasting? Then answer, Yes.

Do you desire that this child should be baptized in this faith, and do you promise to use your endeavors that it may be trained up in the nurture and admonition of the Lord? Then answer, Yes.

Baptism is not simply water, but it is the water comprehended in God's command, and connected with God's Word.

Then shall the Minister say:

Name this child.

Then shall he baptize it, saying:

N. I baptize thee in the name of the Father, and of the Son, and of the Holy Ghost. Amen.

Then laying his right hand upon the head of the child, he shall say:

Almighty God, the Father of our Lord Jesus Christ, Who hath begotten thee again of water and the Holy Ghost, and hath forgiven thee all thy sin, strengthen thee with His grace unto life everlasting. Amen.

Peace be with thee.

Let us pray:

Almighty and most merciful God and Father, we thank Thee that Thou dost graciously preserve and extend Thy Church, and hast granted to this child the new birth in holy Baptism, planted it in Jesus Christ our Lord and Saviour and made it Thy child and heir to Thy heavenly kingdom. And as this child hath now become Thine own, we humbly beseech Thee to defend and keep it in this grace, that according to all Thy good pleasure it may be faithfully and savingly brought up to the praise and honor of Thy holy name, and finally, with all Thy saints, receive the promised inheritance; through Jesus Christ our Lord. Amen.

The Minister may say:

The Lord bless thee and keep thee.
The Lord make His face shine upon thee, and be gracious unto thee.
The Lord lift up His countenance upon thee, and give thee peace. Amen.

2. The Baptism of Adults

The Baptism of adults shall, except in cases of sickness, always be administered in the church, in the presence of the congregation. The candidate having presented himself, the Minister, standing at the altar, shall say:

In the name of the Father, and of the Son, and of the Holy Ghost. Amen.

Dearly Beloved: We learn from the Word of God and from the experience of our own lives, that all men are conceived and born in sin, and that we must all assuredly perish, except our blessed Lord and Saviour, the only-begotten Son of God, deliver us from our sins and guilt. Inasmuch as this person, who now desires to be baptized, is of like sinful and depraved nature, and our Lord Jesus Christ has borne in His own body the sins of the whole world, and has redeemed and delivered us from death and from everlasting damnation: I beseech you to call upon God, through our Lord Jesus Christ, that of His goodness and mercy He will receive this person, truly repenting and coming unto Him by faith, into the kingdom of His grace, and bestow upon him everlasting life; confidently believing that He will accept your offering and intercession of love, and will assuredly hear our prayer.

Let us pray:

Almighty and immortal God, the aid of all that need, the helper of all that flee to Thee for succor, the life of them that believe, and the resurrection of the dead; we call upon Thee for this thy servant who seeketh the gift of Thy Baptism and Thine everlasting grace through regeneration by the Holy Ghost. Receive Him, O Lord, according to Thy Word and promise: Ask, and it shall be given you; seek, and ye shall find; knock, and it shall be opened unto you. So give now Thy heavenly good to him that asketh; let him that seeketh, find; and open the gate to him that knocketh; that he may have the everlasting benediction of Thy heavenly washing, and receive the promised kingdom of Thy grace; through Jesus Christ our Lord. Amen.

Then shall the Minister say:

Hear the words of our Lord:

All power is given unto Me, in heaven and on earth. Go ye therefore and teach all nations, baptizing them in the name of the Father, and of the Son, and of the Holy Ghost; teaching them to observe all things, whatsoever I commanded you; and lo, I am with you always, even unto the end of the world.

In like manner He says: He that believeth and is baptized shall be saved; but he that believeth not shall be damned.

In accordance with this command of our Lord Jesus, this person has been instructed in the saving doctrines of the Gospel, and now desires holy Baptism. Therefore let us with the laying on of hands invoke God's blessing.

Let us pray:

Our Father, Who art in heaven; etc.

Then shall the Minister say to the person to be baptized:

The Lord preserve thy coming in and thy going out from this time forth, and even forevermore.

The Minister shall then ask:

Do you renounce the devil, and all his works, and all his ways? Then answer, Yes.

Do you believe in God the Father Almighty, Maker of heaven and earth? And in Jesus Christ, His only Son, our Lord; Who was conceived by the Holy Ghost, born of the Virgin Mary; suffered under Pontius Pilate, was crucified, dead and buried; He descended into hell; the third day He rose again from the dead; He ascended into heaven, and sitteth on the right hand of God the Father Almighty; from thence He shall come to judge the quick and the dead? Do you believe in the Holy Ghost; the Holy Christian Church; the Communion of Saints; the forgiveness of sins; the Resurrection of the body; and the Life everlasting. Then answer: Yes.

Do you desire to be baptized? Then answer: Yes.

Will you continue steadfast in the true Christian faith, as it is confessed by our Evangelical Lutheran Church, and serve the Lord Jesus Christ by a godly life, even unto the end? Then answer: Yes, I will, by the help of God.

The Minister shall then turn to the font and say:

Baptism is not simply water, but it is the water comprehended in God's Command, and connected with God's Word.

Then shall the person to be baptized kneel, and the Minister shall baptize him, saying:

N. I baptize thee in the name of the Father, and of the Son, and of the Holy Ghost. Amen.

Then laying his right hand upon the head of the person baptized, he shall say:

Almighty God, the Father of our Lord Jesus Christ, Who through water and the Holy Spirit has forgiven thee all thy sins, strengthen and keep thee by His grace unto life everlasting.

Let us pray:

Almighty and most merciful God the Father, we thank Thee that Thou dost graciously preserve and extend Thy Church, and hast granted to this Thy servant the grace of the new birth in holy Baptism, planted him in Jesus Christ, our Lord and Saviour, and made him Thy child, and heir to Thy heavenly kingdom. And as he hath now become Thine own, we humbly beseech Thee to defend and keep him steadfast in this grace, that according to all Thy good pleasure he may walk in Thy ways, to the praise and honor of Thy holy name, and finally, with all Thy saints, receive the promised inheritance; through Jesus Christ our Lord. Amen.

The service may be closed with a Hymn and the Benediction.

EVANGELICAL LUTHERAN AUGUSTANA SYNOD OF NORTH AMERICA

(Members: 340,000)

Ritual: *

In the Name of the Father, and of the Son, and of the Holy Spirit.

Beloved in the Lord. From the Word of God we learn that all men are born in sin, but also that Jesus Christ has come into the world to save sinners. Our Lord and Saviour has testified and said: "Except one be born of water and the Spirit, he cannot enter into the kingdom of God" (John 3:5). Therefore, according to His commandment, we receive this child (these children) into the Christian Church through the washing of regeneration, and beseech our Lord and Saviour graciously to receive him (her, or them) and endue him (her, or them) with the power of the Holy Spirit unto a living faith and true godliness. To this end may God grant His blessing for the sake of Jesus Christ. Amen.

Lift up your hearts unto God.

Our Lord Jesus Christ Himself instituted Holy Baptism, when He said to His disciples:

"All authority hath been given unto Me in heaven and on earth. Go ye therefore, and make disciples of all the nations, baptizing them into the Name of the Father, and of the Son, and of the Holy Spirit: teaching them to observe all things whatsoever I commanded you: and lo, I am with you always, even unto the end of the world" (Matt. 28:18-20).

Hear also the holy and comforting Gospel according to St. Mark (Mark 10:13-16).

Then the Minister shall place his hand upon the head of the child and pray:

The Lord's Prayer.

The Merciful and Eternal God, Who alone saves from all evil; and Who has graciously called thee to be a partaker of the inheritance of the saints in light, through our Saviour Jesus Christ, deliver thee from the power of darkness and preserve thee in His truth and fear, now and forevermore. Amen.

Let us hear the Christian faith, which we confess, and into which this child is (these children are) to be baptized.

I believe in God the Father Almighty, Maker of heaven and earth.

And in Jesus Christ, His only Son, our Lord: Who was conceived by the Holy Spirit; born of the Virgin Mary; suffered under Pontius Pilate; was crucified, dead, and buried; He descended into hell; the third day He rose again from the dead; He ascended into heaven; and sitteth on the right hand of God the Father Almighty; from thence He shall come to judge the quick and the dead.

* *The Church Service Book,* of the Evangelical Lutheran Augustana Synod of North America (Augustana Book Concern, Rock Island, Ill., 1928), pp. 151-153. The form for adults is essentially the same, with few and minor differences. This rite is not optional but obligatory for all ministers of this sect.

I believe in the Holy Spirit; the Holy Christian Church; the Communion of saints; the forgiveness of sins; the Resurrection of the body; and the Life everlasting.

The Minister shall continue:

Do you desire that this child (these children) shall upon this confession be baptized, and by baptism be received into the Communion of Christ and His Church?

The Parents or Sponsors answer:

Yes.

Then the Minister shall three times pour water upon child's head and say:

I baptize thee, N. N., into the Name of the Father, and of the Son, and of the Holy Spirit. Amen.

Then shall the Minister say:

Let us give thanks and pray:

Almighty, Eternal God, our Heavenly Father, we give Thee hearty thanks that Thou dost continually preserve and increase Thy holy Christian Church, and that Thou hast now permitted this child (these children) to receive the washing of regeneration unto eternal life. We pray thee to preserve him (her, or them) in the grace of baptism, so that he (she, or they) may grow up in Thy fear, and in the power of Christ's resurrection walk in newness of life, ever pleasing to Thee, and finally receive the inheritance of the saints in heaven; through the same, Thy Son, Jesus Christ, our Lord. Amen.

The Minister shall pronounce the Benediction upon the child:

The Lord bless thee, and keep thee. The Lord make His face shine upon Thee, and be gracious unto thee. The Lord lift up His countenance upon thee, and give thee peace. In the Name of the Father, and of the Son, and of the Holy Spirit. Amen.

Thereupon the Minister shall admonish the Sponsors as follows:

Dearly Beloved. This child (these children) through the washing of regeneration, has (have) become a child (children) of God and joint heir(s) with Jesus Christ. It becomes you who have witnessed this sacred act diligently to assist this child (these children) with Christian love and faithful prayers. Take solemnly to heart the obligation of the Church, especially in the event of the death of the parents before the child is (these children are) of age, to rear this child (these children) in the fear and admonition of the Lord, to the end that it (they) may faithfully keep the gifts of grace received in Holy Baptism.

The Minister shall continue:

Let us now hear the exhortation of God's Word to us who have received the grace of baptism (Col. 2:6, 7):

Glory be to the Father, and to the Son, and to the Holy Spirit; as it was in the beginning, is now, and ever shall be, world without end. Amen.

Then the Minister shall say to the Sponsors:

Depart in peace.

NORWEGIAN LUTHERAN CHURCH

(Members: 536,000)

Ritual: *

Baptism of Infants

When a stanza of a Baptismal Hymn has been sung, the Minister shall say:

Hath this child been privately baptized?

If the child has not been privately baptized, the Minister shall proceed as follows:

Dearly Beloved: Forasmuch as by one man sin entered into the world, and death by sin, and so death passed upon all men, for that all have sinned, so, by the offense of one, judgment came upon all men to condemnation. For which reason we are all by nature the children of wrath, and have come short of the glory of God. But as by one man's disobedience many were made sinners, so, by the obedience of one, namely, Jesus Christ, shall many be made righteous. For as sin hath reigned unto death, even so might grace reign through righteousness unto eternal life by Jesus Christ, Who was delivered for our offenses, and was raised again for our justification.

But our Lord Jesus Christ, in order that we may obtain right and access to this divine grace, hath instituted the Sacrament of Holy Baptism, which is the washing of regeneration, and renewing of the Holy Ghost. For Baptism is not the putting away of the filth of the flesh, but the answer of a good conscience toward God, by the resurrection of Jesus Christ. In order, then, that this child (these children) which is (are) conceived in sin and born in iniquity, may see the kingdom of God, into which our Lord Jesus Christ Himself hath said that none can enter, except he be born again of water and of the Spirit, we will now, in the Name of our Lord Jesus, receive it (them) through holy Baptism into His believing Church, that it (they), as a member (members) of His Body, may partake of His salvation.

Let us hear God's Word and command concerning holy Baptism.

Our Lord Jesus Christ saith in the 28th chapter of St. Matthew:

All power is given unto Me in heaven and in earth. Go ye therefore, and make disciples of all the nations, baptizing them in the Name of the Father, and of the Son, and of the Holy Ghost; teaching them to observe all things whatsoever I have commanded you; and, lo, I am with you always, even unto the end of the world.

The Sign of the Cross

Receive the sign of the holy cross, upon thy brow, and upon thy breast, in token that thou shalt believe on the crucified Lord Jesus Christ.

* *Abridgment of the Ministerial Acts of the Norwegian Lutheran Church* (Minneapolis, Minn.: Augsburg Publishing House), pp. 3-10. The doctrine of this sect is clearly contained in the ritual.

Let Us Pray

Almighty and everlasting God, the Father of our Lord Jesus Christ: We call upon Thee for this child (these children) which seeketh (seek) the gift of Thy Baptism unto regeneration and everlasting life. Lord receive it (them). And, as Thou hast said: Ask, and it shall be given you; seek, and ye shall find; knock, and it shall be opened unto you; bestow Thy gifts upon the one which now asketh (upon those which now ask), and open the door unto the one (unto those) which knocketh (which knock), that it (they) may receive the everlasting blessing in this heavenly washing, and may inherit Thy kingdom which Thou hast promised unto us all; through Jesus Christ, our Lord.

The Sponsors and the Assistant (Precentor) shall say: Amen.

Let us hear the Holy Gospel as written by St. Mark:

And they brought young children to Jesus, that He should touch them; and His disciples rebuked those that brought them, but when Jesus saw it, He was much displeased and said unto them: Suffer the little children to come unto Me, and forbid them not; for of such is the kingdom of God. Verily I say unto you, whosoever shall not receive the kingdom of God as a little child, he shall not enter therein. And He took them up in His arms, put His hands upon them, and blessed them.

Therefore, by devout prayer to God, let us help this little child (these little children) to obtain such blessing.

The Minister laying his right hand upon the head of the child (the heads of the children) shall say:

Our Father, Who art in heaven; hallowed be Thy Name; Thy kingdom come; Thy will be done on earth, as it is in heaven; give us this day our daily bread; and forgive us our trespasses, as we forgive those who trespass against us; and lead us not into temptation; but deliver us from evil; for Thine is the kingdom, and the power, and the glory, for ever and ever. Amen.

The Sponsors and the Assistant (Precentor) shall say: Amen.

The child is now brought nearer to the Font (each child separately, if there be several). The Minister shall then say:

The Lord preserve thy coming in and thy going out, from this time forth even for evermore.

The Sponsors and the Assistant (Precentor) shall say: Amen.

The Minister shall then ask the child's name.

Minister:

N. Dost thou renounce the devil, and all his works, and all his ways?

The one who carries the child shall answer:

I do.

Minister:

Dost thou believe in God, the Father Almighty, Maker of heaven and earth?

Answer, I do.

Dost thou believe in Jesus Christ, His only Son, our Lord; Who was conceived by the Holy Ghost, born of the Virgin Mary; suffered under Pontius

Pilate; was crucified, dead, and buried; descended into hell; the third day rose again from the dead; ascended into heaven, and sitteth on the right hand of God, the Father Almighty; whence He shall come to judge the quick and the dead?

Answer, I do.

Dost thou believe in the Holy Ghost; the Holy Christian Church; the Communion of Saints; the forgiveness of sins; the Resurrection of the body; and the Life everlasting?

Answer, I do.

Wilt thou be baptized in this faith?

Answer, I will.

The Minister shall then apply water three times upon the child's head, and shall say:

N. I baptize thee in the Name of the Father, and of the Son, and of the Holy Ghost.

The Sponsors and the Assistant (Precentor) shall say: Amen.

The christening cap is now put upon the child's head, after which the Minister, with the laying on of hands, shall say:

Almighty God, the Father of our Lord Jesus Christ, Who hath begotten thee again of water and the Holy Ghost, and hath forgiven thee all thy sins, strengthen thee with His grace unto life everlasting.

Sponsors and Assistant: Amen.

Minister: Peace be with thee.

Sponsors and Assistant: Amen.

The child (children) having thus been baptized, the Minister shall say:

Blessed be the God and Father of our Lord Jesus Christ, Who according to His abundant mercy hath begotten us again unto a lively hope by the resurrection of Jesus Christ from the dead.

Sponsors and Assistant: Amen.

The Minister shall then say to the Sponsors:

Dear Christian Friends: You, who have been sponsors for this child (these children), are to be witnesses that it has (they have) been baptized in the Name of the Holy Trinity. You are also to remember it (them) in your prayers before God; and, if the parents should die before it has (they have) arrived at the age of discretion, you should, as far as possible, see that it is (they are) instructed in the Catechism, so that, in riper years, it (they) may abide in Christ, even as now, through Baptism, it has (they have) been grafted into Him.

Minister: Peace be with thee.

Sponsors and Assistant: Amen.

Instead of this Salutation of Peace the Minister shall pronounce the Benediction, when Baptism is not administered in connection with the regular Service. The baptismal Act shall then, as at the regular Service, begin and close with a stanza of a suitable Hymn.

THE LUTHERAN FREE CHURCH

(Members: 48,000)

Doctrine:

The Lutheran Free Church is one in doctrine with the other Lutheran churches of this country. That is, it unreservedly accepts the historic confessions of the Lutheran Church, Luther's small catechism, the unaltered Augsburg confession.

In regard to Baptism, it teaches that it is a sacrament of regeneration, which includes forgiveness of sin and the new birth.

Ritual: *

ORDER FOR THE BAPTISM OF INFANTS

Hymn.

Hath this child been privately baptized?

Dearly Beloved: Forasmuch as by one man sin entered into the world, and death by sin, and so death passed upon all men, for that all have sinned, so by the offense of one, judgment came upon all men unto condemnation. We are all, therefore, by nature the children of wrath, and have come short of the glory of God. But as through one man's disobedience many were made sinners, so through the obedience of one shall many be made righteous. For as sin reigned unto death, even so might grace reign through righteousness unto eternal life by Jesus Christ our Lord, Who was delivered for our offenses and was raised again for our justification.

But in order that we might have right and access to this divine grace, our Lord Jesus Christ hath instituted the sacrament of Holy Baptism, which is the washing of regeneration and the renewing of the Holy Spirit. For Baptism is not the putting away of the filth of the flesh, but the answer of a good conscience toward God, through the resurrection of Jesus Christ. Therefore, in order that this child, which is conceived in sin and born in iniquity, may see the kingdom of God, into which our Lord Jesus Christ Himself hath said that none can enter except he be born anew of water and of the Spirit, we will now, in the name of our Lord Jesus, receive it through Holy Baptism into His believing Church, that it, as a member of His body, may partake of His salvation.

Let us hear the word and command of God concerning this Sacrament. Our Lord Jesus Christ saith in the 28th Chapter of St. Matthew:

All authority hath been given unto Me in heaven and on earth. Go ye therefore, and make disciples of all nations, baptizing them into the Name of the Father, and of the Son, and of the Holy Spirit: teaching them to observe all things whatsoever I have commanded you. And lo, I am with you alway, even unto the end of the world.

(Sign of the cross.)

* *Altar Book* (pocket edition, Minneapolis, Minn.: Augsburg Publishing House), pp. 1-8. This ritual is also used by the Norwegian Lutheran Church of America.

Receive the sign of the holy cross, upon thy brow and upon thy breast, as a token that thou shalt believe on the crucified Lord Jesus Christ.

Let us pray.

Almighty and everlasting God, the Father of our Lord Jesus Christ; we call upon Thee for this child who seeketh the gift of Thy Baptism unto regeneration and everlasting life. Lord, receive it! And, as Thou hast said, Ask, and it shall be given you; seek, and ye shall find; knock, and it shall be opened unto you; bestow Thy gifts upon the one who now asketh, and open the door unto the one who knocketh, that it may receive the everlasting benediction in this heavenly washing, and may inherit Thy kingdom, which Thou hast promised unto us all; through Jesus Christ our Lord.

Sponsors and Assistant: Amen.

Let us hear the holy Gospel as it is written by St. Mark:

And they were bringing unto Him little children, that He should touch them: And the disciples rebuked those that brought them. And when Jesus saw it, He was moved with indignation, and said unto them, Suffer the little children to come unto Me; and forbid them not; for to such belongeth the kingdom of God. Verily I say unto you, whosoever shall not receive the kingdom of God as a little child, he shall in no wise enter therein. And He took them in His arms, and blessed them, laying His hands upon them.

Let us therefore, by devout prayer to God, help this little child to obtain such blessing.

(With laying on of hands):

Our Father, Who art in heaven; hallowed by Thy Name; Thy kingdom come; Thy will be done on earth as it is in heaven; give us this day our daily bread; and forgive us our trespasses, as we forgive those who trespass against us; and lead us not into temptation; but deliver us from evil; for Thine is the kingdom, and the power, and the glory, for ever and ever. Amen.

The Lord preserve thy coming in and thy going out, from this time forth even forevermore.

Sponsors and Assistant: Amen.

(The name of the child is here asked.)

N., Dost thou renounce the devil, and all his works, and all his ways?

Answer, I do.

Dost thou believe in God, the Father Almighty, Maker of heaven and earth?

Answer, I do.

Dost thou believe in Jesus Christ, His only Son, our Lord; Who was conceived by the Holy Ghost, born of the Virgin Mary; suffered under Pontius Pilate; was crucified, dead, and buried; descended into hell; the third day He rose again from the dead; ascended into heaven, and sitteth at the right hand of God, the Father Almighty; when He shall again come to judge the quick and the dead?

Answer, I do.

Dost thou believe in the Holy Ghost; the Holy Christian Church; the Communion of Saints; the forgiveness of sins; the resurrection of the body; and the life everlasting?

Answer, I do.

Wilt thou be baptized into this Christian faith?

Answer, I will.

** N., I baptize thee in the Name of the Father, and of the Son, and of the Holy Ghost.

(With laying on of hands): Almighty God, the Father of our Lord Jesus Christ, Who hath begotten thee again of water and the Holy Ghost and hath forgiven thee all thy sins, strengthen thee with His grace unto life everlasting.

Sponsors and Assistant: Amen.

Peace be with thee.

Sponsors and Assistant: Amen.

Blessed be the God and Father of our Lord Jesus Christ, Who according to His abundant mercy hath begotten us again unto a lively hope by the resurrection of Jesus Christ from the dead.

Sponsors and Assistant: Amen.

Dear Christian Friends: As sponsors for this child you are to be witnesses that it hath been baptized in the Name of the Holy Trinity. You are also to remember it before God in prayer; and, if the parents die before it shall have arrived at the age of discretion, you shall as far as possible see to it that it is instructed in the catechism, so that in riper years it may abide in Christ, even as now through Baptism it hath been grafted into Him. Peace be with you.

Sponsors and Assistant: Amen.

Hymn.

Baptism of Children in Church

The pastor shall beforehand ascertain which children have been privately baptized and which children are to be baptized.

The act begins with a baptismal hymn.

Thereupon the pastor says:

Dear Christians! Let us hear the command of our Lord Jesus Christ concerning Holy Baptism:

All authority hath been given unto me in heaven and on earth. Go ye therefore, and make disciples of all the nations, baptizing them into the name of the Father, and of the Son, and of the Holy Spirit: teaching them to observe all things whatsoever I commanded you: and lo, I am with you always, even unto the end of the world.

Let us next hear how graciously our Lord Jesus Christ receives little children and opens the door of the Kingdom of God for them:

And they were bringing unto Him little children, etc. (cf. above).

So in thankfulness and in faith we bring our children to the Lord in Holy Baptism, in order that they may share in His blessing and though they are sin-

** The customary manner of administering Baptism is not immersion nor sprinkling, but pouring the water on the child's head.

ful human beings under the law of sin and of death, may become children of God by grace in the washing of regeneration and renewing of the Holy Spirit.

Let us pray:

Eternal and Almighty God! We thank Thee that in Thy Church Thou hast instituted Baptism into Thy holy name, and that in Baptism Thou dost promise to be our Father, to save us from sin by Thy Son, our Redeemer, and to regenerate and sanctify us by Thy Spirit.

We pray Thee, receive this child (children) which we today bring before Thee and let it (them) receive the eternal blessings of Holy Baptism. Grant that it (they) may grow up in Thy Church as Thy child (children). Let the fear and love of God prevail in its (their) home. Teach it to fear and love Thee and preserve it (them) from all evil until it (they) shall come unto Thee in Thy heavenly Kingdom! Amen.

Let us confess the renunciation and the faith into which we baptize our children:

I renounce the Devil and all his works and all his ways.

I believe in God the Father Almighty, Maker of heaven and earth.

I believe in Jesus Christ His only Son, our Lord; Who was conceived by the Holy Spirit, born of the Virgin Mary; suffered under Pontius Pilate, was crucified, dead, and buried; He descended into hell; the third day He arose again from the dead; He ascended into heaven, and sitteth on the right hand of God the Father Almighty; from thence He shall come to judge the quick and the dead.

I believe in the Holy Spirit; the holy Christian Church, the Communion of Saints; the forgiveness of sins; the resurrection of the body, and the life everlasting. Amen.

The child—if there are several, then each separately—is then brought forward to the baptismal font, and its sponsors and parents, if they are present, likewise step forward or rise.

The pastor says to the sponsors and parents:

Will ye that this child shall be baptized into the name of the Father, and of the Son, and of the Holy Spirit and be reared in the Christian renunciation and faith?

The one holding the child answers aloud:

I will.

The pastor says:

The Lord keep thy coming in and thy going out from this time forth and for ever more!

Receive the sign of the holy cross upon thy brow and upon thy breast as a token that thou shalt believe on the crucified Lord Jesus Christ.

The pastor asks for the name of the child. Thereupon he pours water upon the child's head three times and says:

N. (child's name), I baptize thee into the name of the Father, and of the Son, and of the Holy Spirit. Amen.

Placing his hand upon the child's head:

The Almighty God, the Father of our Lord Jesus Christ, Who hath made thee His child in Holy Baptism and hath received thee into His believing Church, strengthen thee with His grace unto life everlasting!

Peace be with thee!

When the child (children) has thus been baptized, the pastor says:

Blessed be the God and Father of our Lord Jesus Christ, Who according to His great mercy begat us again unto a living hope by the resurrection of Jesus Christ from the dead!

Let us pray:

Our Father, etc. . . . Amen.

You who are sponsors for this child are to be witnesses that it has been baptized into the name of the Father, and of the Son, and of the Holy Spirit. You are also to remember it before God in your prayers, and, as far as possible assist in rearing it in the faith and fear of God, so that it may abide in Christ when it grows up, even as now through Baptism it has been grafted into Him!

Peace be with you! Amen.

Thereupon the baptismal act closes with an appropriate hymn.

LUTHERAN—MISSOURI SYNOD

(Members: 1,200,000)

Manner of Administering Baptism: *

1. The Baptism of Infants

First Form

Dearly Beloved: (We learn from the Word of God that all men from the fall of Adam are conceived and born in sin, and so are under the wrath of God, and would be lost forever, unless delivered by Our Lord Jesus Christ.

This child, then, is also by nature sinful and under the wrath of God. But the Father of all mercy and grace hath promised and sent His Son Jesus Christ, Who hath borne the sins of the whole world, and redeemed and saved little children, no less than others, from sin, death, and everlasting condemnation. He also commanded that little children should be brought to Him, and graciously received and blessed them.

Wherefore I beseech you, out of Christian love, to intercede for *this child*, to bring *him* to the Lord Jesus, and to ask for *him* the forgiveness of sin and the grace and salvation of Christ's kingdom, nowise doubting that our dear Lord favorably regardeth such work of love, and certainly heareth our prayers.

And) Forasmuch as our Lord hath commanded Baptism, saying to His disciples, in the last chapter of Matthew: "Go ye, therefore, and teach all na-

* *Liturgy and Agenda* (St. Louis, Mo.: Concordia Publishing House, 1936), pp. 329-340. This ritual is also used in the Finnish American Evangelical Lutheran National Church, and in the Norwegian Synod of the American Evangelical Lutheran Church.

tions, baptizing them in the name of the Father, and of the Son, and of the Holy Ghost"; and also hath given promise, in the last chapter of Mark: "He that believeth and is baptized shall be saved": it is meet and right that, in obedience to His command, and trusting in His promise, you shall bring *this child* to be baptized in His name.

(The Exhortation to the Sponsors [see below after Mark 10] may be read at this place.)

Then the Minister may make the sign of the cross on the child's forehead and breast, saying:

Receive the sign of the holy cross, both upon the fore head ✠ and upon the breast, ✠ in token that thou hast been redeemed by Christ the Crucified.

Let us pray.

1

Almighty and eternal God, Father of our Lord Jesus Christ, we pray Thee, bestow upon this N., here presented for Holy Baptism, Thine everlasting grace through regeneration by the Holy Ghost. Receive *him*, O Lord, according to Thy Word and promise: "Ask, and it shall be given you; seek, and ye shall find; knock, and it shall be opened unto you"; and grant that *he* may obtain the everlasting blessing of this heavenly washing and come to the kingdom which Thou hast promised; through Jesus Christ, our Lord. Amen.

2

Almighty and everlasting God, Who according to Thy righteous judgment didst destroy the unbelieving world by the Flood, and according to Thy great mercy didst save faithful Noah and his family; Who didst drown obdurate Pharaoh with all his host in the Red Sea, and didst safely lead Thy people Israel through the midst thereof, prefiguring thereby this washing of Thy Holy Baptism; and who, by the Baptism of Thy beloved Son, our Lord Jesus Christ, didst sanctify and ordain Jordan and all waters for a saving flood and an abundant washing away of sin: we beseech Thee, of Thine infinite mercy to look with favor upon *this child* and to bless *him* in the Spirit with true faith, that, by this salutary flood, there may be drowned and destroyed in *him* all that *he* hath inherited from Adam, and *himself* added thereto; and that, being separated from the number of the únbelieving, *he* may be securely kept in the holy ark of the Christian Church, and ever serve Thy name with fervent spirit and joyful hope, to the end that, together with all believers, *he* may be accounted worthy to attain to everlasting life; through Jesus Christ, our Lord. Amen.

Hear the Holy Gospel of St. Mark which saith: "And they brought young children to Jesus, that He should touch them; and His disciples rebuked those that brought them. But when Jesus saw it, He was much displeased, and said unto them, Suffer the little children to come unto Me, and forbid them not; for of such is the kingdom of God. Verily, I say not enter therein. And He took them up in His arms, put His hands upon them, and blessed them" (Mark 10:13-16).

It also behooves you as sponsors, while confessing in this sacred act the faith of the Christian Church in the Triune God, in Whose name *this child* is to be baptized, to bear witness publicly in the *child's* stead that by Holy Baptism as a means of grace *he* obtains and possesses the saving faith in the one true God, and renounces the devil and his wicked works. Moreover, after *this child* has been baptized, you should at all times remember *him* in your prayers, put *him* in mind of *his* Baptism, and, as much as in you lies, lend your counsel and aid (especially if *he* should lose *his* parents), that *he* may be brought up in the true knowledge and fear of God, according to the teachings of the Lutheran Church, and faithfully keep the baptismal covenant unto the end. This, then, you intend gladly and willingly to do?

Answer: Yes.

May God enable you both to will and to do this charitable work, and with His grace fulfill what we are unable to do. Amen.

In order to implore the blessing of our Lord Jesus Christ upon *this child,* let us pray:

Then the Minister, laying his right hand upon the head of the child, shall say, and the Sponsors and all present may say with him:

Our Father, Who art in heaven; hallowed be Thy name; Thy kingdom come; Thy will be done on earth as it is in heaven; give us this day our daily bread; and forgive us our trespasses, as we forgive those who trespass against us; and lead us not into temptation; but deliver us from evil; for Thine is the kingdom, and the power, and the glory, forever and ever. Amen.

The Lord preserve thy coming in and thy going out from this time forth and even forevermore. ✠ Amen.

Then may the Minister say to the Sponsors:

I now ask you to answer, in the name and in the stead of *this child,* the questions which I address to *him,* to signify thereby that which God in and through Baptism works in *him.*

N., Dost thou renounce the devil, and all his works, and all his ways?

Answer: I do.

Dost thou believe in God the Father Almighty, Maker of heaven and earth?

Answer: I do.

Dost thou believe in Jesus Christ, His only Son, our Lord; Who was conceived by the Holy Ghost; born of the Virgin Mary; suffered under Pontius Pilate; was crucified, dead and buried; He descended into hell; the third day He rose again from the dead; He ascended into heaven; and sitteth on the right hand of God the Father Almighty; from thence He shall come to judge the quick and the dead?

Answer: I do.

Dost thou believe in the Holy Ghost; the holy Christian Church; the Communion of Saints; the forgiveness of sins; the resurrection of the body; and the life everlasting?

Answer: I do.

Wilt thou be baptized into this Christian faith?

Answer: I will.

Then shall the Minister apply water three times upon the head of the child, as he names each person of the Holy Trinity:

N., I baptize thee in the name of the Father, and of the Son, and of the Holy Ghost. ✠ Amen.

Then the Minister, laying his right hand upon the head of the child, shall say:

Almighty God, the Father of our Lord Jesus Christ, Who hath begotten thee again of water and the Spirit, and hath forgiven thee all thy sins, strengthen thee with His grace unto life everlasting. Amen.

Peace be with thee. ✠ Amen.

The Minister may add:

Let us pray.

Almighty and most merciful God and Father, we thank and praise Thee that Thou dost graciously preserve and extend Thy Church, and hast granted to *this child* the new birth in Holy Baptism, and made *him a member* of Thy dear Son, our Lord Jesus Christ, and *an heir* of Thy heavenly kingdom. We humbly beseech Thee, that, as *he* hath now become Thy *child,* Thou wouldst keep *him* in *his* baptismal grace, that, according to all Thy good *he* may be faithfully brought up to lead a godly life to the praise and honor of Thy holy name, and finally, with all Thy saints, obtain the promised inheritance in heaven, through Jesus Christ, our Lord. Amen.

Second Form

(Without Sponsors)

Dearly Beloved: In bringing this child to Baptism, you are observing the will of the Lord, Who commanded Baptism, saying in the last chapter of Matthew: "Go ye and teach all nations, baptizing them in the name of the Father, and of the Son, and of the Holy Ghost." We should, indeed, value this Sacrament highly, particularly since it is the only means of grace God has given us for little children. Little children, though seemingly innocent, are by birth and nature sinful, and without forgiveness would be lost forever. We know that God gave His Son into death to atone for the sins of all, that whosoever believeth in Him should not perish, but have everlasting life. But as little children are as yet unable to understand the Gospel, faith cannot be worked in them by telling them of Christ. We can never sufficiently thank God, therefore, that He has made Baptism a means whereby He works in little children with His divine grace, turning their hearts to faith, cleansing away their sins, and receiving them into His kingdom. The simple act of Baptism has such wonderful power because the Almighty God Himself works in it through His Word. "Baptism is not simple water only, but it is the water comprehended in God's command and connected with God's Word." The divine Word makes Baptism what Paul calls it, Titus 3, "the washing of regeneration and renewing of the Holy Ghost." For this reason Christ says in the last chapter of Mark: "He that believeth and is baptized shall be saved."

It is meet and right, therefore, that we should here, in the sight of God, administer and employ this blessed Sacrament in the fear of God, with due reverence, and with sincere devotion.

Receive the sign of the holy cross, both upon the forehead ✠ and upon the breast, ✠ in token that thou hast been redeemed by Christ the Crucified.

Hear the holy Gospel of St. Mark, which saith (Mark 10:13-16):

In order to ask this blessing of our Lord Jesus Christ upon this child, let us pray:

Almighty and most merciful God, Whose promises are unto us and unto our children, we heartily beseech Thee to look upon this child with Thy tender mercy, and to renew him by Thy Holy Spirit in the Sacrament of Baptism, that he may be Thy child and an heir of everlasting life; through Jesus Christ, our Lord. Amen.

Our Father, Who art in heaven; etc.

The Lord preserve thy coming in and thy going out from this time forth and even forevermore. ✠ Amen.

Let us now confess our Christian faith, into which this child is to be baptized:

I believe in God the Father Almighty, Maker of heaven and earth.

And in Jesus Christ, His only Son, our Lord; Who was conceived by the Holy Ghost; born of the Virgin Mary; suffered under Pontius Pilate; was crucified, dead, and buried; He descended into hell; the third day He rose again from the dead; He ascended into heaven, and sitteth on the right hand of God the Father Almighty; from thence He shall come to judge the quick and the dead.

I believe in the Holy Ghost; the holy Christian Church; the Communion of Saints; the forgiveness of sins; the resurrection of the body; and the life everlasting. Amen.

N., I baptize thee in the name of the Father, and of the Son, and of the Holy Ghost. ✠ Amen.

Almighty God, the Father of our Lord Jesus Christ, who hath begotten thee again of water and the Spirit, and hath forgiven thee all thy sins, strengthen thee with His grace unto life everlasting. Amen.

Peace be with thee. ✠ Amen.

Let us pray.

We thank Thee, gracious Father, that Thou hast received this child through Holy Baptism into the covenant and kingdom of Thy grace, in which we have forgiveness of sin and everlasting life. Grant, we beseech Thee, that, being buried with Christ in Baptism, he may be dead unto sin and made alive unto righteousness, that in the end, together with his parents and all saints, he may obtain the promised inheritance in heaven; through Jesus Christ, our Lord. Amen.

2. The Baptism of Adults

There may be held an Address and a brief Examination of the person to be baptized, and then the Minister may say:

Dearly Beloved: Our Lord and Saviour said to Nicodemus: "Except a man be born of water and of the Spirit, he cannot enter into the kingdom of God. That which is born of the flesh is flesh; and that which is born of the Spirit is spirit." All men, from the fall of Adam, being conceived and born in sin, are under the wrath of God and would be lost forever, had not the Father of all mercy and grace given His only-begotten Son Jesus Christ for the blotting out of our sins. In order that all men might come to the knowledge of the truth as it is in Christ Jesus, He has entrusted to His Church the means of grace for our salvation, saying, in the last chapter of Matthew: "Go ye, and teach all nations, baptizing them in the name of the Father, and of the Son, and of the Holy Ghost; teaching them to observe all things whatsoever I have commanded you"; and again, in the last chapter of Mark: "Go ye into all the world, and preach the Gospel to every creature. He that believeth and is baptized shall be saved; but he that believeth not shall be damned."

Whereas, then, in obedience to Christ's command, and trusting in His promise, after due instruction in the principal doctrine of the Christian religion, this present person desires to be baptized, let us call upon our heavenly Father to grant him all the promised blessings of the Sacrament.

O almighty and everlasting God, we bless Thee for Thy great mercy in calling this Thy servant unto faith in Thee, and we beseech Thee, remove from him all blindness of heart, and open unto him the gates of Thy mercy, that by the washing of regeneration and renewing of the Holy Ghost, the life which has already been begun in him may be increased, strengthened, and confirmed, and he may be sealed unto eternal life, growing daily in grace, fighting the good fight of faith, and being steadfast and unmovable unto the end; through Jesus Christ, Thy dear Son, our Lord. Amen.

Our Father, Who art in heaven; etc.

N., I now ask thee in the presence of God and these witnesses to answer the following questions:

Dost thou renounce the devil, and all his works, and all his ways?

Answer: I do.

Dost thou believe in God the Father Almighty, Maker of heaven and earth?

Dost thou believe in Jesus Christ, His only Son, our Lord; Who was conceived by the Holy Ghost; born of the Virgin Mary; suffered under Pontius Pilate; was crucified, dead, and buried; He descended into hell; the third day He rose again from the dead; He ascended into heaven, and sitteth on the right hand of God the Father Almighty; from thence He shall come to judge the quick and the dead?

Dost thou believe in the Holy Ghost; the holy Christian Church; the Communion of Saints; the forgiveness of sins; the resurrection of the body; and the life everlasting?

Answer: I do.

Dost thou desire to be baptized into this Christian faith?

Answer: I do.

Wilt thou, then, continue steadfast in the true Christian faith as it is confessed by our Evangelical Lutheran Church, and lead a godly life, even unto the end?

Answer: I will, with the help of God.

Then shall the person to be baptized kneel, and the Minister baptize him with water, saying:

N., I baptize thee in the name of the Father, and of the Son, and of the Holy Ghost. ✠ Amen.

Then the Minister, laying his right hand on the head of the person baptized, shall say:

The Almighty God and Father, Who through the washing of Holy Baptism hath sealed in thee the new birth unto eternal life, and hath confirmed to thee the forgiveness of all thy sins unto salvation, strengthen and keep thee in His grace, and, finally, crown thee with everlasting glory. Amen.

In the name of the Church of Christ, I also invite thee, as a baptized and instructed member of the Evangelical Lutheran Church, to participate with us in the reception of the Lord's Supper, for the strengthening of thy faith, for thy furtherance in holiness of life, and in testimony of the communion of faith.

Peace be with thee. ✠ Amen.

Let us pray:

Heavenly Father, we give Thee hearty thanks that Thou hast vouchsafed to call us to the knowledge of Thy grace and to faith in Thee; and we beseech Thee, increase this knowledge, and confirm this faith in us ever more. Bestow Thy Holy Spirit upon this person, that, being born again and made an heir of everlasting salvation through our Lord Jesus Christ, he may continue Thy servant and attain Thy promises; through the same Lord Jesus Christ, Thy Son, Who liveth and reigneth with Thee, in the unity of the Holy Spirit, world without end. Amen.

The service may then be closed with the singing of a Hymn and the Benediction.

EVANGELICAL LUTHERAN JOINT SYNOD OF WISCONSIN AND OTHER STATES

(Members: 235,400)

Doctrine: *

Baptism is not simple water only, but it is water used by God's command and connected with God's Word.

It works forgiveness of sins, delivers from death and the devil, and gives eternal salvation to all who believe, as the words and promise of God declare.

* *Doctor Martin Luther's Small Catechism*, edited by C. Gausewitz (Northwestern Publishing House, Milwaukee, Wis., 1942), pp. 16, 17.

It is not the water that does (these things), but the Word of God which is in and with the water, and faith which trusts this Word of God in the water.

For without the Word of God the water is simple water, and no Baptism; but with the Word of God it is Baptism; that is, a gracious water of life and a washing of regeneration in the Holy Ghost.

Baptism with water signifies that the old Adam in us is to be drowned by daily contrition and repentance, and is to die with all sins and evil lusts; and that again a new man should daily come forth and arise who shall live before God in righteousness and purity forever.

Manner of Administering Baptism: **

BAPTISM OF INFANTS

Hymn No. 230, verses 1-3.

The following introduction up to the asterisk (*) may be omitted when the baptism is performed in a public service.

Dearly Beloved: We learn from the Word of God, and know from our own experience, that all men are conceived and born in sin, and so are under the wrath of God, and would be lost forever, unless delivered by our Lord Jesus Christ.

This child, then, is also by nature sinful and corrupt, and in like manner under the wrath of God; but the Father of all mercy and grace hath promised and sent His Son Jesus Christ, Who hath borne the sins of the whole world, and redeemed and saved little children, no less than others, from sin, death, and everlasting condemnation. He also commanded that little children should be brought to Him, and graciously received and blessed them.

Wherefore I beseech you, out of Christian love, to intercede for *this child,* to bring *it* to the Lord Jesus, and to implore for *it* the forgiveness of sin, and the grace and salvation of His kingdom; nothing doubting that He favorably regardeth such work of love, and certainly heareth our prayers. And *

(Dearly Beloved): Forasmuch as our Lord hath enjoined and commanded Baptism, saying to His disciples: "Go ye therefore and teach all nations, baptizing them in the Name of the Father, and of the Son, and of the Holy Ghost"; and also hath given promise: "He that believeth and is baptized shall be saved"; it is meet and right that, in obedience to His command, and trusting in His promise, you should bring *this child* to be baptized into His Name.

Here the Minister may make the sign of the cross on the child's forehead and breast, in token that it is redeemed by Christ crucified, saying: "Receive the sign of the Holy Cross."

Let us pray:

Almighty and everlasting God, the Aid of all that need, the Helper of all that flee to Thee for succor, the Life of them that believe and the Resurrection

** *Agenda* of the Joint Evangelical Lutheran Synod of Wisconsin and other States (Northwestern Publishing House, Milwaukee, Wis., 1926), pp. 117-122.

NOTE: Only the recitation of the words of institution and the application of the water to the person to be baptized are considered essential. All else in the ritual is not considered obligatory, though usually the entire ritual is carried out.

of the dead: We call upon Thee for *this child* which *seeketh* the gift of Thy baptism and Thine everlasting grace through regeneration by the Holy Ghost. Receive *him,* O Lord, according to Thy Word and promise: Ask, and it shall be given you; seek, and ye shall find; knock, and it shall be opened unto you. Give now to *him* that *asketh*; let *him* that *seeketh* find; and open to *him* that *knocketh,* that *he* may enjoy the everlasting benediction of Thy heavenly washing, and come to the eternal kingdom which Thou hast promised; through Jesus Christ, our Lord. Amen.

Hear the holy Gospel, which saith: "They brought young children to Him, that He should touch them: and His disciples rebuked those that brought them. But when Jesus saw it, He was much displeased, and said unto them: Suffer the little children to come unto Me, and forbid them not, for of such is the kingdom of God. Verily I say unto you, whosoever shall not receive the kingdom of God as a little child, he shall not enter therein. And He took them up in His arms, put His hands upon them, and blessed them" (Mark 10:13-16).

Then the Minister, laying his right hand upon the head of the child, shall say:

Our Father, Who art in heaven; hallowed be Thy Name; Thy kingdom come; Thy will be done on earth, as it is in heaven; give us this day our daily bread; and forgive us our trespasses, as we forgive those who trespass against us; and lead us not into temptation; but deliver us from evil; for Thine is the kingdom, and the power, and the glory, forever and ever. Amen.

The Lord preserve thy coming in and thy going out, from this time forth even for evermore.

The Minister shall then say to the Sponsors:

But you sponsors I admonish in the Lord to consider that you are here taking a stand against the devil and all his kingdom; that you are not only to be witnesses of this holy baptism, but also in the name of *this child* to renounce the devil and all his works and all his ways, and to confess the Christian faith for *this child.*

Furthermore, in order that the promises you here make for your *godchild* may be duly fulfilled, it is your duty to pray for *it*; to remind *it* later on of *its* baptism; and to help as much as is in our power, especially if *it* lose *its* parents, to bring *it* up in the fear of the Lord according to the Lutheran faith.

Are you willing to take upon yourselves this solemn duty? Then answer, Yes.

N., Dost thou renounce the devil, and all his works, and all his ways?

Answer: Yes, I renounce.

N., Dost thou believe in God, the Father Almighty, Maker of heaven and earth?

Dost thou believe in Jesus Christ, His only Son, our Lord: Who was conceived by the Holy Ghost, born of the Virgin Mary; suffered under Pontius Pilate, was crucified, dead, and buried; descended into hell; the third day rose again from the dead; ascended into heaven, and sitteth on the right hand of God the Father Almighty, when He shall come to judge the quick and the dead?

Dost thou believe in the Holy Ghost; the Holy Christian Church; the Communion of Saints; the forgiveness of sins; the resurrection of the body; and the life everlasting?

Answer: Yes, I believe.

N., Wilt thou be baptized into this Christian Faith?

Answer: Yes, I will.

The Minister shall then baptize the child by applying the water three times upon its head, as he pronounces each of the three Holy Names, as follows:

N., I baptize thee in the Name of the Father, . . . and of the Son, . . . and of the Holy Ghost. ✠ . . . Amen.

Then laying his right hand upon the head of the child, he shall say:

Almighty God, the Father of our Lord Jesus Christ, Who hath begotten thee again of water and the Holy Ghost, and hath forgiven thee all thy sins, strengthen thee with His grace unto life everlasting. Amen.

Peace be with thee. ✠ Amen.

Let us pray:

Almighty and most merciful God and Father: We thank Thee that Thou dost graciously preserve and extend Thy Church, and hast granted to *this child* the new birth in Holy Baptism, planted *it* in Jesus Christ, our Lord and Saviour, and made *it* Thy *child,* and *heir* to Thy heavenly kingdom. And as *this child* hath now become Thine own, we humbly beseech Thee to defend and keep *it* in this grace, that, according to all Thy good pleasure, *it* may be faithfully and savingly brought up to the praise and honor of Thy holy Name, and finally, with all Thy saints, receive the promised inheritance; through Jesus Christ our Lord. Amen.

Hymn No. 230, verses 6, 7.

The Lord bless thee, and keep thee.

The Lord make His face shine upon thee, and be gracious unto thee.

The Lord lift up His countenance upon thee, and give thee peace. Amen.

THE GENERAL CONFERENCE OF THE MENNONITE CHURCH OF NORTH AMERICA

(Members: Over 26,000)

Ritual: *

One of the ordinances of the Christian Church is baptism, for the administering and receiving of which we have the most ample warrant not only in the example of the early saints but also and primarily in the explicit command of our Saviour. You have been taught its meaning. Following upon a clear experience and confession of faith, the sacrament is to be the outward seal of the covenant into which one has entered with God by faith in Jesus Christ. It is

* *Forms of Service for the Use of Ministers* (Berne, Indiana: Mennonite Book Concern).

the outward symbol of the washing from sin by the soul-cleansing blood of Christ. Under another figure it signifies our being crucified and buried with Christ according to the old man and the entering with Christ into a new life, a life of victory over sin and death. These spiritual blessings, of which baptism is the outward symbol and seal, are vouchsafed to them that receive them in humble, trustful faith. Such faith you have already professed. Do you now desire to be baptized upon this faith and to be received into the Church of Jesus Christ?

Answer: I do.

The candidate kneels. The officiating elder (pastor) either cups his hands upon the head of the candidate and a deacon or co-pastor pours the water into the cup; or the elder dips the water with the cupped hand out of an appropriate vessel and releases it on the head with these words:

"Upon thy profession of faith in the Lord Jesus Christ as thy personal Saviour from sin, and thy vow of consecration to Him and His service, I baptize thee in the name of the Father, and of the Son, and of the Holy Spirit. The Lord Jesus baptize thee with the Spirit and with fire from above!"

Taking the right hand of the rising one, the elder says:

In the name of Christ and His Church, I now extend to you the right hand of fellowship and welcome you as a brother (sister) in the Church of Christ.

WESLEYAN METHODIST CONNECTION OF AMERICA

(Members: Over 26,000)

Doctrine: *

Justification of Man

We are accounted righteous before God only for the merit of our Lord and Saviour Jesus Christ, by faith, and not our own works or deservings: Wherefore, that we are justified by faith only is a most wholesome doctrine, and very full of comfort.

Regeneration

Regeneration is that work of the Holy Spirit by which the pardoned sinner becomes a child of God; this work is received through faith in Jesus Christ, whereby the regenerate are delivered from the power of sin which reigns over all the unregenerate, so that they love God and through grace serve Him with the will and affections of the heart,—receiving the Spirit of adoption whereby we cry, Abba Father.

The Sacraments

Sacraments ordained of Christ are not only tokens of Christian profession, but they are certain signs of grace and God's good will toward us, by which He doth work invisibly in us, and doth not only quicken but also strengthen and confirm our faith in Him.

* *Discipline* (Wesleyan Methodist Connection [or Church] of America, Syracuse, N. Y.: Wesleyan Methodist Publishing Association, 1943), pp. 15-18.

There are two sacraments ordained of Christ our Lord in the Gospel: that is to say, Baptism, and the Supper of the Lord.

Baptism

Baptism is not only a sign of profession and mark of difference whereby Christians are distinguished from others who are not baptized, but it is also a sign of regeneration or new birth. The baptism of young children is to be retained in the Church.

Ritual: **

Baptism

Let every adult person, and the parents of every child to be baptized, have the choice either of immersion, sprinkling, or pouring.

Of Infants

The parents or parent of the child presented for baptism shall be asked the following questions:

Question: Hast thou renounced the devil and all his works, the vain pomp and glory of the world, with all covetous desires of the same, and the carnal desires of the flesh, so that thou dost not follow or art not led by them?

Answer: I have renounced them all, and by God's help will endeavor not to follow or be led by them.

Question: Dost thou believe in God the Father Almighty, Maker of heaven and earth; and in Jesus Christ His only-begotten Son, our Lord; that He took man's nature in the womb of the Virgin Mary, and was born of her; that He suffered under Pontius Pilate, was crucified, dead, and buried; that He arose again on the third day; that He ascended into heaven, and sitteth at the right hand of God the Father Almighty, and that He shall come again at the end of the world to judge the quick and the dead? And dost thou believe in the Holy Ghost, the Communion of Saints, the remission of sins, the regeneration of our fallen nature, the resurrection of the body, and everlasting life after death?

Answer: All this I steadfastly believe.

Question: Wilt thou have this child baptized in this faith?

Answer: This is my desire.

Question: Wilt thou, then, diligently teach it God's holy Word, and cause it to walk in obedience to His holy will and commandments, until it come to years to assume in its own person the faith, vows and obligations of baptism?

Answer: I will endeavor to do so, the Lord being my helper.

(Then shall the Minister baptize the child and conclude the service with an appropriate prayer.)

Or This Form May Be Used:

By this act of presenting this child for consecration to God, you thereby signify your faith in the Christian religion, and that baptism is an ordinance

** *Discipline*, pp. 248-252.

of the same, and also your desire that he (or she) shall receive the benefits of consecration to God, and of the prayers of the church and congregation, that he (or she) may early learn to know and follow the will of God; and thus doing may live and die a Christian, attaining in the end of this earthly life to everlasting life in the Kingdom of God.

But in order that this may be accomplished in the life of this child, it will be your duty as his (or her) parents (or guardians) to early teach him (or her) the fear of the Lord; to watch over his (or her) education, that he (or she) may not be led astray by false teachings or doctrines, to direct his (or her) mind to the Holy Scriptures as expressing the will and authority of God for all mankind, also to direct his (or her) feet to the sanctuary; to restrain him (or her) from evil associates or habits; and, as much as in you lieth, to "bring him (or her) up in the nurture and admonition of the Lord."

Question: Will you endeavor to do so, by the help of God?

Answer: I will.

Then shall the Minister read the following Scripture lesson:

"And they brought young children unto Him, that He should touch them, etc. . . . And He took them up in His arms, put His hands upon them, and blessed them" (Mark 10:13-16).

Then shall the Minister ask the name of the child.

N.N., I baptize thee in the name of the Father, and of the Son, and of the Holy Ghost. Amen.

The Minister shall then offer an appropriate prayer.

Of Such As Are of Riper Years

The Minister shall demand of each of the persons to be baptized severally:

Question: Dost thou renounce the devil and all his works, the vain pomp and glory of the world, with all covetous desires of the same, and the carnal desires of the flesh, so that thou wilt not follow or be led by them?

Answer: I renounce them all.

Question: Dost thou believe in God the Father Almighty, Maker of heaven and earth; and in Jesus Christ, His only-begotten Son, our Lord; and that He was conceived by the Holy Ghost, born of the Virgin Mary; that He suffered under Pontius Pilate, was crucified, dead, and buried; that He arose again on the third day; that He ascended into heaven, and sitteth at the right hand of God the Father Almighty, and from thence shall come again at the end of the world, to judge the quick and the dead? And dost thou believe in the Holy Ghost; the remission of sins, the resurrection of the body, and everlasting life after death?

Answer: All this I steadfastly believe.

Question: Wilt thou be baptized in this faith?

Answer: This is my desire.

Question: Wilt thou then obediently keep God's holy will and commandments and walk in the same all the days of thy life?

Answer: I will endeavor so to do, God being my helper.

(Then shall the Minister baptize by sprinkling, pouring, or immersion, as the candidate may choose, saying):

N., I baptize thee in the name of the Father, and of the Son, and of the Holy Ghost. Amen.

(Then shall be said an appropriate prayer, or the Lord's prayer.)

THE METHODIST CHURCH *

(Total Membership: 5,800,000)

Doctrine: **

Of the Sacraments: Sacraments ordained of Christ are not only badges or tokens of Christian men's profession, but rather they are certain signs of grace, and God's good will toward us, by which He doth work invisibly in us, and doth not only quicken, but also strengthen and confirm, our faith in Him.

There are two Sacraments ordained of Christ our Lord in the Gospel; that is to say, Baptism and the Supper of the Lord.

Of Baptism: Baptism is not only a sign of profession and mark of difference whereby Christians are distinguished from others that are not baptized; but it is also a sign of regeneration or the new birth. The baptism of young children is to be retained in the Church.

Ritual: **

(Let every adult person, and the parents of every child to be baptized, have the choice of sprinkling, pouring, or immersion.

It is proper and desirable that this Sacrament should not only be accompanied by prayer, admonition, and the reading of Scripture, as herein provided, but that it should be administered in the presence of the people, and most suitably in the house of God.)

The Baptism of Infants

Dearly Beloved, forasmuch as all men are heirs of life eternal and subjects of the saving grace of the Holy Spirit; and that our Saviour Christ saith, Suffer the little children to come unto Me, and forbid them not, for of such is the kingdom of God, I beseech you to call upon God the Father, through our Lord Jesus Christ, that of His bounteous goodness He will grant unto this child, now to be baptized, the continual replenishing of His grace that he become a worthy member of Christ's holy Church.

Then shall the Minister say:

Let us pray.

* The doctrine and ritual quoted apply to the Primitive Methodist Church, the Methodist Episcopal Church, the Methodist Episcopal Church, South, and the Methodist Protestant Church.

** *Doctrines and Discipline of the Methodist Church* (New York: The Methodist Publishing House, 1940), pp. 76-77; 602-613.

Almighty and Everliving God, we beseech Thee, that of Thine infinite goodness Thou wilt look upon this child and grant that by the aid of Thy Holy Spirit he may be steadfast in faith, joyful through hope, and rooted in love, and that he may so live the life which now is, that he may enter triumphantly the life which is to come; through Jesus Christ our Lord. **Amen.**

Then shall the Minister address the Parents or Sponsors, as follows:

Dearly Beloved, forasmuch as this Child is now presented by you for Christian baptism, and is thus consecrated to God and to His Church, it is your part to learn, the meaning and purpose of this holy Sacrament; that he be instructed in the principles of our holy faith and the nature of the Christian life; that he shall be trained to give reverent attendance upon the public and private worship of God and the teaching of the Holy Scripture, and that in every way, by precept and example, you shall seek to lead him into the love of God and the service of our Lord Jesus Christ.

Do you solemnly promise to fulfill these duties so far as in you lies, the Lord being your helper?

We do.

Then shall the People stand and the Minister shall say:

Hear the words of the Gospel written by St. Mark.

And they brought young children to Him, etc.

Then shall the Minister, who may here take the Child in his arms, say to the Parents or Sponsors:

What name shall be given to this child?

And then repeating the name, he shall baptize the Child, saying:

N., I baptize thee in the Name of the Father, and of the Son, and of the Holy Spirit. **Amen.**

Then shall the Minister say:

Let us pray.

O God, our Heavenly Father, grant that this child, as he grows in years, may also grow in grace and in knowledge of the Lord Jesus Christ, and that by the restraining and renewing influence of Thy Holy Spirit he may ever be a true child of God, serving Thee faithfully all his days, through Jesus Christ our Lord. **Amen.**

Almighty God, Fount of all love and wisdom, Source of all power, so guide and uphold the parents (or sponsors) of this child, that, by loving care, wise counsel, and holy example, they may lead him into that life of faith whose strength is righteousness and whose fruit is everlasting joy and peace; through Jesus Christ our Lord. **Amen.**

Or the Minister may offer extemporary Prayer.

Then may the Minister and the People say:

The Lord's Prayer.

Then may be sung a Hymn, such as:

406—"Friend of the home: as when in Galilee."

407—"See Israel's gentle Shepherd stand."

440—"I think when I read."

Then may the Minister say:

Now unto Him that is able to keep you from falling, and to present you faultless before the presence of His glory with exceeding joy, to the only wise God our Saviour, be glory and majesty, dominion and power, now and evermore. **Amen.**

The Order for the Baptism of Children and Youth

The Minister, coming to the Font, shall say:

Hear the words of the Gospel, written by St. Matthew, in the twenty-eighth chapter, beginning at the sixteenth verse.

Then the eleven disciples went away into Galilee, etc.

Amen.

Then shall the Minister say:

Let us pray.

Almighty and Everliving God, Whose most dearly beloved Son Jesus Christ gave Himself for our salvation, and did command His disciples that they should go teach all nations, and baptize them in the name of the Father, and of the Son, and of the Holy Spirit: regard, we beseech Thee, the supplications of Thy congregation; and grant that these persons now to be baptized may so open their hearts to Thee that they may receive the fullness of Thy grace, and may ever remain in the number of Thy faithful children, through Jesus Christ our Lord. **Amen.**

Then the Minister shall say to the Persons to be baptized:

Well beloved, who are come hither, desiring to receive holy Baptism, you have heard how the congregation hath prayed that God would assist you to open your hearts to His love and direction, that you may be faithful disciples of our Lord.

Wherefore, for your part, it is needful that in the presence of Almighty God and the hearing of this congregation, you should now make known your purpose to accept the obligations of this holy Sacrament, by answering the following questions:

Will you faithfully put away from you every known sin, of thought, word, or deed, and accept and confess Jesus Christ as your Saviour and Lord?

God helping me, I will.

Will you diligently study the Bible as God's Holy Word, and in all things strive to make it the rule of your life?

God helping me, I will.

Having been taught how the Spirit of our Lord separates right from wrong, will you faithfully endeavor to live so as to be pleasing unto Him?

God helping me, I will.

Will you be baptized in this faith?

This is my desire.

Then shall the Minister ask each Person his name, and shall baptize him, saying:

N., I baptize thee in the name of the Father, and of the Son, and of the Holy Spirit. **Amen.**

Here the Minister shall offer an extemporary Prayer.

The Order for the Baptism of Adults

The Minister, addressing the People, shall say:

Dearly Beloved, forasmuch as our Saviour Jesus Christ sent forth His disciples to teach all nations and baptize them in the name of the Father, and of the Son, and of the Holy Spirit; and wherefore these persons come now to be baptized, I beseech you to call upon God the Father that of His bounteous goodness He will grant unto them the renewing power of the Holy Spirit and enable them by divine grace to attain unto the fullness of salvation in Jesus Christ our Lord.

Let us pray.

Almighty and immortal God, the aid of all that need, the helper of all that flee to Thee for succor, the life of them that believe, and the resurrection of the dead: we call upon Thee for these persons now to be baptized. May they be filled with Thy Holy Spirit and may they find in Thee their refuge, their strength, their wisdom, and their joy. May they be faithful to Thee all the days of their life and finally come to the eternal kingdom which Thou has promised, through Jesus Christ our Lord. **Amen.**

Then may the Minister read one or more of the following Lessons:

Peter said unto them, Repent, and be baptized, etc.

And it came to pass, that, while Apollos was at Corinth, etc.

There was a man of the Pharisees, named Nicodemus, etc.

For this cause I bow my knees unto the Father, etc.

Then shall the Minister say to the Persons to be baptized:

Dearly Beloved, who have come hither desiring to receive holy Baptism, the Congregation gives thanks to God for your coming, and prays that the Holy Spirit may dwell within you, and that your faith may not fail. In the hearing of this Congregation you should now make known your purpose to accept the obligations of this holy Sacrament.

Do you truly repent of your sins and accept and confess Jesus Christ as your Saviour and Lord?

I do.

Will you earnestly endeavor to keep God's Holy Will and commandments?

I will.

Do you desire to be baptized in this faith?

I do.

Then shall the Minister say:

O merciful God, grant that all sinful affections may die in these persons, and that all things belonging to the Spirit may live and grow in them. **Amen.**

Then the Minister, asking the name of each Person, shall baptize him, repeating the name and saying:

N., I baptize thee in the Name of the Father, and of the Son, and of the Holy Spirit. **Amen.**

Our Father, Who art in heaven, etc.

Then may be sung one or more stanzas of a Hymn, such as:

223—"Blessed Master, I have promised."

226—"O Jesus, I have promised."

257—"My gracious Lord, I own Thy right."

Now unto Him that is able to keep you from falling, and to present you faultless before the presence of His glory with exceeding joy, to the only wise God our Saviour, be glory and majesty, dominion and power, now and evermore. **Amen.**

THE COLORED METHODIST EPISCOPAL CHURCH

(Members: 365,000)

Doctrine: *

Baptism is not only a sign of profession and mark of difference, whereby Christians are distinguished from others that are not baptized; but it is also a sign of regeneration, or new birth. The baptism of young children is to be retained in the church.

Ritual: **

The Administration of Baptism to Adults

(The minister coming to the font, which is to be filled with pure water, shall use the following, or some other suitable exhortation):

Dearly Beloved, forasmuch as all men are conceived and born in sin (and that which is born of the flesh is flesh, and they that are in the flesh cannot please God, but live in sin, committing many actual transgressions), and that our Saviour Christ saith, Except a man be born of water and of the Spirit, he cannot enter into the kingdom of God; I beseech you to call upon God the Father, through our Lord Jesus Christ, that of his bounteous goodness he will grant to *these persons* that which by nature *they* cannot have; that *they* may be baptized with water and the Holy Ghost and received into Christ's holy Church, and be made lively *members* of the same.

(Then shall the Minister say):

Almighty and immortal God, the aid of all that need, the helper of all that flee for succor, the life of them that believe, and the resurrection of the dead;

* *Discipline,* Colored Methodist Episcopal Church (Jackson, Tenn.: General Board of Religious Education).

** *The Ritual,* Colored Methodist Episcopal Church (Jackson, Tenn.: General Board of Religious Education), pp. 1-4.

we call upon Thee for *these persons* now to be baptized. Receive *them,* O Lord, as Thou hast promised by Thy well-beloved Son, saying, Ask and ye shall receive; seek and ye shall find; knock and it shall be opened to you, so give now unto us that ask; let us that seek find; open the gate unto us that knock; that these persons may enjoy the everlasting benediction of Thy heavenly washing, and may come to the eternal kingdom which Thou hast promised by Christ our Lord. AMEN.

(Then shall the people stand, and the Minister shall say):

Hear the words of the Gospel, written by Saint John in the third chapter, beginning at the first verse.

There was a man of the Pharisees, named Nicodemus, a ruler of the Jews. The same came to Jesus by night, and said unto Him, Rabbi, we know that Thou art a teacher come from God; for no man can do these miracles that Thou doest, except God be with him. Jesus answered and said unto him, Verily, verily, I say unto you, Except a man be born again he cannot see the kingdom of God. Nicodemus saith unto him, How can a man be born when he is old? Can he enter the second time into his mother's womb, and be born? Jesus answered, Verily, verily, I say unto thee, Except a man be born of water and of the Spirit, he cannot enter into the kingdom of God. That which is born of the flesh is flesh; and that which is born of the Spirit is spirit. Marvel not that I said unto thee, Ye must be born again. The wind bloweth where it listeth, and thou hearest the sound thereof, but canst not tell whence it cometh, and whither it goeth; so is every one that is born of the Spirit.

(Then the Minister shall speak to the persons to be baptized on this wise):

Well Beloved, who are come hither, desiring to receive holy baptism, *ye have* heard how the congregation hath prayed that our Lord Jesus Christ, would vouchsafe to receive *you,* and bless *you,* to release *you* of your sins, to give *you* the kingdom of heaven, and everlasting life. And our Lord Jesus Christ hath promised in His Holy Word to grant all those things that we have prayed for: which promise He for His part will most surely keep and perform.

Wherefore after this promise made by Christ, ye must also faithfully, for *your* part, promise, in the presence of this whole congregation, that ye will renounce the devil and all his works, and constantly believe God's Holy Word, and obediently keep His commandments.

(Then shall the Minister demand of each of the persons to be baptized severally):

Doth thou renounce the devil and all his work, the vain pomp and glory of the world with all covetous desires of the same, and the carnal desires of the flesh, so that thou wilt not follow or be led by them?

Ans. *I renounce them all.*

Ques. Dost thou believe in God the Father Almighty, maker of heaven and earth? and in Jesus Christ, His only-begotten Son, our Lord? and that He was conceived by the Holy Ghost, born of the Virgin Mary? that He suffered under Pontius Pilate, was crucified, dead, and buried? that He rose again the third day? that He ascended into heaven, and sitteth at the right hand of God the Father Almighty, and from thence shall come again at the end of the world to judge the quick and the dead?

And dost thou believe in the Holy Ghost, the Holy Catholic Church, the Communion of Saints, the remission of sins, the resurrection of the body, and everlasting life after death?

Ans. *All this I steadfastly believe.*

Ques. Wilt thou be baptized in this faith?

Ans. *This is my desire.*

Ques. Wilt thou then obediently keep God's Holy Will and commandments, and walk in the same all the days of thy life?

Ans. *I will endeavor so to do, God being my helper.*

(Then shall the Minister say):

O merciful God, grant that the old Adam in *these* persons may be so buried, that the new man may be raised up in *them*. AMEN.

Grant that all carnal affections may die in *them*, and that all things belonging to the Spirit may live and grow in *them*. AMEN.

Grant that *they* may have power and strength to have victory, and to triumph against the devil, the world, and the flesh. AMEN.

Grant that *they*, being here dedicated to Thee by our office and ministry, may also be endued with heavenly virtues, and everlastingly rewarded, through Thy mercy, O blessed Lord God, Who dost live and govern all things, world without end. AMEN.

Almighty, everliving God, Whose most dearly beloved Son Jesus Christ, for the forgiveness of our sins, did shed out of His most precious side both water and blood; and gave commandment to His disciples, that they should go teach all nations, and baptize them in the name of the Father, and of the Son, and of the Holy Ghost; regard, we beseech Thee, the supplications of this congregation; and grant that the *persons* now to be baptized may receive the fullness of Thy grace, and ever remain in the number of Thy faithful and elect children, through Jesus Christ our Lord. AMEN.

(Then shall the Minister take each person to be baptized by the right hand: and placing him conveniently by the font, according to his discretion, shall ask the name; and then shall sprinkle or pour water upon him [or if he shall desire it, shall immerse him in water], saying):

N., I baptize thee in the name of the Father, and of the Son, and of the Holy Ghost. AMEN.

(The Minister may, at his discretion, lay hands on the subject, accompanying the act with a suitable invocation.)

The Administration of Baptism to Infants

(The Minister, coming to the font, which is to be filled with pure water, shall use the following, or some other suitable exhortation):

Dearly Beloved, forasmuch as all men are conceived and born in sin, and that our Saviour Christ saith, Except a man be born of water and of the Spirit, he can not enter into the kingdom of God: I beseech you to call upon God the Father, through our Lord Jesus Christ, that of His bounteous mercy He will grant to *this* child that which by nature *he* cannot have; that he may be baptized with water and the Holy Ghost, and received into Christ's holy Church, and be made a lively member of the same.

(Then shall the Minister say, Let us pray):

Almighty and everlasting God, we beseech Thee for Thine infinite mercies, that Thou wilt look upon *this child*; wash *him* and sanctify *him* with the Holy Ghost that *he*, being delivered from Thy wrath, may be received into the ark of Christ's Church, and being steadfast in faith, joyful through hope, and rooted in love, may so pass the waves of this troublesome world, that finally *he* may come to the land of everlasting life, there to reign with Thee, world without end, through Jesus Christ our Lord. AMEN.

O merciful God, grant that the old Adam in *this child* may be so buried that the new man may be raised up in *him*. AMEN.

Grant that all carnal affections may die in *him*, and that all things belonging to the Spirit may live and grow in *him*. AMEN.

Grant that *he* may have power and strength to have victory, and to triumph against the devil, the world, and the flesh. AMEN.

Grant that whosoever is dedicated to Thee by our office and ministry may also be endued with heavenly virtues, and everlastingly rewarded through Thy mercy, O blessed Lord God, Who dost live and govern all things, world without end. AMEN.

Almighty, everliving God, Whose most dearly beloved Son Jesus Christ, for the forgiveness of our sins did shed out of His most precious side both water and blood, and gave commandment to His disciples that they should go teach all nations, and baptize them in the name of the Father, and of the Son, and of the Holy Ghost; regard, we beseech Thee, the supplications of Thy congregation; and grant that *this child*, now to be baptized, may receive the fullness of Thy grace, and ever remain in the number of Thy faithful and elect children, through Jesus Christ our Lord. AMEN.

(Then shall the people stand, and the Minister shall say):

Hear the words of the Gospel written by Saint Mark in the tenth chapter, at the thirteenth verse.

They brought young children to Christ that He should touch them. And His disciples rebuked those that brought them; but when Jesus saw it, He was much displeased, and said unto them, Suffer the little children to come unto Me, and forbid them not, for of such is the kingdom of God. Verily I say unto you, Whosoever shall not receive the kingdom of God as a little child, he shall not enter therein. And he took them up in His arms, put His hands upon them, and blessed them.

(Then the Minister, addressing the parents or others presenting the child, shall say):

In causing *this child* to be brought by baptism into the Church of Christ, it is your duty to teach *him* to renounce the devil and all his works, the vain pomp and glory of the world, with all covetous desires of the same, and the carnal desires of the flesh, so that *he* may not follow or be led by them; to believe all the articles of the Christian faith; and to obediently keep God's holy will and commandments all the days of his *life*.

(Then the Minister shall take the child into his hands, if convenient, and say to the friends of the child): Name this child.

N., I baptize thee in the name of the Father, and of the Son, and of the Holy Ghost. AMEN.

(The Minister may, at his discretion, lay hands on the subject, accompanying the act with a suitable invocation, and then, all kneeling, close with extemporaneous devotions and the Lord's Prayer):

Our Father, Who art in heaven, hallowed by Thy name; Thy kingdom come; Thy will be done on earth, as it is in heaven; give us this day our daily bread; and forgive us our trespasses, as we forgive those who trespass against us; and lead us not into temptation, but deliver us from evil. AMEN.

THE MORAVIAN CHURCH

(Members: 37,000)

Doctrine: *

Our Church has never emphasized theological minutiae. Especially since the time of Count Zinzendorf 200 years ago, our emphasis has been on the simple acceptance of Bible doctrine and a personal experience of the saving grace of the Redeemer.

Baptism is a sacrament instituted by Christ Himself; we neither affirm nor deny baptismal regeneration or any other point on which Christian believers differ. We believe every believer should be publicly baptized in obedience to the command of Christ, without raising the question whether a believer could be saved without baptism. Some of our ministers tend toward a sacramentarian view, and others to a symbolic view of baptism.

So long as a minister in administering baptism does so in faithful obedience to the command of the Saviour, we would never question the validity of the act, even if personally he should hold one or the other of several theological views of the meaning of baptism, none of which are obligatory in our doctrinal standards nor denied in them.

Baptism: **

1. Where receptiveness for the preached Word shows itself, where this Word awakens knowledge of sin and longing for salvation in Jesus Christ, and, so far as can be seen, also the resolve to forsake the vain manner of life handed down

* Statement by Rev. S. H. Gapp, President, The Society of the United Brethren for Propagating the Gospel among the heathen, the Moravian Church (69 West Church Street, Bethlehem, Pa.)

** *Book of Order of the Moravian Church* (1938), p. 31.

from their fathers, there the Sacrament of Baptism shall be administered. As we understand Scripture, more than this is not requisite for Baptism, but so much must be earnestly insisted on.

2. Touching the Baptism of adults—men and women—the rule is that such as live in polygamous relations are not to be admitted to Baptism. However, the Provincial Mission Boards are authorized to allow exceptions; for example, to grant Baptism to those women for whom, though in heart truly awakened and converted, the dissolution of the polygamous relation is impossible; but a person in this position may not hold office in the Church. Polyandrists are in no circumstances to be admitted to Baptism.

3. In the Baptism of children the following principles hold good; children may only be baptized when a Christian education can be looked for, e. g., when at least one of the parents belong to the Christian Church.

4. As a rule children over five years old are not baptized until they are twelve years old, and then as adults. But exceptions may be allowed in certain cases, for instance, when the Baptism of a whole family takes place.

5. Baptism of the Roman and Greek Churches is recognized by us on principle. In cases where recognition seems impossible, the individual Missionary must apply to the provincial authority which is empowered to decide if the Baptism is to be recognized or not.

6. Adult Baptism must always be preceded by Christian instruction, which, however, should not be unduly prolonged.

7. Those baptized as adults receive with their baptism the right to partake of the Lord's Supper: but the first partaking must be preceded by brief instruction on the significance of the Supper.

8. As is usual in our home congregations, those baptized as children are confirmed at their own desire before they are admitted to the Communion.

Administration: ***

1. Our children are already by their birth in the Christian Church called of God to a participation in the Kingdom of Jesus Christ, 1 Cor. 7:14, and Christ Himself blessed little children and declared them to be of those who belonged to the Kingdom of God. In the Moravian Church it is, therefore, the duty to present their children for Baptism at the earliest age, as soon as circumstances permit. The Congregation, in whose midst a child is baptized, ought, by its participation in the act, practically to show that, with the parents of the child, it undertakes the duty of bringing it up as a child of the Church in the nurture and admonition of the Lord.

2. Baptism is to be administered with due solemnity, and, if at all possible, at a public meeting of the Congregation, on which occasions the children especially should also be in attendance.

3. As witnesses, or sponsors, only such persons should be selected who are able to appreciate the real significance of the matter. While no legal obligation

*** *Book of Order of the Moravian Church* (1938), p. 140.

devolves upon them to care for the children at whose Baptism they are invited to stand as witnesses, they should nevertheless recognize it as a duty of Christian love to make such children special subjects of prayer, and to look after them faithfully should they be left orphans.

4. All candidates for Adult Baptism shall receive a preparatory course of instruction before they are baptized, and are received by their Baptism into the Church of Christ as communicant members.

5. The mode of administering Baptism shall be that of pouring or sprinkling. In special cases only, and by way of exception, immersion shall be allowed; provided, that there is not combined with the desire for this mode of Baptism a rejection of Infant Baptism, and that the sanction of the Provincial Elders' Conference be secured in every case.

Manner of Administering Baptism: ****

The Baptism of Children

The service shall begin with the singing of a hymn, and a short discourse by the Minister, setting forth the meaning and obligations of this sacrament.

Then, all standing, the Minister shall say and the congregation respond:

Christ, thou Lamb of God, which takest away the sins of the world,

Leave Thy peace with us: Amen.

By Thy holy sacraments,

Bless us, gracious Lord and God.

Baptism was instituted by our Lord Jesus Christ, Who said unto His disciples, Go ye, and teach all nations, baptizing them in the name of the Father, and of the Son, and of the Holy Ghost; teaching them to observe all things whatsoever I have commanded you.

Baptism is the answer of a good conscience toward God, Who hath saved us by washing of regeneration and renewing of the Holy Ghost, which is shed on us abundantly through Jesus Christ our Saviour.

He also gave this promise: He that believeth and is baptized shall be saved.

Children may be made partakers of this grace; for Christ hath said: Suffer little children to come unto Me, and forbid them not, for of such is the kingdom of heaven.

(Then the Minister shall ask and the parents shall answer:

Is it your sincere desire, by the grace of God, as much as lieth in you, to bring up this child in the fear and admonition of the Lord?

It is.)

Then shall be sung one of the following hymns:

**** *The Liturgy of the American Province of the Unitas Fratrum or the Moravian Church* (Moravian Publication Office, Bethlehem, Pa., 1890), pp. 15-19.

L. M. Tune 90.

An infant we present to Thee
As Thy redeemed property,
And Thee most fervently entreat
Thyself this child to consecrate
By baptism, and its soul to bless,
Out of the fullness of Thy grace.

L. M. Tune 22.

The Saviour's blood and righteousness
Our beauty is, our glorious dress;
Thus well arrayed we need not fear,
When in His presence we appear.

Then after a prayer, the Minister shall say and the congregation respond:

Ye who are baptized into Christ Jesus, how were ye baptized?

Into His death.

Then the Minister shall name the child, and pour, or sprinkle, water on its head thrice, saying:

In the death of Jesus I baptize thee, in the name of the Father, and of the Son, and of the Holy Ghost.

Here the sponsors shall join the Minister in the imposition of hands.

Now art thou buried with Him by baptism into His death:

In the name of Jesus: Amen.

Then the Minister shall continue and say:

Now therefore live, yet not thou, but Christ live in thee; and the life which thou now livest in the flesh, live by the faith of the Son of God, Who loved thee, and gave Himself for thee.

The Lord bless thee, and keep thee:

The Lord make His face shine upon thee, and be gracious unto thee;

The Lord lift up His countenance upon thee, and give thee peace;

In the name of Jesus: Amen.

Then may be sung the Doxology:

11s. Tune 39.

The Lamb, Who by blood our salvation obtained,
Took on Him our curse, and death freely sustained,
Is worthy of praises, let with one accord
All people say, Amen, O praise ye the Lord.

THE BAPTISM OF ADULTS

After a short discourse, shall follow these petitions:

Lord God, our Father, which art in heaven,

Hallowed be Thy name; Thy kingdom come; Thy will be done in earth, as it is in heaven; give us this day our daily bread; and forgive us our trespasses, as we forgive them that trespass against us; and lead us not into temptation, but deliver us from evil: for thine is the kingdom, and the power, and the glory, for ever and ever. Amen.

Lord God, Son, thou Saviour of the world,

Be gracious unto us.

Lord God, Holy Ghost,

Abide with us forever.

By Thy divine presence,

By Thy holy sacraments,

Bless us, gracious Lord and God.

Then the Minister shall ask, the candidate responding:

Dost thou believe in God the Father, almighty Maker and Preserver of heaven and earth?

I do.

Dost thou believe in Jesus Christ, the only-begotten Son of God, our Lord, Who loved us, and gave Himself for us?

I do.

Dost thou believe in the Holy Ghost, the holy Christian church, the forgiveness of sins, the resurrection of the body, and the life everlasting?

I do.

Dost thou believe that thou art a sinful creature, deserving of wrath and eternal punishment?

I verily believe it.

Dost thou believe that Jesus Christ is thy Lord, Who redeemed thee a lost and undone human creature, from sin, from death, and from the power of the devil, with His innocent suffering and dying, and with His holy and precious blood?

I verily believe it.

Dost thou in this faith desire to be baptized into the death of Jesus, to be washed from thy sins, and to be embodied into the congregation of the faithful?

This is my sincere desire.

Dost thou in this faith renounce the service of sin and Satan, and determine to live under Christ in His kingdom, and serve Him in holiness and righteousness all the days of thy life?

I do most heartily, in the strength of Jesus Christ, my Lord, and of His Spirit.

Then shall be sung one of the following hymns:

C. M. Tune 14.

Jesus, as water well applied
Will make the body clean,
So in the fountain of Thy side
Wash thou this soul from sin.

S. M. Tune 582.

Rejoice, ye contrite hearts,
The blood which Jesus spilt,
While we with water you baptize,
Will wash away your guilt.

While with repenting tears
Your sins you now deplore,
Christ with His blood will blot them out,
Remember them no more.

Here the candidate for baptism kneeling, the Minister shall offer prayer, and then say, the congregation responding:

Ye who are baptized into Christ Jesus, how were ye baptized?

Into His death.

Then the Minister shall name the candidate, and pour, or sprinkle, water on him thrice, saying:

Into the death of Jesus I baptize thee, in the name of the Father, and of the Son, and of the Holy Ghost.

During the imposition of hands the Minister shall continue:

Now art thou washed, justified, and sanctified by the blood of Christ: therefore live, yet not thou, but Christ live in thee; and the life, which thou now livest in the flesh, live by the faith of the Son of God, Who loved thee, and gave Himself for thee.

The Lord bless thee and kep thee;
The Lord make His face shine upon thee, and be gracious unto thee;
The Lord lift up His countenance upon thee, and give thee peace:
In the name of Jesus: Amen.

Then shall be sung one of the following doxologies:

L. M. Tune 22.

All power and glory doth pertain
Unto the Lamb, for He was slain,
And hath redeemed us by His blood,
And made us kings and priest to God.

7s. Tune 11.

Praise on earth to Thee be given
Never-ceasing praise in heaven;
Boundless wisdom, power divine,
Love unspeakable are Thine.

PENTÉCOSTAL HOLINESS CHURCH

(Members: 24,000)

Doctrine: *

Baptism:

All who unite with any local church on the profession of their faith in Christ shall further confess Christ by receiving water baptism as early as convenient. All candidates for baptism shall have the right of choice between the various modes as practiced by the various evangelical denominations, and baptism shall be administered according to the divine command of our blessed Lord, "In the name of the Father, and of the Son, and of the Holy Ghost." Christian parents and guardians shall have liberty of conscience in the baptism of their children. (Matt. 28: 19, 20.)

Regeneration:

We believe, teach and firmly maintain the Scriptural doctrine of justification by faith alone.

The new birth is the impartation of spiritual life; to be renewed spiritually by the Holy Ghost; the moral image of God upon the heart recovered.

Discipline: *

The candidate shall have the right to choose whatever mode of baptism he prefers. The minister may read a lesson of his own selection from the Word, after which he shall address the congregation, saying:

Dearly Beloved: The last command of our risen Lord was to go into all the world and preach the gospel to every creature, and His representative, the blessed Holy Spirit, throughout the Book of Acts enforced this command through the apostles in relation to all who believe in Christ; therefore it is our bounden duty as possessors of His grace to conform to this great commission, both in the preaching of the Word and the administration of the ordinance of baptism, as opportunity affords.

Here let the candidates for baptism be invited to stand before the congregation, the minister addressing them as follows:

Dearly Beloved: This act of yours, coming seeking baptism in the name of the Lord, is a public testimony of your professed subjection to Christ and the grace vouchsafed to you in the pardon and cleansing of your soul from sin. But that you may further declare your determination to walk in the commandments of the Lord and in the faith of Christ, you shall in the presence of God and of this congregation, give answer to the following questions:

1. Have you faith in Christ? Ans. I have.

2. Have you the witness of the Spirit to your acceptance with God? Ans. I have.

* *Discipline of the Pentecostal Holiness Church* (Publishing House of the Pentecostal Holiness Church: Franklin Springs, Ga., 1941). pp. 29; 10; 44-46.

3. Will you endeavor to walk in the fear of God and in the way of His commandment to the end of life? Ans. I will endeavor to do so by His grace.

4. Will you endeavor to seek after all the fullness of God, till all His will and good pleasure are fulfilled in you? Ans. I will do so by His grace helping me.

5. Will you attend divine services as opportunity affords, and contribute of your means for the spread of the full gospel? Ans. I will.

6. Do you desire to be baptized in this faith? Ans. That is my desire.

Here the minister shall proceed to administer the ordinance to the candidate, saying:

In obedience to the command of the Word of God, I baptize thee in the name of the Father, and of the Son, and of the Holy Ghost, and may the blessings of the Triune God rest upon you.

After the baptism of the candidate, the congregation shall sing a hymn, following which prayer shall be offered and the service closed with the benediction.

PILGRIM HOLINESS CHURCH

(Members: Over 23,000)

Doctrine: *

The Sacraments

Sacraments ordained of Christ are not only badges or tokens of Christian men's profession, but rather they are certain signs of grace and God's good will toward us, by the which He doth work invisibly in us, and doth not only quicken, but also strengthen and confirm our faith in Him. The Sacraments were not ordained of Christ to be gazed upon, or to be carried about, but that we should duly use them, and in such only as worthily receive the same they have a wholesome effect or operation; but they that receive them unworthily purchase unto themselves condemnation, as St. Paul saith (1 Cor. 11:29).

Baptism

This is an outward sign of an inward work wrought by the Holy Ghost in the soul. As to the mode, let every one be fully persuaded in his own mind, and no preacher or layman shall insist on any certain mode. The baptism of children shall be retained in the Church.

(Matt. 28:19; Acts 2:38; Col. 2:12; Acts 8:36-38; 16:33; 1 Pet. 3:21.)

Ritual: **

Let the minister read Matt. 3; John 3:1-8.

Prayer.

* *Manual of the Pilgrim Holiness Church* (revised edition, Indianapolis, Ind.: The Pilgrim Publishing House, 1942), pp. 21-22.

** *Op. cit.*, pp. 120-121.

Let the candidates be questioned as follows:

Dost thou renounce the devil and all his works, the vain pomp and glory of the world, with all covetous desires of the same, and the carnal desires of the flesh, so that thou wilt not be led by them?

Ans. I renounce them all.

Dost thou believe in God the Father and in Jesus Christ, His Son, our Lord; in the Holy Ghost, and in the Church of God in general; the remission of sins, the resurrection of the body, and everlasting life after death?

Ans. All this I steadfastly believe.

Wilt thou be baptized in this faith?

Ans. This is my desire.

Wilt thou obediently keep God's holy commandments and walk in them daily?

Ans. I will do so, God being my helper.

The minister, asking the name of the candidate, shall baptize him, saying: N....., I baptize thee in the name of the Father, and of the Son, and of the Holy Ghost. Amen.

Repeat the Lord's Prayer, closing with extemporary prayer.

Baptism of Children

Where parents so desire, let baptism be administered, using the following form:

Read Mark 15:13-16, and Matthew 18:1-6.

Then shall the minister take the child into his hands and say to the parents:

Name this child.

And then naming it after them, he shall baptize it, saying:

N....., I baptize thee in the name of the Father, and of the Son, and of the Holy Ghost. Amen.

Then shall the Lord's Prayer be repeated, closing with extemporary prayer.

THE PRESBYTERIAN CHURCH IN THE UNITED STATES OF AMERICA *

(Members: 1,971,000)

Doctrine: **

I. Baptism is a Sacrament of the New Testament, ordained by Jesus Christ, not only for the solemn admission of the party baptized into the visible Church, but also to be unto him a sign and seal of the covenant of grace, of

* The Orthodox Presbyterian Church also holds to the same doctrine and rite. Membership exceeds 5,000.

** *Constitution of the Presbyterian Church in the United States of America* (Philadelphia, Pa.: Westminster Press, 1943), pp. 109-112.

his ingrafting into Christ, of regeneration, of remission of sins, and of his giving up unto God, through Jesus Christ, to walk in newness of life: which Sacrament is, by Christ's own appointment, to be continued in His Church until the end of the world.

II. The outward element to be used in this Sacrament is water, wherewith the party is to be baptized in the name of the Father, and of the Son, and of the Holy Ghost, by a minister of the gospel, lawfully called thereunto.

III. Dipping of the person into the water is not necessary; but Baptism is rightly administered by pouring or sprinkling water upon the person.

IV. Not only those that do actually profess faith in, and obedience unto Christ, but also the infants of one or both believing parents are to be baptized.

V. Although it be a great sin to contemn or neglect this ordinance, yet grace and salvation are not so inseparably annexed unto it, as that no person can be regenerated or saved without it, or that all that are baptized are undoubtedly regenerated.

VI. The efficacy of Baptism is not tied to that moment of time wherein it is administered; yet, notwithstanding, by the right use of this ordinance the grace promised is not only offered, but really exhibited and conferred by the Holy Ghost, to such (whether of age or infants) as that grace belongeth unto, according to the counsel of God's own will, in His appointed time.

VII. The Sacrament of Baptism is but once to be administered to any person.

Manner of Administering Baptism: ***

THE BAPTISM OF INFANTS

Baptism is not to be unnecessarily delayed; not to be administered, in any case, by any private person; but by a minister of Christ, called to be the steward of the mysteries of God. It is usually to be administered in the church, in the presence of the congregation; and it is convenient that it be performed

*** *The Book of Common Worship* (revised ed., For Voluntary Use, Philadelphia, Pa.: Presbyterian Board of Christian Education, 1943), pp. 57-63.

In the *Directory for the Worship of God*, which is contained in the work entitled, *Constitution of the Presbyterian Church in the United States of America*, the essential requirements of the administration of baptism which are obligatory are noted (Chapter viii, p. 446-448):

I. Baptism is not to be unnecessarily delayed; not to be administered, in any case, by any private person; but by a minister of Christ, called to be the steward of the mysteries of God.

It is usually to be administered in the church, in the presence of the congregation; and it is convenient that it be performed immediately after sermon.

Of the expediency of performing this service in other places than the church, the minister shall be the judge.

II. Of the administration of baptism to infants:

After previous notice is given to the minister, the child to be baptized is to be presented, by one or both the parents, signifying their desire that the child may be baptized.

Before baptism, let the minister use some words of instruction respecting the institution, nature, use, and ends of this ordinance; showing:

"That it is instituted by Christ, that it is a seal of the righteousness of faith; that the seed of the faithful have no less a right to this ordinance, under the gospel, that the seed of Abraham to circumcision, under the Old Testament; that Christ commanded all nations to be baptized; that He blessed little children, declaring that of such is the kingdom of heaven; that children are federally holy, and therefore ought to be baptized; that we are by nature sin-

immediately after the sermon. Of the expediency of performing this service in other places than the church, the minister shall be the judge.—Directory for Worship, Chap. viii, 1.

After previous notice is given to the minister, the child to be baptized is to be presented, by one or both the parents, signifying their desire that the child may be baptized.—Directory for Worship, Chap. viii, 2.

While the parents are bringing the children to be baptized a baptismal hymn may be sung: or the following Sentences may be read by the minister.

The mercy of the Lord is from everlasting to everlasting upon them that fear Him, and His righteousness unto children's children,

To such as keep His covenant, and to those that remember His commandments to do them.

He shall feed His flock like a shepherd, He shall gather the lambs with His arm and carry them in His bosom.

For the promise is unto you and to your children, and to all that are afar off, even as many as the Lord, our God shall call.

Glory be to the Father and to the Son: and to the Holy Ghost;

As it was in the beginning, is now, and ever shall be: world without end. *Amen.*

The Minister shall address the Parents in this wise:

ful, guilty, and polluted, and have need of cleansing by the blood of Christ, and by the sanctifying influences of the Spirit of God."

The minister is also to exhort the parents to the careful performance of their duty, requiring:

"That they teach the child to read the Word of God, that they instruct him in the principles of our holy religion, as contained in the Scriptures of the Old and New Testaments; an excellent summary of which we have in the Confession of Faith of this Church, and in the Larger and Shorter Catechisms of the Westminster Assembly, which are to be recommended to them, as adopted by this Church, for their direction and assistance in the discharge of this important duty; that they pray with and for the child; that they set an example of piety and godliness before him, and endeavor by all the means of God's appointment to bring up their child in the nurture and admonition of the Lord."

Then the minister is to pray for a blessing to attend this ordinance; after which, calling the child by name, he shall say:

"I baptize thee, in the name of the Father, and of the Son, and of the Holy Ghost."

As he pronounces these words, he is to baptize the child with water, by pouring or sprinkling it on the head of the child, without adding any other ceremony; and the whole shall be concluded with prayer.

III. Of the administration of baptism to adult:

When unbaptized persons are to be admitted into the Church, they shall, in ordinary cases, after giving satisfaction with respect to their knowledge and piety, make a public profession of their faith in the presence of the congregation; and thereupon be baptized.

Before baptism, let the minister use some words of instruction respecting the institution, nature, use, and ends of this ordinance, showing:

"That it is instituted by Christ; that our Lord commanded His disciples to baptize believers of every nation; that it is a sacrament wherein the washing with water, in the name of the Father, and of the Son, and of the Holy Ghost, doth signify and seal our engrafting into Christ, and partaking of the benefits of the covenant of grace, and our engagement to be the Lord's; that it is not to be administered to any that are out of the visible Church till they profess their faith in Christ and obedience to Him; that it becomes an effectual means of salvation, not from any virtue in it, or in him that doth administer it, but only by the blessing of Christ, and the working of His Spirit in them that by faith receives it."

The minister shall then propose to the person to be baptized the following or similar questions, to wit:

"Do you believe that Jesus Christ is the only-begotten Son of God and the only Saviour from sin?"

"Is it your desire to be baptized in this faith?"

Then the minister shall baptize the candidate by pouring or sprinkling water upon his head, calling him by name, and using these words:

"I baptize thee, in the name of the Father, and of the Son, and of the Holy Ghost."

The administration of the sacrament shall be concluded with prayer.

Beloved in Christ: Baptism is a sacrament given by our Lord to His Church as a sign and seal of the remission of sins and our union with Christ. It is to be administered not only to believers, but also to their children, to signify their membership in the household of faith. Our Saviour called the children unto Him, and blessed them, saying: Suffer the little children to come unto Me, and forbid them not: for of such is the Kingdom of God.

For as much as you desire and claim this blessing for your *Child,* you will now engage, on your part, to perform those things which God requires of you, that the good will and pleasure of your Heavenly Father may be known to your *Child.*

Here the Minister shall address the following Questions to the Parents; and the Parents, each of them, shall make answer:

Question: Do you acknowledge your faith in Christ and therein consecrate your *Child* to Him?

Answer: I do.

Question: Do you promise to instruct your *Child* in the principles of our holy religion, as contained in the Scriptures, to pray with *him* and for *him,* and to bring *him* up in the nurture and admonition of the Lord?

Answer: I do.

Then the Minister shall say:

Grant, O Lord, to *these* Thy *servants* grace to perform the things *they have* promised before Thee:

And sanctify with Thy Spirit *this Child* now to be baptized according to Thy Word; through Jesus Christ our Lord. *Amen.*

Then all present reverently standing, the Minister shall say to the Parents:

What is the given name of this Child?

Then the Minister (taking the Child in his arms, or leaving it in the arms of the Parent), pronouncing the name of the Child, shall pour or sprinkle water upon it, saying:

N____, I baptize thee in the Name of the Father, and of the Son, and of the Holy Spirit. *Amen.*

Then the Minister, addressing the People, shall say:

This Child, thus acknowledged as a *member* of Christ's Church, *is* commended to your love and care. Whosoever shall receive one such little child in My Name receiveth Me.

Then the Minister shall say:

Let Us Pray

Most holy and merciful Father, we give Thee hearty thanks that Thou hast numbered us amongst Thy people, and dost also call our children unto Thee, marking them with this Sacrament, as a singular token and badge of Thy love. Wherefore, we beseech Thee to confirm Thy favor more and more toward us, and to take into Thy tuition and defense *this Child,* whom we offer and present unto Thee with common supplications. Grant that *he* may know

Thee *his* Heavenly Father, through Thy Holy Spirit working in *his heart,* and that *he* may not be ashamed to confess the faith of Christ crucified; but may continue His good and faithful servant, and so prevail against evil that in the end *he* may obtain the victory, and be exalted into the liberty of Thy kingdom; through Jesus Christ our Lord. *Amen.*

The Lord's Prayer

Our Father, Who art in heaven, hallowed be Thy Name. Thy kingdom come. Thy will be done, on earth as it is in heaven. Give us this day our daily bread. And forgive us our debts, as we forgive our debtors. And lead us not into temptation, but deliver us from evil: For Thine is the kingdom, and the power, and the glory, for ever. *Amen.*

Then the Minister shall say:

The grace of the Lord Jesus Christ, and the love of God, and the communion of the Holy Spirit, be with you all. *Amen.*

Infants descending from parents, either both or but one of them professing faith in Christ and obedience to Him, are within the covenant of promise, and are to be baptized.—Larger Catechism, 166.

The efficacy of Baptism is not tied to that moment of time wherein it is administered; yet, notwithstanding, by the right use of this Sacrament the grace promised is not only offered, but really exhibited and conferred by the Holy Ghost, to such (whether of age or infants) as that grace belongeth unto, according to the counsel of God's own will, in His appointed time. Grace and salvation are, however, not so inseparably annexed unto Baptism as that none can be regenerated or saved without it, or that all that are baptized are undoubtedly regenerated.—Confession of Faith, Chap. xxviii, 5, 6.

When, by death of the parents or otherwise, children are removed from their custody, the guardian or other person who has undertaken to rear them may present them for Baptism, provided he possess the qualifications requisite for having his own children baptized, and is willing to assume the obligations made by parents in the foregoing service.—Minutes of the Synod of 1786.

THE BAPTISM OF ADULTS AND THEIR RECEPTION TO THE LORD'S SUPPER

When unbaptized persons apply for admission into the Church, they shall, in ordinary cases, after giving satisfaction with respect to their knowledge and piety, make a public profession of their faith in the presence of the congregation; and thereupon be baptized.—Directory for Worship, Chap. viii, 3.

The Minister shall say:

These persons desiring to profess *their* faith in Christ *have* been examined, and approved by the Session as to their knowledge and piety, and will now present *themselves* for baptism and reception to the Lord's Supper: (Names).

The Candidates appearing before the Minister, he shall say:

Hear the words of the Lord Jesus concerning this Sacrament, spoken to His disciples, before His ascension to the right hand of God:

"All power is given unto Me in heaven and in earth. Go ye, therefore, and teach all nations, baptizing them in the name of the Father, and of the Son, and of the Holy Ghost: teaching them to observe all things whatsoever I have commanded you: and, lo, I am with you always, even unto the end of the world."

Hence St. Peter, on the day of Pentecost, called upon the people, saying, "Repent, and be baptized, every one of you, in the name of Jesus Christ, for the remission of sins, and ye shall receive the gift of the Holy Ghost. For the promise is unto you, and to your children, and to all that are afar off, even as many as the Lord our God shall call."

Doubt ye not, therefore, but earnestly believe, that He will number among His people *these* present *persons,* truly repenting and coming unto Him by faith, and that this Baptism with water in His Name shall be unto *them* the sign and seal of the washing away of *their* sins, *their* union with Christ, *their* regeneration by His Holy Spirit, and *their* engagement to be the Lord's.

The Minister shall then say to the persons to be baptized, and each shall answer, as follows:

Dearly beloved, you are now faithfully, for your part, in the presence of God and of His congregation, to answer to the following questions.

Question: Do you receive and profess the Christian faith, and in this faith do you desire to be baptized?

Answer: I do.

Question: Do you confess your sins, and repent of them, and put all your trust in the mercy of God, which is in Christ Jesus; and do you promise in His strength to lead a sober, righteous, and godly life?

Answer: I do.

The question here following is to be omitted at this point in case this Order for Baptism is used in connection with that for Reception to the Lord's Supper, page 72.

Question: Now desiring to be received to the Lord's Supper, do you promise to make diligent use of the means of grace, giving your whole heart to the service of Christ and His kingdom in the world, and continuing in the peace and fellowship of the people of God?

Answer: I do.

Then the Minister shall say:

Let Us Pray

We beseech Thee, O Lord, that it may please Thee to receive, and to sanctify with Thy Spirit, *these persons* now to be baptized according to Thy Word; that *they* may obtain the fullness of Thy grace, and ever remain in the number of Thy faithful children; through Jesus Christ our Lord. *Amen.*

Then, all present reverently standing, and each person to be baptized kneel-

ing, the Minister, pronouncing his name, shall pour or sprinkle water upon his forehead, saying:

N......, I baptize thee in the Name of the Father, and of the Son, and of the Holy Spirit. *Amen.*

Then the Minister shall say:

We receive *this person* into the congregation of Christ's flock; in the confidence that *he* will never be ashamed to confess the faith of Christ crucified, and to continue Christ's faithful follower and servant unto his life's end.

Here, if persons who have been baptized in infancy are to be received to the Lord's Supper, they may be called to come forward; and the Minister, omitting the remainder of this Order, may proceed with the Order for Reception to the Lord's Supper, the newly baptized persons still standing in their places before him.

Then the Minister (laying his hand, if such be his discretion, upon the head of every one in order kneeling before him) shall say:

Defend, O Lord, this Thy Child with Thy heavenly grace; that he may continue Thine for ever; and daily increase in Thy Holy Spirit more and more, until he come unto Thy everlasting kingdom. *Amen.*

Let Us Pray

O Lord and Father of us all, we give Thee thanks, and praise for Thy loving-kindness to these Thy servants, to whom Thou givest shelter within the covenant of Thy peace, and whom Thou makest to sit down at Thy table. We entreat Thee of Thy great mercy to perfect in them the good work Thou hast begun; that they, being defended by Thy fatherly hand, and strengthened with power through Thy Spirit in the inward man, may be enabled to keep this covenant without spot, unrebukable, until the day of the appearing of our Lord Jesus Christ. *Amen.*

Now unto him that is able to keep you from falling, and to present you faultless before the presence of his glory with exceeding joy; to the only wise God our Saviour, be glory and majesty, dominion and power, both now and ever. *Amen.*

PRESBYTERIAN CHURCH OF THE UNITED STATES

(Members: 532,000)

Doctrine: *

Baptism is a sacrament of the New Testament, ordained by Jesus Christ, not only for the solemn admission of the party baptized into the visible church, but also to be unto him a sign and seal of the covenant of grace, of his ingrafting into Christ, of regeneration, of remission of sins, and of his

* *The Constitution of the Presbyterian Church in the United States* (revised edition, Richmond, Va.: Presbyterian Committee of Publication), *Confession of Faith* (revised, 1932), chapter 28.

giving up unto God, through Jesus Christ, to walk in newness of life: which sacrament is, by Christ's own appointment, to be continued in His church until the end of the world.

II. The outward element to be used in this sacrament is water, wherewith the party is to be baptized in the name of the Father, and of the Son, and of the Holy Ghost, by a minister of the gospel, lawfully called thereunto.

III. Dipping of the person into the water is not necessary; but baptism is rightly administered by pouring, or sprinkling water upon the person.

IV. Not only those that do actually profess faith in, and obedience unto Christ, but also the infants of one or both believing parents are to be baptized.

V. Although it be a great sin to contemn or neglect this ordinance, yet grace and salvation are not so inseparably annexed unto it, as that no person can be regenerated or saved without it, or that all that are baptized, are undoubtedly regenerated.

VI. The efficacy of baptism is not tied to that moment of time wherein it is administered; yet, notwithstanding, by the right use of this ordinance the grace promised is not only offered, but really exhibited and conferred by the Holy Ghost, to such (whether of age or infants) as that grace belongeth unto, according to the counsel of God's own will, in his appointed time.

VII. The sacrament of baptism is but once to be administered to any person.

Administration: **

BAPTISM OF INFANTS

343.—It is the duty and privilege of parents to dedicate their children to God in baptism, thereby claiming God's covenant promises to parents and children.

344.—Baptism is not to be unnecessarily delayed, nor to be administered in any case by any private person, but by a minister of Christ, called to be the steward of the mysteries of God.

345.—Baptism is ordinarily to be administered in the church in the presence of the congregation; yet there may be occasions when it is expedient to administer this ordinance elsewhere, of which the minister is to be the judge.

346.—After previous notice is given to the minister, the child to be baptized is to be presented, by one or both the parents, or some other responsible person, signifying the desire that the child be baptized.

347.—Before baptism, let the minister use some words of instruction, respecting the institution, nature, use and ends of this ordinance, showing:

That it is instituted by Christ; that it is a seal of the righteousness of faith; that the seed of the faithful have no less a right to this ordinance, under the gospel than the seed of Abraham to circumcision, under the Old Testament; that Christ commanded all nations to be baptized; that He blessed little children, declaring that of such is the kingdom of Heaven; that the promise of the

** *The Constitution of the Presbyterian Church in the United States* (revised edition, Richmond, Va.: Presbyterian Committee of Publication), *Book of Church Order* (revised, 1938), chapter 10.

gospel is to the believer and his house; that household baptism was practiced by the apostles; that we are, by nature, sinful, guilty, and polluted, and have need of cleansing by the blood of Christ, and by the sanctifying influence of the Spirit of God.

The minister is also to exhort the parents to the careful performance of their duty, requiring;

That they teach the child to read the Word of God; that they instruct it in the principles of our holy religion, as contained in the Scriptures of the Old and New Testaments, an excellent summary of which we have in the Confession of Faith, and in the Larger and Shorter Catechisms of the Westminster Assembly, which are to be recommended to them, as adopted by the Church, for their direction and assistance, in the discharge of this important duty; that they pray with and for it; that they set an example of piety and godliness before it; and endeavor, by all the means of God's appointment, to bring up their child in the nurture and admonition of the Lord.

348.—The minister may then propose the following, or like questions:

(1) Do you acknowledge your child's need of the cleansing blood of Jesus Christ, and the renewing grace of the Holy Spirit?

(2) Do you claim God's covenant promises in (his) behalf, and do you look in faith to the Lord Jesus Christ for (his) salvation, as you do for your own?

(3) Do you now unreservedly dedicate your child to God, and promise, in humble reliance upon divine grace, that you will endeavor to set before (him) a godly example, that you will pray with and for (him), that you will teach (him) the doctrines of our holy religion, and that you will strive, by all the means of God's appointment, to bring (him) up in the nurture and admonition of the Lord?

349.—Then the minister is to pray for a blessing to attend this ordinance, after which, calling the child by name, he shall say:

I baptize thee in the name of the Father, and of the Son, and of the Holy Ghost.

As he pronounces these words, he is to baptize the child with water, by pouring or sprinkling it on the head of the child, without adding any other ceremony; and the whole shall be concluded with prayer.

Admission of Persons to Sealing Ordinances
(Baptism of Adults) ***

354.—The time having come for the making of a public profession, and those who have been approved by the Session having taken their places in the presence of the congregation, the minister may state that:

(1) Of the number of those who were baptized in infancy as members of the Church of God by birthright, and heirs of the covenant promises, and who were then dedicated to God by their parents, or some other responsible per-

*** *Book of Church Order* (revised, 1938), chapter 11.

son, in solemn vows, the Session has examined and approved A, B and C, who come now to assume for themselves the full privileges and responsibilities of their inheritance in the household of faith.

(2) If there be present any candidates for baptism, the minister may state that: As applicants for admission into the Church of God by baptism, which is a sign and seal of our engrafting into Christ, and of our engagement to be the Lord's, the Session has examined and approved D, E and F, who are cordially welcomed into the goodly fellowship of the household of faith.

(3) The minister may then address those making a profession in the following terms: (All of) you being here present to make a public profession of faith, are to assent to the following declarations and promises, by which you enter into a solemn covenant with God and His Church;

1. Do you acknowledge yourselves to be sinners in the sight of God, justly deserving His displeasure, and without hope save in His sovereign mercy?

2. Do you believe in the Lord Jesus Christ as the Son of God, and Saviour of sinners, and do you receive and rest upon Him alone for salvation as He is offered in the Gospel?

3. Do you now resolve and promise, in humble reliance upon the grace of the Holy Spirit, that you will endeavor to live as becometh the followers of Christ?

4. Do you promise to support the Church in its worship and work to the best of your ability?

5. Do you submit yourselves to the government and discipline of the Church, and promise to study its purity and peace?

The minister may now briefly admonish those making a profession of faith as to the importance of the solemn obligations they have assumed; then baptism may be administered, if there be present any candidates for the ordinance, and the whole concluded with prayer.

CUMBERLAND PRESBYTERIAN CHURCH

(Members: 73,000)

Doctrine: *

Water-baptism is a sacrament of the New Testament, ordained by Jesus Christ as a sign or symbol of the baptism of the Holy Spirit, and as the seal of the Covenant of Grace.

The outward element to be used in this sacrament is water, wherewith the party is to be baptized into the name of the Father, and of the Son, and of the Holy Spirit, by an ordained minister of the gospel.

Baptism is rightly administered by pouring or sprinkling water upon the person, yet the validity of this sacrament does not depend upon any particular mode of administration.

* *Confession of Faith* and Government of the Cumberland Presbyterian Church (Revised), Adopted, 1883 (Nashville, Tenn.: Cumberland Presbyterian Publishing House, 1928), pp. 58-60, 34-36, 149-150.

The proper subjects of water-baptism are believing adults; also infants, one or both of whose parents or guardians are believers.

There is no saving efficacy in water-baptism, yet it is a duty of all believers to confess Christ in this solemn ordinance, and it is also the duty of all believing parents to consecrate their children to God in baptism.

Regeneration: Those who believe in the Lord Jesus Christ are regenerated, or born from above, renewed in spirit, and made new creatures in Christ.

The necessity for this moral purification arises out of the enmity of the human heart against God, its insubordination to His law, and its consequent incapacity to love and glorify God.

Regeneration is of God's free grace alone, and is the work of the Holy Spirit, who, by taking of the things which are Christ's and showing them unto the sinner, enables him to lay hold on Christ. This renewal of the heart by the Holy Spirit is not of the nature of a physical but of a moral work—a purification of the heart by faith.

All infants dying in infancy, and all persons who have never had the faculty of reason, are regenerated and saved.

Ritual: *

Baptism is not to be unnecessarily delayed, and should be administered by an ordained minister of the gospel.

When a child is to be baptized, it should be presented before the minister by one or both of the parents.

Before baptism, let the minister use some words of instruction respecting the institution, nature, use, and ends of this ordinance—showing:

That it is instituted by Christ; that it is a seal of the righteousness of faith; that the children of the faithful have no less right to the ordinance of the gospel than the children of Abraham to circumcision under the Old Testament; that Christ commanded all nations to be baptized; that he blessed little children, declaring that of such is the kingdom of heaven; that we are, by nature, polluted, and have need of cleansing by the blood of Christ, and by the sanctifying influences of the Holy Spirit.

The minister is also to exhort the parents to the careful performance of their duty—requiring:

That they teach the child to read the word of God; that they instruct it in the principles of our holy religion, as contained in the Scriptures of the Old and the New Testament, an excellent summary of which we have in the Confession of Faith of this Church, and in the Catechism, which are to be recommended to them as adopted by the Church for their direction and assistance in the discharge of this important duty; that they pray with and for it; that they set an example of piety and godliness before it; and endeavor, by all the means of God's appointment, to bring up their child in the nurture and admonition of the Lord.

Then the minister is to pray for a blessing to attend this ordinance; after which, calling the child by its name, he shall say:

I baptize thee into the name of the Father, and of the Son, and of the Holy Spirit.

As he pronounces these words, he is to baptize the child with water, by pouring or sprinkling it on the face of the child, without adding any other ceremony, and the whole shall be concluded with prayer.

When unbaptized adults apply for baptism, the ordinance shall be administered upon profession of their faith in Christ, they having given satisfactory evidence of their conversion to God.

PROTESTANT EPISCOPAL CHURCH

(Members: 1,996,000)

Ritual: *

The Minister of every Parish shall often admonish the People, that they defer not the Baptism of their Children, and that it is most convenient that Baptism should be administered upon Sundays and other Holy Days. Nevertheless, if necessity so require, Baptism may be administered upon any other day. And also he shall warn them that, except for urgent cause, they seek not to have their Children baptized in their houses.

There shall be for every Male-child to be baptized, when they can be had, two Godfathers and one Godmother; and for every Female, one Godfather, and two Godmothers; and Parents shall be admitted as Sponsors, if it be desired.

When there are Children to be baptized, the Parents or Sponsors shall give knowledge thereof to the Minister. And then the Godfathers and Godmothers, and the People with the Children, must be ready at the Font, either immediately after the Second Lesson at Morning or Evening prayer, or at such other time as the Minister shall appoint.

When any such Persons as are of riper years are to be baptized, timely notice shall be given to the Minister; that so due care may be taken for their examination, whether they be sufficiently instructed in the Principles of the Christian Religion; and that they may be exhorted to prepare themselves, with Prayers and Fasting, for the receiving of this holy Sacrament. And Note, That at the time of the Baptism of an Adult, there shall be present with him at the Font at least two Witnesses.

The Minister, having come to the Font, which is then to be filled with pure Water, shall say as followeth, the People all standing,

Hath this Child (Person) been already baptized, or no?

If they answer, No: then shall the Minister proceed as followeth.

Dearly Beloved, forasmuch as our Saviour Christ saith, None can enter into the kingdom of God, except he be regenerate and born anew of Water and of the Holy Ghost; I beseech you to call upon God the Father, through our Lord

* *The Book of Common Prayer* and Administration of the Sacraments and Other Rites and Ceremonies of the Church, According to the Use of the Protestant Episcopal Church in the United States of America (New York: Oxford University Press, 1935), pp. 273-281.

Jesus Christ, that of His bounteous mercy He will grant to this Child (this Person) that which by nature he cannot have; that he may be baptized with Water and the Holy Ghost, and received into Christ's holy Church and be made a living member of the same.

Then shall the Minister say, Let us pray.

Almighty and immortal God, the aid of all who need, the helper of all who flee to Thee for succor, the life of those who believe, and the resurrection of the dead; we call upon thee for this Child (this Thy Servant), that he, coming to Thy holy Baptism, may receive remission of sin, by spiritual regeneration. Receive him, O Lord, as Thou hast promised by Thy well-beloved Son, saying, Ask, and ye shall have; seek, and ye shall find; knock, and it shall be opened unto you. So give now unto us who ask; let us who seek, find; open the gate unto us who knock; that this Child (this Thy Servant) may enjoy the everlasting benediction of Thy heavenly washing, and may come to the eternal kingdom which Thou hast promised by Christ our Lord. Amen.

Then the Minister shall say as followeth:

Hear the words of the Gospel, written by Saint Mark, in the tenth Chapter, at the thirteenth Verse. . . .

Or this:

Hear the words of the Gospel, written by Saint John, in the third Chapter, at the first Verse. . . .

Or this:

Hear the words of the Gospel, written by Saint Matthew, in the twenty-eighth Chapter, at the eighteenth Verse. . . .

Then shall the Minister say:

And now, being persuaded of the good will of our heavenly Father toward this Child (this person) declared by His Son Jesus Christ; let us faithfully and devoutly give thanks unto Him, and say:

Almighty and everlasting God, heavenly Father, we give Thee humble thanks, that Thau hast vouchsafed to call us to the knowledge of Thy grace, and faith in Thee: Increase this knowledge, and confirm this faith in us evermore. Give Thy Holy Spirit to this Child (this Thy Servant), that he may be born again, and be made an heir of everlasting salvation; through our Lord Jesus Christ, Who liveth and reigneth with Thee and the same Holy Spirit, now and forever. Amen.

Minister and People

When the Office is used for Children, the Minister shall speak unto the Godfathers and Godmothers on this wise.

Dearly Beloved, ye have brought this Child here to be baptized; ye have prayed that our Lord Jesus Christ would vouchsafe to receive him, to release him from sin, to sanctify him with the Holy Ghost, to give him the kingdom of heaven, and everlasting life.

Dost thou, therefore, in the name of this Child, renounce the devil and all his works, the vain pomp and glory of the world, with all covetous desires of the same, and the sinful desires of the flesh, so that thou wilt not follow, nor be led by them?

Answer. I renounce them all; and, by God's help, will endeavor not to follow, nor be led by them.

Minister. Dost thou believe all the Articles of the Christian Faith, as contained in the Apostles' Creed?

Answer. I do.

Minister. Wilt thou be baptized in this Faith?

Answer. That is my desire.

Minister. Wilt thou then obediently keep God's holy will and commandments, and walk in the same all the days of thy life?

Answer. I will, by God's help.

Minister. Having now, in the name of this Child, made these promises, wilt thou also on thy part take heed that this Child learn the Creed, the Lord's Prayer, and the Ten Commandments, and all other things which a Christian ought to know and believe to his soul's health?

Answer. I will, by God's help.

Minister. Wilt thou take heed that this Child, so soon as sufficiently instructed, be brought to the Bishop to be confirmed by him?

Answer. I will, God being my helper.

When the Office is used for Adults, the Minister shall address them on this wise, the Persons to be baptized answering the questions for themselves.

Well-beloved, you have come hither desiring to receive holy Baptism. We have prayed that our Lord Jesus Christ would vouchsafe to receive you, to release you from sin, to sanctify you with the Holy Ghost, to give you the kingdom of heaven, and everlasting life.

Dost thou renounce the devil and all his works, the vain pomp and glory of the world, with all covetous desires of the same, and the sinful desires of the flesh, so that thou wilt not follow, nor be led by them?

Answer. I renounce them all; and, by God's help, will endeavor not to follow, nor be led by them.

Minister. Dost thou believe in Jesus the Christ, the Son of the Living God?

Answer. I do.

Minister. Dost thou accept him, and desire to follow him as thy Saviour and Lord?

Answer. I do.

Minister. Dost thou believe all the Articles of the Christian Faith, as contained in the Apostles' Creed.

Answer. I do.

Minister. Wilt thou be baptized in this Faith?

Answer. That is my desire.

Minister. Wilt thou then obediently keep God's holy will and commandments, and walk in the same all the days of thy life?

Answer. I will, by God's help.

Then shall the Minister say:

O Merciful God, grant that like as Christ died and rose again, so this Child (this Thy Servant) may die to sin and rise to newness of life. Amen.

Grant that all sinful affections may die in him, and that all things belonging to the Spirit may live and grow in him. Amen.

Grant that he may have power and strength to have victory, and to triumph, against the devil, the world, and the flesh. Amen.

Grant that whosoever is here dedicated to thee by our office and ministry, may also be endued with heavenly virtues, and everlastingly rewarded, through Thy mercy, O blessed Lord God, Who dost live, and govern all things, world without end. Amen.

Minister. The Lord be with you.

Answer. And with thy spirit.

Minister. Lift up your hearts.

Answer. We lift them up unto the Lord.

Minister. Let us give thanks unto our Lord God.

Answer. It is meet and right so to do.

Then the Minister shall say:

It is very meet, right, and our bounden duty, that we should give thanks unto Thee, O Lord, Holy Father, Almighty, Everlasting God, for that Thy dearly beloved Son Jesus Christ, for the forgiveness of our sins did shed out of His most precious side both water and blood; and gave commandment to His disciples, that they should go teach all nations, and baptize them in the Name of the Father, and of the Son, and of the Holy Ghost. Regard, we beseech Thee, the supplications of Thy congregation; sanctify this Water to the mystical washing away of sin; and grant that this Child (this Thy Servant), now to be baptized therein, may receive the fullness of Thy grace, and ever remain in the number of Thy faithful children; through the same Jesus Christ our Lord, to Whom, with Thee, in the unity of the Holy Spirit, be all honor and glory, now and evermore. Amen.

Then the Minister shall take the Child into his arms, and shall say to the Godfathers and Godmothers:

Name this Child.

And then, naming the Child after them, he shall dip him in the Water discreetly, or shall pour Water upon him, saying:

N., I baptize thee In the Name of the Father, and of the Son, and of the Holy Ghost. Amen.

But NOTE, That if the Person to be baptized be an Adult, the Minister shall take him by the hand, and shall ask the Witnesses the Name; and then shall dip him in the Water, or pour Water upon him, using the same form of words.

Then the Minister shall say:

We receive this Child (Person) into the congregation of Christ's flock; and do * sign him with the sign of the Cross, in token that hereafter he shall not be ashamed to confess the faith of Christ crucified, and manfully to fight under His banner, against sin, the world, and the devil; and to continue Christ's faithful soldier and servant unto his life's end. Amen.

Then shall the Minister say:

* *Here the Minister shall make a Cross upon the Child's (or Person's) forehead.*

Seeing now, dearly beloved brethren, that this Child (this Person) is regenerate, and grafted into the body of Christ's Church, let us give thanks unto Almighty God for these benefits; and with one accord make our prayers unto Him, that this Child (this Person) may lead the rest of his life according to this beginning.

Then shall be said:

Our Father, Who art in heaven, Hallowed by Thy Name. Thy kingdom come. Thy will be done, On earth as it is in heaven. Give us this day our daily bread. And forgive us our trespasses, As we forgive those who trespass against us. And lead us not into temptation, But deliver us from evil. For Thine is the kingdom, and the power, and the glory, for ever and ever. Amen.

Then shall the Minister say:

We yield Thee hearty thanks, most merciful Father, that it hath pleased Thee to regenerate this Child (this Thy Servant) with Thy Holy Spirit, to receive him for Thine own Child, and to incorporate him into Thy holy Church. And humbly we beseech Thee to grant, that he, being dead unto sin, may live unto righteousness, and being buried with Christ in His death, may also be partaker of His resurrection; so that finally, with the residue of Thy holy Church, he may be an inheritor of Thine everlasting kingdom; through Christ our Lord. Amen.

Then the Minister shall add:

The Almighty God, the Father of our Lord Jesus Christ, of Whom the whole family in heaven and earth is named; Grant you to be strengthened with might by His Spirit in the inner man; that, Christ dwelling in your hearts by faith, ye may be filled with all the fullness of God. Amen.

It is expedient that every Adult, thus baptized, should be confirmed by the Bishop, so soon after his Baptism as conveniently may be; that so he may be admitted to the Holy Communion.

Private Baptism

When in consideration of extreme sickness, necessity may require, then the following form shall suffice:

The Child (or Person) being named by some one who is present, the Minister shall pour Water upon him, saying these words:

N., I baptize thee In the Name of the Father, and of the Son, and of the Holy Ghost. Amen.

After which shall be said the Lord's Prayer, and the Thanksgiving from this Office, beginning, We yield Thee hearty thanks, *etc.*

But NOTE, *That in the case of an Adult, the Minister shall first ask the questions provided in this Office for the Baptism of Adults.*

THE REFORMED CHURCH IN AMERICA

(Members: 163,000)

Ritual: *

THE principal parts of the doctrine of Holy Baptism are these three:

First. That we, with our children, are conceived and born in sin, and therefore are children of wrath, insomuch that we cannot enter into the kingdom of God, except we are born again. This the dipping in or sprinkling with water teaches us, whereby the impurity of our souls is signified, and we are admonished to loathe and humble ourselves before God, and seek for our purification and salvation without ourselves.

Secondly. Holy Baptism witnesseth and sealeth unto us the washing away of our sins, through Jesus Christ. Therefore we are baptized in the Name of the Father, and of the Son, and of the Holy Ghost. For when we are baptized in the Name of the Father, God the Father witnesseth and sealeth unto us that He doth make an eternal covenant of grace with us, and adopts us for His children and heirs, and therefore will provide us with every good thing, and avert all evil or turn it to our profit. And when we are baptized in the Name of the Son, the Son sealeth unto us that He doth wash us in His blood from all our sins, incorporating us into the fellowship of His death and resurrection, so that we are freed from all our sins and accounted righteous before God. In like manner, when we are baptized in the Name of the Holy Ghost, the Holy Ghost assures us, by this holy Sacrament, that He will dwell in us, and sanctify us to be members of Christ, applying unto us that which we have in Christ, namely, the washing away of our sins and the daily renewing of our lives, till we shall finally be presented without spot or wrinkle among the assembly of the elect in life eternal.

Thirdly. Whereas in all covenants there are contained two parts, therefore are we by God, through Baptism, admonished of and obliged unto new obedience, namely, that we cleave to this one God, Father, Son, and Holy Ghost; that we trust in Him and love Him with all our heart, with all our soul, with all our mind, and with all our strength; that we forsake the world, crucify our old nature, and walk in a new and holy life.

And if we sometimes, through weakness, fall into sin, we must not despair of God's mercy nor continue in sin, since Baptism is a seal and undoubted testimony that we have an eternal covenant of grace with God.

I—To Infants

AND although our young children do not understand these things, we may not therefore exclude them from Baptism; for as they are, without their knowledge, partakers of the condemnation in Adam, so are they again received unto grace in Christ; as God speaketh unto Abraham, the father of all the faithful, and therefore unto us and our children (Gen. xvii: 7), saying, "I will establish

* *The Liturgy of the Reformed Church in America* (New York: The Board of Publication, 156 Fifth Avenue, 1940), pp. 10-17.

My covenant between Me and thee and thy seed after thee in their regenerations, for an everlasting covenant; to be a God unto thee, and to thy seed after thee." This also the Apostle Peter testified, with these words (Acts ii: 39): "For the promise is unto you, and to your children, and to all that are afar off, even as many as the Lord our God shall call." Therefore God formerly commanded them to be circumcised, which was a seal of the covenant, and of the righteousness of faith; and therefore Christ also embraced them, laid His hands upon them and blessed them (Mark x: 16).

Since then Baptism is come in the place of circumcision, infants are to be baptized as heirs of the kingdom of God and of His covenant. And parents are in duty bound further to instruct their children herein, when they shall arrive at years of discretion.

THAT therefore this holy ordinance of God may be administered to His glory, to our comfort, and to the edification of His Church, let us call upon His holy Name.

Prayer

O ALMIGHTY and eternal God, we beseech Thee that Thou wilt be pleased, of Thine infinite mercy, graciously to look upon these children, and incorporate them by Thy Holy Spirit into Thy Son Jesus Christ, that they may be buried with Him into His death and be raised with Him in newness of life; that they may daily follow Him, joyfully bearing their cross, and cleave unto Him in true faith, firm hope, and ardent love; that they may, with a comfortable sense of Thy favor, leave this life, which is nothing but a continual death, and at the last day may appear without terror before the judgment seat of Christ Thy Son; through Jesus Christ our Lord, Who with Thee and the Holy Ghost, one only God, lives and reigns forever. Amen.

An Exhortation to the Parents, and Those Who Come With Them to Baptism

BELOVED in the Lord Jesus Christ, you have heard that Baptism is an ordinance of God, to seal unto us and to our seed His covenant. Therefore it must be used for that end, and not out of custom or superstition. That it may then be manifest that you are thus minded, you are to answer sincerely to these questions:

First. Do you acknowledge that although our children are conceived and born in sin, and therefore are subject to all miseries, yea, to condemnation itself; yet that they are sanctified in Christ, and therefore, as members of His Church, ought to be baptized?

Secondly. Do you acknowledge the doctrine which is contained in the Old and New Testaments, and in the Articles of the Christian Faith, and which is taught here in this Christian Church, to be the true and perfect doctrine of salvation?

Thirdly. Do you promise and intend to see these children, when they come to the years of discretion, instructed and brought up in the aforesaid doctrine, or to help or cause them to be instructed therein, to the utmost of your power?

Answer. Yes.

Then the Minister of God's Word, in baptizing, shall say:

N., I baptize thee in the Name of the Father, and of the Son, and of the Holy Ghost. Amen.

Thanksgiving

ALMIGHTY God and merciful Father, we thank and praise Thee, that Thou hast forgiven us and our children all our sins, through the blood of Thy beloved Son Jesus Christ, and received us through Thy Holy Spirit, as members of Thy only-begotten Son, and adopted us to be Thy children, and sealed and confirmed the same unto us by Holy Baptism. We beseech Thee, through the same Son of Thy love, that Thou wilt be pleased always to govern these baptized children by Thy Holy Spirit; that they may be piously and religiously educated, increase and grow up in the Lord Jesus Christ; that they then may acknowledge Thy fatherly goodness and mercy, which Thou hast shown to them and us, and live in all righteousness, under our only Teacher, King, and High Priest, Jesus Christ; and manfully fight against and overcome sin, the devil, and his whole dominion, to the end that they may eternally praise and magnify Thee, and Thy Son Jesus Christ, together with the Holy Ghost, the one only True God. Amen.

II—To Adults

HOWEVER children of Christian parents, although they understand not this mystery, must be baptized by virtue of the covenant; yet it is not lawful to baptize those who have come to years of discretion, except they first be sensible of their sins, and make confession both of their repentance and their faith in Christ. For this cause not only did John the Baptist preach, according to the command of God, the Baptism of repentance, and baptize for the remission of sin those who confessed their sins (Mark i: 4); but our Lord Jesus Christ also commanded His disciples to teach all nations, and then to baptize them in the Name of the Father, and of the Son, and of the Holy Ghost, adding this promise: "He that believeth and is baptized shall be saved." According to which rule the Apostles (Acts ii, x, xvi) baptized none who were of years of discretion, but such as made confession of their faith and repentance. Therefore it is not lawful now to baptize any other adult persons, than such as have been taught the mysteries of Holy Baptism by the preaching of the Gospel, and are able to give an account of their faith by the confession of the mouth.

SINCE therefore you, N—, are also desirous of Holy Baptism, to the end it may be to you a seal of your engrafting into the Church of God: that it may appear that you do not only receive the Christian religion, in which you have been privately instructed by us, and of which also you have made confession before us, but that you, through the grace of God, intend and purpose to lead a life according to the same; you are sincerely to give answer before God and His Church:

First. Dost thou believe in the only True God, distinct in three persons, Father, Son and Holy Ghost, Who hath made heaven and earth, and all that in them is, of nothing, and still maintains and governs them, insomuch that nothing comes to pass, either in heaven or on earth, without His divine will?

Answer. Yes.

Secondly. Do thou believe that thou art conceived and born in sin, and therefore art a child of wrath by nature, wholly incapable of doing any good and prone to all evil; and that thou hast frequently, both in thought, word, and deed, transgressed the commandments of the Lord; and art thou heartily sorry for these sins?

Answer. Yes.

Thirdly. Dost thou believe that Christ, Who is the True and Eternal God, and Very Man, Who took His human nature on Him out of the flesh and blood of the Virgin Mary, is given thee of God to be thy Saviour; and that thou dost receive, by this faith, remission of sins in His blood; and that thou art made, by the power of the Holy Ghost, a member of Jesus Christ and of His Church?

Answer. Yes.

Fourthly. Dost thou assent to all the Articles of the Christian religion, as they are taught here in this Christian Church, according to the Word of God; and purpose steadfastly to continue in the same doctrine to the end of thy life; and also dost thou reject all heresies and schisms, repugnant to this doctrine, and promise to persevere in the communion of our Christian Church, not only in the hearing of the Word, but also in the use of the Lord's Supper?

Answer. Yes.

Fifthly. Hast thou taken a firm resolution always to lead a Christian life; to forsake the world and its evil lusts, as is becoming the members of Christ and His Church; and to submit thyself to all Christian admonitions?

Answer. Yes.

THE good and great God mercifully grant His grace and blessing to this thy purpose, through Jesus Christ. Amen.

Then the Minister of God's Word, in baptizing, shall say:

N—, I baptize thee, in the Name of the Father, and of the Son, and of the Holy Ghost. Amen.

Thanksgiving

ALMIGHTY God, our heavenly Father, we give Thee most humble and hearty thanks, that Thou hast called us to the knowledge of Thy grace, and unto the faith of Thy Son, and unto the covenant of salvation, wherein we are sealed by Holy Baptism. Give Thy Holy Spirit to these Thy servants, that, being born again and made heirs of God, they may keep themselves in Thy love, and receive the fulfillment of Thy promises; through our Lord Jesus Christ, Who, with Thee, O Father, and the Holy Ghost, the one only True God, liveth and reigneth, world without end. Amen.

AMERICAN UNITARIAN ASSOCIATION

(Members: 63,000)

Doctrine: *

In general: The Unitarians have never adopted a creed and do not require of members or ministers profession of a particular doctrine. The most distinguishing marks of Unitarianism today are its insistence upon absolute freedom of belief, its reliance upon the supreme guidance of reason, its tolerance of difference in religious opinion, its devotion to education and philanthropy and its emphasis upon character, as the principles of fundamental importance in religion. There is, however, a general consensus upon the unipersonality of God, the strict humanity of Jesus, the essential dignity and perfectibility of human nature, the natural character of the Bible, and the hope for the ultimate salvation of all souls.

Baptism: **

Baptism is not considered a sacrament. It is not universally practiced in the different churches. Where it is used it is customarily looked upon as a service symbolically introducing a child or adult into the Christian tradition. In the case of infant Baptism, most ministers would consider it more a service of consecration and dedication for the parents than for the child.

Administration: ***

Three forms of baptism are used, two for children, and one for adults. There is variation of the actual formula which is used because no particular words are considered necessary to make the service valid.

UNITED BRETHREN IN CHRIST

(Members: Over 15,000)

Doctrine: ****

The Sacraments

We believe that the sacraments, baptism and the Lord's Supper, are to be used in the Church, and should be practiced by all Christians; but the mode of baptism and the manner of observing the Lord's Supper are always to be left to the judgment and understanding of each individual. Also, the baptism of children shall be left to the judgment of believing parents.

* *Census of Religious Bodies, 1936,* II, pp. 1622-1623.

** Statement by Dan Huntington Fenn, Director, Department of Ministry, American Unitarian Association (25 Beacon Street, Boston, Mass.).

*** *Ministers Handbook, Services of Religion for Special Occasions* (Boston, Mass.: The Beacon Press, 1943).

**** *Discipline of the Church of the United Brethren in Christ,* 1941-1945 (Dayton, Ohio: United Brethren Publishing House, The Otterbein Press, 1941), p. 14.

Justification

We believe that penitent sinners are justified before God only by faith in our Lord Jesus Christ, and not by works; yet that good works in Christ are acceptable to God, and spring out of a true and living faith.

Regeneration and Adoption

We believe that regeneration is the renewal of the heart of man after the image of God, through the Word, by the act of the Holy Ghost, by which the believer receives the spirit of adoption, and is enabled to serve God with the will and the actions.

Ritual: **

Baptism of Adults

When the applicants (or applicant) on call of the minister, have presented themselves (himself or herself) before him, the minister shall say:

Our Lord commanded His apostles, saying "Go ye therefore, and make disciples of all the nations, baptizing them into the name of the Father, and of the Son, and of the Holy Spirit" (Matt. 28:19). On the day of Pentecost, the multitude, under the preaching of the Word, "were pricked in their heart, and said unto Peter and the rest of the apostles, Brethren, what shall we do? And Peter said unto them, Repent ye, and be baptized every one of you in the name of Jesus Christ unto the remission of your sins, and ye shall receive the gift of the Holy Spirit" (Acts 2:37, 38).

Philip, the evangelist, went down to the city of Samaria, and preached Christ to the people. And "when they believed Philip preaching good tidings concerning the kingdom of God and the name of Jesus Christ, they were baptized, both men and women" (Acts 8:12).

Dearly beloved, it has pleased God, in His infinite mercy, to awaken you to a sense of your guilt and danger, and to lead you, as we humbly trust, to repentance and faith in our Lord Jesus Christ. By presenting yourselves (or yourself) for this holy sacrament, you declare your purpose to lead a new life, and to seek an inheritance with the righteous in the "house not made with hands, eternal in the heavens."

Do you now solemnly consecrate yourselves (yourself) to Christ and his service; and will you endeavor henceforth to keep God's holy commandments and to walk in the same all the days of your life? If so, answer, "I will endeavor so to do, the Lord being my helper."

The minister shall then baptize the candidate, repeating in each case his (or her) name and saying:

I baptize thee in the name of the Father, and of the Son, and of the Holy Spirit. Amen.

The service shall be concluded with a short prayer and benediction.

** *Discipline*, pp. 236-240.

Baptism of Children
(From Nine to Twelve Years)

This service is appointed for the baptism of children who have already received the grace of God in a definite acceptance of the Lord Jesus Christ as their Saviour, and who have been duly instructed in the meaning of the Christian life.

Hymn, "By Cool Siloam's Shady Rill."

This hymn, or some other appropriate one, may be sung as the candidates present themselves before the minister at the chancel of the church. The minister shall then say:

Hear ye the words from the Holy Bible: The mercy of the Lord is from everlasting to everlasting upon them that fear Him, and His righteousness unto children's children. He will feed His flock like a shepherd, He will gather the lambs in His arm and carry them in His bosom, etc. . . . Verily I say unto you, Whosoever shall not receive the kingdom of God as a little child, he shall in no wise enter therein.

Dearly Beloved: I now welcome you as you come here to enter this sacrament of cleansing and divine fellowship unto eternal life. The sacrament of baptism is the outward and visible sign of an inward and spiritual grace. It signifies the entrance into a new life of fellowship with Jesus Christ and the saints of God. By receiving baptism, you confess repentance toward God and faith in Christ unto salvation. You also confess that you love God sincerely and supremely and that you will be true and faithful disciples as long as you live. I admonish you that you continue in the faith and the consecration of your life to God and His Church. As you are baptized with water, so may you also be baptized with the Holy Spirit.

Let us pray.

O Christ of God, and Saviour of all mankind. Thy love for us is wonderful and everlasting. Having loved His own, He loved them unto the end. Help us to love Thee with a love like that. We give glory to Thee, O Lord God, for these children who have sought Thee early and found Thee as the Saviour and Shepherd of their souls. We bring them now to Thee, and pray for them, that through the renewing of the Holy Spirit in holy baptism they may become Thy true disciples and ever witness a good confession. May they continue steadfast in faith, joyful through hope and always rooted in love. Grant that they may evermore be kept in purity and faithfulness, and have their inheritance in that eternal kingdom which Thou hast promised. Through Jesus Christ our Lord. Amen.

The minister shall then say to the children to be baptized:

Dearly Beloved: We greatly rejoice with you that the grace of God has brought you to this confession of faith in Him, and that you now desire to be His disciples and serve Him in the fellowship of His Church. It is fitting and right that you should openly confess your faith and purpose in the presence of His people.

Question. Do you truly repent of your sins and resolve to lead a Christian life, loving God with all your heart?

Answer. I do.

Question. Do you now receive the Lord Jesus Christ as your Saviour, and do you purpose that He shall have your life and love as long as you live?

Answer. I do.

Question. Will you be baptized in this faith?

Answer. I will.

The minister shall then administer the sacrament of baptism. He shall repeat the name of the candidate and as he sprinkles or pours the water on the head, he shall use these words:

N—, Upon confessing faith in the Lord Jesus Christ and your love for Him, I baptize you in the name of the Father, and of the Son, and of the Holy Spirit. Amen.

The candidates shall then kneel together at the altar chancel and the minister will lift his hands over them in blessing and say:

Defend and keep, O Lord God, these Thy children with heavenly grace. May they increase daily in the power of the Holy Spirit and in the beauty and favor of the Christian life. Grant, that they may continue Thine evermore, until they come at last unto Thy everlasting kingdom. Amen.

Benediction:

The grace of the Lord Jesus Christ, and the love of God, and the Communion of the Holy Spirit, be with you all. Amen.

If it is desired, a hymn, such as "Saviour, Like a Shepherd Lead Us," may be sung as the candidates return to their seats.

Baptism of Infants

When the sponsors have presented themselves with the child (or children) before the minister at his call, he shall say:

"And they were bringing unto Him little children, that He should touch them: etc. . . . And He took them in His arms, and blessed them, laying His hand upon them" (Mark 10:13-16).

In presenting this child for baptism, you not only signify your faith in the Christian religion, of which baptism is a sacrament, but also your desire that he (or she) may early know and follow the will of God, may live and die a Christian, and attain until everlasting life.

In order to do this it will be your duty, as parents (or guardians) to teach him (or her) early the fear of the Lord; to watch over his (or her) education, that he (or she) be not led astray; to direct his (or her) youthful mind to the Holy Scriptures, and his (or her) feet to the sanctuary; to restrain him (or her) from evil associates and habits; and, as much as in you lies, to bring him (or her) up in the nurture and admonition of the Lord.

Will you endeavor so to do, by the help of God? If so, answer, "I will."

The minister shall then baptize the child, repeating the full name of the same, and saying:

I baptize thee in the name of the Father, and of the Son, and of the Holy Spirit. Amen.

All to be followed by a short prayer by the minister.

VOLUNTEERS OF AMERICA

(Members: Over 10,000)

Ritual: *

ORDER FOR THE ADMINISTRATION OF BAPTISM TO INFANTS

The ordained officer before the font, which is to be filled with pure water. shall use the following:

Comrades and Friends of the Faith: Forasmuch as all men by nature are sinners and that our Saviour Jesus Christ saith, "Except a man be born of water and of the Spirit he cannot enter the Kingdom of God," I beseech you to call upon God the Father, through our Lord Jesus Christ, that having, of His bounteous mercy, redeemed this child by the blood of His Son, He will grant that he, being baptized with water, may also be baptized with the Holy Ghost, be received into Christ's holy Church and become a lively member of the same.

Then shall the ordained officer offer a prayer, asking God's blessing upon the child to be baptized.

A short and suitable hymn may be sung.

The officiating officer will offer the following prayer:

Almighty, Everlasting God, Whose most dearly beloved Son Jesus Christ, for the forgiveness of our sins, did shed out of His most precious side both water and blood, regard, we beseech Thee, our supplications. Sanctify this water for this Holy Sacrament, and grant that this child now to be baptized, may receive the fullness of Thy faithful and elect children, through Jesus Christ our Lord. Amen.

The officiating officer shall then address the Parents or Guardians as follows:

Dearly Beloved: Forasmuch as this child is now presented by you for Christian Baptism, you must remember that it is your part and duty to see that he be taught as soon as he shall be able to learn, the nature and end of this Holy Sacrament. And that he may know these things the better, you shall call upon him to give reverent attendance upon the appointed means of grace, such as the ministry of the Word, and the public and private worship of God; and further, you shall provide that he shall read the Holy Scriptures, and learn the Lord's Prayer, the Ten Commandments, the Apostles' Creed, the Catechism, and all other things which a Christian ought to know and believe to his soul's health, in order that he may be brought up to lead a virtuous and holy life, remembering always that Baptism doth represent unto us that inward purity which dis-

* *Discipline* (New York, N. Y.), pp. 57-61.

poseth us to follow the example of our Saviour Christ; that He died and rose again for us, so should we, who are baptized, die unto sin and rise again unto righteousness, continually fortifying all corrupt affections and daily proceeding in all virtue and godliness.

Do you therefore solemnly engage to fulfill these duties so far as in you lies, the Lord being your helper?

Ans. We do.

Then shall the people stand up, and the officer shall say:

Hear the words of the Gospel, written by St. Mark (Chap. 10:13-16): "They brought young children to Christ, etc."

Then the officer shall take the child into his hands, and say to the friends of the child:

Name this child.

And then naming it after them, he should sprinkle or pour water upon it, saying:

(Name), I baptize thee in the name of the Father, and of the Son, and of the Holy Ghost. Amen.

Then shall the officer offer the following prayer, the people kneeling:

O God of infinite mercy, the Father of all the faithful seed, be pleased to grant unto this child an understanding mind, a sanctified heart. May Thy providence lead him through the dangers, temptations and ignorance of his youth, that he may never run into folly nor into any evil. We pray Thee so to order the course of his life, that by good education, by holy examples, and by Thy restraining and renewing grace, he may be led to serve Thee faithfully all his days, so that when he has glorified Thee in his generation, and has served the Church on earth, he may be received into Thine eternal kingdom, through Jesus Christ our Lord. Amen.

Almighty and merciful Father, let Thy loving mercy and compassion descend upon these, Thy servant and handmaid, the parents (or guardians) of this child. Grant unto them, we beseech Thee, Thy Holy Spirit, that they may, like Abraham, command their household to keep the way of the Lord. Direct their actions, and sanctify their hearts, words and purposes, that their whole family may be united to our Lord Jesus Christ in the bonds of faith, obedience, and charity and that they all, being in this life Thy holy children by adoption and grace, may be admitted into the Church of the first-born in heaven, through the merits of Thy dear Son, our Saviour and Redeemer. Amen.

Then may the officer offer extemporary prayer. Then shall be said, by all kneeling:

Our Father, Who art in heaven, hallowed by Thy name, etc.

Order for the Administration of Baptism to Such As Are of Riper Years

Dearly Beloved: Forasmuch as all men are conceived and born in sin; and that which is born of the flesh is flesh, and they that are in the flesh cannot please God, but live in sin, committing many actual transgressions; and our Saviour Christ saith, except a man be born of water and of the Spirit he cannot enter into the kingdom of God; I beseech you to call upon God, the Father, through our Lord Jesus Christ that of His bounteous goodness He will grant to these persons that which by nature they cannot have; that they being baptized with water, may also be baptized with the Holy Ghost, and being received into Christ's holy Church, may continue lively members of the same.

Then shall the officer say:

Let us pray.

Almighty and Immortal God, the aid of all that need, the helper of all that flee to Thee for succor, the life of them that believe, and the resurrection of the dead; we call upon Thee for these persons, that they coming to Thy Holy Baptism, may also be filled with Thy Holy Spirit. Receive them, O Lord, as Thou hast promised by Thy well-beloved Son, saying: "Ask, and ye shall receive; seek, and ye shall find; knock, and it shall be opened unto you"; so give now unto us that ask; let us that seek, find; open the gate unto us that knock; that these persons may enjoy the everlasting benediction of Thy heavenly washing, and may come to the eternal kingdom which Thou hast promised, by Christ our Lord. Amen.

Then shall the people stand up, and the ordained officer shall say:

Hear the words of the Gospel, written by St. John (Chap. 3:1-8): "There was a man of the Pharisees, Nicodemus, a ruler of the Jews: etc."

Then shall the officer speak to the persons to be baptized on this wise:

Well-Beloved, who have come hither desiring to receive holy baptism, you have heard how the congregation hath prayed that our Lord Jesus Christ would vouchsafe to receive you, to bless you, and to give you the kingdom of heaven, and everlasting life. And our Lord Jesus Christ hath promised in His holy Word to grant all those things that we have prayed for; which promise He for His part will most surely keep and perform.

Wherefore, after this promise made by Christ, you must also faithfully, for your part, promise in the presence of this whole congregation, that you will renounce the devil and all his works, and constantly believe God's holy Word, and obediently keep His commandments.

Then shall the officer demand of each of the persons to be baptized:

Quest. Dost thou renounce the devil and all his works, the vain pomp and glory of the world, with all covetous desires of the same, and the carnal desires of the flesh, so that thou wilt not follow nor be led by them?

Ans. I renounce them all.

Quest. Dost thou believe in God the Father Almighty, maker of heaven and earth?

And in Jesus Christ, His only Son, our Lord; Who was conceived by the Holy Ghost, born of the Virgin Mary; suffered under Pontius Pilate, was crucified, dead, and buried; the third day He rose from the dead; He ascended into heaven, and sitteth at the right hand of God the Father Almighty; from thence He shall come to judge the quick and the dead.

And dost thou believe in the Holy Ghost; the Holy Catholic or general Christian Church; the Communion of Saints; the forgiveness of sins; the resurrection of the body; and the life everlasting after death?

Ans. All this I steadfastly believe.

Quest. Wilt thou be baptized in this faith?

Ans. Such is my desire.

Quest. Wilt thou then obediently keep God's holy will and commandments, and walk in the same all the days of thy life?

Ans. I will endeavor to do so, God being my helper.

Then shall the ordained officer say:

O Merciful God, grant that all carnal affections may die in these persons, and that all things belonging to the Spirit may live and grow in them. Amen.

Grant that they may have power and strength to have victory, and triumph against the devil, the world and the flesh. Amen.

Grant that they, being here dedicated to Thee by our Office and Ministry, may also be endued with heavenly virtues, and everlastingly rewarded, through Thy mercy, O blessed Lord God, Who dost live, and govern all things, world without end. Amen.

Almighty, Everlasting God, Whose most dearly beloved Son Jesus Christ, for the forgiveness of our sins, did shed out of His most precious side both water and blood; and gave commandments to His disciples that they should go teach all nations, and baptize them in the name of the Father, and of the Son, and of the Holy Ghost; regard, we beseech Thee, our supplications; and grant that the persons now to be baptized may receive the fullness of Thy grace, and ever remain in the number of Thy faithful and elect children, through Jesus Christ our Lord. Amen.

Then shall the ordained officer ask the name of each person to be baptized; and shall sprinkle or pour water upon him (or, if he shall desire it, shall immerse in water), saying:

(Name), I baptize thee in the name of the Father, and of the Son, and of the Holy Ghost. Amen.

Then shall be said the Lord's Prayer, by all while kneeling.

Rituals of Three Sects Outside the United States of America

DIE CHRISTKATHOLICSCHEN KIRCHE DER SCHWEIZ: *

Ritus für Spendung der Sakramente

I. Taufe

(Lieder Nr. 168-170)

Priester. Im Namen des Vaters und des Sohnes ✠ und des heiligen Geistes. Amen.

Jesus sprach zu seinen Jüngern: Mir ist alle Gewalt im Himmel und auf Erden gegeben. Gehet hin und lehret alle Völker und taufet sie im Namen des Vaters, des Sohnes und des heiligen Geistes, und lehret sie alles halten, was ich euch befohlen habe; und siehe, ich bin bei euch alle Tage bis ans Ende der Welt.

Ein anderes Mal brachten die Leute Kindlein zu Jesu, dass er sie berühren möchte. Die Jünger aber drohten denen, die sie brachten. Als nun Jesus sie sah, ward er unwillig und sprach zu ihnen: Lasset die Kindlein zu mir kommen und wehret es ihnen nicht; denn solcher ist das Himmelreich. Wahrlich, ich sage euch, wer das Reich Gottes nicht aufnimmt wie ein Kind, wird in dasselbe nicht eingehen. Und er schloss sie in seine Arme und legte ihnen die Hände auf und segnete sie.

Solchen Worten gemäss bringen Sie, im Herrn Geliebte, dieses Kind hieher, damit es nach Christi Anordnung die heilige Taufe empfange und ein Mitglied der Gemeinschaft seiner Gläubigen werde.

Es soll . . . heissen.—N.N., es komme auf dich herab die allmächtige Kraft des Vaters, des Sohnes ✠ und des heiligen Geistes, auf dass die Sündhaftigkeit von unsern Stammeltern her und der Geist des Bösen nichts über dich vermöge!

Verleihe, Vater unseres Herrn Jesu Christi, diesem deinem Kinde, mit Kraft gestärkt, zu werden dem innern Menschen nach durch deinen Geist, auf dass Christus wohne durch den Glauben in seinem Herzen und es fest gewurzelt und gegründet sei in der Liebe.

Anwesende. Amen.

P. (Den Täufling anhauchend): Wie der Schöpfer den Adam anhauchte, ihn zu beleben, und Jesus seine Jünger anhauchte, ihnen den heiligen Geist mitzuteilen, so verleihe dir nun der himmlische Vater ein höheres und heiliges Leben durch die Wiedergeburt aus dem Wasser und dem heiligen Geiste, damit du seiest ein lebendiges Mitglied seines Reiches.

A. Amen.

* *Corpus Confessionum,* Die Bekenntnisse der Christenheit. Sammlung Grundlegender Urkunden aus allen Kirchen der Gegenwart. hrsg. von D. Caius Fabricius (24 vols., 1935—, Berlin und Leipzig: Verlag von Walter de Gruyter & Co.). Vol. 6, pp. 119-121.

P. (Stirn und Brust des Täuflings mit dem Kreuze bezeichnend): Empfange auf deiner Stirne das Zeichen des heiligen Kreuzes, ✠ zur Erinnerung daran, dass du deinen Glauben an Christum, den Gekreuzigten, offen bekennen und dich in nichts rühmen sollest, als allein im Kreuze unseres Herrn Jesu Christi—und auf deiner Brust, ✠ zur Erinnerung daran, dass du den, welcher für dich am Kreuze gestorben ist, von Herzen lieben und nach seinem Vorbild willig dein Kreuz auf dich nehmen sollest. A. Amen.

P. (Dem Täufling die Hand auflegend): Wie Jesus die ihm dargebrachten Kleinen unter Auflegung seiner Hände gesegnet hat, so sei auch du jetzt im Namen Jesu von mir gesegnet.

Beschirme, o Herr, diesen deinen Diener N. (diese deine Dienerin N.); entferne von ihm (ihr) alle Fisternisse des Geistes, verleihe, dass er (sie) dich erkenne, den alleinigen, wahren Gott, und den du gesandt hast, Jesum Christum, und lass ihn (sie) also nach dem Worte deines Sohnes gelangen zum ewigen Leben. A. Amen.

P. (Dem Täufling etwas Salz auf die Lippen legend): N., nimm hin dieses Salz als Sinnbild der Weisheit.—Siehe gnädig herab, o Gott, auf diesen deinen Diener (diese deine Dienerin) N.; bewahre ihn (sie) vor aller Verderbnis der Sünde und erhalte ihn (sie) stets in deiner Furcht, welche ist der Anfang aller Weisheit. Durch Jesum Christum, unsern Herrn. A. Amen.

P. (Dem Täufling die Stola auflegend): N., komm herein in die Kirche Gottes, in die Gemeinschaft der Heiligen. Möge dich Christus, der Herr, wie heute in die Gemeinschaft seiner Gläubigen, so einst am Tage des Gerichtes als seinen treuen Diener (seine treue Dienerin) aufnehmen in das Reich der Seligen. A. Amen.

Beim Taufstein

P. Lasset uns beten! Allmächtiger, gütiger Gott, der du diesem Kinde das Dasein unter den Lebendigen gegeben hast und es nun durch die heilige Taufe in die Gemeinschaft Jesu, deines Sohnes, aufnehmen willst, wir bitten dich: Erhalte es in diesem Leben, wenn es deinem heiligen Willen gemäss ist. Lass es aufwachsen zu deiner Ehre, zur Freude seiner Eltern, zum Heile seiner Mitmenschen, zur Zierde deiner Kirche. Erfülle es mit deinem heilgen Geiste, dass es dich von ganzem Herzen liebe, auf den Pfaden deiner heiligen Gebote wandle und niemals mehr getrennt werden möge von dem, dem es nun angehören wird, Christo, deinem Sohne, unserm Herrn. A. Amen.

P. Vater unser, der du bist in den Himmeln, geheiligt werde dein Name. Zu uns komme dein Reich. Dein Wille geschehe, wie im Himmel, also auch auf Erden. Unser tägliches Brot gib uns heute und vergib uns unsere Schulden, wie auch wir vergeben unsern Schuldigern. Und führe uns nicht in Versuchung.

A. Sondern erlöse uns von dem Übel. Amen.

P. (Ohren und Mund des Täuflings mit dem Finger berührend): Epheta, das ist, tue dich auf! Der Herr öffne deine Ohren und löse das Band deiner Zunge, damit du Gottes Wort hörest und freudig sein Lob verkündest.

Nach den Worten des Glaubensbekenntnisses, welches von den apostolischen Zeiten her als kurzer Inbegriff der christlichen Lehre in der Kirche im Gebrauche ist, frage ich dich nun:

N., glaubst du an Gott den Vater, den Allmächtigen, den Schöpfer Himmels und der Erde?

Die Paten (antworten im Namen des Täuflings): Ich glaube.

P. Glaubst du auch an Jesum Christum, seinen eingeborenen Sohn, unsern Herrn, der empfangen ist von dem heiligen Geiste, geboren aus Maria, der Jungfrau, gelitten unter Pontius Pilatus, gekreuzigt, gestorben und begraben, abgestiegen zur Hölle, am dritten Tage wieder auferstanden von den Toten; aufgefahren gen Himmel, sitzet zur Rechten Gottes, des allmächtigen Vaters, von dannen er kommen wird, zu richten die Lebendigen und die Toten? Paten: Ich glaube.

P. Glaubst du auch an den heiligen Geist, eine heilige, allgemeine Kirche, Gemeinschaft der Heiligen, Nachlass der Sünden, Auferstehung des Fleisches und ein ewiges Leben? Paten: Ich glaube.

P. N., widersagst du allem, was Gott missfällt und Sünde ist, dem Geiste des Bösen, allen seinen Werken und aller seiner Pracht? Paten: Ich widersage.

P. N., gelobst du, gemäss dem Gebote Christi, den Herrn, deinen Gott, zu lieben von ganzem Herzen, von ganzer Seele und von ganzem Gemüte und deinen Nächsten wie dich selbst? Paten: Ich gelobe es.

P. (Den Täufling auf der Brust mit Katechumenen-Öl salbend): Ich salbe dich mit dem Öle des Heiles in Christo Jesu, unserm Herrn.

Zum Kampfe gegen das Böse, zur Übung des Guten, zur Geduld in Leiden stärke dich die Gnade dessen, der uns von der Sünde erlöst hat. A. Amen.

P. (Giesst dreimal kreuzweise das Taufwasser auf das Haupt des Täuflings): *N., ich taufe dich im Namen des Vaters ✠ und des Sohnes ✠ und des heiligen Geistes.* ✠

A. Amen.

P. (Den Scheitel des Täuflings mit Chrisam salbend): Der allmächtige Gott, der Vater unseres Herrn Jesu Christi, der dich wiedergeboren hat aus dem Wasser und dem heiligen Geiste, salbe dich mit dem Chrisam des Heiles in Christo Jesu, unserm Herrn. A. Amen.

P. (Dem Täufling ein weisses Gewand oder das Ende der Stola auflegend): N., empfange das weisse Gewand der Unschuld. Erhalte es rein und unbefleckt auf den Tag Jesu Christi, damit du eingehest in das ewige Leben. A. Amen.

P. (Den Paten eine brennende Kerze darreichend): N., nimm hin diese brennende Kerze als ein Sinnbild des durch die Liebe lebendigen Glaubens. Öffne die Augen dem Lichte wahrer Erkenntnis und folge nach Christo, dem Lichte der Welt, damit du niemals wandelst in der Finsternis und im Schatten des Todes. A. Amen.

P. Der Herr selbst hat gesagt: Das ist das ewige Leben, dass die Menschen dich erkennen, den alleinigen, wahren Gott, und den du gesandt hast, Jesum Christum. Und: Wenn du zum Leben eingehen willst, so halte die Gebote: Du sollst den Herrn, deinen Gott, lieben von ganzem Herzen, von ganzer Seele und von ganzem Gemüte und deinen Nächsten wie dich selbst.—N., gehe hin in Frieden; der Herr sei mit dir und geleite dich bis ans Ende deiner Tage. A. Amen.

CHURCH OF ENGLAND*

The Ministration of Publick Baptism of Infants to Be Used in the Church (1662)

And the Priest coming to the Font (which is then to be filled with pure water), and standing there shall say:

Hath this child been already baptized, or no?

If they answer, No: then shall the Priest proceed as followeth:

Dearly beloved, forasmuch as all men are conceived and born in sin; and that our Saviour Christ saith, None can enter into the kingdom of God, except he be regenerate and born anew of water and of the Holy Ghost; I beseech you to call upon God the Father, through our Lord Jesus Christ, that of His bounteous mercy He will grant to *this child* that nothing which by nature he cannot have; that *he* may be baptized with Water and the Holy Ghost, and received into Christ's Holy Church, and be made *a lively member* of the same.

Then shall the Priest say:

Let us pray.

Almighty and everlasting God, Who of Thy great mercy didst save Noah and his family in the ark from perishing by water; and also didst safely lead the children of Israel Thy people through the Red Sea, figuring thereby Thy Holy Baptism; and by the Baptism of Thy well-beloved Son Jesus Christ, in the river Jordan, didst sanctify water to the mystical washing away of sin: We beseech Thee, for Thine infinite mercies, that Thou wilt mercifully look upon *this child*; wash *him* and sanctify *him* with the Holy Ghost; that *he*, being delivered from Thy wrath, may be received into the ark of Christ's Church; and being steadfast in faith, joyful through hope, and rooted in charity, may so pass the waves of this troublesome world, that finally *he* may come to the land of everlasting life, there to reign with thee world without end; through Jesus Christ our Lord. *Amen.*

Almighty and immortal God, the aid of all that need, the helper of all that flee to Thee for succour, the life of them that believe, and the resurrection of the dead: We call upon Thee for *this infant*, that *he*, coming to Thy Holy Baptism, may receive remission of his sins by spiritual regeneration. Receive *him*, O Lord, as Thou hast promised by Thy well-beloved Son, saying, Ask, and ye shall have; seek, and ye shall find; knock, and it shall be opened unto you: So give now unto us that ask; let us that seek, find; open the gate unto us that knock; that *this infant* may enjoy the everlasting benediction of Thy heavenly

* The rite of Baptism is found in the Book of Common Prayer with the Additions and Deviations proposed in 1928.—*Corpus Confessionum,* Vol. 17, pp. 212-226.

washing, and may come to the eternal kingdom which Thou hast promised by Christ our Lord. *Amen.*

Then shall the people stand up, and the Priest shall say:

Hear the words of the Gospel, written by Saint Mark, in the tenth chapter, at the thirteenth verse.

They brought young children to Christ, that He should touch them; and His disciples rebuked those that brought them. But when Jesus saw it, He was much displeased, and said unto them, Suffer the little children to come unto Me, and forbid them not; for of such is the kingdom of God. Verily I say unto you, Whosoever shall not receive the kingdom of God as a little child, he shall not enter therein. And He took them up in His arms, put His hands upon them, and blessed them.

After the Gospel is read, the Minister shall make this brief Exhortation upon the words of the Gospel.

Beloved, ye hear in this Gospel the words of our Saviour Christ, that He commanded the children to be brought unto Him; how He blamed those that would have kept them from Him; how He exhorteth all men to follow their innocency. Ye perceive how by His outward gesture and deed He declared His good will toward them; for He embraced them in His arms, He laid His hands upon them, and blessed them. Doubt ye not therefore, but earnestly believe, that He will likewise favourably receive *this* present *infant*; that He will embrace *him* with the arms of His mercy; that He will give unto *him* the blessing of eternal life, and make *him* partaker of His everlasting kingdom. Wherefore we being thus persuaded of the good will of our heavenly Father towards *this infant,* declared by His Son Jesus Christ; and nothing doubting but that He favourably alloweth this charitable work of ours in bringing *this infant* to His Holy Baptism; let us faithfully and devoutly give thanks unto Him, and say:

Almighty and everlasting God, heavenly Father, We give Thee humble thanks, For that Thou hast vouchsafed to call us to the knowledge of Thy grace, and faith in Thee: Increase this knowledge, and confirm this faith in us evermore. Give Thy Holy Spirit to *this infant,* That *he* may be born again, And be made *an heir* of everlasting salvation; Through our Lord Jesus Christ, Who liveth and reigneth with Thee and the Holy Spirit, now and for ever. *Amen.*

Then shall the Priest speak unto the Godfathers and Godmothers on this wise.

Dearly beloved, ye have brought *this child* here to be baptized, ye have prayed that our Lord Jesus Christ would vouchsafe to receive *him,* to lease *him* of *his* sins, to sanctify *him* with the Holy Ghost, to give *him* the kingdom of heaven, and everlasting life. Ye have heard also that our Lord Jesus Christ hath promised in His Gospel to grant all these things that ye have prayed for: which promise He, for His part, will most surely keep and perform. Wherefore, after this promise made by Christ, *this infant* must also faithfully, for *his* part, promise by you that are *his* sureties (until *he* come of age to take it upon *himself*), that *he* will renounce the devil and all his works, and constantly believe God's holy Word, and obediently keep His commandments.

I demand therefore,

Dost thou, in the name of this child, renounce the devil and all his works, the vain pomp and glory of the world, with all covetous desires of the same, and the carnal desires of the flesh, so that thou wilt not follow, nor be led by them?

Answer. I renounce them all.

Minister:

Dost thou believe in God the Father Almighty, Maker of heaven and earth?

And in Jesus Christ His only-begotten Son our Lord? And that He was conceived by the Holy Ghost; born of the Virgin Mary; that He suffered under Pontius Pilate, was crucified, dead, and buried; that He went down into hell, and also did rise again the third day; that He ascended into heaven, and sitteth at the right hand of God the Father Almighty; and from thence shall come again at the end of the world, to judge the quick and the dead?

And dost thou believe in the Holy Ghost; the Holy Catholick Church; the Communion of Saints; the Remission of sins; the Resurrection of the flesh; and everlasting life after death?

Answer. All this I steadfastly believe.

Minister:

Wilt thou be baptized in this faith?

Answer. That is my desire.

Minister:

Wilt thou then obediently keep God's holy will and commandments, and walk in the same all the days of thy life?

Answer. I will.

Then shall the Priest say:

O Merciful God, grant that the old Adam in *this child* may be so buried, that the new man may be raised up in *him*. *Amen.*

Grant that all carnal affections may die in *him*, and that all things belonging to the Spirit may live and grow in *him*. *Amen.*

Grant that *he* may have power and strength to have victory, and to triumph, against the devil, the world, and the flesh. *Amen.*

Grant that whosoever is here dedicated to Thee by our office and ministry may also be endued with heavenly virtues, and everlastingly rewarded, through Thy mercy, O blessed Lord God, Who dost live, and govern all things world without end. *Amen.*

Almighty, everliving God, Whose most dearly beloved Son Jesus Christ, for the forgiveness of our sins, did shed out of His most precious side both water and blood; and gave commandment to His disciples, that they should go teach all nations, and baptize them In the name of the Father, and of the Son, and of the Holy Ghost: Regard, we beseech Thee, the supplications of Thy congregation; sanctify this water to the mystical washing away of sins; and grant that *this child,* now to be baptized therein, may receive the fulness of Thy grace, and ever remain in the number of Thy faithful and elect children; through Jesus Christ our Lord. *Amen.*

Then the Priest shall take the child into his hands, and shall say to the Godfathers and Godmothers:

Name this child.

And then naming it after them (if they shall certify him that the child may well endure it) he shall dip it in the water discreetly warily, saying:

N., I baptize thee In the name of the Father, and of the Son, and of the Holy Ghost. *Amen.*

But if they certify that the child is weak, it shall suffice to pour water upon it, saying the foresaid words:

N., I baptize thee In the name of the Father, and of the Son, and of the Holy Ghost. *Amen.*

Then the Priest shall say:

We receive this child into the congregation of Christ's flock,** and do sign *him* with the sign of the Cross, in token that hereafter *he* shall not be ashamed to confess the faith of Christ crucified, and manfully to fight under His banner, against sin, the world, and the devil; and to continue Christ's faithful soldier and servant unto *his* life's end. *Amen.*

Then shall the Priest say:

Seeing now, dearly beloved brethren, that *this child is* regenerate, and grafted into the body of Christ's Church, let us give thanks unto Almighty God for these benefits; and with one accord make our prayers unto Him, that *this child* may lead the rest of *his* life according to this beginning.

Then shall be said, all kneeling:

Our Father, Which art in heaven, Hallowed be Thy name; Thy kingdom come; Thy will be done; In earth as it is in heaven. Give us this day our daily bread. And forgive us our trespasses, As we forgive them that trespass against us. And lead us not into temptation; But deliver us from evil. *Amen.*

Then shall the Priest say:

We yield Thee hearty thanks, most merciful Father, that it hath pleased Thee to regenerate *this infant* with Thy Holy Spirit, to receive *him* for Thine own *child* by adoption, and to incorporate *him* into Thy holy Church. And humbly we beseech Thee to grant, that *he,* being dead unto sin, and living unto righteousness, and being buried with Christ in His death, may crucify the old man, and utterly abolish the whole body of sin; and that, as *he is* made *partaker* of the death of Thy Son, *he* may also be *partaker* of His resurrection; so that finally, with the residue of Thy holy Church, *he* may be *an inheritor* of Thine everlasting kingdom; through Christ our Lord. *Amen.*

Then, all standing up, the Priest shall say to the Godfathers and Godmothers this Exhortation following.

Forasmuch as *this child hath* promised by you *his* sureties to renounce the

** Here the Priest shall make a Cross upon the Child's forehead.

devil and all his works, to believe in God, and to serve Him; ye must remember, that it is your parts and duties to see that *this infant* be taught, so soon as *he* shall be able to learn, what a solemn vow, promise, and profession, *he hath* here made by you. And that *he* may know these things the better, ye shall call upon *him* to hear sermons; and chiefly ye shall provide, that *he* may learn the Creed, the Lord's Prayer, and the Ten Commandments, in the vulgar tongue, and all other things which a Christian ought to know and believe to his soul's health; and that *this child* may be virtuously brought up to lead a godly and a Christian life; remembering always, that Baptism doth represent unto us our profession; which is, to follow the example of our Saviour Christ, and to be made like unto Him; that, as He died, and rose again for us, so should we, who are baptized, die from sin, and rise again unto righteousness; continually mortifying all our evil and corrupt affections, and daily proceeding in all virtue and godliness of living.

Then shall he add and say:

Ye are to take care that *this child* be brought to the Bishop to be confirmed by him, so soon as *he* can say the Creed, the Lord's Prayer, and the Ten Commandments, in the vulgar tongue, and be further instructed in the Church Catechism set forth for that purpose.

An Alternative Order of the Ministration of Publick Baptism of Infants

Which may be used at the discretion of the Minister unless the parents require the use of the Form of 1662.

The Priest, coming to the Font (which is then to be filled with pure water), and standing there, shall say:

Hath this child been already baptized or no?

If they answer, No: then shall the Priest proceed as followeth:

Beloved in Christ Jesus, seeing that all men are from their birth prone to sin, but that God willeth all men to be saved, for God is love: and that our Saviour Christ saith, None can enter into the kingdom of God, except he be born anew of water and of the Holy Ghost; I beseech you to call upon God the Father, through our Lord Jesus Christ, that of His bounteous mercy He will grant to *this child,* that thing which by nature *he* cannot have, that *he* may be baptized with water and the Holy Ghost, and received into Christ's holy Church, and be made *a living member* of the same.

Then shall the Priest say, all standing:

Almighty and everlasting God, Who by the Baptism of Thy well-beloved Son Jesus Christ, in the river Jordan, didst sanctify water to the mystical washing away of sin: Mercifully look upon *this child*; wash *him* and sanctify *him* with the Holy Spirit, that *he* may be received into the ark of Christ's Church; and being steadfast in faith, joyful through hope, and rooted in charity, may so pass the waves of this troublesome world, that finally *he* may come to the land of everlasting life, there to reign with Thee world without end; through Jesus Christ our Lord. *Amen.*

Or this

Almighty and immortal God, the aid of all that need, the helper of all that flee to Thee for succour, the life of them that believe, and the resurrection of the dead: We call upon Thee for *this infant* that *he,* coming to Thy Holy Baptism, may receive remission of sin by spiritual regeneration. Receive *him,* O Lord, as Thou hast promised by Thy well-beloved Son, saying, Ask, and ye shall have; seek, and ye shall find; knock, and it shall be opened upon you: So give now unto us that ask; let us that seek, find; open the gate unto us that knock; that *this infant,* being washed from sin, may enjoy Thy heavenly benediction, and may come to the eternal kingdom, which Thou hast promised by Christ our Lord. *Amen.*

Then shall the Priest say:

Hear the words of the Gospel, written by Saint Mark, in the tenth chapter, at the thirteenth verse.

Answer. Glory be to Thee, O Lord. Cf. above.

Answer. Praise be to Thee, O Christ.

Then shall the Priest read this brief Exhortation upon the words of the Gospel.

You hear in this Gospel the words of our Saviour Christ, when He commanded the children to be brought unto Him. You perceive how He took them in His arms, and blessed them. Jesus Christ is the same yesterday, and today, and for ever. Doubt not, therefore, but earnestly believe, that He loveth *this child,* that He approveth this work of ours in bringing *him* to Holy Baptism, that He is ready to receive *him,* to embrace *him* with the arms of His mercy, and to give *him* the blessing of eternal life. Wherefore, we being thus persuaded of the good will of our heavenly Father towards *this* infant, declared by His Son Jesus Christ, let us faithfully and devoutly give thanks unto Him, and say:

Then shall the Priest and people, still standing, say:

Almighty and everlasting God, heavenly Father, We give Thee humble thanks, For that Thou hast called us to the knowledge of Thy grace, and to faith in Thee: Increase this knowledge, and confirm this faith in us ever more. Give Thy Holy Spirit to *this infant,* That *he* may be born again, and be made *an heir* of everlasting salvation; through our Lord Jesus Christ, Who liveth and reigneth with Thee and the Holy Spirit, now and for ever. *Amen.*

The Promises

Then shall the Priest speak unto the Godfathers and Godmothers on this wise:

Dearly beloved, you have brought *this child* here to be baptized, you have prayed that our Lord Jesus Christ would be pleased to receive *him,* to cleanse *him,* and to sanctify *him.* Our Lord hath promised in His Gospel to grant all these things that you have prayed for; which promise He, for His part, will most surely keep and perform.

You, on your part, must undertake on behalf of *this infant* three things:

first that *he* will renounce the devil and all his works; secondly, that *he* will constantly believe God's holy Word; and thirdly, that *he* will obediently keep His commandments.

Dost thou, in the name of this child, renounce the devil and all his works, the vain pomp and glory of the world, with all covetous desires of the same, and the sinful desires of the flesh, so that thou wilt not follow nor be led by them?

Answer. I do.

Dost thou in the name of this child profess the Christian Faith?

Answer. I do.

Then shall be said by the Priest and the Godparents the Apostles' Creed as followeth:

I believe in God the Father Almighty, Maker of heaven and earth:

And in Jesus Christ His only Son our Lord, Who was conceived by the Holy Ghost, Born of the Virgin Mary, Suffered under Pontius Pilate, Was crucified, dead, and buried, He descended into hell; The third day He rose again from the dead, He ascended into heaven, And sitteth on the right hand of God the Father Almighty; From thence He shall come to judge the quick and the dead.

I believe in the Holy Ghost; The holy Catholick Church; The Communion of Saints; The Forgiveness of sins; The Resurrection of the body, And the Life everlasting. *Amen.*

Dost thou in the name of this child promise obedience to God's holy will and commandments?

Answer. I do.

Dost thou in the name of this child ask for baptism?

Answer. I do.

Then shall the Priest say:

O Merciful God, grant that the old Adam in *this child* may be so buried that the new man may be raised up in *him*. *Amen*.

Grant that all evil desires of the flesh may die in *him*, and that all things belonging to the Spirit may live and grow in *him*. *Amen*.

Grant that *he* may have power and strength to have victory, and to triumph, against the devil, the world, and the flesh. *Amen*.

Grant that whosoever is here dedicated to Thee by our office and ministry may also be endued with heavenly virtues, and everlastingly rewarded, through Thy mercy, O blessed Lord God, Who dost live, and govern all things, world without end. *Amen*.

The Blessing of the Water

After which the Priest shall proceed, saying:

The Lord be with you;

Answer. And with thy spirit.

Priest. Lift up your hearts;

Answer. We lift them up unto the Lord.

Priest. Let us give thanks unto our Lord God;

Answer. It is meet and right so to do.

Priest. It is very meet, right, and our bounden duty, that we should give thanks unto Thee, O Lord, Holy Father, Almighty, Everlasting God, for that Thy most dearly beloved Son Jesus Christ, for the forgiveness of our sins, did shed out of His most precious side both water and blood; and gave commandment to His disciples, that they should go teach all nations, and baptize them In the name of the Father, and of the Son, and of the Holy Ghost, Hear, we beseech Thee, the prayer of Thy people; sanctify this water to the mystical washing away of sin; and grant, that *this child,* now to be baptized therein, may receive the fulness of Thy grace, and ever remain in the number of Thy faithful and elect children; through Jesus Christ our Lord, to Whom with Thee in the unity of the Holy Spirit, be all honour and glory, now and evermore. *Amen.*

The Baptism

Then shall the Priest take the child into his arms, or by the hand, and shall say to the Godfathers and Godmothers:

Name this child.

And then naming it after them, he shall dip it in the water, or pour water upon it, saying:

N., I baptize thee In the name of the Father, and of the Son, and of the Holy Ghost. *Amen.*

Then shall the Priest say:

We receive this child into the congregation of Christ's flock,*** and do sign *him* with the sign of the Cross, in token that hereafter *he* shall not be ashamed to confess the faith of Christ crucified, and manfully to fight under His banner, against sin, the world, and the devil; and to continue Christ's faithful soldier and servant unto *his* life's end. *Amen.*

The Thanksgiving

Then shall the Priest say:

Seeing now, dearly beloved brethren, that *this child is* born again, and received into the family of Christ's Church, let us give thanks unto Almighty God for these benefits; and with one accord make our prayers unto Him, that *this child* may lead the rest of *his* life according to this beginning.

Then shall be said by all, standing:

Our Father, Which art in heaven, Hallowed by Thy name; Thy kingdom come; Thy will be done; In earth as it is in heaven. Give us this day our daily bread. And forgive us our trespasses, As we forgive them that trespass against us. And lead us not into temptation; But deliver us from evil: For Thine is the kingdom, The power, and the glory, For ever and ever. *Amen.*

Then shall the Priest say:

*** Here the Priest shall make a Cross upon the Child's forehead.

We yield Thee hearty thanks, most merciful Father, that it hath pleased Thee to regenerate *this infant* with Thy Holy Spirit, to receive *him* for Thine own *child* by adoption, and to make *him* a member of Thy holy Church. *Amen.*

Grant, O Lord, that, being buried with Christ by baptism into His death, *he* may also be made *partaker* of His resurrection; so that, serving Thee here in newness of life, *he* may finally, with the rest of Thy holy Church, be *an inheritor* of Thine everlasting kingdom; through Jesus Christ our Lord. *Amen.*

Then may follow this Prayer for the Home.

Almighty God, our heavenly Father, Whose blessed Son did share at Nazareth the life of an earthly home: Bless, we beseech Thee, the home of *this child,* and grant wisdom and understanding to all who have the care of *him*: that *he* may grow up in Thy constant fear and love; through the same Thy Son Jesus Christ our Lord. *Amen.*

The Duties of the Godfathers and Godmothers

Then the Priest shall say to the Godfathers and Godmothers and Parents this Exhortation following:

You who have brought *this child* to be baptized into the family of Christ's Church, must see that *he* be taught the Creed, the Lord's Prayer, and the Ten Commandments, as set forth in the Church Catechism, and all other things which a Christian ought to know and believe to his soul's health.

See also that *he* be virtuously brought up to lead a godly and Christian life.

See also that *he* be brought to the Bishop to be confirmed by him; so that, strengthened with the gift of the Holy Spirit, he may come with due preparation to receive the Holy Communion of the Body and Blood of Christ, and go forth into the world to serve God faithfully in the fellowship of His Church.

Will you help *him* to learn and to do all these things?

Answer. I will, the Lord being my helper.

Remember always that Baptism doth represent unto us our Christian profession, which is to follow the example of our Saviour Christ, and to be made like unto Him; that as He died and rose again for us, so should we, who are baptized, die unto sin and rise again unto righteousness, continually mortifying all evil desires, and daily advancing in all virtue and godliness of living.

LIBERAL CATHOLIC CHURCH*

Holy Baptism

Baptism is a Sacrament by which the recipient is solemnly admitted to membership of Christ's holy Church and "grafted into His mystical body."

The Exorcism is intended to deaden the germs of evil in infants, or to effect a preliminary purification in those more advanced in years.

* *Corpus Confessionum,* Vol. 6, pp. 338-349.

The first Anointing is, as indicated, for the strengthening and safeguarding of the candidate, and is followed immediately by the Baptism in the Name of the Trinity, and then by the second Anointing with holy chrism, still further to strengthen him.

Where there is doubt about the validity or completeness of a former Baptism, the Sacrament is re-administered conditionally.

The pouring of the water symbolizes both the washing away of sin and the downpouring of power from on high. The font is usually placed near the entrance of the church to show that by Baptism we gain admission to the Church of God.

So far as is convenient, holy Baptism should be administered publicly in the presence of a congregation.

Form to Be Used for Infants

Instructions to Parents

The head of the child should be uncovered, and the dress so arranged that the oil of catechumens can be applied on the neck or breast before and at the nape of the neck behind.

It is customary that the "white vesture" shall be a white silk handkerchief, presented by the godparents. This is to be blessed by the Priest and is retained by the child in memory of his Baptism.

For each child to be baptized there should be a godfather and godmother, who say the words of presentation respectively, according to whether the child be male or female.

The Invocation

Priest. In the Name of the Father, ✠ and of the Son, and of the Holy Ghost. *R.* Amen.

The Presentation

The child is presented as follows:

Sponsor. Reverend Father, we present to you this child, praying that you will receive *him* into the fellowship of Christ's Church.

P. Brethren, our fair Father Christ, in His great loving kindness, hath ordained that His mystic Bride, our holy Mother the Church, shall guide and protect her children at every stage from the cradle to the grave. To this end is the Sacrament of the holy Baptism ordained, that in His Name the Church may give welcome and blessing to *him* who is newly come into this world of pilgrimage, and that the soul may dwell in a body purified from the taint of evil, sanctified and set apart for the services of Almighty God.

Addressing the sponsors and congregation:

Therefore, brethren of Christ's catholic Church, I pray you to join with me in this our holy rite, whereby this child shall be made partaker of these heavenly gifts and a member of His mystical body.

Hear the words of the Gospel written by St. Mark, in the tenth chapter, at the thirteenth verse.

They brought young children to Christ, that He should touch them; and His disciples rebuked those that brought them. But when Jesus saw it, He was much displeased, and said unto them: Suffer the little children to come unto Me, and forbid them not; for of such is the kingdom of God. Amen, I say unto you, whosoever shall not receive the kingdom of God as a little child, he shall not enter therein. And He took them up in His arms, put His hands upon them, and blessed them.

The Priest places his right hand on the head of the child, and says:

Let us pray.

O God, Omnipotent and Omnipresent, Whose power worketh in every living creature, Who alone art the source of all life and goodness, deign to shed upon this Thy servant, who has been called to the rudiments of the faith, a ray of Thy light; drive out from *him* all blindness of heart, break all the chains of iniquity wherewith *he* has been bound; open to *him,* O Lord, the gate of Thy glory, that being replenished with the spirit of Thy wisdom and strengthened by Thy mighty power, *he* may be free from the taint of evil desire, and steadfastly advancing in holiness may joyfully serve Thee in the course Thou hast appointed for *him*. Through Christ our Lord. *R*. Amen.

The Exorcism

P. In the Name which is above every name, in the power of the ✠ Father, and of the ✠ Son, and of the Holy ✠ Ghost, I exorcise all influences and seed of evil; I lay upon them the spell of Christ's holy Church, that they may be bound fast as with iron chains and cast into outer darkness, that they trouble not this servant of God;

He again places his hand on the head of the child.

For He Who is the Lord of Love and Compassion hath deigned to call *him* to His holy grace and blessing and to the font of Baptism.

The Priest then proceeds as follows:

Ephphatha: that is, Be thou opened.

Here the Priest makes the sign of the cross over the brow, the throat, the heart, and the navel of the child.

Let thy mind and thy heart be opened to the most holy Spirit of the living God, that thy whole nature may be dedicated forever to His service; so mayest thou have power to receive the heavenly precepts and to be such in thy conduct that thou mayest be a pure temple of the living God.

He stretches out his right hand towards the child, and says:

Do Thou, O Lord, with Thy ever-abiding power, watch over this Thy chosen servant, whom we dedicate to Thy service, that, using well the beginnings of Thy glory and heedfully observing Thy holy laws, *he* may be found worthy to attain to the fullness of the new birth. Through Christ our Lord. *R*. Amen.

The Priest places the end of his stole upon the child's shoulder, and says:

Come into the temple of God, that thou mayest have part with Christ unto life eternal.

The First Anointing

The Priest takes upon his right thumb a little of the oil of catechumens. At the first two crosses the Priest touches respectively the child's breast or throat and the nape of his neck, making a small cross at each with the oil; he then makes two crosses respectively before and behind the child, reaching to the entire length of the body.

P. In the Name of Christ our Lord, I ✠ ✠ anoint thee with oil for thy safeguarding; may His holy Angel ✠ go before thee, and ✠ follow after thee; may he be with thee in thy downsitting and thine uprising and keep thee in all thy ways.

The Baptism

While the godparents hold the child over the font, the Priest pours some of the consecrated baptismal water over the head and forehead of the child thrice. At the same time he pronounces the words:

N., I baptize thee in the Name of the ✠ Father, and of the ✠ Son, and of the Holy ✠ Ghost. Amen.

The Anointing with Chrism

The Priest takes upon his thumb some of the sacred chrism, and, anointing the child on the top of the head in the form of a cross, says:

With Christ's holy chrism do I ✠ anoint thee, that His strength may prevent thee in thy going out, thy coming in, and may guide thee into life everlasting.

The Reception

With his thumb, still moist with chrism, the Priest makes a cross upon the child's brow; at the last clause he lays his hand upon the infant's head.

P. I receive this child into the fellowship of Christ's holy Church and do ✠ sign *him* with the sign of the cross in token that hereafter *he* shall not be ashamed to confess the faith of Christ our Lord, to acknowledge Him when He shall come, and manfully to fight under His banner against sin and selfishness, and that *he* shall continue Christ's faithful soldier and servant throughout the ages of ages. *R.* Amen.

A white silk handkerchief is brought and the Priest, having blessed it, places it upon the shoulders of the child, saying:

Receive from holy Church this white vesture as a pattern of the spotless purity and brightness of Him Whose service thou hast entered today, and for a token of thy fellowship with Christ and His holy Angels, that thy life may be filled with His peace.

Delivering a lighted candle to the child, the Priest says:

Take this burning light, enkindled from the fire of God's holy Altar, for a sign of the ever-burning light of thy spirit. God grant that hereafter His love shall so shine through thy heart that thou mayest continually enlighten the lives of thy fellow men.

The Priest places his hand on the head of the child, saying:

N., Go in peace, and may the Lord be with thee. *R.* Amen.

The Charge to Sponsors

P. Ye who have brought this child here to be baptized, seeing that now *he* is regenerate of water and the Holy Spirit and grafted into the mystical body of Christ's Church, remember that there lies upon you a duty not lightly to be cast aside. It is your part to see that so soon as *he* is old enough to understand, *he* is taught God's holy will and commandment, as it was spoken by our Lord Himself when He said: "Thou shalt love the Lord thy God with all thy heart and with all thy soul and with all thy mind and with all thy strength. This is the first and great commandment; and the second is like unto it: Thou shalt love thy neighbor as thyself. On these two commandments hang all the law and the prophets."

Also *he* shall be taught the doctrine of the holy Catholic Church, into which *he* has this day been admitted, and shall be brought in due course before the Bishop to be confirmed by him.

Form to be Used for Children

This form is to be used for children of four or five and upwards, who are able in some measure to understand the service.

Invocation, cf. above.

The Presentation, cf. above.

Address to people, cf. above.

Prayer, cf. above.

The Exorcism

In the Name which is above every name, in the power of the ✠ Father, and of the ✠ Son, and of the Holy ✠ Ghost, be you so purified that you may be rightly prepared to receive this first Sacrament of Christ's holy Church; (*the Priest places his hand on the head of the child*).

Cf. above.

The First Anointing, cf. above.

The Baptism

While the child leans, or is held, over the font, the Priest pours some of the consecrated baptismal water over the head and forehead of the child thrice. At the same time he pronounces the words:

N., I baptize thee in the Name of the ✠ Father, and of the ✠ Son, and of the Holy ✠ Ghost. Amen.

If the Baptism be sub conditione *the following is the formula:*

N., If thou art not already baptized, then do I baptize thee in the Name of the ✠ Father, and of the ✠ Son, and of the Holy ✠ Ghost. Amen.

The Anointing with Chrism, cf. above.

The Reception

Same as above, with the exception that the words "receive you into the fellowship of Christ's holy Church and do" are usually to be omitted when the person has already received baptism in some other Church or by lay ministration.

The Final Charge

The Priest then addresses the neophyte, saying:

You who have come here to be baptized, seeing that now you are regenerate of water and the Holy Spirit, and grafted into the mystical body of Christ's Church, remember that there lies upon you the duty of following God's holy will and commandment, as it was spoken by our Lord Himself, when He said: "Thou shalt love the Lord thy God with all thy heart and with all thy soul and with all thy mind and with all thy strength. This is the first and great commandment; and the second is like unto it: Thou shalt love thy neighbor as thyself. On these two commandments hang all the law and the prophets."

Also you shall further study the doctrine of the holy Catholic Church, into which you have been admitted, and come in due course before the Bishop to be confirmed by him.

Form to be Used for Adults

Invocation: cf. above.

The candidate comes forward and kneels.

The Exorcism

P. In the Name which is above every name, In the power of the ✠ Father, and of the ✠ Son, and of the Holy ✠ Ghost, be you so purified that you may be rightly prepared to receive this first Sacrament of Christ's holy Church; (*the Priest places his hand on the head of the candidate*) for He Who is the Lord of Love and Compassion hath deigned to call you to His holy grace and blessing, and to the font of Baptism.

The Priest stretches out his right hand towards the candidate, and says:

Do thou, etc., cf. above.

The First Anointing, cf. above.

The Baptism

While the candidate leans over the font the Priest pours some of the consecrated baptismal water thrice over his head and forehead, pronouncing these words:

N., I baptize thee in the Name of the ✠ Father, and of the ✠ Son, and of the Holy ✠ Ghost. Amen.

If the Baptism be sub conditione *the following is the formula:*

N., if thou art not already baptized; then do I baptize thee in the Name of the ✠ Father, and of the ✠ Son, and of the Holy ✠ Ghost. Amen.

The Anointing with Chrism, cf. above.

The Reception, cf. above.

The giving of the white vesture and light may then follow (or not) at the option of the Priest.

He places his hand on the head of the neophyte, saying:

N., go in peace, and may the Lord be with thee. *R.* Amen.

The Final Charge

The following charge is also optional: Cf. above.

APPENDIX II

Sects Which Observe Baptism But Which Recognize No Official Ritual

ASSEMBLIES OF GOD

(Members: 198,834)

Doctrine: *

The ordinance of Baptism by a burial with Christ should be observed as commanded in the Scriptures, by all who have really repented and in their hearts have truly believed on Christ as Saviour and Lord. In so doing, they have the body washed in pure water as an outward symbol of cleansing, while their heart has already been sprinkled with the blood of Christ as an inner cleansing. They declare to the world that they have died with Jesus and that they have also been raised with Him to walk in newness of life (Matt. 28:19; Acts 10:47, 48; Rom. 6:4; Acts 20:21; Heb. 10:22).

Administration: **

All ministers of the Assemblies of God practice the rite of baptism by immersion. Sprinkling and pouring is considered to be inadequate to express the symbol of Romans 6, "Therefore, we are buried with Him by baptism into death."

NORTHERN BAPTIST CONVENTION

(Members: 1,543,976)

Doctrine:

* In general: Although various groups and assemblies, at various times have endeavored to formulate "Confessions of Faith" such as the "New Hampshire Confession"; and although many local churches have "Articles of Faith" and "Church Covenants" these last are adopted by the individual churches, are for their own use locally, and are binding on no other churches than the ones which adopted them. Even in the local church there is wide liberty of

* *The Origin and Development of the Assemblies of God* (pamphlet), (Springfield, Mo.: The Gospel Publishing House, 1942), p. 21.

** Official statement by J. Roswell Flower, General Secretary, The General Council, Assemblies of God. This sect has no ritual.

* Statement by Dr. Clarence M. Gallup, Recording Secretary, Northern Baptist Convention, New York, N. Y., in *Census of Religious Bodies, 1936,* II, 110.

opinion permitted concerning these doctrinal statements. The number and length of them tends steadily to decrease. One reason for this light hold of creedal statement is that Baptists generally hold to the view that the Bible itself, especially the New Testament, is the only proper compendium for faith and practice; and the individual conscience and intelligence enlightened by the Divine Spirit, is the proper interpreter thereof.

Baptists, in general, believe in religious freedom, the validity and inspiration of the Scriptures, the Lordship of Christ, the immortality of the soul, the brotherhood of man, the future life, the need of redemption from sin, and the ultimate triumph of the Kingdom of God. Various groups and individuals hold to other items of conviction, which are not so universally accepted, and by many are regarded as secondary.

While for centuries, Baptists generally have stood for the validity and value of two ordinances, baptism and the Lord's Supper, their insistence has been limited to those two; and their views as to the vital efficacy of those ordinances have gradually shaded into a conviction of their value as an aid to Christian witness and comfort, rather than as a vital necessity for Christian character. This increasing liberalism is especially characteristic of Northern Baptists, and has come about more or less through the increase of scholarship and the association and conference in the north of many more diverse groups than are found elsewhere in the land.

So-called fundamentalism, or reactionary and conservative bodies of thought revolving around the Scriptures and theology, is found somewhat among Northern Baptists; but this phenomenon is not peculiar to them, being found also in practically all evangelical communions.

** Baptism: The Northern Baptist Convention includes the Baptist churches in the northern part of the United States. There is very little difference in views concerning baptism, between northern and southern Baptists, or Baptists in the entire world, of which four-fifths are in the United States.

The only baptism recognized in the New Testament is that by immersion. The denomination does not recognize any mystical or magical effect of this ordinance, which never is called a "sacrament." Its value in the Baptist church is symbolic; and the symbolism, according to the writings of St. Paul, are those of burial and resurrection—a burial to a life of sin and a resurrection to a newness of life.

** *Administration:* As aforesaid, the exact rite of administering baptism is by immersion in water. We have no book of discipline in the Baptist church, every church being a law unto itself in all matters of administration. The rite is not *obligatory* on ministers, but is universally performed by Baptist ministers, and customarily in baptistries within the church buildings, which contain sufficient water to permit of complete submersion of the body of the baptized person. Some Baptist churches receive members without this form of immersion, if they have received sprinkling or affusion, in other evangelical de-

** Statement furnished by Clarence M. Gallup, Recording Secretary, Northern Baptist Convention, 152 Madison Avenue, New York, N. Y.

nominations; and occasionally there is a Baptist church which, under a form of "associate" membership, will receive members without *any* form of baptism. But these cases are very rare.

It is perfectly correct to assume that whenever a minister of a Baptist church performs the rite of baptism, his intention is to imitate the method by which Christ Himself was baptized. In the Baptist church, it is not asserted that Christ "instituted" any rites whatever, but did approve of even His own baptism by saying, "Thus it becometh us to fulfill all righteousness." He was baptized by John the Baptist, who practiced immersion after the custom of the order of the Essenes.

SOUTHERN BAPTIST CONVENTION

(Members: 4,949,174)

Doctrine: *

In general: In doctrine the Southern Baptist churches are in harmony with those of the North, although in general they are more strictly Calvinistic, and the New Hampshire Confession of Faith is more firmly held than in the Northern churches. In polity, likewise, there is no essential difference. The Northern and Southern churches interchange membership and ministry on terms of perfect equality, and their separation is purely administrative in character, not doctrinal or ecclesiastical.

** Baptism: Baptism is by emersion of a believer in Christ. We consider this to be an act of obedience to Christ but we do not attach any saving efficacy to baptism. Among us, only ordained ministers administer the ordinance of baptism. He performs the rite in obedience to the command of Christ and upon profession of faith of the candidate in Christ as his Saviour.

Administration: ***

Christian baptism is the immersion of a believer in water in the name of the Father, the Son, and the Holy Spirit. The act is a symbol of our faith in a crucified, buried and risen Saviour. It is prerequisite to the privileges of a church relation and to the Lord's Supper, in which the members of the church, by the use of bread and wine, commemorate the dying love of Christ.

The formula used is as follows: "In obedience to the command of my Lord and Saviour Jesus Christ, and upon your profession of faith in Him as your Saviour, I baptize you, my brother (or sister), in the name of the Father, and of the Son, and of the Holy Ghost (or Holy Spirit)."

* *Census of Religious Bodies, 1936,* II, 141.

** Statement by Austin Crouch, Executive Secretary, The Executive Committee, Southern Baptist Convention (127 Ninth Avenue, North; Nashville, Tenn.).

*** Statement by Austin Crouch; *The Baptist Faith and Message* (pamphlet), a statement adopted by the Southern Baptist Convention, 1925, published by the Sunday School Board, Southern Baptist Convention, Nashville, Tenn., p. 11.

SEVENTH DAY BAPTIST GENERAL CONFERENCE

(Members: 6,876)

Doctrine: *

The Seventh Day Baptists are evangelical and except for the Sabbath, are in harmony with other Baptists, especially those of the Northern and Southern Baptist Conventions. Salvation is attained through personal faith in Christ, and the believer's baptism upon his confession of faith. Only two sacraments are recognized. The seventh day of the week is observed as the Sabbath. Church membership is extended only to those who have been immersed.

The organization is very weak: the officers and boards have very little authority. They function in an advisory capacity only.

The Sacraments

We believe that baptism of believers by immersion is a witness to the acceptance of Jesus Christ as Saviour and Lord, and is a symbol of death to sin, a pledge to a new life in Christ. We believe that the Lord's Supper commemorates the suffering and death of the world's Redeemer, and is a symbol of Christian fellowship and a pledge of renewed allegiance to our risen Lord.

These are not merely human institutions, deriving their sole value from the actions of men. What is presented in a sacrament has been derived not from men, but from God. This does not mean that a sacrament holds a magic charm and produces its effect upon life by the mere fact of its being employed. Its value depends upon the attitude of the recipient. In other words, it is valueless without faith. The Sacrament, whether baptism or the Lord's Supper, may not be administered purely as an external rite, and the one receiving the ordinance then be dismissed as though the external act had bestowed a spiritual benefit. We are saved by faith alone. The ordinances are aids and reminders. Each is a symbol, keeping before the believer's mind essential elements in a Christian experience. The ordinances can serve to fortify the life of the spirit only as they stimulate in the one receiving them greater faith and a purer life.

In the sacraments God elevates objects to the level of signs and witnesses, and, where rightly understood, these become channels of His grace.

Baptism

The origin of baptism is uncertain. Baptism is older than Christianity, with which it is now so closely associated. . . . Baptism was a seal of the new life. Christ Himself was baptized by John in Jordan (Matthew 3:12-17). So fitting was this rite as a symbol of repentance and remission of sins that Christ carried it over into His teachings and gave express command to His disciples that they baptize all nations (Matthew 28:19, 20).

* *Census of Religious Bodies, 1936,* II, 164; *Seventh Day Baptist Beliefs* (Plainfield, N. J.: American Sabbath Tract Society), pp. 69-74.

For the one who has been brought up in a Christian home, and who has believed in Christ from the time of understanding, baptism is alike significant. As the latter comes to the time in his life when he makes his decision to accept Christ as his personal Saviour and to join the church and help to carry on the work of the kingdom of God on earth, he asks that baptism be administered to him as a witness to this decision and to this high purpose (Acts 8:35-38). The ordinance becomes to him a witness in his own heart and of his new allegiance to Christ, and by the same token he gives evidence to others of his decision and of his positive stand for Christ and the church. It is an act of personal consecration to God and is a witness to others of that dedication. Baptism signifies our union with Christ and attests our status as children of God.

We hold that Baptism is wholly symbolic in nature, its physical performance a public proclamation to the world of the fact of the repentance, regeneration and reconciliation of a soul, which by nature, and by willful violation of the laws of God, has become alienated from Him. This experience must come about by the exercise of the will. Therefore the implication is that an infant under the age of responsibility is not capable of this experience, therefore not a subject for baptism.

Administration: **

The Seventh Day Baptist clergy are quite unanimous in the use of the formula for administering baptism as suggested in the Great Commission in Matt. 28. While the minister and the candidate are standing in the water ready the minister reads appropriate Scripture on the subject, prays, and then asks the candidate:

Minister—"John, do you believe on the Lord Jesus Christ and accept Him as your Lord and Saviour?"

John—"I do."

Minister—"Upon this profession of your faith, I baptize you in the name of the Father, the Son and the Holy Ghost."

(Candidate is completely immersed once only.)

Minister—"Amen."

AMERICAN BAPTIST ASSOCIATION

(Members: 260,876)

Doctrine:

* In General: The American Baptist Association accepts the New Hampshire Confession of Faith that has been so long held by American Baptists. They believe in: the infallible verbal inspiration of the whole Bible; the Triune God; the Genesis account of creation; the Deity of Jesus Christ; the virgin

** According to an official statement by Edward M. Holston, Chairman, Seventh Day Baptist General Conference.

* Statement by J. E. Cobb, Secretary-Treasurer, American Baptist Association, Texarkana, Ark.-Texas, as quoted in *Religious Bodies, 1936*, II, 249.

birth of Christ; the sufferings and death of Christ as vicarious and substitutionary; the bodily resurrection of Christ and the bodily resurrection and glorification of His saints; they believe in the second coming of Christ personal and bodily as the crowning event of the gospel age, and that His coming will be premillenial; the Bible doctrine of eternal punishment of the wicked; that in the carrying out of the commands of Jesus in the great commission, the churches are the only units, all exercising equal authority, and that responsibility should be met by them according to their several abilities; that all co-operative bodies such as conventions, associations, etc., are only advisory bodies and cannot exercise any authority whatsoever over the churches. They believe furthermore that salvation is wholly by grace through faith without any admixture of law or works, and that the church was instituted during the personal ministry of Jesus Christ on the earth.

** Baptism: We do not believe that baptism is a saving rite or ordinance; it is the obedience of a believer in Christ, one who is already saved. Its design is to show forth in emblematic form the burial and resurrection of Christ, and to show one's faith in his own resurrection from the dead.

Administration: ** It is our belief that when a Baptist minister baptizes a candidate by the authority of a Baptist church he is administering the rite or ordinance which Christ gave to His church; See Matt. 28:18-20.

We believe immersion is the only Scriptural act of baptism. It is obligatory upon all who desire to unite with a Baptist church to be immersed in water.

FIRST BRETHREN CHURCH

(Members: 17,300)

Doctrine: *

Christian water baptism was instituted by our Lord Jesus Christ in His parting commission to His disciples (Matt. 28:19, 20; Mark 16:15, 16). Baptism is never anything more than a symbol of certain great Biblical truths having to do with salvation and the work of the God-head in redemption. It is erroneous and unscriptural to say that it is essential to salvation, or that it adds to salvation. It is triple or triune immersion in water.

Believers should be baptized because the Lord Jesus Christ commands it (Matt. 28:19; Mark 16:15, 16); because it publicly identifies the believer with Christ; because it is considered the door into the visible local church.

The time in life when different children feel the pangs of conscience for the first time, know the distinct difference between right and wrong, and can intelligently accept Christ as their own personal Saviour, will vary greatly. Any child under this age of accountability should not be baptized. The mind

** Statement furnished by J. E. Cobb, Secretary-Treasurer, America Baptist Association, 214 East Broad Street, Texarkana, Ark.-Texas.

* *What Do Brethren Believe?* (pamphlet) by L. Llewellyn Grubb (Hagerstown, Md.), pp. 9-15.

of a child at this age is not capable of grasping this profound symbolism. Parents should be reassured by the knowledge that every babe born into the world, though depraved in its nature, is still under the blessed covering and power of Christ's vicarious atonement; and thus, until it reaches the age of accountability, is absolutely secure in Him. However, Christian parents, do well to dedicate their children to Christ and actually to lead them to a practical acceptance of Him as their Saviour in the earliest possible years.

Administration:

Triple or triune immersion in the name of the Father, and of the Son and of the Holy Ghost.

CHURCH OF GOD, CLEVELAND, TENN.

(Members: 18,351)

Doctrine: *

We baptize just because Jesus and the disciples baptized and instructed us to do likewise. This is not the baptism which John the Baptist preached, but it is baptism because Jesus gave authority to do it and commanded it to be done. Paul took some of the disciples that had been baptized unto John's baptism and baptized them again.

The great commission points out baptism for the whole world. This commission was given the eleven disciples by Jesus after His resurrection. It makes a broad sweep and covers the whole world. It calls for all nations to be taught, and baptized in the name of the Father, and of the Son, and of the Holy Ghost. If any have been baptized any other way they will yet have to be baptized this way if they live long enough.

Manner of Administration: *

This sacred ordinance was instituted by Jesus the same as all other practices. The applicant for baptism is taken down in the water by the minister who is to administer the ceremony, or his assistants. When they get in the water about waist deep they stop. The minister steps to one side and gently places one hand on the back of the applicant's neck, and with the other hand he takes hold of his hands and presses them up to his breast. In this position the minister raises his right hand toward heaven and repeats after Jesus, "I now baptize thee in the name of the Father, and of the Son, and of the Holy Ghost." Then he baptizes him by pressing him backwards into the water until his whole body is completely submerged. Then he lifts him up. He is baptized and comes up out of the water.

* *Water Baptism* (pamphlet), by A. J. Tomlinson (Cleveland, Tenn.: White Wing Publishing House, 1938). This sect has no ritual. The approved doctrine and manner of administering baptism is cited above. Because of the separation of the matter and form, this baptism may easily be questioned as regards its validity.

DISCIPLES OF CHRIST

(Members: 1,659,000)

Doctrine: *

We have no statements of creed. As to creed we accept only the statement of the Apostle Peter when he said, "Thou art the Christ, the Son of the living God."

The Disciples of Christ have made a great deal of the rite of Christian baptism. However, we do not look upon it as having magical significance. We look upon it as a rite to which a penitent believer commits himself "to fulfill all righteousness." In the experience of Christian baptism, the candidate symbolizes his death and burial to a life of sin and his rebirth to a life of righteousness in Christ.

Administration: *

Since the Disciples of Christ came into existence early in the nineteenth century as a revolt movement against ecclesiasticism and ritualism, we have no book of rituals.

When a candidate presents himself for baptism and membership in the church, the only question asked him is this, "Do you believe that Jesus is the Christ, the Son of the living God and do you accept Him as your personal Saviour?"

Baptism is by immersion only.

When a candidate is led into the baptismal water, the minister states only the following simple formula: "I baptize you, John Doe, into the name of the Father and of the Son and of the Holy Spirit. Amen."

APOSTOLIC EPISCOPAL CHURCH

(The Holy Eastern Catholic and Apostolic Orthodox Church in America.
Members: 6,389)

Doctrine: *

New Birth: Our Lord said: "Ye must be born again" (John iii, 7). A man must therefore accept Christ as his own personal Saviour, and be born again of water and of the Holy Ghost in the Sacrament of Baptism; whereby he is incorporated into Christ, and becomes a member of His Mystical Body the Church.

Sacraments: We believe that Christ and His Apostles instituted seven sacraments. A sacrament is an outward sign of inward grace, the sign being a channel through which the grace is mediated. Christ is the true minister of

* Statement by Willard M. Wickizer, Executive Secretary, Division of Home Missions (Missions Building, 222 Downey Avenue, Indianapolis, Ind.), Disciples of Christ.

* *The Ecclesia* (pamphlet), published by the Apostolic Episcopal Church, Hollis, L. I., New York, pp. 5, 6.

all Sacraments, and the Holy Ghost gives life and validity to what would otherwise be a mere form. By means of the Sacraments, Christians are enabled to make progress in spiritual life.

Baptism: It is the sacrament whereby we are made members of Christ, and therefore of His Church, and are cleansed from the taint of "original" sin. Baptism is by triune immersion or affusion with water "In the Name of the Father, and of the Son, and of the Holy Ghost."

Administration: **

The exact rite consists of a profession of the Christian faith, the taking of the vows of baptism, the blessing of the water with the invocation of the Holy Ghost, the act of baptizing with this water in the Name of the Father and of the Son and of the Holy Ghost, followed by the anointing with oil in the sign of the cross, with the declaration that the person is received into the ark of Christ's holy church.

The intention of the priest (or if no priest is available in an emergency, then a layman *Christian*) is certainly to baptize, as the Church hath taught and shown her teaching in the formula, which is sufficiently clear.

THE CHURCH OF JESUS CHRIST OF LATTER-DAY SAINTS (MORMONS)

(Members: 680,000)

Doctrine: *

In the theology of the Church of Jesus Christ of Latter-Day Saints, water baptism ranks as the third principle and the first essential ordinance of the Gospel. Baptism is the gateway leading into the fold of Christ, the portal to the Church, the established rite of naturalization in the kingdom of God. The candidate for admission into the Church, having obtained and professed faith in the Lord Jesus Christ and having sincerely repented of his sins, is properly required to give evidence of this spiritual sanctification by some outward ordinance, prescribed by authority as the sign or symbol of his new profession. The initiatory ordinance is baptism by water, to be followed by the higher baptism of the Holy Spirit; and, as a result of this act of obedience, remission of sins is granted.

The establishment of Baptism dates from the time of the earliest history of the race.

** Official statement by Most Rev. Arthur Wolford Brooks, D.D., Bishop titular of Sardis, presiding bishop, the Apostolic Episcopal Church. The writer was unable to obtain the ritual of the sect, containing the baptismal service.

* *A Study of the Articles of Faith,* James E. Talmage (12. ed., Salt Lake City, Utah: The Church of Jesus Christ of Latter Day Saints, 1924), pp. 120-145.

NOTE: This sect has no ritual for use in the administration of baptism. The same doctrine, manner of administering, and lack of ritual apply also to the Reorganized Church of Jesus Christ of Latter Day Saints. Cf. *Doctrines and Covenants,* by the Reorganized Church of Jesus Christ of Latter Day Saints (Independence, Mo.: Board of Publication, 1941), 17: 7, 21; *Census of Religious Bodies, 1936,* II, 815-822; *The Priesthood Journal,* October, 1939, Vol. 5, No. 4.

The special purpose of baptism is to afford admission to the Church of Christ with remission of sins.

Fit Candidates for Baptism—The prime object of baptism being admission to the Church with remission of sins, and this coming only through faith in God and true repentance before Him, it naturally follows that baptism can in justice be required of those only who are capable of exercising faith and of working repentance. . . . By revelation the Lord had designated eight years as the age at which children may be properly baptized into the Church; and parents are required to prepare their children for the ordinances of the Church by teaching them the doctrines of faith, repentance, baptism, and the laying on of hands for the gift of the Holy Ghost. Failure in this requirement is accounted by the Lord as a sin resting upon the heads of the parents.

Infant Baptism—The Latter-Day Saints are opposed to the practice of infant baptism, which indeed they believe to be a sacrilege. No one having faith in the word of God can look upon the child as cupably wicked; such an innocent being needs no initiation into the fold, for he has never strayed therefrom; he needs no remission of sins for he has committed no sin; and should he die before he has become contaminated by the sins of earth he will be received without baptism into the paradise of God.

Baptism Essential to Salvation—. . . baptism is necessary for salvation; for, inasmuch as remission of sins constitutes a special purpose of baptism, and as no soul can be saved in the kingdom of God with unforgiven sins, it is plain that baptism is essential to salvation. . . . Baptism is required of all who have attained to years of accountability; none are exempt.

Method of Administering Baptism:

The Latter-Day Saints hold that the Scriptures are devoid of ambiguity regarding the acceptable mode of baptism; and they boldly declare their belief that bodily immersion by a duly commissioned servant or representative of the Saviour is the only true form.

In a revelation concerning Church government, dated April, 1830, the Lord prescribed the exact mode of baptism as He desires the ordinance administered in the present dispensation. He said: "Baptism is to be administered in the following manner unto all those who repent—The person who is called of God and has authority from Jesus Christ to baptize, shall go down into the water with the person who has presented himself or herself for baptism, and shall say, calling him or her by name: *Having been commissioned of Jesus Christ, I baptize you in the name of the Father, and of the Son, and of the Holy Ghost. Amen.* Then shall he immerse him or her in the water, and come forth again out of the water."

The Lord would not have prescribed the words of this ordinance had He not intended that this form only should be used; therefore elders and priests of the Church of Jesus Christ of Latter-Day Saints have no personal authority to change the form given of God, by additions, omissions, or alterations of any kind.

OLD ORDER AMISH MENNONITE CHURCH

(Members: Over 11,000)

Doctrine: *

Regarding baptism, we confess that all penitent believers, who through faith, the new birth and renewal of the Holy Ghost, have become united with God, and whose names are recorded in heaven, must, on such scriptural confession of their faith, and renewal of life, according to the command and doctrine of Christ, and the example and custom of the apostles, be baptized with water in the ever adorable name of the Father, and of the Son, and of the Holy Ghost, to the burying of their sins, and thus to become incorporated into the communion of the saints; whereupon they must learn to observe all things whatever the Son of God taught, left on record, and commanded His followers to do (Matt. 3:15; *28:19, 20;* Mark 16:15, 16; Acts 2:38; 8:12, 38; 9:18; 10:47; 16:33; Rom. 6:3, 4; Col. 2:12).

MENNONITE BRETHREN CHURCH OF NORTH AMERICA

(Members: Over 8,000)

Doctrine: *

We believe and confess, that Christian baptism is a holy, visible, evangelical, sacred act and ordinance (institution) of Christ, commanded by the Lord Himself for a sacred sign of regeneration and embodiment in Him and His church. Holy baptism is not the putting away of the filth of the flesh, but for the honest believer a blessed representation of the purging from the inner sinful uncleanness of the soul by the blood of Christ, through which forgiveness of sin has been received, and the answer of a good conscience toward God. (Cf. 1 Cor. 12:27; 1 Pet. 3:21; Rev. 1:5.)

The practice of baptism consists in this, that all that hear the Gospel and in repentance of heart and living faith accept it, on their confession of a new life from God (Col. 2:12-13) are baptized (immersed) in water according to the command of Christ: All power is given unto me in heaven and in earth. Go ye, therefore, and teach all nations, baptizing them in the name of the Father, and of the Son, and of the Holy Ghost: teaching them to observe all things whatsoever I have commanded you: and lo, I am with you alway, even unto the end of the world.—Go ye into all the world and preach the Gospel to every creature. He that believeth and is baptized shall be saved; but he that believeth not shall be damned. (Matt. 28:18-20; Mark 16:15-16; John 3:22.)

This command of the Lord the Apostles have carried out and thereby many

* *Confession of Faith* (S. F. Coffman, editor, Scottdale, Pa.: Mennonite Publishing House, 1941), p. 30, art. VII. These Mennonites have no ritual.

* *Confession of Faith of the Mennonite Brethren of North America* (American edition, Hillsboro, Kansas, Mennonite Brethren Publishing House), pp. 28-32.

have been brought into the faith and have been baptized, both men and women, as especially on the day of the outpouring of the Holy Spirit, on the day of Pentecost at Jerusalem. And they, which gladly received the words of Peter and the other apostles were baptized; and the same day there were added unto them about three thousand souls. (Acts, chapters 2, 8, 10, 16.)

The children of believers (Acts 2:39) shall continually be brought before the Lord in prayer by the parents and the church, and shall be brought up in the nurture and admonition of the Lord and instructed in the Scriptures according to the measure of their understanding. . . . When later they have advanced so far that they can comprehend the calling voice of the holy Gospel, and accept the Word with a repentant heart and take faith in the Lord Jesus, it becomes them unto their own desire and free confession to receive holy baptism, as says the apostle Paul: So then faith cometh by hearing, and hearing by the Word of God. (Luke 2:52; Acts 8:5, 6, 12; 10:33-48; 16:14, 31-34; Rom. 10:17; John 3:5-8; Matt. 4:1; 2 Tim. 2:19.)

Baptism shall rightfully be administered once in the life of the believer.

The believers are bound together through baptism as having died unto sin to walk in the newness of life as taught by the apostle Paul: How shall we, that are dead to sin, live any longer therein? Know ye not, that so many of us as were baptized into Jesus Christ were baptized into His death? Therefore we are buried with Him by baptism into death: that like as Christ was raised up from the dead by the glory of the Father, even so we also should walk in newness of life. The believers have in baptism put on Christ (Gal. 3:27). Therefore every one must contribute according to his calling and gifts toward the support and betterment of the body of Christ in spiritual and temporal things with diligence. As true members of the household of God and children of the kingdom, they shall carefully guard the holy privileges of divine citizenship and duties received of Christ their head and be subject to all the commandments of their King and obedient to them according to His Word: Teach them to observe all things whatsoever I commanded to you.

THE PENTECOSTAL CHURCH, INC.

(Members: Over 15,000)

Doctrine: *

The scriptural mode of baptism is immersion, and is only for those who have fully repented, having turned from their sins, and a love of the world. It should be administered by a duly authorized minister of the gospel, by the authority, and in the *Name* of our Lord Jesus Christ, according to the Acts of the Apostles 2:38; 8:16; 10:48; 19:5, thus obeying and fulfilling Matthew 28:19.

* *Discipline of the Pentecostal Church* (Houston, Texas), *Baptism*. It is important to remember that the formula, "I baptize thee in the Name of the Lord Jesus," is invalid.

THE PENTECOSTAL ASSEMBLIES OF JESUS CHRIST

(Members: Over 16,000)

Doctrine: **

Water baptism is essential to New Birth. It is the act by which a penitent sinner partakes of the death and burial of the Lord Jesus Christ.

Administration: **

Our manner of administering baptism is by immersion in the name of the Lord Jesus Christ for the remission of sins. This is necessary as a means of entering into the invisible church and is obligatory.

The intention of the minister, when he baptizes, is to follow out the above, according to the instructions of the Apostle Peter, as recorded in the Book of Acts, 2nd chapter and 38th verse.

PENTECOSTAL ASSEMBLIES OF THE WORLD

(Members: Over 5,000)

Doctrine: *

Repentance and Remission of Sins

The only grounds upon which God will accept a sinner is Repentance from the heart for the sins that he has committed. A broken and a contrite heart He will not despise (Ps. 15:17). John preached Repentance, Jesus proclaimed it, and before His ascension commanded that Repentance and Remission of Sins should be preached in His name, beginning at Jerusalem (Luke 24:47). And Peter fulfilled this command on the Day of Pentecost. See Acts 2:38.

Membership—How Obtained

As members of the Body of Christ, which is the true Church, the Word of God declares but one way of entrance, therein and that is, "By one spirit are we all baptized into one Body," and that is a baptism of "water and spirit.".

Administration **

That in administering baptism in Jesus' Name our formula should include "In the name of the Lord Jesus Christ for the remission of sins" (1930). We believe Baptism once in the Name of the Lord Jesus Christ for the remission of sins for persons who have reached the age of understanding, and *no baptism* of infants under any condition.

** From an official statement by W. T. Witherspoon, General Chairman, the Pentecostal Assemblies of Jesus Christ.

* *Ministerial Record, Codified Rules and Minutes of the Pentecostal Assemblies of the World* (Indianapolis, Indiana), pp. 4, 5, 25.

** *Op. cit., Appendix*, n. 38.

APPENDIX III

General Statistics on Baptism as Observed By Religious Bodies in the United States of America

BAPTISM BY IMMERSION

Adventist Bodies	(3-48)
Assyrian Jacobite Apostolic Church	(75)
Baptist Bodies	(83-265)
Calvary Pentecostal Church	(1359)
Christadelphians	(356)
Christian and Missionary Alliance, The	(358)
Church of Armenia in America	(383)
Church of Christ (Holiness) U. S. A.	(389)
Church of Christ (Temple Lot)	(827)
Church of God	(407)
Church of God (Apostolic)	(656)
Church of God (Headquarters, Anderson, Ind.)	(415)
Church of God (Salem, W. Va.)	(424)
Church of God and Saints of Christ	(439)
Church of God in Christ	(448)
Church of Jesus Christ (Bickertonites)	(831)
Church of Jesus Christ of Latter-Day Saints	(812)
Church of the Gospel	(1267)
Churches of Christ	(470)
Churches of God, Holiness	(477)
Churches of the Living God	(486-497)
Disciples of Christ	(542)
Eastern Orthodox Churches	(549-604)
Faith Tabernacle	(1270)
General Eldership of the Churches of God in North America	(485)
German Baptist Brethren (Dunkers)	(266-290)
House of God, the Holy Church of the Living God, the Pillar and Ground of the Truth, House of Prayer for All People	(1251)
International Pentecostal Assemblies	(1342)
Italian Bodies	(747-755)
Krimmer Mennonite Brueder-Gemeinde	(1069)

Numbers in brackets refers to pages in Vol. II, *Religious Bodies, 1936* (U. S. Dept. of Commerce, Bureau of Census).

OPTIONAL FORM OF BAPTISM

INFANT BAPTISM

SECTS WHICH DO NOT OBSERVE BAPTISM

APPENDIX IV

Questionnaire on Baptism

1. Is natural water used in administering baptism?

2. Is the water applied by pouring, immersion, or sprinkling?

3. To what part of the body is the water applied?

4. Is water used in sufficient quantity for it to actually *flow* on the skin?

5. If applied to the head, does the water touch the *skin* of the head, and not merely the hair?

6. What is the exact formula recited in administering baptism?

7. Does the minister pronounce this formula at exactly the same time when he applies the water?

8. If not, when is this formula recited relative to the time when the water is applied? (Immediately before, immediately after.)

9. Does the same person apply the water and pronounce the formula of baptism?

10. Is it the constant and accepted doctrine of your church that the minister confers the baptism which Jesus Christ commanded to be administered?

11. If not, what is the intent and purpose in administering baptism?

BIBLIOGRAPHY

Sources

Acta Apostolicae Sedis, Commentarium Officiale, Romae, 1909—

Acta et Decreta Concilii Plenarii Baltimorensis Tertii, MDCCCLXXXIV, Baltimorae: Typis Joannis Murphy et Sociorum, 1886.

Acta et Decreta Concilii Provincialis Portlandensis in Oregon Quarti, Portlandiae in Ecclesia Metropolitana Celebrati diebus VIII, IX, X Septembris, MCMXXXII.

Acta et Decreta Concilii Provincialis Torontini Secundi, Toronti in Ecclesia Metropolitana celebrati diebus XIII, XIV, XV Decembris, MCMXXXVIII.

Acta et Decreta Quatuor Conciliorum Provincialium Cincinnatensium, 1855-1882, Cincinnati: Benziger, 1886.

Acta et Decreta Sacrorum Conciliorum Recentiorum, Collectio Lacensis, 7 vols., Friburgi Brisgoviae: Herder, 1870-1890.

Acta Sanctae Sedis, 41 vols., Romae, 1865-1908.

Bouscaren, T. Lincoln, *The Canon Law Digest*, 2 vols., Milwaukee: Bruce, 1934-1943.

Bullarii Romani Continuatio, 10 vols., Prati, 1840-1856.

Bullarium Benedicti XIV, 4 vols., Prati, 1845.

Bullarum Diplomatum et Privilegiorum S. R. Pontificum Taurinensis Editio, 20 vols., Augustae Taurinorum, 1857-1872; 5 vols., Neapoli, 1867-1885.

Canones et Decreta Sacrosancti Oecumenici Concilii Tridentini, Romae: Bernhardi Tauchnitz, 1863.

Codicis Iuris Canonici Fontes cura Emi Petri Card. Gasparri editi, 9 vols., Romae (postea Civitate Vaticana), Typis Polyglottis Vaticanis, 1923-1939. (Vols. VII-IX, ed. *cura et studio Emi Justiniani Card. Serédi*).

Collectanea S. Congregationis de Propaganda Fide, Romae: Typographia Polyglotta, S. C. de Propaganda Fide, 1893.

Collectanea S. Congregationis de Propaganda Fide, 2 vols., Romae: Typographia Polyglotta, S. C. de Propaganda Fide, 1907.

Concilii Plenarii Baltimorensis II, in Ecclesia Metropolitana Baltimorensi, a die VII ad diem XXI Octobris A. D. MDCCCLXVI Habiti et a Sede Apostolica Recogniti, Acta et Decreta, ed. 2a, Baltimorae: Ioannes Murphy, 1894.

Concilii Tridentini Diariorum, Actorum, Epistolarum, Tractatuum Nova Collectio, ed. Societas Goerresiana, 13 vols., Friburgi Brisgoviae: B. Herder, 1901-1938.

Corpus Iuris Canonici, ed. Lipsiensis secunda, post Aemilii Ludovici Richteri curas instruxit Aemilius Friedberg, 2 vols., Lipsiae: Ex Officina Bernhardi Tauchnitz, 1879-1881. Editio anastatice repetita, Lipsiae, 1922.

Corpus Iuris Civilis, 3 vols., ed. Krueger-Mommsen-Schoell-Kroll, Berolini, 1928-1929.

Decreta Authentica Congregationis Sacrorum Rituum, 5 vols., Romae: Ex Typographia Polyglotta, 1898-1901. Appendix I, 1912; Appendix II, 1927.

Decretales D. Gregorii Papae IX, una cum glossis restitutae, Romae, 1582.

Decretum Gratiani Emendatum et Notationibus illustratum una cum glossis, Romae, 1582.

Decretum Gratiani Emendatum et Notationibus illustratum una cum glossis, Venetiis, 1605.

Enchiridion Symbolorum et Definitionum, Denziger-Bannwart-Umberg, editio 21-23, Friburgi Brisgoviae: Herder & Co., 1937.

Formula Facultatum Quae Sacerdotibus Dioeceseos Neo-Eboracensis Concedi Solent, 11 febr. 1942.

Jaffé, Philippus, *Regesta Pontificum Romanorum ab condita Ecclesia ad annum post Christum natum MCXCVIII,* ed. 2a, cura Wattenbach, Löwenfeld, Kaltenbrunner, Ewald, 2 vols. in 1, Lipsiae, 1885-1888.

Liber Sextus Decretalium D. Bonifacii Papae VIII, una cum Clementinis et Extravagentibus tum D. Joannis XXII tum Communibus, una cum earum glossis, Romae, 1582.

Mansi, J. D., *Sacrorum Conciliorum Nova et Amplissima Collectio,* 53 vols. in 59, Parisiis, 1901-1927.

Ordo administrandi sacramenta et alia quaedam officia peragendi, London: Burns, Oates & Washbourne, 1915.

Quinque Compilationes Antiquae, ed. Aemilius Friedberg, Lipsiae, 1881.

Potthast, A., *Regesta Pontificum Romanorum,* 2 vols., Berolini, 1874-1875.

Rituale Romanum Pauli V Pontificis Maximi iussu editum aliorumque Pontificum cura recognitum atque auctoritate SSmi D.N. Pii Papae XI ad normam Codicis Iuris Canonici accommodatum, editio iuxta typicam vaticanam, Mechliniae: Typis H. Dessain, 1926.

Rituale Parvum, ed. Rev. J. B. O'Connell, ed. 2a, Dublin: Jas. Duffy & Co., 1929.

Schroeder, H. J., *Canons and Decrees of the Council of Trent,* St. Louis: B. Herder Book Co., 1941.

Synodus Dioecesana Fargensis I diebus 29 et 30 Septembris 1941 habita, Bruce: Milwaukee, 1941.

S. Romanae Rotae Decisiones seu Sententiae (ab anno 1909), Romae, 1912—

Statuta Dioecesis Seattlensis Lata ac Promulgata ab Excellentissimo ac Reverendissimo Geraldo Shaughnessy, S.M., Episcopo Seattlensi in Synodo Dioecesana Seattlensi Quinta die prima mensis Junii, A. D. 1938, celebrata in Ecclesia Cathedrali Sancti Jacobi apud Seattle, Washington, Seattle, Washington: Typis Metropolitan Press Printing Company, 1938.

The Priest's New Ritual, compiled by Rev. Paul Griffith, revised edition, Baltimore, Md.: John Murphy Co., 1940.

Thesaurus Resolutionum S. C. Concilii ab anno 1718, 167 vols., Urbino, 1718-1749; Romae, 1843-1908.

Reference Works

Aertnys, Jos.-Damen, C. A., *Theologia Moralis,* ed. 13a, 2 vols., Taurini, Romae: Marietti, 1939.

Aquinas, St. Thomas, *Summa Theologica,* ed. Marietti, 6 vols., Taurini, Romae: Marietti, 1937.

Attwater, Donald, *A Catholic Dictionary,* The Catholic Action Society of the College of St. Robert Bellarmine, Hethrop, New York: Macmillan Co., 1941.

Avanzini, Petrus, *De Constitutione Apostolicae Sedis,* ed. 2a, Romae, 1874.

Ayrinhac, H. A.-Lydon, P. J., *Penal Legislation in the New Code of Canon Law,* revised edition, New York: Benziger Bros., 1936.

Ayrinhac, H. A., *Legislation on the Sacraments in the New Code of Canon Law,* New York: Longmans, Green & Co., 1928.

(Bachofen), Charles Augustine, *A Commentary on the New Code of Canon Law,* 8 vols., St. Louis: Herder & Co., 1925-1938. Vol. I, 6. ed., 1931; Vol. II, 6. ed., 1936; Vol. III, 5. ed., 1938; Vol. IV, 3. ed., 1925; Vol. V, 5. ed., 1935; Vol. VI, 3. ed., 1931; Vol. III, 3. ed., 1930; Vol. VIII, 2. ed., 1924.

Barbosa, Augustinus, *De Officio et Potestate Episcopi,* Lugduni, 1656.

Benedictus XIV (Prosper Lambertini), *Institutiones Ecclesiasticae,* 3 vols., Romae, 1784.

———, *De Synodo Dioecesana,* 2 vols., Romae, 1806.

Berutti, Christophorus, *Institutiones Iuris Canonici,* Vol. VI, *De Delictis et Poenis,* Taurini, Romae: Marietti, 1938.

Beste, Udalricus, *Introductio in Codicem,* Collegeville, Minn.: St. John's Abbey Press, 1938.

Blat, A., *Commentarium Textus Codicis Iuris Canonici,* 5 vols. in 7, Romae: Collegio "Angelico," 1921-1938. Vol. I, 1921; Vol. II, Pars I, ed. 2a, 1921; Vol. II, Partes II et III, ed. 3a, 1938; Vol. III, Pars I, ed. 2a, 1924; Vol. III, Partes II-VI, ed. 2a, 1934; Vol. IV, 1927; Vol. V, 1924.

Bouix, D., *Tractatus De Episcopo,* 2 vols. in 1, ed. 2a, Paris, 1873.

Buchanan, Henry D., *Art of Persuasion in Pastoral Theology,* Philadelphia: The Dolphin Press, 1940.

Cappello, Felix M., *Tractatus Canonico-Moralis De Censuris iuxta Codicem Iuris Canonici,* ed. 2a, Taurinorum Augustae: Marietti, 1925.

———, *Tractatus Canonico-Moralis de Sacramentis,* 3 vols. in 6, Vol. I, ed 3a, 1938; Vol. II, Pars I, 1926, Romae: Marietti.

Cerato, Prosdocimus, *Censurae Vigentes Ipso Facto a Codice Iuris Canonici Excerptae,* ed. 2a, Patavii: Typis Seminarii, 1921.

Chelodi, Ioannes, *Ius Poenale et Ordo Procedendi in Iudiciis Criminalibus iuxta Codicem Iuris Canonici,* ed. 4a, recognita et aucta a Vigilio Dalpiaz, Tridenti: Libr. Edit. Tridentum, 1935.

Cicognani, Amleto, *Canon Law,* authorized English version, by J. O'Hara and F. Brennan, Philadelphia: Dolphin Press, 1934.

Cipollini, Albertus D., *De Censuris Latae Sententiae iuxta Codicem Iuris Canonici,* Taurini: Marietti, 1925.

Claeys-Bouuaert, F.-Simenon, G., *Manuale Iuris Canonici,* 3 vols., Gandae et Leodii: Dessain, Vol. I et III, ed. 3a, 1930; Vol. II, 1931.

Cocchi, Guidus, *Commentarium in Codicem Iuris Canonici,* 5 vols. in 8, Taurinorum Augustae: Marietti, 1922-1930; Vol. VIII, *De Delictis et Poenis,* ed. 2a, 1928.

Corblet, Jules, *Histoire Dogmatique, Liturgique et Archéologique du Sacrament de Baptême,* 2 vols., Genève, 1881-1882.

Coronata, Matthaeus Conte a, *Institutiones Iuris Canonici,* 5 vols., Taurini: Marietti: 1928-1936; Vol. IV, *De Delictis et Poenis,* 1935.

Crnica, Antonius, *Modificationes in Tractatu de Censuris per Codicem Iuris Canonici Introductae,* S. Mauritii Agaunensis: Typis Op. S. Augustini, 1919.

D'Annibale, Joseph Card., *Commentarium in Constitutionem Apostolicae Sedis,* ed. 5a, Prati, 1894.

De Meester, Alphonsus, *Iuris Canonici et Iuris Canonico-Civilis Compendium,* nova editio, 3 vols. in 4, Brugis: Desclée, De Brouwer et Sii, 1921-1928.

De Smet, Aloysius, *De Sacramentis in Genere—De Baptismo et Confirmatione,* ed. 2a, Brugis: Car. Beyaert, 1925.

Del Bene, Thomas, *De Officio S. Inquisitionis,* 2 vols., Lugduni, 1666.

Devoti, Ioannes, *Institutionum Canonicarum Libri IV,* Venetiis, 1827.

Doheny, William J., *Canonical Procedure in Matrimonial Cases,* Milwaukee: Bruce, 1938.

Duskie, John Aloysius, *The Canonical Status of Orientals in the United States,* The Catholic University of American Canon Law Studies, n. 48, Washington, D. C.: The Catholic University of America, 1929.

Fagnanus, Prosper, *Commentaria in Quinque Libros Decretalium,* 4 vols., Venetiis, 1709.

Farinacius, Prosper, *Tractatus De Haeresi,* Romae, 1616.

Ferraris, F. Lucius, *Bibliotheca,* ed. novissima, Romae, 1885.

Fortescue, Adrian-O'Connell, J., *The Ceremonies of the Roman Rite Described,* 6. ed. revised, London: Burns, Oates & Washbourne, 1937.

Garcias, Nicolaus, *De Beneficiis Ecclesiasticis,* Caesaraugustae, 1609.

Genicot, Eduardus-Salsmans, I., *Institutiones Theologiae Moralis,* ed. 14a, 2 vols., Dedebec: Desclée, De Brouwer, Buenos Aires, 1939.

Gonzalez-Tellez, Emmanuel, *Commentaria Perpetua in Singulos Textus Quinque Librorum Decretalium Gregorii IX,* 5 vols. in 4, Lugduni, 1715.

Haring, Johann, *Grundzüge des katholischen Kirchenrechtes,* 2 vols., Graz: Ulrich Moser, 1924.

Hefele, Carolus-Leclercq, Henricus, *Histoire des Conciles,* 10 vols. in 19, Paris: Letauzey et Ané, 1907-1938.

Hergenröther, Joseph-Kaulen, Franz, *Kirchenlexikon,* 2. ed., 13 vols., Freiburg in Breisgau: Herder, 1882-1903.

Hinschius, Paulus, *Decretales Pseudo-Isidorianae et Capitula Angilramni,* Leipzig, 1863.

Hostiensis, Cardinalis (Henricus de Segusio), *Commentaria in Quinque Decretalium Libros,* 5 vols. in 3, Venetiis, 1581.

———, *Summa Aurea,* Venetiis, 1570.

Lacroix, Claudius, *Theologia Moralis,* 3 vols., Venetiis, 1753.

Lahousse, Gustavus, *Tractatus De Sacramentis,* 2 vols., Brugis, 1899.

Lehmkuhl, Augustinus, *Theologia Moralis,* ed. 2a, 2 vols., Friburgi Brisgoviae, 1884.

Leone, Marcus Paulus, *Praxis ad Litteras Maioris Poenitentiarii et Officii Sacrae Poenitentiariae Apostolicae,* ed. 2a, Mediolani, 1655.

Lydon, P. J., *Ready Answers in Canon Law,* San Francisco: Benziger Bros., 1934.

MacKenzie, Eric, *The Delict of Heresy in Its Commission, Penalization, Absolution,* The Catholic University of America Canon Law Studies, n. 77, Washington, D. C.: The Catholic University of America, 1932.

Maroto, Philippus, *Institutiones Iuris Canonici ad Normam Novi Codicis,* 2 vols., Vol. I, ed. 3a, Romae: Apud Commentarium Pro Religiosis, 1921.

Martene, Edmundus, *De Antiquis Ecclesiae Ritibus,* 4 vols., Rotomagi, 1700.

Mazzella, Camillus, *De Virtutibus Infusis,* Romae, 1879.

McCloskey, Joseph A., *The Subject of Ecclesiastical Law According to Canon 12,* The Catholic University of America Canon Law Studies, n. 165, Washington, D. C.: The Catholic University of America Press, 1943.

Merkelbach, Benedictus Henricus, *Summa Theologiae Moralis,* ed. 3a, 3 vols., Parisiis: Desclée, De Brouwer et Soc., Buenos Aires, 1942.

Michiels, Gommarus, *Normae Generales Iuris Canonici,* 2 vols., Lublin: Universitas Catholica, 1929.

———, *De Delictis et Poenis,* Vol. I, *De Delictis,* Lublin: Universitas Catholica, 1934.

Migne, Jacques Paul, *Patrologiae Cursus Completus, Series Graeca,* 161 vols., Parisiis, 1856-1866.

———, *Patrologiae Cursus Completus, Series Latina,* 221 vols., Parisiis, 1844-1864.

Monin, Arthur, *De Curia Romana,* Lovanii: J. Van Linthout, 1912.

Moriarty, Francis, *The Extraordinary Absolution from Censures,* The Catholic University of America Canon Law Studies, n. 113, Washington, D. C.: The Catholic University of America, 1938.

Mothon, Joseph Pie, *Institutions Canoniques,* 3 vols., Lille, Bruges: Desclée, De Brouwer & Cie., 1922-1924.

Noldin, H.-Schmitt, A., *Summa Theologiae Moralis iuxta Codicem Iuris Canonici,* ed. 25a, 3 vols., Oeniponte: Rauch, 1938.

Ojetti, B., *Synopsis Rerum Moralium et Iuris Pontificii,* 3 vols., ed. 3a, Romae. Vol. I, 1909; Vol. II, 1911; Vol. III, 1912.

O'Kane, James-Fallon, Michael, *Notes on the Rubrics of the Roman Ritual,* new edition completely revised in accordance with the latest (1925) *Editio Typica* of the *Rituale Romanum* and the Decrees of the Sacred Congregations, Dublin: James Duffy & Co., Ltd., 1938.

Pallavicino, Sforza, *Istoria del Concilio di Trento,* ed. Francesco Antonio Zaccaria, 4 vols., Romae, 1883.

Panormitanus, Abbas (Nicolaus de Tudeschis), *Commentaria in Quinque Libros Decretalium,* 5 vols. in 7, Venetiis, 1588.

Payen, G., *De Matrimonio,* 3 vols., ed. 2a, Zi-ka-weî: T'oo-sè-wè, 1935.

Pennacchi, Joseph, *Commentaria in Constitutionem Apostolicae Sedis,* 2 vols., Romae, 1883.

Petra, Vincentius Cardinalis, *Commentaria ad Constitutiones Apostolicas,* 5 vols. in 2, Venetiis, 1729.

Petrani, A., *De Relatione Juridica Inter Diversos Ritus in Ecclesia Catholica,* Taurini, Romae: Marietti, 1930.

Pignatelli, Jacobus, *Consultationes Canonicae,* 6 vols., Coloniae Allobrogum, 1700.

Pirhing, Ernricus, *Ius Canonicum Nova Methodo Explicatum,* 5 vols. in 4, Dilingae, 1674-1678.

Pistocchi, Mario, *I Canoni Penali del Codice Ecclesiastico Esposti e Commentati,* Torino, Roma: Marietti, 1925.

Pourrat, P., *Theology of the Sacraments,* translated from 4. French ed., St. Louis: B. Herder Book Co., 1930.

Prümmer, Dominicus M., *Manuale Iuris Canonici,* ed. 3a, Fribourgi Brisgoviae: Herder & Co., 1922.

———, *Manuale Theologiae Moralis,* 3 vols., ed. 4a et 5a, Friburgi Brisgoviae: Herder & Co., 1929.

Rabanus Maurus, *De Institutione Clericorum,* ed. Aloysius Knoepfler (Veröffentlichungen aus dem kirchenhistorischen Seminar München, hrsg. von Alois Knoepfler, n. 5), München, 1900.

Raymundus de Pennafort, *Summa,* Veronae, 1744.

Reiffenstuel, Anacletus, *Jus Canonicum Universum,* 5 vols. in 7, Parisiis, 1864-1870.

Roberti, Franciscus, *De Delictis et Poenis,* Vol. I, Romae: Libraria Pontificii Instituti Utriusque Iuris, 1938.

Rufinus, *Summa Decretorum,* hrsg. von D. Heinrich Singer (*Die Summa Decretorum des Magister Rufinus*), Paderborn: 1902.

Sabetti, Aloysius-Barrett, Timotheus, *Compendium Theologiae Moralis,* ed. 27a, New York: Frederick Pustet Co., Inc., 1919.

Salmanticenses, *Cursus Theologicus,* 20 vols., editio nova, correcta, Genève, 1870-1883.

Salucci, Raffaele, *Il Diritto Penale secondo il Codice di Diritto Canonico,* 2 vols. in 1, Subiaco: Tipografia dei Monasteri, 1926-1930.

Sanchez, Thomas, *Disputationes De Sancto Matrimonii Sacramento*, 3 vols. in 1, Antverpiae, 1626.

Schenk, Francis J., *The Matrimonial Impediments of Mixed Religion and Disparity of Cult*, The Catholic University of America Canon Law Studies, n. 51, Washington, D. C.: The Catholic University of America, 1929.

Schmalzgrueber, Franciscus, *Jus Ecclesiasticum Universum*, 5 vols. in 12, Romae, 1843-1845.

Schöllig, Otto, *Die Verwaltung der heiligen Sakramente unter pastoralen Gesichtspunkten*, Freiburg im Breisgau: Herder & Co., 1936.

Schulze, Frederick, *A Manual of Pastoral Theology*, 3. ed., revised and enlarged, St. Louis: B. Herder Book Co., 1923.

Sipos, Stephanus, *Enchiridion Iuris Canonici*, ed. 3a, Pécs: "Haladáas R. T.," 1936.

Slater, Thomas, *A Manual of Moral Theology*, New York: Benziger Bros., 1908.

Smith, S. B., *Elements of Ecclesiastical Law*, 3 vols., Vol. I, 9. ed., 1887; Vol. II, 5. ed., 1887; Vol. III, 3. ed., 1888.

Sole, Iacobus, *De Delictis et Poenis—Praelectiones in Lib. V Codicis Iuris Canonici*, Romae: Fredericus Pustet, 1920.

Suarez, Franciscus, *Opera Omnia*, 26 vols., Parisiis, 1856-1866.

Tanquerey, A., *Synopsis Theologiae Dogmaticae*, 3 vols., Parisiis: Desclée et Socii, 1930-1934.

Téphany, Joseph-Marie, *Constitution "Apostolicae Sedis" Commentaire*, Tours, 1883.

Van der Stappen, J. F., *Sacra Liturgia*, Vol. IV, *Tractatus De Administratione Sacramentorum et De Sacramentalibus*, Mechliniae: H. Dessain, 1900.

Van Hove, A., *Commentarium Lovaniense in Codicem Iuris Canonici*, 1 vol. in 5 (Vol. II, *De Legibus Ecclesiasticis*, 1930), Mechliniae, Romae: H. Dessain, 1928-1939.

Van Noort, G., *De Fontibus Revelationis*, ed. 2a, Amstelodami: C. L. Van Langenhuysen, 1911.

Vecchiotti, S. M., *Institutiones Canonicae ex Operibus Cardinalis Soglia Excerptae*, 2 vols., Augustae Taurinorum, 1867.

Vermeersch, Arthurus, *Theologiae Moralis Principia, Responsa, Consilia*, 4 vols., ed. 3a, Roma: Università Gregoriana, 1933-1937.

Vermeersch, A.-Creusen, J., *Epitome Iuris Canonici*, 3 vols., Mechliniae, Romae: H. Dessain, Vol. I, ed. 6a, 1937; Vol. II, ed. 5a, 1934; Vol. III, ed. 5a, 1936.

Weaver, Francis, *Hints for the Instruction of Converts*, London: Burns, Oates & Washbourne, Ltd., 1933.

Wernz, F.-Vidal, P., *Ius Canonicum*, 7 vols. in 8, Romae: Universitas Gregoriana, 1923-1938.

Woywod, Stanislaus, *A Practical Commentary on the Code of Canon Law*, 3. ed., 2 vols., New York: Wagner, 1929.

Zoesius, Henricus, *Jus Canonicum Universum*, Venetiis, 1757.

Periodicals

American Ecclesiastical Review, The, Philadelphia, 1889-1944; Washington, D. C., 1944—

Analecta Ecclesiastica, Romae, 1893-1911.

Apollinaris, Romae, 1928—

Archiv für katholisches Kirchenrecht, Innsbruck, 1857-1861; Mainz, 1862—

Collationes Brugenses, Bruges, 1896—

Conference Bulletin of the Archdiocese of New York, New York, 1923—

Ephemerides Theologicae Lovanienses, Brugis, 1924—

Gregorianum, Romae, 1920—

Homiletic and Pastoral Review, The, New York, 1900—

Jurist, The, Washington, D. C., 1941—

Jus Pontificium, Romae, 1921—

Nouvelle Revue Théologique, Paris, 1869—

Periodica de Re Canonica et Morali, Brugis, 1905—; ab anno, 1927: *Periodica de Re Canonica, Morali, Liturgica,* Romae, 1937—

Revue Ecclésiastique de Liège, Leodii, 1908—

Theologisch-Praktische Quartalschrift, Linz, 1832—

Principal Articles

Boehm, F., "Konversion eines vierzehnjährigen Mädchens—*LQS,* LXXVI (1923), 118-121.

Bouscaren, T. L., "De Validitate Baptismi Apud Baptistas"—*Gregorianum,* VIII (1927), 41-51.

Castillon, P., "Le Baptême de Valeur Douteuse et Les Obligations Qu' il Produit" —*NRTh,* XLVI (1914-1919), 581-598.

Ciprotti, Pius, "De Consummatione Delictorum Attento Eorum Elemento Objectivo"—*Apollinaris,* VIII (1935), 224-248.

Connell, Francis, "Priestly Ministry of the Essentials of Faith"—*AER,* LXXVI (1927), 570-579.

De Schepper, R., "De Haereticis relate ad Leges Ecclesiasticas"—*Collationes Brugenses,* XXIV (1924), 209-213.

Gillman, Franz, "Die *anni discretionis* im Kanon *Omnis utriusque sexus*"—*AKKR,* CVIII (1928), 556-617.

Leroux, E., "Les Baptêmes d'Adultes"—*Revue Ecclésiastique de Liège,* XXV (1925-1926), 341-352.

Pappafava dei Carraresi, "Quaestio Quaedam Circa Haeresim"—*Jus Pontificium,* XI (1931), 52-53.

Schaaf, Valentine, "The Validity of Protestant Baptisms"—*AER,* LXXVII (1927), 496-504.

———, "The Right to Baptize Converts"—*AER,* XCIV (1936), 531.

Slater, T., "Sacramental Ministration to Non-Catholics"—*AER,* LXIV (1921), 255-260.

Teodori, I., "Condiciones ad Censuram Incurrendam"—*Apollinaris,* II (1929), 218-220.

Umberg, Joh. B., "Quo Jure Haereticis et Schismaticis Sacramenta Sint Neganda"—*Periodica,* XVIII (1929), 97*-122*.

Vermeersch, A., "Practica Disquisitio de Sacramentis Conferendis vel Negandis Acatholico"—*Periodica,* XVIII (1929), 123*-148*.

Woywod, Stanislaus, "The Legislation of the Code on Baptism"—*Homiletic and Pastoral Review,* XX (1920), 1037-1043; 1145-1152; XXI (1921), 16-25.

ABBREVIATIONS

AAS—Acta Apostolicae Sedis
AER—The American Ecclesiastical Review
AKKR—Archiv für katholisches Kirchenrecht
ASS—Acta Sanctae Sedis
C—Codex Justinianus
CIC—Commissio Ad' Codicis Canones Authenice Interpretandos
Collect.—Collectanea S. C. de Propaganda Fide
Coll. Lac.—Collectio Lacensis
D. B.—Denziger-Bannwart-Umberg, *Enchiridion Symbolorum et Definitionum*
Fontes—Codicis Iuris Canonici Fontes
Hefele—*Histoire des Conciles*
LQS—Theologisch-Praktische Quartalschrift
MPG—Migne, *Patrologia Graeca*
MPL—Migne, *Patrologia Latina*
NRTh—Nouvelle Revue Theologique
S.C.C.—Sacra Congregatio Concilii
S. C. de Prop. Fide—Sacra Congregatio de Propaganda Fide
S. C. S. Off.—Suprema Congregatio Sancti Officii
S.R.C.—Sacra Congregatio Rituum

ALPHABETICAL INDEX

BIOGRAPHICAL NOTE

JOSEPH GERARD GOODWINE was born in New York City on January 4, 1916. He received his primary education at St. Joseph's parochial school, New York City. He completed his high school and college studies in St. Joseph's College and Seminary, New York City and Yonkers, from which institution he received the degree of Bachelor of Arts in 1937. In October, 1937, he was appointed to the North American College, Rome, Italy, to make his theological studies at the Pontifical Gregorian University, where he received the Baccalaureate in Theology in 1939. He made the last two years of his theological studies at St. Joseph's Seminary, Yonkers, and was ordained to the priesthood on June 7, 1941. In September, 1941, he entered the Canon Law School at the Catholic University of America, Washington, D. C., where he received the Baccalaureate in Canon Law in June, 1942, and the Licentiate in Canon Law in May, 1943.

CANON LAW STUDIES *

1. Freriks, Rev. Celestine A., C.PP.S., J.C.D., Religious Congregations in Their External Relations, 121 pp., 1916.
2. Galliher, Rev. Daniel M., O.P., J.C.D., Canonical Elections, 117 pp., 1917.
3. Borkowski, Rev. Aurelius L., O.F.M., J.C.D., De Confraternitatibus Ecclesiasticis, 136 pp., 1918.
4. Castillo, Rev. Cayo, J.C.D., Disertacion Historico-Canonica sobre la Potestad del Cabildo en Sede Vacante o Impedida del Vicario Capitular, 99 pp.; 1919 (1918).
5. Kubelbeck, Rev. William J., S.T.B., J.C.D., The Sacred Penitentiaria and Its Relation to Faculties of Ordinaries and Priests, 129 pp., 1918.
6. Petrovits, Rev. Joseph, J.C., S.T.D., J.C.D., The New Church Law on Matrimony, X-461 pp., 1919.
7. Hickey, Rev. John J., S.T.B., J.C.D., Irregularities and Simple Impediments in the New Code of Canon Law, 100 pp., 1920.
8. Klekotka, Rev. Peter J., S.T.B., J.C.D., Diocesan Consultors, 179 pp., 1920.
9. Wanenmacher, Rev. Francis, J.C.D., The Evidence in Ecclesiastical Procedure Affecting the Marriage Bond, 1920 (Printed 1935).
10. Golden, Rev. Henry Francis, J.C.D., Parochial Benefices in the New Code, IV-119 pp., 1921 (Printed 1925).
11. Koudelka, Rev. Charles J., J.C.D., Pastors, Their Rights and Duties According to the New Code of Canon Law, 211 pp., 1921.
12. Melo, Rev. Antonius, O.F.M., J.C.D., De Exemptione Regularium, X-188 pp., 1921.
13. Schaaf, Rev. Valentine Theodore, O.F.M., S.T.B., J.C.D., The Cloister, X-180 pp., 1921.
14. Burke, Rev. Thomas Joseph, S.T.D., J.C.D., Competence in Ecclesiastical Tribunals, IV-117 pp., 1922.
15. Leech, Rev. George Leo, J.C.D., A Comparative Study of the Constitution "Apostolicae Sedis" and the "Codex Juris Canonici," 179 pp., 1922.
16. Motry, Rev. Hubert Louis, S.T.D., J.C.D., Diocesan Faculties According to the Code of Canon Law, II-167 pp., 1922.
17. Murphy, Rev. George Lawrence, J.C.D., Delinquencies and Penalties in the Administration and the Reception of the Sacraments, IV-121 pp., 1923.
18. O'Reilly, Rev. John Anthony, S.T.B., J.C.D., Ecclesiastical Sepulture in the New Code of Canon Law, II-129 pp., 1923.

---

* Below n. 100 only the following numbers are still available: No. 3, 4, 9, 25, 34, 57 and 75. Beginning with n. 100 only the following are unavailable: No. 100-111 inclusive, and n. 113.

19. Michalicka, Rev. Wenceslas Cyrill, O.S.B., J.C.D., Judicial Procedure in Dismissal of Clerical Exempt Religious, 107 pp., 1923.

20. Dargin, Rev. Edward Vincent, S.T.B., J.C.D., Reserved Cases According to the Code of Canon Law, IV-103 pp., 1924.

21. Godfrey, Rev. John A., S.T.B., J.C.D., The Right of Patronage According to the Code of Canon Law, 153 pp., 1924.

22. Hagedorn, Rev. Francis Edward, J.C.D., General Legislation on Indulgences, II-154 pp., 1924.

23. King, Rev. James Ignatius, J.C.D., The Administration of the Sacraments to Dying Non-Catholics, V-141 pp., 1924.

24. Winslow, Rev. Francis Joseph, O.F.M., J.C.D., Vicars and Prefects Apostolic, IV-149 pp., 1924.

25. Correa, Rev. Jose Servelion, S.T.L., J.C.D., La Potestad Legislativa de la Iglesia Catolica, IV-127 pp., 1925.

26. Dugan, Rev. Henry Francis, A.M., J.C.D., The Judiciary Department of the Diocesan Curia, 87 pp., 1925.

27. Keller, Rev. Charles Frederick, S.T.B., J.C.D., Mass Stipends, 167 pp., 1925.

28. Paschang, Rev. John Linus, J.C.D., The Sacramentals According to the Code of Canon Law, 129 pp., 1925.

29. Piontek, Rev. Cyrillus, O.F.M., S.T.B., J.C.D., De Indulto Exclaustrationis necnon Saecularizationis, XIII-289 pp., 1925.

30. Kearney, Rev. Richard Joseph, S.T.B., J.C.D., Sponsors at Baptism According to the Code of Canon Law, IV-127 pp., 1925.

31. Bartlett, Rev. Chester Joseph, A.M., LL.B., J.C.D., The Tenure of Parochial Property in the United States of America, V-108 pp., 1926.

32. Kilker, Rev. Adrian Jerome, J.C.D., Extreme Unction, V-425 pp., 1926.

33. McCormick, Rev. Robert Emmett, J.C.D., Confessors of Religious, VIII-266 pp., 1926.

34. Miller, Rev. Newton Thomas, J.C.D., Founded Masses According to the Code of Canon Law, VII-93 pp., 1926.

35. Roelker, Rev. Edward G., S.T.D., J.C.D., Principles of Privilege According to the Code of Canon Law, XI-166 pp., 1926.

36. Bakalarczyk, Rev. Richardus, M.I.C., J.U.D., De Novitiatu, VIII-208 pp., 1927.

37. Pizzuti, Rev. Lawrence, O.F.M., J.U.L., De Parochis Religiosis, 1927. (Not Printed.)

38. Bliley, Rev. Nicholas Martin, O.S.B., J.C.D., Altars According to the Code of Canon Law, XIX-132 pp., 1927.

39. Brown, Mr. Brendan Francis, A.B., LL.M., J.U.D., The Canonical Juristic Personality with Special Reference to its Status in the United States of America, V-212 pp., 1927.

40. Cavanaugh, Rev. William Thomas, C.P., J.U.D., The Reservation of the Blessed Sacrament, VIII-101 pp., 1927.

41. DOHENY, REV. WILLIAM J., C.S.C., A.B., J.U.D., Church Property: Modes of Acquisition, X-118 pp., 1927.
42. FELDHAUS, REV. ALOYSIUS H., C.PP.S., J.C.D., Oratories, IX-141 pp., 1927.
43. KELLY, REV. JAMES PATRICK, A.B., J.C.D., The Jurisdiction of the Simple Confessor, X-208 pp., 1927.
44. NEUBERGER, REV. NICHOLAS J., J.C.D., Canon 6 or the Relation of the Codex Juris Canonici to the Preceding Legislation, V-95 pp., 1927.
45. O'KEEFE, REV. GERALD MICHAEL, J.C.D., Matrimonial Dispensations, Powers of Bishops, Priests, and Confessors, VIII-232 pp., 1927.
46. QUIGLEY, REV. JOSEPH A. M., A.B., J.C.D., Condemned Societies, 139 pp., 1927.
47. ZAPLOTNIK, REV. JOHANNES LEO, J.C.D., De Vicariis Foraneis, X-142 pp., 1927.
48. DUSKIE, REV. JOHN ALOYSIUS, A.B., J.C.D., The Canonical Status of the Orientals in the United States, VIII-196 pp., 1928.
49. HYLAND, REV. FRANCIS EDWARD, J.C.D., Excommunication, Its Nature, Historical Development and Effects, VIII-181 pp., 1928.
50. REINMANN, REV. GERALD JOSEPH, O.M.C., J.C.D., The Third Order Secular of Saint Francis, 201 pp., 1928.
51. SCHENK, REV. FRANCIS J., J.C.D., The Matrimonial Impediments of Mixed Religion and Disparity of Cult, XVI-318 pp., 1929.
52. COADY, REV. JOHN JOSEPH, S.T.D., J.U.D., A.M., The Appointment of Pastors, VIII-150 pp., 1929.
53. KAY, REV. THOMAS HENRY, J.C.D., Competence in Matrimonial Procedure, VIII-164 pp., 1929.
54. TURNER, REV. SIDNEY JOSEPH, C.P., J.U.D., The Vow of Poverty, XLIX-217 pp., 1929.
55. KEARNEY, REV. RAYMOND A., A.B., S.T.D., J.C.D., The Principles of Delegation, VII-149 pp., 1929.
56. CONRAN, REV. EDWARD JAMES, A.B., J.C.D., The Interdict, V-163 pp., 1930.
57. O'NEILL, REV. WILLIAM H., J.C.D., Papal Rescripts of Favor, VII-218 pp., 1930.
58. BASTNAGEL, REV. CLEMENT VINCENT, J.U.D., The Appointment of Parochial Adjutants and Assistants, XV-257 pp., 1930.
59. FERRY, REV. WILLIAM A., A.B., J.C.D., Stole Fees, V-136 pp., 1930.
60. COSTELLO, REV. JOHN MICHAEL, A.B., J.C.D., Domicile and Quasi-Domicile, VII-201 pp., 1930.
61. KREMER, REV. MICHAEL NICHOLAS, A.B., S.T.B., J.C.D., Church Support in the United States, VI-136 pp., 1930.
62. ANGULO, REV. LUIS, C.M., J.C.D., Legislation de la Iglesia sobre la intencion en la application de la Santa Misa, VII-104 pp., 1931.
63. FREY, REV. WOLFGANG NORBERT, O.S.B., A.B., J.C.D., The Act of Religious Profession, VIII-174 pp., 1931.

64. Roberts, Rev. James Brendan, A.B., J.C.D., The Banns of Marriage, XIV-140 pp., 1931.
65. Ryder, Rev. Raymond Aloysius, A.B., J.C.D., Simony, IX-151 pp., 1931.
66. Campagna, Rev. Angelo, Ph.D., J.U.D., Il Vicario Generale del Vescovo, VII-205 pp., 1931.
67. Cox, Rev. Joseph Godfrey, A.B., J.C.D., The Administration of Seminaries, VI-124 pp., 1931.
68. Gregory, Rev. Donald J., J.U.D., The Pauline Privilege, XV-165 pp., 1931.
69. Donohue, Rev. John F., J.C.D., The Impediment of Crime, VII-110 pp., 1931.
70. Dooley, Rev. Eugene A., O.M.I., J.C.D., Church Law on Sacred Relics, IX-143 pp., 1931.
71. Orth, Rev. Clement Raymond, O.M.C., J.C.D., The Approbation of Religious Institutes, 171 pp., 1931.
72. Pernicone, Rev. Joseph M., A.B., J.C.D., The Ecclesiastical Prohibition of Books, XII-267 pp., 1932.
73. Clinton, Rev. Connell, A.B., J.C.D., The Paschal Precept, IX-108 pp., 1932.
74. Donnelly, Rev. Francis B., A.M., S.T.L., J.C.D., The Diocesan Synod, VIII-125 pp., 1932.
75. Torrente, Rev. Camilo, C.M.F., J.C.D., Las Procesiones Sagradas, V-145 pp., 1932.
76. Murphy, Rev. Edwin J., C.PP.S., J.C.D., Suspension Ex Informata Conscientia, XI-122 pp., 1932.
77. MacKenzie, Rev. Eric F., A.M., S.T.L., J.C.D., The Delict of Heresy in its Commission, Penalization, Absolution, VII-124 pp., 1932.
78. Lyons, Rev. Avitus E., S.T.B., J.C.D., The Collegiate Tribunal of First Instance, XI-147 pp., 1932.
79. Connolly, Rev. Thomas A., J.C.D., Appeals, XI-195, pp., 1932.
80. Sangmeister, Rev. Joseph V., A.B., J.C.D., Force and Fear as Precluding Matrimonial Consent, V-211 pp., 1932.
81. Jaeger, Rev. Leo A., A.B., J.C.D., The Administration of Vacant and Quasi-Vacant Episcopal Sees in the United States, IX-229 pp., 1932.
82. Rimlinger, Rev. Herbert T., J.C.D., Error Invalidating Matrimonial Consent, VII-79, pp. 1932.
83. Barrett, Rev. John D. M., S.S., J.C.D., A Comparative Study of the Third Plenary Council of Baltimore and the Code, IX-221 pp., 1932.
84. Carberry, Rev. John J., Ph.D., S.T.D., J.C.D., The Juridical Form of Marriage, X-177 pp., 1934.
85. Dolan, Rev. John L., A.B., J.C.D., The Defensor Vinculi, XII-157 pp., 1934.
86. Hannan, Rev. Jerome D., A.M., S.T.D., LL.B., J.C.D., The Canon Law of Wills, IX-517 pp., 1934.

87. LEMIEUX, REV. DELISE A., A.M., J.C.D., The Sentence in Ecclesiastical Procedure, IX-131 pp., 1934.
88. O'ROURKE, REV. JAMES J., A.B., J.C.D., Parish Registers, VII-109 pp., 1934.
89. TIMLIN, REV. BARTHOLOMEW, O.F.M., A.M., J.C.D., Conditional Matrimonial Consent, X-381 pp., 1934.
90. WAHL, REV. FRANCIS X., A.B., J.C.D., The Matrimonial Impediments of Consanguinity and Affinity, VI-125 pp., 1934.
91. WHITE, REV. ROBERT J., A.B., LL.B., S.T.B., J.C.D., Canonical Ante-Nuptial Promises and the Civil Law, VI-152 pp., 1934.
92. HERRERA, REV. ANTONIO PARRA, O.C.D., J.C.D., Legislacion Ecclesiastica sobra el Ayuno y la Abstinencia, XI-191 pp., 1935.
93. KENNEDY, REV. EDWIN J., J.C.D., The Special Matrimonial Process in Cases of Evident Nullity, X-165 pp., 1935.
94. MANNING, REV. JOHN J., A.B., J.C.D., Presumption of Law in Matrimonial Procedure, XI-111 pp., 1935.
95. MOEDER, REV. JOHN M., J.C.D., The Proper Bishop for Ordination and Dimissorial Letters, VII-135 pp., 1935.
96. O'MARA, REV. WILLIAM A., A.B., J.C.D., Canonical Causes for Matrimonial Dispensations, IX-155 pp., 1935.
97. REILLY, REV. PETER, J.C.D., Residence of Pastors, IX-81 pp., 1935.
98. SMITH, REV. MARINER T., O.P., S.T.Lr., J.C.D., The Penal Law for Religious, VIII-169 pp., 1935.
99. WHALEN, REV. DONALD W., A.M., J.C.D., The Value of Testimonial Evidence in Matrimonial Procedure, XIII-297 pp., 1935.
100. CLEARY, REV. JOSEPH F., J.C.D., Canonical Limitations on the Alienation of Church Property, VIII-141 pp., 1936.
101. GLYNN, REV. JOHN C., J.C.D., The Promoter of Justice, XX-337 pp., 1936.
102. BRENNAN, REV. JAMES H., S.S., M.A., S.T.B., J.C.D., The Simple Convalidation of Marriage, VI-135 pp., 1937.
103. BRUNINI, REV. JOSEPH BERNARD, J.C.D., The Clerical Obligations of Canons 139 and 142, X-121 pp., 1937.
104. CONNOR, REV. MAURICE, A.B., J.C.D., The Administrative Removal ot Pastors, VIII-159 pp., 1937.
105. GUILFOYLE, REV. MERLIN JOSEPH, J.C.D., Custom, XI-144 pp., 1937.
106. HUGHES, REV. JAMES AUSTIN, A.B., A.M., J.C.D., Witnesses in Criminal Trials of Clerics, IX-140 pp., 1937.
107. JANSEN, REV. RAYMOND J., A.B., S.T.L., J.C.D., Canonical Provisions for Catechetical Instruction, VII-153 pp., 1937.
108. KEALY, REV. JOHN JAMES, A.B., J.C.D., The Introductory Libellus in Church Court Procedure, XI-121 pp., 1937.
109. MCMANUS, REV. JAMES EDWARD, C.SS.R., J.C.D., The Administration of Temporal Goods in Religious Institutes, XVI-196 pp., 1937.

110. MORIARTY, REV. EUGENE JAMES, J.C.D., Oaths in Ecclesiastical Courts, X-115 pp., 1937.
111. RAINER, REV. ELIGIUS GEORGE, C.SS.R., J.C.D., Suspension of Clerics, XVII-249 pp., 1937.
112. REILLY, REV. THOMAS F., C.SS.R., J.C.D., Visitation of Religious, VI-195 pp., 1938.
113. MORIARTY, REV. FRANCIS E., C.SS.R., J.C.D., The Extraordinary Absolution from Censures, XV-334 pp., 1938.
114. CONNOLLY, REV. NICHOLAS P., J.C.D., The Canonical Erection of Parishes, X-132 pp., 1938.
115. DONOVAN, REV. JAMES JOSEPH, J.C.D., The Pastor's Obligation in Prenuptial Investigation, XII-322 pp., 1938.
116. HARRIGAN, REV. ROBERT J., M.A., S.T.B., J.C.D., The Radical Sanation of Invalid Marriages, VIII-208 pp., 1938.
117. BOFFA, REV. CONRAD HUMBERT, J.C.D., Canonical Provisions for Catholic Schools, VII-211 pp., 1939.
118. PARSONS, REV. ANSCAR JOHN, O.M.Cap., J.C.D., Canonical Elections, XII-236 pp., 1939.
119. REILLY, REV. EDWARD MICHAEL, A.B., J.C.D., The General Norms of Dispensation, XII-156 pp., 1939.
120. RYAN, REV. GERALD ALOYSIUS, A.B., J.C.D., Principles of Episcopal Jurisdiction, XII-172 pp., 1939.
121. BURTON, REV. FRANCIS JAMES, C.S.C., A.B., J.C.D., A Commentary on Canon 1125, X-222 pp., 1940.
122. MIASKIEWICZ, REV. FRANCIS SIGISMUND, J.C.D., Supplied Jurisdiction According to Canon 209, XII-340 pp., 1940.
123. RICE, REV. PATRICK WILLIAM, A.B., J.C.D., Proof of Death in Prenuptial Investigation, VIII-156 pp., 1940.
124. ANGLIN, REV. THOMAS FRANCIS, M.S., J.C.D., The Eucharistic Fast, VIII-183 pp., 1941.
125. COLEMAN, REV. JOHN JEROME, J.C.D., The Minister of Confirmation, VI-153 pp., 1941.
126. DOWNS, REV. JOHN EMMANUEL, A.B., J.C.D., The Concept of Clerical Immunity, XI-163 pp., 1941.
127. ESSWEIN, REV. ANTHONY ALBERT, J.C.D., Extrajudicial Penal Powers of Ecclesiastical Superiors, X-144 pp., 1941.
128. FARRELL, REV. BENJAMIN FRANCIS, M.A., S.T.L., J.C.D., The Rights and Duties of the Local Ordinary Regarding Congregations of Women Religious of Pontifical Approval, V-195 pp., 1941.
129. FEENEY, REV. THOMAS JOHN, A.B., S.T.L., J.C.D., Restitutio in Integrum, VI-1169 pp., 1941.
130. FINDLAY, REV. STEPHEN WILLIAM, O.S.B., A.B., J.C.D., Canonical Norms Governing the Deposition and Degradation of Clerics, XVII-279 pp., 1941.

131. Goodwine, Rev. John, A.B., S.T.L., J.C.D., The Right of the Church to Acquire Property, VIII-119 pp., 1941.
132. Heston, Rev. Edward Louis, C.S.C., Ph.D., S.T.D., J.C.D., The Alienation of Church Property in the United States, XII-222 pp., 1941.
133. Hogan, Rev. James John, A.B., S.T.L., J.C.D., Judicial Advocates and Procurators, XIII-200 pp., 1941.
134. Kealy, Rev. Thomas M., A.B., Litt.B., J.C.D., Dowry of Women Religious, IX-152 pp., 1941.
135. Keene, Rev. Michael James, O.S.B., J.C.D., Religious Ordinaries and Canon 198, V-164 pp., 1942.
136. Kerin, Rev. Charles A., S.S., M.A., S.T.B., J.C.D., The Privation of Christian Burial, XVI-279 pp., 1941.
137. Louis, Rev. William Francis, M.A., J.C.D., Diocesan Archives, X-101 pp., 1941.
138. McDevitt, Rev. Gilbert Joseph, A.B., J.C.D., Legitimacy and Legitimation, X-247 pp., 1941.
139. McDonough, Rev. Thomas Joseph, A.B., J.C.D., Apostolic Administrators, X-217 pp., 1941.
140. Meier, Rev. Carl Anthony, A.B., J.C.D., Penal Administrative Procedure Against Negligent Pastors, XI-240 pp., 1941.
141. Schmidt, Rev. John Rogg, A.B., J.C.D., The Principles of Authentic Interpretation in Canon 17 of the Code of Canon Law, XII-331 pp., 1941.
142. Slafkosky, Rev. Andrew Leonard, A.B., J.C.D., The Canonical Episcopal Visitation of the Diocese, X-197 pp., 1941.
143. Swoboda, Rev. Innocent Robert, O.F.M., J.C.D., Ignorance in Relation to the Imputability of Delicts, IX-271 pp., 1941.
144. Dubé, Rev. Arthur Joseph, A.B., J.C.D., The General Principles for the Reckoning of Time in Canon Law, VIII-299 pp., 1941.
145. McBride, Rev. James T., A.B., J.C.D., Incardination and Excardination of Seculars, XX-585 pp., 1941.
146. Król, Rev. John T., J.C.D., The Defendant in Ecclesiastical Trials, XII-207 pp., 1942.
147. Comyns, Rev. Joseph J., C.SS.R., A.B., J.C.D., Papal and Episcopal Administration of Church Property, XIV-155 pp., 1942.
148. Barry, Rev. Garrett Francis, O.M.I., J.C.D., Violation of the Cloister, XII-260 pp., 1942.
149. Bolduc, Rev. Gatien, C.S.V., A.B., S.T.L., J.C.D., Les Études dans les Religions Cléricales, VIII-155 pp., 1942.
150. Boyle, Rev. David John, M.A., J.C.D., The Juridic Effects of Moral Certitude on Pre-Nuptial Guarantees, XII-188 pp., 1942.
151. Canavan, Rev. Walter Joseph, M.A., Litt.D., J.C.D., The Profession of Faith, XII-143 pp., 1942.
152. Desrochers, Rev. Bruno, A.B., Ph.L., S.T.B., J.C.D., Le Premier Concile Plénier de Québec et le Code de Droit Canonique, XIV-186 pp., 1942.

153. DILLON, REV. ROBERT EDWARD, A.B., J.C.D., Common Law Marriage, X-148 pp., 1942.
154. DODWELL, REV. EDWARD JOHN, Ph.D., S.T.B., J.C.D., The Time and Place for the Celebration of Marriage, X-156 pp., 1942.
155. DONNELLAN, REV. THOMAS ANDREW, A.B., J.C.D., The Obligation of the Missa pro Populo, VII-131 pp., 1942.
156. ELTZ, REV. LOUIS ANTHONY, A.B., J.C.L., Cooperation in Crime.
157. GASS, REV. SYLVESTER FRANCIS, M.A., J.C.D., Ecclesiastical Pensions, XI-206 pp., 1942.
158. GUINIVEN, REV. JOHN JOSEPH, C.SS.R., J.C.D., The Precept of Hearing Mass, XIV-188 pp., 1942.
159. GULCZYNSKI, REV. JOHN THEOPHILUS, J.C.D., The Desecration and Violation of Churches, X-126 pp., 1942.
10. HAMMILL, REV. JOHN LEO, M.A., J.C.D., The Obligations of the Traveler According to Canon 14, VIII-204 pp., 1942.
161. HAYDT, REV. JOHN JOSEPH, A.B., J.C.D., Reserved Benefices, XI-148 pp., 1942.
162. HUSER, REV. ROGER JOHN, O.F.M., A.B., J.C.D., The Crime of Abortion in Canon Law, XII-187 pp., 1942.
163. KEARNEY, REV. FRANCIS PATRICK, A.B., S.T.L., J.C.L., The Principles of Canon 1127.
164. LINAHEN, REV. LEO JAMES, S.T.L., J.C.D., De Absolutione Complicis In Peccato Turpi, 114 pp., 1942.
165. MCCLOSKEY, REV. JOSEPH ALOYSIUS, A.B., J.C.D., The Subject of Ecclesiastical Law According to Canon 12, XVII-246 pp., 1942.
166. O'NEILL, REV. FRANCIS JOSEPH, C.SS.R., J.C.D., The Dismissal of Religious in Temporary Vows, XIII-220 pp., 1942.
167. PRINCE, REV. JOHN EDWARD, A.B., S.T.B., J.C.D., The Diocesan Chancellor, X-136 pp., 1942.
168. RIESNER, REV. ALBERT JOSEPH, C.SS.R., J.C.D., Apostates and Fugitives from Religious Institutes, IX-168 pp., 1942.
169. STENGER, REV. JOSEPH BERNARD, J.C.D., The Mortgaging of Church Property, 186 pp., 1942.
170. WALDRON, REV. JOSEPH FRANCIS, A.B., J.C.D., The Minister of Baptism, XII-197 pp., 1942.
171. WILLETT, REV. ROBERT ALBERT, J.C.D., The Probative Value of Documents in Ecclesiastical Trials, X-124 pp., 1942.
172. WOEBER, REV. EDWARD MARTIN, M.A., J.C.D., The Interpellations, XII-161 pp., 1942.
173. BENKO, REV. MATTHEW ALOYSIUS, O.S.B., M.A., J.C.L., The Abbot *Nullius.*
174. CHRIST, REV. JOSEPH JAMES, M.A., S.T.L., J.C.L., Dispensation from Vindicative Penalties, XIII-285 pp., 1943.
175. CLANCY, REV. PATRICK M. J., O.P., A.B., S.T.Lr., J.C.D., The Local Religious Superior, X-229 pp., 1943.

176. Clarke, Rev. Thomas James, J.C.D., Parish Societies, XII-147 pp., 1943.
177. Connolly, Rev. John Patrick, S.T.L., J.C.D., Synodal Examiners and Parish Priest Consultors, X-223 pp., 1943.
178. Drumm, Rev. William Martin, A.B., J.C.L., Hospital Chaplains, XI-175 pp., 1943.
179. Flanagan, Rev. Bernard Joseph, A.B., S.T.L., J.C.D., The Canonical Erection of Religious Houses, X-147 pp., 1943.
180. Kelleher, Rev. Stephen Joseph, A.B., S.T.B., J.C.D., Discussions with Non-Catholics: Canonical Legislation, X-93 pp., 1943.
181. Lewis, Rev. Gordian, C.P., J.C.D., Chapters in Religious Institutes, XII-169 pp., 1943.
182. Marx, Rev. Adolph, J.C.D., The Declaration of Nullity of Marriages Contracted Outside the Church, X-151 pp., 1943.
183. Matulenas, Rev. Raymond Anthony, O.S.B., A.B., J.C.L., Communication, a Source of Privileges.
184. O'Leary, Rev. Charles Gerard, C.SS.R., J.C.L., Religious Dismissed After Perpetual Profession.
185. Power, Rev. Cornelius Michael, J.C.L., The Blessing of Cemeteries, XII-231 pp., 1943.
186. Shuhler, Rev. Ralph Vincent, O.S.A., J.C.D., Privileges of Religious to Absolve and Dispense, XII-195 pp., 1943.
187. Ziolkowski, Rev. Thaddeus Stanislaus, A.B., J.C.D., The Consecration and Blessing of Churches, XII-151 pp., 1943.
188. Heneghan, Rev. John Joseph, S.T.D., J.C.L., The Marriages of Unworthy Catholics: Canons 1065 and 1066.
189. Carroll, Rev. Coleman Francis, M.A., S.T.L., J.C.L., Charitable Institutions.
190. Ciesluk, Rev. Joseph Edward, Ph.B., S.T.L., J.C.L., National Parishes in the United States.
191. Coburn, Rev. Vincent Paul, A.B., J.C.L., Marriages of Conscience.
192. Connors, Rev. Charles Paul, C.S.Sp., A.B., J.C.L., Extra-Judicial Procurators in the Code of Canon Law.
193. Coyle, Rev. Paul Raymond, A.B., J.C.L., Judicial Exceptions.
194. Fair, Rev. Bartholomew Francis, A.B., S.T.L., J.C.L., The Impediment of Abduction.
195. Gallagher, Rev. Thomas Raphael, O.P., A.B., S.T.Lr., J.C.L., The Examination of the Qualities of the Ordinand.
196. Gannon, Rev. John Mark, S.T.L., J.C.L., The Interstices Required for the Promotion to Orders.
197. Goldsmith, Rev. J. William, B.C.S., S.T.L., J.C.L., The Competence of Church and State Over Marriages—Disputed Points.
198. Goodwine, Rev. Joseph Gerard, A.B., S.T.B., J.C.L., The Reception of Converts.
199. Kowalski, Rev. Romuald Eugene, O.F.M., A.B., J.C.L., Sustenance of Religious Houses of Regulars.

200. McCoy, Rev. Alan Edward, O.F.M., J.C.L., Force and Fear in Relation to Delictual Imputability and Penal Responsibility.

201. McDevitt, Rev. Vincent John, Ph.B., S.T.L., J.C.L., Perjury.

202. Martin, Rev. Thomas Owen, Ph.D., S.T.D., J.C.L., Adverse Possession, Prescription and Limitation of Actions: The Canonical "Praescriptio."

203. Miklosovic, Rev. Paul John, A.B., J.C.L., Attempted Marriages and Their Consequent Juridic Effects.

204. Mundy, Rev. Thomas Maurice, A.B., S.T.L., J.C.L., The Union of Parishes.

205. O'Dea, Rev. John Coyle, A.B., J.C.L., The Matrimonial Impediment of Nonage.

206. Olalia, Rev. Alexander Ayson, S.T.L., J.C.L., A Comparative Study of the Christian Constitution of States and the Constitution of the Philippine Commonwealth.

207. Poisson, Rev. Pierre-Marie, C.S.C., A.B., Ph.L., Th.L., J.C.L., Droits Patrimoniaux des Maisons et des Eglises Religieuses.

208. Stadalnikas, Rev. Casimir Joseph, M.I.C., J.C.L., Reservation of Censures.

209. Sullivan, Rev. Eugene Henry, S.T.L., J.C.L., Proof of the Reception of the Sacraments.

210. Vaughan, Rev. William Edward, J.C.L., Constitutions for Diocesan Courts.

211. Lyons, Rev. Joseph Henry, J.C.L., The Joinder of Issue in Canonical Trials.

www.ingramcontent.com/pod-product-compliance
Lightning Source LLC
LaVergne TN
LVHW050258080826
844660LV00012B/655

* 9 7 8 0 8 1 3 2 2 3 8 5 8 *